AMERICAN LAW: THE THIRD CENTURY

The Law Bicentennial Volume

Editor
Bernard Schwartz
Edwin D. Webb, Professor of Law
New York University School of Law

PUBLISHED FOR
NEW YORK UNIVERSITY
SCHOOL OF LAW
by
Fred B. Rothman & Co.
South Hackensack, N.J.
1976

L. C. Card No. 76-50507
ISBN. 0-8377-0204-6.

Printed in the U.S.A.

TABLE OF CONTENTS

INTRODUCTION

Bernard Schwartz

The Bicentennial of American independence is also the Bicentennial of American law. It is true that even before 1776 a body of American law had developed distinct from the English law from which it was derived. As early as 1704, indeed, an *Abridgement of the Laws in Force and Use in Her Majesty's Plantations* was printed in London, devoted to the laws of Virginia, Maryland, and Massachusetts, together with a smattering of items from New York and the Carolinas. Before independence, also, the law had already begun to play its crucial role in American society. We need only refer to Burke's famous words on the extent of legal influence in the American colonies: "In no country, perhaps, in the world, is the law so general a study. The profession itself is numerous and powerful, and in most provinces it takes the lead. The greater number of deputies sent to the [continental] Congress were lawyers."

Before 1776, nevertheless, the law, like the nation, could not be considered independent. In vital respects, the American system was still a legal dependency of the mother country—a situation that continued until the voting of independence. With the need to replace the royal governments which they had ousted, the Americans could fashion their own political and legal institutions. Now came the formative era of American law, when the foundations of the new legal system were fixed. This was the classical era of constitution making, with its basic American contribution to public law—the concept of fundamental law to define and limit government and its powers. It was also a period of ferment in private law, when the details of the marriage between the common law and the people and conditions of the new nation were worked out.

Celebration of the nation's Bicentennial would scarcely be

complete without commemoration of the two centuries of American law. The crucial role of the law in our society has been apparent to all observers—from Burke before independence, to Alexis de Tocqueville, to the present day. The true American contribution to human progress has not been technology, economics, or culture; it has been the development of the notion of law as a check on power. American society has been dominated by law as has no other society in history. Struggles over power that in other countries have called forth regiments of troops in this country call forth battalions of lawyers. As United States Attorney General Richard Rush put it in 1815, "The *Constitution* with Captain Hull in her, did not come down upon the *Guerriere* in a spirit of more daring and triumphal energy than the Philadelphia or New York lawyers will sometimes do upon a statute that happens to run a little amiss!"

This volume commemorates the Bicentennial of American law. It is based upon the papers delivered at the Bicentennial Conference held at the New York University School of Law, April 27-30, 1976. That Conference was the major legal event of the Bicentennial year.

The Bicentennial should be more than an occasion for congratulatory retrospective. This volume attempts both to project basic legal trends in the next century and to consider law from a broader perspective. In the first part, outstanding judges, lawyers, and law professors discuss different areas of the law as they foresee them during the nation's Third Century. In the second part, the law will be considered from the perspective of many nonlegal disciplines. The authors are all leaders in their fields, who bring to the volume points of view those engaged in the law hear only too rarely. The volume concludes with papers by the Lord Chief Justice of the country from which our legal system is inherited and the Chief Justice of the United States.

The present volume will remain a notable reminder of the Bicentennial of American law. It would, however, be a pity if it were treated as merely another Bicentennial souvenir—kept as a memento on coffee table or shelf, but never opened for serious purposes. The papers deserve a better fate. They are of a much higher caliber than those normally contained in a commemorative volume. Many of them make a real contribution to the fields to which they are devoted. The remainder of this Introduction will try to point out these contributions. Hopefully it will help rescue these papers from the obscurity which is too often the fate of such *festschrift*-type writings.

I

The history of American law is a history of the effort to mold legal institutions and doctrines to meet the felt necessities of each period in the nation's development. The effort has not always succeeded; at times there has been an all-too-large gap between the law and public needs. Yet the gap has always ultimately been narrowed, as judges, lawyers, and legislators have worked out new principles and doctrines better adapted to the changed conditions of the day.

Will the same prove true during the Third Century?

There is no doubt that substantial changes will be required in American law to meet the needs of the next century. Virtually all the contributors to the first part of this volume agree on this point. It may surprise some that the most radical proposals for change are put forward by some of the judges who have contributed papers. Judges are, of course, conservative by tradition. They can normally not be radical innovators and remain true to the demands imposed upon the judicial process. But these are scarcely normal times. Transforming thought which implies some break with the past is needed now, even by those entrusted by society with enforcing its laws.

The papers of the federal judges who deal with the courts and judicial administration are particularly suggestive. Judge Frankel's paper makes recommendations that would alter the present adversary justice model and transform it from the legal counterpart of Adam Smith in action to a system in which public responsibility for seeking truth would become the dominant feature. Judge Kaufman puts forth suggestions that would also make for far-reaching changes. Among his recommendations deserving of further study are proposals for a Congressional office to assess the impact of legislation on the courts (with "court impact" statements comparable to the environmental impact statements now required), increased use of parajudges and professional staff, use of experts retained by the courts, an Office of Science Advisor to the Courts (this should be compared with the proposal, now a focus of public attention, for a Science Court, by Dr. Arthur Kantrowitz of Avco Everett Research Laboratory), as well as for diverting cases from the courts (as by his suggestive proposal for a no-fault approach to consumer law). Judge Friendly projects drastic changes in federal court jurisdiction, such as the elimination of diversity jurisdiction, which will make the most important role for the federal courts the control of governmental action so that it does not infringe the Constitution or federal law.

The other papers in Part I are devoted, after a magisterial overview of the Third Century by Dean Redlich, to different areas of public law (Professor Dorsen paints with a broad brush in covering current and projected issues in separation of powers and federalism, Judge Higginbotham's moving paper deals with race, Judge Bazelon writes of the need to protect basic values in the area of civil liberties, Professor Rusk makes an eloquent plea for a meaningful role for international law, and Dean Morris contributes a provocative criminal law survey), private law (contracts, torts, and property are surveyed by acknowledged masters of those basic subjects, and there is an analysis of codification, which potentially brings all these subjects together, by Dean Mentschikoff), then to procedure and practice (with Judge Frankel's paper on trials and procedure, Judge Walsh's survey, from the perspective of his presidency of the American Bar Association, and Judge Fuchsberg's on legal services, with his plea for expansion in the profession's role of serving the public), the courts and judicial administration (Judge Friendly on the federal courts, Judge Mosk on the state courts, with his provocative prognosis of a meaningful role for those courts in the federal system), public interest law (by the man who, almost single handed, made that so relevant a subject in today's law), legal education (with Dean McKay's masterful survey), and the ends of law.

Of course, any projection of future legal trends may scarcely be taken as more than an informed guess. Judge Mosk well compares the contributor to this volume to a hieromancer who reads animal entrails for portents of the future. Or, as an editorial in the *Shreveport (La.) Times* once put it, with regard to the present writer's effort to predict future Supreme Court tendencies, "He would be on much safer ground trying to forecast the winner of the 1958 Kentucky

Derby, for which nominations have not even been made as yet."

It is, at the same time, significant that so many of the jurists contributing to this volume emphasize similar points. If there is one recurring question raised, it is that of whether the law is not trying to do too much—whether we are not imposing on the courts and the legal order tasks which are beyond the scope of the ends which may properly be attained through the law. One who reads the examples given by Judge Friendly is bound to wonder whether the judge who acts as a super-board of corrections or super-EPA is not contributing to the malaise in the legal world that is so prominent a feature in this Bicentennial year.

The judicial contributors, as well as others such as Dean Morris, join in urging that a primary need in the Third Century is to develop methods for dispute resolution outside the courts. Unless substantial measures are taken along those lines, the legal system will scarcely be able to perform its proper role. The courts cannot long continue trying to do more and more with less and less. The continuing expansion of the role of law is increasingly accompanied by increasing skepticism about its ability to keep up with society's needs.

The ends of law are starting to come full circle. The overexpansion of the legal order has militated against proper performance of the core functions of the law. The ever-more-inclusive ends sought to be attained may be rendered meaningless by the failure effectively to further the public interest in the general security. A major part of the current dissatisfaction with the law is based on the ineptitude of our legal institutions in fulfilling the elementary end of any legal order: to keep the peace.

This brings us directly to the themes enunciated by the two Chief Justices—particularly Lord Widgery. Before we discuss their concluding papers, however, we should survey the substantial contribution made by the nonlegal papers in Part II of this volume.

II

It is now almost two decades since C. P. Snow delivered his Rede Lecture, *The Two Cultures,* with its seminal expression of concern for the everincreasing gap between science and letters. Yet, as Snow himself recognizes, "The number 2 is a very dangerous number. . . . Attempts to divide anything into two ought to be regarded with much suspicion." In truth, there are not two cultures, but as many as there are intellectual disciplines. In the second part of this volume twelve cultures are represented. All of them are directly relevant to the law, whose operation in particular cases may involve virtually every aspect of societal life. All too often, however, the law and these other disciplines remain separate worlds; between them there are gulfs of mutual incomprehension—sometimes even hostility and dislike, most of all lack of understanding.

In Part II of this book, the law is considered from the perspective of twelve other disciplines, ranging from history to philosophy. Such a look at the law from a broader perspective is also appropriate in a volume commemorating the Bicentennial of American law. From its beginnings American law has drawn its concepts and inspirations from nonlegal sources. We have only to evidence the leadership role of the clergy in the early New England polity and the part played by Biblical inspiration in the drafting of legislation there, notably in the 1641 Massachusetts Body of Liberties. Even during the nineteenth century, when American law was developing in what its molders thought of as a self-contained system, uninfluenced by nonlegal modes of thought, the picture of splendid legal isolation was inconsistent with reality. The general culture of the society, in its different spheres of intellectual activity, has always been the secret root from which American law has drawn its life. Even the black-letter judge has, perhaps unknowingly, been influenced by more than the letter of the law alone. To paraphrase Holmes's famous words, the felt necessities of the time, the prevalent philosophical theories, intuitions of what best served the public interest—all had more to do with the development of American law than the strictly analytical jurisprudence the judges professed to be applying. Our judges have always known too much to sacrifice good sense to the syllogism.

In our own day, of course, the interdisciplinary approach to law has become fully established; the black-letter judge has become an anomaly, increasingly replaced by the man of statistics and the master of economics and other disciplines.

During this century we have become increasingly aware of the proper dependence of the law upon all the other intellectual disciplines. The theme in this respect was set just before the turn of the century in the 1892 introductory lecture delivered at Cambridge by the poet A. E. Housman—a theme that may also serve for Part II of this volume: "There is no rivalry between the studies of Arts and Laws and Science but the rivalry of fellow-soldiers in striving which can most victoriously achieve the common end of all, to set back the frontier of darkness."

The list of contributors of Part II reads like a *Who's Who of Intellectual Attainment.* Each is preeminent in the field on which he writes and each brings a unique nonlegal perspective to the law. Each has something to say about the law which should broaden the understanding of both the lawyer and lay reader. The former particularly should profit by being able to approach the law from perspectives not commonly seen by those trained in the law school.

Part II starts with Professor Morris's provocative comparison of the methodology and objectives of history and law. Of especial interest is his recognition that, while history is inevitably important in the decision of legal issues, it should not be the decisive factor in judicial decision-making. This, we shall note, is a theme that recurs in other papers as well. Senator Packwood points out what too many lawyers forget—how important British constitutional history was in the development of American public law. All too few people realize the extent to which our modern liberties are based upon the crucial battles waged by our English forebears, from Magna Carta down.

Mr. Rosenthal discusses the apparent conflict between the First Amendment and the duty to ensure a fair trial from the journalist's point of view. Even after the Supreme Court's decision in *Nebraska Press Association v. Stuart* the whole question of the relations between law and journalism remains one that still must be resolved.

Two papers of particular interest to a legal reader are those by Father Greeley and Professor Commoner. Greeley emphasizes the limited role that sociology should play in the decision of cases. The disclaimer by a leading sociologist is of the greatest significance. Ever since *Brown v. Board of Educa-*

tion, with its famous footnote 11, both jurists and sociologists have overmagnified the contribution which sociological studies can make to the law. In fact, the studies referred to by Chief Justice Warren were far from having the crucial impact on the *Brown* decision that some have urged. Edmond Cahn showed this convincingly some years ago and Chief Justice Warren himself later publicly confirmed it.

Of equal interest is Professor Commoner's *mea culpa.* From the person who more than any other was responsible for awakening the national consciousness to ecology and its implications, it is revealing to have such a statement of the practical results, in terms of the bureaucratic apparatus spawned by the laws passed to protect the environment. Commoner has helped give effect to T.S. Eliot's rallying cry, "Clear the air! clean the sky! wash the wind!", but the consequence has been an administrative machine that may defeat the very purpose of ecological legislation.

The other nonlegal papers also have much to tell the reader. It is most suggestive to have a Nobel laureate like Professor Leontief note the inadequacies of laws like the antitrust laws in dealing with economic matters, to have Dr. Wallis show us the same with regard to medicine, and to have an eminent psychiatrist like Dr. Szasz so eloquently point out the dangers in undue reliance on psychiatry as the "revealed religion" of our day. These papers may be balanced by the inspiring papers of Rev. Boyd, who reminds us of the essential need for law to be based upon ethics, and Dr. Asimov who points the way to the contribution which the law can make to the conquest of space—the great frontier of the next century. Professor Ellison's paper is the rare discussion of the law by a leading literary figure—the converse, as it were, of Cardozo's noted essay, LAW AND LITERATURE. Last of all there is Professor Hart's perceptive paper on jurisprudence—a field that has threatened during this century to preempt the title of "the dismal science" from another discipline, but which is anything but that in Professor Hart's graceful hands.

To the legal reader, perhaps the most significant thing about the papers in Part II is their depreciation of the role the different disciplines should play in the decision of cases. The lawyer and the judge have too easily succumbed to this century's "cult of the expert." Legal issues in the courts are, more often than not, resolved after parades of expert witnesses who give their opinions based on arcane studies conducted by them. In the papers in Part II, the experts themselves place the role of expertise, particularly in the social sciences, in proper perspective: other disciplines are a useful tool in resolving legal issues, but they should not be given undue weight by the judge in a specific case; to use a common aphorism about experts, they "should be kept on tap, but not on top."

III

The volume concludes with the papers of the two Chief Justices—the one the highest judicial officer of the United States, the other of the country from which American law is derived. With Lord Widgery's paper we are back to the point already mentioned, that of the legal system coming full circle, with increasing emphasis upon the public interest in maintaining the general security. The Lord Chief Justice's subject is the rule of law; but he rightly stresses the need for it not only in the marble palace but also in the streets. Some may find his emphasis upon "law and order" and the deterrent value of punishment old-fashioned. It may be questioned, however, whether they are the people who themselves suffer from the failure of law enforcement that has become pandemic.

It remains for the Chief Justice of the United States to make the Bicentennial summing up. Chief Justice Burger repeats the theme met in many of the other papers—that of whether we are not trying to do too much through the law. Virtually all societal demands are now accompanied by the claim, "There ought to be a law!" Further, the tendency to use the judicial process as a shortcut for the solution of problems, as distinguished from disputes, tends to deflect responsibility from the political organs and thus dilute the democratic bases of our system. The Chief Justice lists the major problems with which the law should concern itself during the next century. Not all will agree with either his catalogue of problems or the solutions which he offers. Particularly controversial are his suggestions for removing disputes from the courts, at a time when strong efforts are being made to expand access to the law, especially for those in the community who have, practically speaking, been forced to live beyond the pale of legal protection. Compare, in this respect, the approach of the Chief Justice, as well as that of the other federal judges in this volume, with Ralph Nader's plea for the lowering of the barriers which prevent millions from entering the legal forum. We may wonder, nevertheless, whether the Chief Justice and the other judges are not correct in their contention that there is only so much that can be accomplished through legal rules and institutions. History shows that there are limits to the effectiveness of legal action; when the law tries to do too much, it leads to increasing skepticism about its ability to meet even the basic needs of a legal order. A primary task during the Third Century will be a narrowing of the goals which we seek to attain through the law.

Chief Justice Burger articulates the needs for in-depth analysis of our legal institutions. That is, of course, the primary purpose of this observance of the Bicentennial of American law. Such a commemoration should enable us to paraphrase Webster's famous question about the Union: "How stands the law now?" The reader of this volume has gotten a very broad picture not only of projected trends and issues during the Third Century, but also a good balance sheet of the law today.

One cannot help reflecting how different the balance sheet would have been if a similar commemoration had been held in 1876, at the Centennial of the nation. The leaders of the Bench and Bar then would have engaged in a stream of gushing self-congratulatory panegyric. The law, they would have said, as James C. Carter did, had progressed to "the last stage. . . . This is the stage of full enlightenment, such as is exhibited in . . . the United States at the present day." Similarly patting themselves figuratively on their backs, they would have repeated Joseph H. Choate's characterization of the American Bar as "the happiest illustration of Darwin's great theory of survival of the fittest", whose leaders were chosen "by a process of natural selection, for merit and fitness, from the whole body of the Bar."

How different it is in this Bicentennial volume! The almost Hegelian arrogance of a hundred years ago has given way to probing critique and radical suggestions for change—the most far-reaching of which are put forth by leaders of the Legal Establishment.

It should not be forgotten that the law's ability to make the changes needed to adapt to the demands of the Third Century is intimately related to the very survival of the American legal system as we know it. In 1970 the Association of the Bar of the City of New York convened a symposium, with the papers delivered published under the title, "Is Law Dead?" The symposium's answer was, as one critic pointed out, as predictable as a conclusion from a Vatican conference on whether God was dead. But the mere fact that the question was asked by the country's most prestigious bar association was significant.

The question of the death of law, like its counterpart of the death of God which agitated theologians not long ago, is more than mere word playing. Of course, we can, with utopians and revolutionaries, repeat the cry of Shakespeare's Dick the Butcher: "The first thing we do, let's kill all the lawyers." That slogan soon gives way to the realization that the law is an indispensable element of any functioning society. The Marxist goal of the disappearance of law does not mean the end of the legal order, of legal bureaucracy, and legal controls. It means instead the end of law as we know it—i.e., of the rule of law. It brings to life Engels' famous thesis that the government of persons would be replaced by the administration of things. Law, in the sense of the rule of law, is to be wholly replaced by administration.

Toward the end of the twentieth century, the danger is not yet so much that the rule of law will formally end in this country, but that it will become increasingly irrelevant. Despite the continuing efforts to modernize the law and legal institutions, the gap between need and performance is widening. Law is not dead, but its institutions are becoming increasingly ineffective.

Or, to put it more accurately, the community is becoming more aware of the inadequacies of its legal institutions. This is but one aspect of the growing hostility toward social institutions that characterizes the contemporary society. During most of the nation's history, Americans took for granted the superiority of their political, legal, economic, social, and other institutions. Now, at all levels of society, people rage at all their institutions. In every area the rise in human expectations leads people to demand more and more of institutions and to want their demands met "Now!" The institutions alter, but never fast enough to meet the demands.

Of course, the complaints about the law's decay are not new. What is new is the institutional crisis of our time. Legal institutions, like all others, are caught in a crossfire between the need for drastic alteration and their inability to keep up with the leaping aspirations of the day. Intransigent frustration is the increasing response of the community.

This frustration is leading Americans, for perhaps the first time in their history, to question the legitimacy of their legal institutions. The twentieth century has been witness to the collapse of traditional religion; the next may see a collapse of traditional law. Whether this will happen depends in large part upon the ability of our legal institutions to transform themselves. Effective institutional reform has become the categorical imperative for survival of the law as Americans know it. "Unless something new and effective is done promptly . . . ," declared Chief Justice Warren in 1967, "the rule of law in this nation cannot endure."

Finally a word of gratitude to those who helped make the New York University Law School Bicentennial commemoration auch a success, particularly to Deans Norman Redlich and Robert B. McKay, and Gerald C. Crane, Bobbie Glover, and Pearl Rosenbaum, of the Office of Law Development, and my secretary, Barbara Ortiz.

I.

The Law of The Next Century

AN OVERVIEW

Norman Redlich*

To contemplate the Third Century of American Law is to attempt to project a vision of what we expect to be as a nation. Although that task is difficult, even for the remarkable group of scholars participating in this Bicentennial celebration, we view this future with considerable help from the past. For law in America has performed a fairly consistent set of tasks since the Revolutionary period and can probably be expected to continue to perform them. The values and interests which American law has furthered have, of course, varied with the changing flow of forces that have shaped American life. These changes have profoundly altered our substantive law and our legal institutions, particularly in the last half century. But the evolution has occurred within the framework of a legal system whose functional role in American life may have changed far less than one might think.

What is that functional role? First, American law has articulated the high ideals of individual political liberty, religious freedom, and human dignity which gave rise to the American nation. Our highest aspirations have been contained in legal documents. The Declaration of Independence was itself a brilliant legal document setting forth the inalienable rights of men and women and then stating, with lawyerlike precision, why a political breaking of the bonds with Great Britain was essential to achieve these rights. The Constitution, the Bill of Rights, the State Constitutions, the post-Civil War Amendments, the great statements of individual liberty which are found in our court decisions—all of this tells us something of one role of American law: it has been the forum for the expression of the best in the American national experience. We have not left these ideals to be expressed in

**Dean, New York University School of Law*

pamphlets and speeches and in religious pronouncements. They have been embodied into law.

That is, by itself, a profoundly important fact. It means that our highest ideals are not merely aspirational. They are not intended to be achieved in heaven. They are woven into our positive law and, as such, have become an essential part of the life of the country, to be dealt with in the here and now. At times we have advanced these principles, at times we have subverted them. But they remain as a force in American law which is difficult permanently to ignore.

As we attempt to cast a light into the future of American law we must project the role of some of these basic rights—of free speech, press and assembly, religious freedom, separation of church and state, racial equality, rights of the accused, the rights of participation in the political process and others-including the expanding concept of sexual equality. But in doing so we must remember that these rights have to be considered as part of our legal system. They will be shaped by an American society acting through legislators, lawyers and judges. If these values are abandoned by America in the next century it will be as a result of actions in the legal arena, either by judicial decision or by constitutional amendment. If they are protected and enlarged, these good works will be in the law.

At this juncture in our history, Americans could well emulate the Biblical commandment to the Jews that each succeeding generation should treat the exodus as if it had been a personal gift to the generation then living. The one safe prediction about the Third Century is that there will be continuous pressure from government and private institutions, perhaps augmented by pressures from abroad, on the fundamental freedoms guaranteed by our Constitution. There are no permanent victories, only perpetual struggle. Because our highest ideals of individual freedom have been written into law, American law has had another function to perform—one which many consider to be its most important and certainly its most uniquely American. That is, of course, the role of law as a check on governmental power. From John Marshall's opinion in *Marbury v. Madison* to Warren Burger's in *Nixon v. United States*, American courts both, federal and state, have defined the limits of legislative and executive power.

This power has, of course, been exercised within the limits of a system which may impose severe political restraints, as we recall from the New Deal constitutional crisis and the *Dred Scott* case. But the willingness of the American political system to permit so broad a role for the judiciary in restricting the executive and the legislature is a component of American law and life whose future is part of the future we contemplate this Bicentennial year. As with the substantive rights that are sought to be enforced, the future of individual freedom in America will be determined by the decisions that are made within the legal structure.

If American law has embodied some of our highest aspirations and has served as a restraint on governmental power, it has also expressed some of our sorriest sentiments. This is because, as expressed by Professor Hurst, ". . . law in the United States [has] dealt with tensions that traced to differences in religion, race, color and social class." Here we have another function of American law which has been with us from the day the first black slave arrived on these shores. That function has been to deal with the moral dilemma arising from the pervasive factor of race and racism in American life. And in performing that function, law has often embodied the very racism it should have eradicated. No survey of American law can ignore this factor in our past and our future. From the yielding to South Carolina in the drafting of the Declaration of Independence to the present controversies over the legality of affirmative action programs, American law has grappled with the realities of racism in a society whose most cherished legal principles cannot tolerate it.

Our record in this area has been a combination of glory and of shame. Whatever may have been the "true" historical origins of the Civil War, it was given meaning at the time, and certainly throughout history, in terms of the struggle to free the slaves. That struggle gave rise to the post-Civil War Amendments which provided not only a legal framework for achieving racial equality but, particularly in the last twenty-five years, the extension of the Bill of Rights to the states. But if America's continuing encounter with race enabled the law to reach the moral level of *Brown v. Board of Education,* we cannot forget the depths of *Plessy v. Ferguson.* Whatever satisfaction we may derive from the Civil Rights legislation since 1957 must be tempered by the knowledge that from

1875 to 1957 not a single piece of civil rights legislation emerged from the Congress. And it is sobering to recall at our Bicentennial how our two founding documents treated the issue of slavery. The Declaration ignored it as a price of unity, and the Constitution recognized it (without mentioning the word "slavery") by its reference to the counting of population for purposes of Congressional representation, and the twenty-year bar to any legislation barring the importation of slaves.

Moreover, we ought not to delude ourselves into thinking that the road to racial equality in American law has been a steady march upward. Who would have predicted, at the Nation's Centennial in 1876, that a Civil Rights Act passed only one year before would be the last such federal statute for another eighty-two years? Or that a few months later, the principles for which the Civil War had been fought would be largely abandoned in the presidential compromise of 1876? Or that the Supreme Court, twenty years later in 1896, with only one dissenter, would legitimate racial segregation?

It would be disappointing if only Judge Higginbotham discussed race and American law, for it is difficult for me to perceive how we can project the public and private law of the Third Century without attempting to predict whether our people and our legal institutions will finally resolve America's moral dilemma.

If American law has reflected the tensions of race, it has also reflected the tensions of American capitalism. A country's legal system will embody that society's underlying economic values and will enforce the institutional arrangements that the particular system demands. Ours has been no exception. It was a system built on the protection of private property and achieving economic growth through the accumulation of private property and the accumulation of private capital. This necessitated a set of laws relating to contract, property, corporations, labor, taxation, finance, and personal injuries which could encourage the development of such a system and protect the products of success. For at least the first half of our history this was the principal role of the American legal system. But the tensions that have always existed in the American economy have given rise, particularly in the past sixty years, to legal institutions and arrangements that reflect increased public and private control over the forces of private industry. Just as an unregulated American economy protected its freedom through legal institutions, the attempt to regulate that economy has been accomplished by dramatic changes in those legal institutions. Thus, we can safely predict that American law of the Third Century will embody the institutional and structural changes which the American economy will undergo.

Even taking into account the important changes of the New Deal and post-World War II periods, our legal institutions have been able to adapt, with great resiliency, to the increased public regulation, and increased power-sharing, of mid-twentieth century capitalism. Perhaps this is because the changes in the economic system have not struck to its fundamentals, but merely to its social and economic excesses. The growth of regulatory laws, the court decisions which allocate economic risks, the legally encouraged growth of the power and rights of tenants, consumers, workers, borrowers, and public shareholders, even the intervention of government through massive military procurement—these developments have not fundamentally altered the underlying structure of American private capitalism. And as long as that system continues to provide for the allocation of resources which the American people finds basically acceptable, then the next hundred years can be expected to provide for more of the same—different forms of attempting to regulate, through public and private legal arrangements, the way in which our system fulfills its mission.

One can be permitted to speculate, however, whether American law will continue to perform this role of regulating and adjusting an economy whose basic institutional structures remain fundamentally unchanged, or whether the next century will see more basic changes in ownership and in decision-making. Those whose lives are almost totally immersed in the legal system which has developed in America can easily lose sight of the extent to which that system is rooted in the economic system of private capitalism. If that economic system should undergo basic changes in the next century, much of what we now accept as constant could be unmoored.

Apart from the embodiment of values and providing the restraints on power, American law, like other systems of law, has provided, and will continue to provide, a method for the peaceful resolution of disputes. The substantive manner in which this is done is one important method by which law reflects our underlying values. But to an increasing extent American law is concerned with how this function is performed. The second century of American law, particularly the last twenty-five years, has seen an impressive expansion of judicially enforceable rights. Viewed from what Edmond Cahn called the "imperial perspective" Americans who are accused of crimes or otherwise involved in litigation have available to them a set of rights and rules which are unmatched in their concern for protecting the individual against excessive governmental power. When viewed from the "consumer perspective," however, these rights have been diluted by a system of judicial administration which still suffers from lack of resources and lack of concern.

And in the setting of a law school, it is particularly important to note that the law teaching community, including that portion of it that is most concerned with human rights, bears a major share of this responsibility. Judicial administration is still an academic stepchild of the law schools. Students are rarely encouraged to consider careers in this area or to probe for solutions for some of the problems in judicial administration—problems which are far more interesting and important than those which occupy the attention of many of our best academic minds.

It benefits little to fight the good fight for individuals' access to the courts if they encounter a hopeless administrative morass once they're in. Very early in the Third Century of American law, judicial administration must catch up with the substantive advances of American law before we are compelled to yield to the pressures, which are gathering momentum, to contract substantive rights to the level of a court system capable of dealing with them.

Perhaps the function of American law which will change most in the Third Century is in an area which most of us scarcely notice. Every country's legal system must develop the institutions which relate that system to those of other countries. This is true even if, as has been the case with our system and that of all other nations, the system has functioned so as to be contained within its own national framework. Actually, our legal institutions have been shaped by events abroad far more than most Americans care to recognize. Consider but a few examples: the alien and sedition laws, our laws regarding immigration, the legal system surrounding the development and survival of Negro slavery, laws regarding the treatment of aliens or, in the case of Japanese and Chinese, even the native-born of foreign ancestry, laws responding to the growth of communism abroad by repressing dissenting expression at home, laws concerning foreign trade—and many, many more.

Yet, although we have responded to pressure from abroad and although our legal system has itself adapted to the increasing involvement of the United States in the affairs of people throughout the world, ours is a country where the focus of decision-making has, both in perception and reality, been centered at home. We tend to think of our legal institutions as either insulated from the rest of the world or as affecting other societies' systems more than theirs affect ours. Those few periods when our institutions had to make profound changes as a result of conditions beyond our control—the Civil War, World War II, and the 1974 energy crisis—were viewed as temporary phenomena. Surely, we cannot contemplate the Third Century without wondering whether our legal institutions will continue to have the relative immunity from events abroad that they have enjoyed in the past. Can we continue to control our own resource allocations in a world where, perhaps, billions of people may actually be dying from lack of food? If continued population and economic growth should not be possible as a result of limits on our available resources—limits which are imposed from abroad—it is illusory to think that this will not cause profound changes in a legal system which has flourished in a society where there have been essentially no legally imposed limits.

The generation of Americans that now celebrates the Bicentennial has become accustomed to speaking about the need for America to "play a role" in the world, or to "meet its responsibilities as a world power." These were the phrases with which, in the past, we countered the arguments of isolationism. The generation of Americans that will convene one hundred years from now will, I suggest, be considering what has happened to our legal institutions as a result of our having been forced to make profound changes in our way of life as a result of world conditions over which our control will have been quite limited.

If American law defines our values, both good and bad, restrains governmental power, writes the regulatory rules of the game for American capitalism, resolves disputes, and copes with this nation's relationships to the world, it also does one more thing which is of great importance to a legal audience. It defines the role of the lawyer. *Marbury v. Madison* assured the lawyer a place at the heart of the great constitutional issues of our history; the growth of a regulated capitalism placed lawyers in pivotal roles in both the government and corporate structures. And a society which resolves disputes through a case-by-case process of litigation, based primarily on common law and statutory interpretations, provides a special place of power for the lawyer. Observers, from at least as far back as deTocqueville, have recognized the influential position occupied by lawyers in America. The profession, despite considerable democratization, still has as its principal financial base the providing of services to a small minority of individuals and corporations at the top of the economic structure. As long as the basic economic and political institutions in American society were accepted without serious question, there was little pressure for lawyers to examine their own roles as well-paid verbal engineers who enabled those institutions to function efficiently in an increasingly complex society.

As we start our Third Century, however, there is serious questioning about the moral quality of our institutions, and it is not surprising that lawyers have been prime targets of criticism. If lawyers had simply perceived of themselves as technicians, and if society had accepted so limited a role for lawyers, the present criticism of the profession would be far less intense. But lawyers have, with justification, held themselves out as something more than scriveners and advocates. They have sought and achieved a role as independent professionals, presumably able to influence clients in the direction of compliance with law, rather than of evasion. They have operated the machinery of an adversary system which, whatever its enormous shortcomings and failures, has had as its fundamental tenet that, in the hands of lawyers following certain rules, it was more likely to produce truth than any other system yet devised for resolving disputes.

If Ralph Nader is correct when he talks about rampant corporate and governmental lawlessness, then the legal profession must seriously contemplate its own responsibility for the actions of its clients. How far into the Third Century will the American people contemplate a government that lies, corporate leadership that bribes, a system where the vast majority of those requiring legal services cannot afford them, a criminal justice system that is a shambles, a legal education system that still trains students primarily to serve the wealthy classes of America—and not start to hold lawyers responsible?

Obviously, it is unfair and inaccurate to hold lawyers alone responsible for the virtues, or the ills, of American society. And in every major reform movement in American history, lawyers have played an essential role. But we cannot have it both ways. We cannot hold the positions of influence which we enjoy and then pretend to be unimportant technicians when the institutions we serve are in trouble. One may seriously question whether, in the Third Century, lawyers should continue to play so important a role in American life. Indeed, if our society manages to create structures which provide legal services for the broad base of the American people, much of the elitism that now surrounds the bar will evaporate. But if the Third Century becomes a period of questioning and change in American life, the leaders of the bar must be in the forefront of those changes and the profession must be restructured to serve people in relation to their needs, not merely their ability to pay.

Finally, we may hear very often during this Bicentennial about the function of law as a synthesizer of other disciplines. Lawyers, judges and teachers recognize that legal rules and institutions cannot be removed from the underlying social, economic, political and moral values of our society. This has been recognized in this volume, with its special emphasis on these other disciplines.

Before we start on the exciting intellectual journey of this Bicentennial, however, let me sound a note for the primacy of law itself. It becomes very easy, particularly in the company of outstanding economists, historians, doctors, physical and social scientists, and political activitsts, to view the law as an empty vessel into which the other values of our society are poured. To a considerable extent, law in America embodies those values and disciplines. But it is something much more. The law has a moral and ethical force of its own which transcends the other forces and disciplines which affect it. Those who compose the legal profession—lawyers, judges, teachers and law students—bring their own value judgments as legal professionals to bear on the events of American life. They will write, interpret, and argue for a system of law that represents their vision of the American future. If law were viewed merely as the neutral recipient of other values in society, then lawyers could easily absolve themselves of their responsibilities for society's shortcomings. Recognizing the power of law and its independent intellectual and moral force makes us all accountable to the society which we claim to serve.

I hope that one hundred years from now a new generation of Americans will look back at the Third Century of American law with pride that, through law, this nation's promise of individual liberty and social justice will have moved closer to reality. If that happens, all of American society can share in the glory. But a special place will be reserved for the role of law and lawyers. Our profession alone cannot assure that the promises of the past will be fulfilled. But the future will be written in law. And lawyers must provide the commitment to freedom and dignity, the moral stature, and the skill, if America's journey into the Third Century is to be worthy of the birth we celebrate this year.

SEPARATION OF POWERS AND FEDERALISM

Two Doctrines with A Single Goal: Confining Arbitrary Authority

Norman Dorsen*

Although customarily viewed as structural arrangements for the allocation of government authority, both the separation of powers and the federal system are deeply rooted in the need to enhance personal liberty. As Justice Brandeis said in *Myers v. United States*,[1] "The doctrine of separation of powers was adopted by the Convention of 1787, not to promote efficiency but to preclude the exercise of arbitrary power. The purpose was, not to avoid friction but, by means of the inevitable friction incident to the distribution of governmental powers among three departments, to save the people from autocracy." Much the same could be said about federalism, which leaves to the states all power that is not assigned to the national government in carefully enumerated ways.

The Constitution, before its amendment by the Bill of Rights, contained only a sprinkling of clauses designed to protect individual rights, including the ex post facto cause, the prohibition against bills of attainder, the grant of trial by jury. Nevertheless, one of the great purposes of the Constitution was to "secure the blessings of liberty for ourselves and our posterity" and the means chosen to achieve this end were the separation of powers and the federal system.

**Professor of Law, New York University School of Law; General Counsel, American Civil Liberties Union; President, Society of American Law Teachers, 1973-75.*

I.

Turning first to the branches of the federal government, the original conception was that the Congress would be dominant. In the Constitutional Convention Madison said that "experience in all the states has evinced a powerful tendency in the legislature to absorb all power into its vortex."[2] And in the Federalist Papers, he again commented on the "tendency of the legislative authority to absorb every other."[3] The reasons are plain: It controls the pursestrings, its powers are the most extensive, and it possesses the warmaking power. The judiciary was widely regarded as the "least dangerous" branch,[4] and so it has been despite rumor to the contrary and some notable exceptions. The President, an untried entity, was an enigma. Madison said that "the executive department is very justly regarded as the source of danger, and watched with all the jealousy which a zeal for liberty ought to inspire."[5] Accordingly, the executive power was "restrained within a narrower compass"[6] as the great experiment was launched in 1789.

The nineteenth century did not disappoint the hopes of the founders. Congress was indeed the dominant branch, except during wartime, and despite several misguided decisions of the Supreme Court, including the infamous *Dred Scott* ruling[7]and the invalidation of the first income tax in 1895.[8] The sporadic assertions of authority by a few presidents, notably Jackson and Lincoln, were quickly assimilated into the overall national plan.

But in the twentieth century, with gathering momentum, the executive branch began to dominate. The aggressiveness of Theodore Roosevelt provided a benchmark for active presidential intervention into the economy under the Sherman and Interstate Commerce Acts, and later other regulatory statutes. The New Deal permanently transformed the domestic landscape, not only by centralizing power theretofore held by the states, but by lodging ever more firmly in the executive offices the motive force in the society. Four major wars settled the matter. Power became concentrated in a presidency which controlled the armed forces, dominated a vast bureaucracy, represented the country in foreign affairs, distributed a hundred ransoms in money and patronage, suffused the national consciousness through the mass media, and had access to secret information that could be used for a variety of ends.

The Congress lay back, timid, politically controlled, and, for the most part, ineffective.[9] A recent comment by Senator Phillip Hart of Michigan, epitomizes the position. In announcing his retirement after 24 years service, he said it was discouraging to see that things in the Congress remained just about the same as they had been when he arrived. As for the Supreme Court, its major assertions of power vis à vis the other branches and the states were a disaster. I refer of course to the rulings of the "old Court" that sought to shore up a *laissez faire* economic system by restricting the national authority under the Commerce Clause and limiting the state governments' capacity through the due process clause of the Fourteenth Amendment. As Justice Robert Jackson said when he was Attorney General, "the Court was poised between two worlds. The older world of *laissez faire* was recognized everywhere outside the Court to be dead. Would the Court then hold any other world powerless to be born?"[10] Although the Court's institutional wounds may have been self-inflicted, as Chief Justice Hughes said,[11] it was the blood of others that ran.

Recent years have wrought new changes. Successive presidents have presided over the Vietnam War, Watergate, and the illegal activities of the intelligence agencies. While the other branches did not distinguish themselves during these episodes, the executive as the principal agent of government action was most responsible for and most affected by what occurred. This is not merely a fact, but an opportunity, for it permits us now, at the threshold of our Third Century, to view the powers of the three branches in a time of relative flux. It would have been a purely academic exercise to have discussed ways of enhancing the presidency in 1876 or 1926. Similarly, it would have been of questionable utility to have considered ways of confining its authority in 1936 or 1966. But now there are concrete proposals afoot which, if adopted, could alter the relationship of the chief executive to the other branches.

My own view is that there should be such an alteration in the direction of reduced presidential power, or more exactly, that there should be greater cooperative effort among the branches that will permit congressional input into decisions that have customarily been made by the executive alone. As Attorney General Levi recently said, separation of powers does not mean that the branches must be "at war with each other."[12]

There are important unresolved domestic issues in which cooperative efforts between the executive and legislative branches will be necessary. These include the proposed guaranteed annual income, the nomination and election process for state and federal officials, the proper balance between economic growth and ecological demands, inflation, racial and sexual discrimination, drug approval and regulation, population control, and many others. It is tempting to discuss these engrossing problems, but instead I shall concentrate on a few major issues of foreign affairs, where the stakes if anything are higher and the pressures correspondingly greater.

It must be conceded that there has been accomodation between the executive and legislative branches over the years. The trouble is that almost all of it has been on one side—Congress has acquiesced in the erosion or limitation of its powers, perhaps out of an unwillingness to accept the responsibility that is the handmaiden of authority. This was surely the case in regard to the Vietnam War. In the Tonkin Gulf Resolution Congress virtually ceded to the President its constitutional power to declare war,[13] and its annual appropriations to finance the war undercut the protests of some congressional leaders that the war was being fought by the President alone without legislative support. Similarly, the Congress for decades turned a blind eye toward the CIA and other intelligence agencies that engaged in admittedly illegal conduct, including planned assassinations, mail openings, and other interferences with the rights of Americans. As the Church Committee recently stated with regard to covert action in Chile between April 1964 and December 1974, "The CIA did not volunteer detailed information; Congress most often did not seek it."[14] And even when Congress managed to act, as in the 1973 War Powers Resolution, it seems at best to have left executive powers where it found them, and at worst to have expanded them by conceding presidents up to 90 days *carte blanche* in the waging of war.[15] Senator Eagleton, an original sponsor of the Resolution, has written that the final bill was a "dangerous piece of legislation which, if enacted, would effectively eliminate Congress' constitutional power to authorize war."[16] The bill of course was enacted, and events alone will tell if Eagleton was correct.

To right the balance that has long been one-sided is no easy task for the Third Century. Initially, one may support steps that will enable Congress to participate more fully with the President in shaping American war and foreign policy.[17] For example, Congress should develop the capacity for periodic review of our use-of-force policy and participate with the President in its shaping even during crisis situations; there should also be systematic consultation between the President and the Congress concerning use of force; and Congress should provide greater legislative direction to the deployment of American armed forces abroad when their imminent involvement in hostilities is NOT indicated.

Turning more generally to foreign affairs, a permanent executive-legislative group should meet regularly for discussions on current problems, and a small agency on the General Accounting Office model should be established to scrutinize the foreign affairs bureaucracy. (All this presupposes, of course, that Congress will receive full information, if necessary on a classified basis, to enable it to perform its oversight function properly.) The President also should involve Congress in the decision-making process before he enters into long term, substantial commitments to foreign governments. And finally, the Congress should enact pending bills that would establish an independent Office of Legal Counsel. This office would be empowered, among other things, to represent the legislative interests of Congress in civil litigation, such as enforcement of subpeonas for information from the executive branch. It is no aspersion on the Justice Department to observe that Congress at times has independent interests that would be represented more single-mindedly by its own lawyers.

These steps, although important, would not be sufficient in the Third Century to assure the kind of joint effort that the Constitution contemplated or that events of the past decade suggest is needed. More decisive legislative action should be taken.

First, Congress should re-enact section 2(c) of the War

Powers Resolution to ensure its operative effect. This section is now described in the Act as part of its "purpose and policy." If it were wholly operative, it would prevent the President from deploying armed forces into actual hostilities, or situations where imminent involvement in hostilities is clearly indicated by the circumstances, except pursuant to (1) a declaration of war, (2) other specific statutory authorization, or (3) a national emergency created by attack upon the United States or its territories or possessions, or perhaps its armed forces. Respectable opinion holds that section 2(c) already achieves this.[18] But the history of the Resolution raises sufficient doubt to warrant new action. Thus, the conference of the two Houses reporting out the bill states that "subsequent sections of the joint resolution are not dependent upon the language of this subsection."[19] This was largely the basis for the defection of Senator Eagleton and others,[20] and while it is hard to be categorial, the better part of wisdom seems to suggest clarifying reenactment.

Secondly, Congress should sharply curtail the nature and occasions for covert activity by American foreign intelligence forces. A minimum legislative program has been outlined by two former high national security officials, Clark Clifford and Cyrus Vance,[21] neither of whom can be dismissed as radicals or unrealistic dreamers. They agree first that the law should authorize covert operations in very limited circumstances—"only when absolutely essential to the national security," in Mr. Vance's phrase. Next, certain methods such as political assassinations should be forbidden altogether. Third, Congress should assure accountability in the executive branch by requiring the express approval of the President for any secret operation. And fourth, one or perhaps two oversight committees of Congress should be told about any covert action contemplated before the President finally approves it. This, I repeat, is a minimum program. Many thoughtful observers believe covert activity by human means should be abolished altogether, that its achievements are insignificant and that such operations are incompatible with our democratic institutions, with public control over foreign policy decisions, with our constitutional rights, and with the principles that the Republic stands for in the world.[22]

A third and related area that urgently needs attention in the Third Century concerns classified or secret information. It is now almost universally accepted that a principal source of recent corruption was the excessive use of classified information to shroud the workings of government from the press and the people. But the malady is not new. Henry Steele Commager, the historian, has reminded us that "The generation that made the nation thought secrecy in government one of the instruments of Old World Tyranny and committed itself to the principle that a democracy cannot function unless the people are permitted to know what their government is doing."[23] There have been modest steps to establish a more open government,[24] but much more is needed. The areas of secrecy should be statutorily limited to three narrowly defined categories of information: first, technical details of military operations or weaponry, knowledge of which would be of benefit to another nation; second, military contingency plans with respect to foreign powers; and third, ongoing diplomatic negotiations of a patently sensitive character. In these categories the information is not essential to an informed public and could be damaging if released.

All other routinely classified information should be available to the public, including: (1) military action that the government is taking or sponsoring; (2) the presence of United States military or paramilitary forces in foreign counties; (3) the provision of United States military or economic assistance to foreign countries; and (4) any decisions or diplomatic commitments that the United States has made to do any of the foregoing.[25] Most of this information is now classified, but because the public through the Congress cannot exercise its responsibilities without information about foreign policy and military affairs, it should not be. I do not believe the genuine national security would be harmed if these recommendations were followed.

There are other actions that Congress should take to clarify and confine the powers of the executive. It should pass the proposed National Emergencies Act which would bring the various "national emergencies" declared in the past into some rational order.[26] It should be careful, however, that in achieving this objective it does not grant the President a wide-open power to declare an emergency whenever he thinks it is necessary to national "well-being."[27] Similarly, the Congress should legislate to require court orders and otherwise to limit the use of electronic surveillance to obtain foreign intelligence information. The Attorney General recently proposed such a bill, but because of concern over some of its provisions it was not enacted in the 94th Congress.[28]

There are two important lacunae in the above discussion. First, assuming that the goals outlined above are desirable, does the Congress have authority under the Constitution to limit the powers of the executive in the described manner? Closely related is the question of the role of the Supreme Court. Until now we have played the game of separation of powers with almost no reference to the third branch of government—the judiciary. This may seem particularly odd in view of the prominence of the courts over the past two decades and the heavy reliance on them for protection of the fabric of government as well as our individual liberties.

The Supreme Court's principal job with respect to separation of powers is to be an umpire, that is, to allocate responsibilities between the executive and legislative branches, to define the respective powers of these branches, and to assure that neither branch exceeds the measure of power granted by the Constitution.[29] It is important to recall, however, that umpires sometimes call players out, just as traffic cops sometimes put people in jail. Accordingly, in the *Steel Seizure*[30] and *Pentagon Papers*[31] cases the Supreme Court called the President out; it did so again, more literally this time, in the *Nixon Tapes* case (although it did grant a prospective right of rehearing to future presidents).[32] On the other hand, the Court took no such action with regard to the legality of the Vietnam War or the excesses of the intelligence agencies. In those instances it did not call the government safe;[33] rather it turned its back to the play and let the players work things out in a good old-fashioned rhubarb.

More important than its sporadic "calls" are the rules that the Court has announced to govern future controversies. It is here we must look to respond to the second question earlier left open—the power of Congress under the Constitution to limit the President's waging of war, keeping of secrets, carrying on covert intelligence activities, declaring national emergencies, and conducting electronic surveillance. We now enter deep water indeed, and I shall not attempt a full exposition of my grounds for believing that the Congress has considerable power in these respects. A summary of the reasons may, however, be briefly offered.

1. In its own right Congress possesses abundant affirmative powers relating to foreign affairs—for example, the powers to raise armies and declare war. The Senate also has the power to advise and consent in the making of treaties. In addition, there are the plenary legislative powers of investigation and appropriation.

2. In 1952 the Supreme Court decisively rejected the idea of an inherent executive power by holding invalid President Truman's seizure of the nation's steel mills to respond to an emergency during the Korean War.[34] It reiterated this principle in the 1972 *Keith* case,[35] where it ruled that the President lacked inherent power to engage in electronic surveillance for domestic security purposes. It is true that the Court has recognized certain special presidential prerogatives in foreign affairs,[36] but there has been no suggestion that these are limitless. It is also true that in the *Nixon Tapes* case the Court recognized an inherent, constitutionally based executive privilege,[37] but it also ruled that the privilege was not absolute and must yield in the balance to superior governmental interests.[38]

3. The Supreme Court made it clear in the *Mink* case,[39] involving the Freedom of Information Act, that Congress could enact legislation to affect this balance by restricting or otherwise changing the classification system. This conclusion built heavily on Justice Jackson's concurring opinion in the *Steel Seizure* decision, where he distinguished three situations in which there might be a confrontation with respect to power asserted by the President not expressly found in the Constitution.[40]

First, there is the situation in which the President is acting pursuant to an express or implied statement by Congress that he can so act—in other words, he is relying on a statute and Congress has not repealed the statute or amended it. In those circumstances, the President's power is at the maximum.

In the next situation the Congress has been silent—there is no statute on the books one way or the other. Here the President's power is ambiguous or, as Jackson describes it, in a "zone of twilight." The third case is where the President is acting contrary to the express will of Congress, announced in some enforceable resolution—such as a statute restricting covert intelligence activities, or a resolution requiring disclosure of certain classified information. Here the President's power is weakest, and this would be the situation if Congress now asserted itself.

4. Congress's authority is enhanced by the Necessary and Proper Clause.[41] It should be particularly noted that its power to make all laws Necessary and Proper for carrying into execution the other powers enumerated in the Constitution applies not only to the powers accorded the legislative branch, but pertains to "all other powers vested by [the] Constitution in the Government of the United States," including the powers of the executive branch.

5. Finally, the Supreme Court has recognized in diverse circumstances a congressional power to alter the substantive content of constitutional provisions. It has held that Congress may validate state laws regulating commerce which, in the absence of federal consent, would violate the Commerce Clause.[42] More recently, the Court has sustained congressional extensions of the Equal Protection Clause, noting that it "was for Congress" to "assess and weigh the various conflicting considerations."[43] Although these situations are distinguishable, they add to the sum of the congressional authority to fashion the limits of executive competence.

These, in summary form, are the reasons that lead me to conclude that the Congress can properly limit the President's authority to wage war, maintain secrets within the executive branch, carry on covert intelligence activities, and otherwise act in this field. Moreover, the Supreme Court has never declared an act of Congress unconstitutional because it encroached on the President's defense or foreign powers.

Despite the above considerations, we must not lose sight of certain inherent weaknesses and limitations in the legislative branch. Congress has a diffuse structure as well as a potential for arbitrariness that has often been fulfilled. The very forces which have prevented the Congress from fulfilling its promise as a strong branch of government, particularly in regard to foreign affairs, will always threaten to overwhelm incipient assertions of legislative authority.[44]

Similarly, one cannot be oblivious to the frequent need for decisive executive action. "Energy in the executive," wrote Hamilton, "is a leading character in the definition of good government. It is essential to the protection of the community against foreign attacks; it is not less essential to the steady administration of the laws."[45] Surely this must be admitted.

But there is no likelihood that the above proposals would eviscerate the executive branch. They are, after all, variants of the cooperative effort contemplated by the separation of powers. Very recently Vice President Rockefeller, returning from a four continent journey, referred to the importance of coordinating foreign policy between the legislative and executive branches and avoiding fragmentation.[46] And Judge Friendly, speaking on a related aspect of the war power, recently stated that the "obvious solution is the untidy one that the President should do the least that is feasible and consult Congress as soon and as fully as is possible."[47]

Even if there is a marginal impairment of the executive's ability to function, we may reasonably conclude that this is the lesser of two evils. It must not be forgotten that the Constitution contemplated an element of inefficiency in preference to autocracy. What it did not contemplate, and we must reject, is the executive's ability to involve the nation in foreign wars and troubles, and especially to be able to do so through covert agents or on the basis of information kept from the Congress and the people.[48] The rule of law requires no less. And if further resort to scripture is needed, Madison pointed out that Montesquieu's famous statement that "There can be no liberty where the legislative and executive powers are united," did not mean that "these departments ought to have no *partial agency* in, or no *control* over, the acts of each other."[49] This is exactly the path I have tried to outline for America's Third Century.

I should not pass to the second subject of this paper without trying to predict the future course of events. My opinion is that Congress eventually will enact some of the legislative proposals suggested above, including institutional arrangements for sharing power with the executive branch and a statute designed to regularize electronic surveillance of foreign intelligence sources. But I do not believe that it will soon face up to its harder responsibilities and cut back on covert activity abroad, or the capacity of the executive to wage unilateral war.[50] It will take another great crisis like the Vietnam War or Watergate to prod the Congress to attempt the last mile.

II.

When one turns from the allocation of authority within the national government to the problem of federalism—the relationship between national and state powers—the difficulties are more subtle. There is no doubt about the need for a fresh look at the start of our Third Century. Writing in 1939, the British political scientist, Harold Laski, declared that "the epoch of federalism is over," and that "only a [centralized] system can affectively (sic) confront the problem of a new time."[51] I hear the same refrain annually in constitutional law classes. But I also hear the contrary, that the national government is too remote from the people and their problems, too bureaucratized and complex, and too inflexible in coping with discrete situations. What is to be done? In fact, what can be done, given the fixed existence of the states in our constitutional system?

First a brief retrospective look. From 1789 until 1933 the federal government functioned more or less according to the original plan. It possessed limited powers and rarely attempted to expand or exceed them. True, a few statutes involved the national government in economic issues that had previously been exclusively in state hands. But enforcement was weak, dislocations relatively minor, and the overall impact small. This was reflected in, among other things, the docket of the Supreme Court. It was observed in 1907 in regard to Commerce Clause doctrine that "The development of the power was for one hundred years rather in a negative way than a positive way. The Court was called upon to say what the States could not do, instead of what Congress could do—except as the one necessarily followed from the other."[52]

The New Deal following hard on the depression changed all that. The first 100 days of Franklin D. Roosevelt's administration were the most active legislative period in American history, with the passage of regulatory laws involving securities, agriculture, labor, welfare, insurance and virtually every other area of national economic life. For a while the "old" Supreme Court thwarted the effort.[53] But that is not surprising when one considers that the Justices were being asked to legitimate a world into which they had not been born, which was foreign to their values, and which contained the seeds of much controversy. In any case, by the end of the Second World War at the latest, Washington was seen to be and in fact was the dominant force on national economic and social issues. Three Republican presidents in diverse ways attempted to turn back the clock or at least slow it down, but their impact was small, as the national budget is perhaps the best testament. As for the tenth amendment to the Constitution, which was supposed to embody federalistic values by reserving to the states powers not delegated to the United States, it was written off by the Supreme Court in 1941 "as a truism" meaning only "that all is retained which has not been surrendered."[54]

We are left with a number of fascinating constitutional problems, all of which are grist for a law professor's mill, but none, it must be said, basic to the way in which this country is governed. One issue is whether there are any limits to the scope of the commerce power, the constitutional source of most federal expansion into both economic and non-economic fields. Or to put the matter more precisely, are there any principles which would have permitted the Supreme Court to implement the tenth amendment by barring the application of national power to transactions that have only the barest connection, if any, with interstate commerce,[55] or to deal with matters such as local crime that traditionally have been subject only to state and local control?[56]

A closely related question is whether there are any subjects which are inherently local, and therefore not subordinate to federal power. The Supreme Court rejected this claim in a 1966 contest between federal and state governments over the estate of an Oregon resident who died intestate in United States Veteran Administration hospital.[57] Justices Douglas and Whittaker dissented on the ground that "nothing [is] more deeply inbedded in the Tenth Amendment . . . than the disposition of the estates of deceased people."[58] A few years later this dissent found an unfortunate echo in an opinion of Justice Black in a case involving a man who died intestate leaving an illegitimate child. A narrowly divided Court upheld Louisiana's rule of law that disinherited the child, saying that "the power to make rules to . . . regulate the disposition of property . . . is committed [to] the legislature of that State."[59] Whatever the truth of that statement in other circumstances, it is unfortunate that it was applied to defeat the claim of a stigmatized and unfortunate child who was not at all responsible for his status.[60]

A third issue is the extent to which the federal government can interfere with or penetrate a state's autonomy by coercing the states to take certain action to achieve federal ends. For instance, in the interest of assuring the proper administration of federal grants in aid, could the Congress determine "which [state officers] may be elected, which others politically appointed, and which must be in a nonpartisan career status."[61] Or could Congress validly enact a law assigning onerous administrative duties to state officials and require a state to expend funds in the administration of a program it opposes? This is not an academic issue; it is the route, for example, selected initially by the sponsors of the proposed national no-fault automobile insurance program.[62] Even more important, the Tenth Amendment received resuscitation recently when the Supreme Court manifested sensitivity to state autonomy concerns by invalidating the extension of the Fair Labor Standards Act to state and local governmental employees.[63]

A final issue concerns the circumstances in which federal courts will interfere with pending or threatened state proceedings in order to protect litigants from unconstitutional state action or to permit federal constitutional claims to be litigated in federal courts.[64] This is a complex problem that is sure to receive more attention.

But the fundamental problem of federalism for the future—I hesitate to say the entire Third Century—is not one of constitutional limits. It is rather the legislative allocation of responsibilities between Washington and other units of government. The charges are familiar: Inefficiency, insensitivity to local problems, lack of coordination, distance from government, and finally cynicism and alienation. These are basic questions of government responsiveness, and we hear them from people in the street as well as presidential candidates. They invite an inquiry as to the prospects for further decentralization of government . . . and the risks.

Although this important question does not ordinarily concern judicially enforceable rights, individual freedom is surely engaged. It is an aspect of freedom to be able to live one's life with a minimum of external control, and this principle would seem applicable to small communities as well as individuals. It is also pertinent that such freedom permits the maximum of local flexibility, underscoring Justice Brandeis's federalist concern that the states be permitted to serve as "laboratories" to "try novel social and economic experiments without risks to the rest of the country."[65]

What Brandeis was referring to, of course, was the ordinary administration of civil and criminal justice—contemporary problems of schools, housing, welfare, and myriad other governmental activities. In seeking to achieve Brandeis's goal, and simultaneously to allay the current dissatisfaction, many proposals have been made.[66] Their common element is transfer of power from Washington to the states, to local governments, and in some cases to regions. Revenue-sharing is one manifestation of the principle.[67] Personally, I am attracted to a model developed by a student writer at the University of St. Louis, who has proposed a two-level metropolitan system of government.[68] The first would centralize in a regional unit the authority to deal with areawide problems, such as mass transit, air and water pollution, and the pooling of funds for largescale projects. The second governmental unit would be essentially local, which would tailor its activities to better delivery of neighborhood services such as sanitation, police and fire protection and consumer assistance. Ironically, the key to the success of this idea would be the federal government, which would have to develop the necessary strategy and provide the impetus for reform by tying federal financial aid to programs of restructuring.[69]

Proposals of this sort, no matter how carefully thought out, present hard problems, which suggest caution in their adoption. Initially, there are the legal and political questions that bypassing existing entities of government would raise. The states are not going to disappear as legal units, since they are mandated by the Constitution.[70] Neither I suspect are the cities and towns of this country, all of which hold substantial and overlapping legal powers that could frustrate any attempt at reform. Second, local units of government are not quite as ideal as some have painted them. Historically, they have been plagued by inefficiency and corruption, insensitivity to many broad problems, lack of innovative drive, and often a poor caliber of personnel.[71] It must not be assumed that a transfer of problems from centralized Washington to smaller units of government will automatically assure their solution.

Finally, and most important for us today, there is valid doubt about the responsiveness of smaller units of government to minorities within their jurisdiction. As Vernon Jordan of the Urban League said recently, "If black folks have made any progress it was not at the hands of the state and local government but the Federal Government."[72] Similarly, Pablo Eisenberg, a consultant to the Center for Community Change, has charged that block grants to local communities have been used "to shore up local budgets" and that the poor and the minorities "tend to get left out."[73] It may have been true in 1787, when the Constitution was drafted, that "the State governments will, in all possible contingencies, afford complete security against invasions of the public liberty by the national authority."[74] The nation was then small, rural and comparatively homogeneous. It is so no longer and, not surprisingly, minorities are often the losers at the local level of government.

If this is correct, we are confronted with what might be called a double problem of freedom in the context of federalism. On the one hand, the desire to enhance individual liberty and creativity and responsive self-government; on the other, to assure that politically weak or isolated groups are not victimized by interests traditionally insensitive to their plight. It would not be unreasonable, in these circumstances, to condition any movement to disperse power on the express requirement that minority groups are protected. One early model is the Minneapolis Metropolitan Council, which has been designated by the United States Bureau of the Budget as a regional clearinghouse for applications by local communities to the federal government for funding assistance. The Council provided by rule that federal assistance should be denied to any community that refuses to take its share of funds for low income housing.[75] Whether this approach can work in other regions or on a broader scale, whether it is desirable in the first place to decentralize government services, and what mechanisms should be employed to achieve this goal are all difficult problems that will have to be faced in the Third Century.

At this point, I would merely stress the close relationship of federalism—and the separation of powers—to these issues of individual freedom and growth. Let us again recall the words of The Federalist:

> It may be a reflection on human nature that such devices should be necessary to control the abuses of government. But what is government itself but the greatest of all reflections on human nature? It men were angels, no government would be necessary. If angels were to govern men, neither external nor internal controls on government would be necessary. In framing a government which is to be administered by men over men, the great difficulty lies in this: you must first enable the government to control the governed; and in the next place oblige it to control itself.[76]

It is with the hope that in the Third Century we somehow can learn to control each other—and ourselves—that I conclude my review of this subject.

FOOTNOTES

1. 272 U.S. 52, 293 (1927).
2. 2 Farrand, The Records of the Federal Convention of 1787, 74 (1911 ed).
3. Federalist No. 71.
4. Federalist No. 78 (Hamilton). Montesquieu wrote, "Of the three powers above mentioned, the Judiciary is next to nothing." 1 The Spirit of the Laws 186 (1748).
5. Federalist No. 48.
6. Id.
7. Dred Scott v. Sandford, 60 U.S. (19 How.) 393 (1857).
8. Pollock v. Farmers' Loan & Trust Co., 157 U.S. 429 (1895).
9. Pritchett, The President's Constitutional Position, in Tugwell and Cronin (eds.), The Presidency Reappraised 26 (1974).
10. Jackson, The Struggle for Judicial Supremacy 85 (Vintage ed. 1941).
11. Hughes, The Supreme Court of the United States 50 (1928). In addition to the Dred Scott and Farmers' Loan cases, cited in notes 7 and 8, supra, the third such wound was the overruling of Hepburn v. Griswold, 8 Wall. 603(1869), which invalidated the legal tender act, by Knox v. Lee, 12 Wall. 457 (1870). See Hughes, *supra*, at 51-53.
12. Testimony of Hon Edward H. Levi before the Senate Government Operations Committee, February 6, 1976, p. 16.
13. P.L. 93-148, 93rd Cong. (Nov. 7, 1973).
14. Hearings before the Senate Select Committee to Study Governmental Operations with respect to Intelligence Activities (hereafter the Church Committee), 94th Cong., 1st Sess., Volume 7, p. 196 (1976).

15. War Powers Resolution section 8.
16. Eagleton, War and Presidential Power 204 (1974).
17. Most of my recommendations in this portion of the paper are adapted from The Powers of the Presidency, the Final Report of the Annual Chief Justice Earl Warren Conference on Advocacy in the U.S.A., June 20-21, 1975.
18. *Id*. at 13 (views of Professor Gerhard Casper and Phillip Kurland).
19. H.R. Rep. No. 546, 93rd Cong., 1st Sess. 8 (1973).
20. See, e.g., Fisher, War Powers: A Need for Legislative Reassertion, in Tugwell and Cronin, op. cit. *supra,* note 9, at 65-67.
21. Final Report of the Church Committee, 94th Cong., 2d Sess., Book 1, pp. 512-517 (1976). See also Lewis, A Test of Seriousness, N.Y. Times, Feb. 9, 1976, p. 27.
22. See statement of Morton H. Halperin before the Church Committee, Final Report, Book 1, p. 520.
23. Quoted from the New York Review of Books in Dorsen and Gillers, None of Your Business: Government Secrecy in America, vi (1974).
24. E.g., the 1974 amendments to the Freedom of Information Act, 5 U.S.C. 552 et seq.
25. The recommendations regarding classified information track closely the policy of the American Civil Liberties Union. See 1976 Policy Guide of the ACLU, Policy #7.
26. H. R. 3884, 94th Cong., 1st Sess.
27. *Id*., section 201(a).
28. S. 3197, 94th Cong., 2nd Sess. See Statement of Attorney General Edward H. Levi before the Senate Judiciary Committee, Subcommittee on Criminal Laws and Procedures, March 29, 1976. Compare Memorandum of the ACLU to Members of the United States Senate, re S. 3197, dated August 26, 1976.
29. See earlier discussions in Freund, Umpiring the Federal System, 54 Colum. L. Rev. 561 (1954); Vile, Constitutionalism and the Separation of Powers (1967).
30. *Youngstown Sheet & Tube Co. v. Sawyer,* 343 U.S. 579 (1952).
31. *New York Times Co. v. United States,* 403 U.S. 713 (1971).
32. *United States v. Nixon,* 418 U.S. 683 (1974).
33. Among the cases in which the Supreme Court declined to review the constitutionality of the Vietnam War are *Mora v. McNamara,* 389 U.S. 934 (1967) and *Massachusetts v. Laird,* 400 U.S. 886 (1970). See generally Friedman and Neuborne, Unquestioning Obedience to the President: The ACLU Case Against the Legality of the War in Vietnam (1972). The Supreme Court likewise has not reviewed the constitutionality of covert intelligence activity.
34. *Youngstown Sheet & Tube Co. v. Sawyer, supra* note 30.
35. *United States v. United States District Court,* 407 U.S. 297 (1972).
36. E.g., *United States v. Curtiss-Wright Export Corp., 299 U.S. 304 (1936); cf. Chicago & Southern Airlines v. Waterman S.S. Corp.,* 333 U.S. 103 (1948).
37. *United States v. Nixon, supra* note 32, 418 U.S. at 705.
38. *Id.*, 705-707.
39. *Environmental Protection Agency v. Mink,* 410 U.S. 73 (1973); see also *United States v. Reynolds,* 345 U.S. 1, 9-10 (1953).
40. *Youngstown Sheet & Tube Co. v. Sawyer, supra* note 27, 343 U.S. at 635-638.
41. U.S. Constitution, Article I, section 8.
42. *In re Rahrer,* 140 U.S. 545 (1891); *Clark Distilling Co. v. Western Maryland R. Co., 242 U.S. 311 (1917).*
43. *Katzenbach v. Morgan,* 384 U.S. 641, 653 (1966). See also *Oregon v. Mitchell,* 400 U.S. 112 (1970).
44. Compare the high hopes reflected in Gelb, Congress Likely to Press Its Role in Foreign Policy, N.Y. Times, April 19, 1976, p.1, and Lewis, The Church Committee: A Return to Basics, N.Y. Times, May 2, 1976, Section 4, p. 1, with Gelb, Spy Inquiries, Begun Amid Public Outrage, End in Indifference, N.Y. Times, May 12, 1976, p. 20 (discussing reasons for congressional lassitude in implement-

ing recommendations of the Church Committee concerning foreign and military intelligence, cited in note 21, *supra.*) And see the depressing analysis in Branch, The Trial of the C.I.A., N.Y. Times Mag. Sept. 12, 1976, p. 35.

45. The Federalist No. 70.
46. N.Y. Times, April 23, 1976, p. 10.
47. Friendly, The Constitution, Address at Convention Hall, Philadelphia, Pa., Jan. 29, 1976, p. 21. (U.S. Dept. of Justice Bicentennial Series—to be published 1977).
48. See generally the Final Report of the Church Committee, Book 1.
49. Quoted in Federalist No. 47 (Madison).
50. See, e.g., Gelb, Spy Inquiries, Begun Amid Public Outrage, End in Indifference, N.Y. Times, May 12, 1976, p. 20. And see the extensive analysis of Henry Steele Commager, 'Intelligence': The Constitution Betrayed, New York Review of Books, Vol. XXIII, No. 15, pp. 32-37 (Sept. 30, 1976), in which Professor Commager, among other things, critically assesses congressional performance in the past and pessimistically views prospects for the future.
51. Laski, The Obsolescence of Federalism, 98 New Republic 367 (1939).
52. Noyes, Development of the Commerce Clause in the Federal Constitution, 16 Yale L.J. 253, 258 (1907); see also Frankfurter, The Constitutional Opinions of Justice Holmes, 29 Harv. L. Rev. 683 (1916).
53. See the luminous discussion in Jackson, The Struggle for Judicial Supremacy (1941).
54. *United States v. Darby,* 312 U.S. 100, 124 (1941). But see *Fry v. United States,* 412 U.S. 542, 547 n. 7 (1975) ("The Amendment expressly declared the constitutional policy that Congress may not exercise power in a fashion that impairs the States' integrity or their ability to function in a federal system.").
55. E.g., *United States v. Sullivan,* 332 U.S. 689 (1948).
56. E.g., *Perez v. United States,* 402 U.S. 146 (1971). See generally Stern, The Commerce Clause Revisited—The Federalization of Intrastate Crime, 15 Ariz. L. Rev. 271 (1973).
57. United States v. Oregon, 366 U.S. 643 (1961).
58. *Id.,* at 654.
59. *Labine v. Vincent,* 401 U.S. 532, 538 (1971).
60. The Supreme Court in its 1976 Term will have an opportunity to overrule *Labine v. Vincent.* See *Trimble v. Gordon,* No. 75-5952, on appeal from the Supreme Court of Illinois.
61. Linde, Justice Douglas on Freedom in the Welfare State, 39 Wash. L. Rev. 4, 30 n. 111 (1964).
62. S. 354, 93d Cong., 2d Sess. (1074). See generally Dorsen, The National No-Fault Motor Vehicle Insurance Act: A Problem in Federalism, 49 N.Y.U.L.Rev. 45 (1974).
63. *National League of Cities v. Usery,* 96 S. Ct. 2465 (1976). The Court in the process overruled *Maryland v. Wirtz,* 392 U.S. 183 (1968).
64. See, e.g., *Younger v. Harris,* 401 U.S. 37 (1971); *Huffman v. Pursue, Ltd.,* 420 U.S. 592 (1975). See also the extensive consideration of the problem in N. Dorsen, P. Bender, & B. Neuborne, 1 Emerson, Haber & Dorsen's Political and Civil Rights in the United States 1577-1618 (4th ed. 1976).
65. *New State Ice Co. v. Liebmann,* 285 U.S. 262, 311 (1932) (dissenting opinion); see also *Anderson v. Dunn,* 19 U.S. (6 Wheat.) 204, 226 (1821) (Johnson, J., "The science of government . . . is the science of experiment").
66. See, e.g., Advisory Commission on Intergovernmental Relations, Alternative Approaches to Government in Metropolitan Areas (1962); Lineberry, Reforming Metropolitan Governance: Requiem or Reality?, 58 Geo. L. J. 675 (1970).
67. See, e.g., Strauss, Revitalizing Our Federal System: The Rationale for Revenue Sharing, 21 De Paul L. Rev. 889 (1972).
68. Comment, Restructuring Urban Government: The Two-Tier Federation and the Role of the Federal Government, 19 St. Louis U.L.J. 78 (1974).
69. *Id.,* See also Fisher, Presidential Spending Power (1975).

70. U.S. Constitution Article II, section 1; Article IV, section 3; passim.
71. See, e.g., Cattanach, Have the States Become an Anachronism in the Federal System? The Case for a Negative Answer, 21 De Paul L. Rev. 649 (1972).
72. See N.Y. Times, March 8, 1976, p. 18.
73. *Id.*
74. The Federalist No. 28 (Hamilton).
75. Urban Transportation Decision Making: 6 - - Minneapolis-St. Paul: A Case Study 15-16 (U.S. Dept. of Transportation 1974).
76. The Federalist No. 51 (Madison).

RACE IN AMERICAN LAW*

A. Leon Higginbotham, Jr.**

There has always been a fundamental ambiguity, some might even suggest a pervasive hypocrisy, on the issue of race and the legal process in America. Before we speculate about how racial issues will or should be dealt with in the constitutional and legislative arenas during the next century, we must first understand the failures and successes of the past since the first blacks came ashore at Jamestown in 1619—a year before the Pilgrims landed on the Mayflower. To the extent that we accurately comprehend the past, we can more adequately assess the magnitude of the present burdens and with such insights we will be able to more rationally identify the problems, the challenges, the options and the alternatives of the future. We must appreciate the

**Some of the materials presented here include excerpts from my forthcoming book Race and the Early American Legal Process: The Colonial and Revolutionary experience, to be published by Oxford University Press, and the thesis of this article has been developed more extensively in my previous articles published in the University of Pennsylvania Law Review, April, 1974, THE ANNALS of the American Academy of Political and Social Science, May 1973, Crisis Magazine, Winter, 1975, Proceedings of the American College Testing Program, Invitational Conference, May, 1972, and the Journal of Negro History, July, 1975.* *I also acknowledge the substantial assistance rendered to me by Thomas M. Gannon, S.J., my law clerk, and Brenda Spears, Esq., my research associate from the University of Pennsylvania, in the preparation of this article. I also wish to acknowledge my substantial reliance on the economic analysis and writings of Professor Bernard Anderson of the Wharton School, University of Pennsylvania.*

***District Judge, Eastern District, Pennsylvania; Adjunct Professor, University of Pennsylvania.*

nature of time as a continuum. Daniel Bell, Chairman of the Commission on the Year 2000, has written:

> "Time, said St. Augustine, is a threefold present as we experience it, the past as a present memory, and the future as a present expectation. By that criterion, the world of the year 2000 has already arrived, for in the decisions we make now, in the way we design our environment and thus sketch the lines of constraints, the future is committed . . . the future is not an overarching leap into the distance; it begins in the present."

The racial polarization of the 1970s has been partially determined by our history of thirty, one hundred, and even three hundred years ago. Similarly, by the positions we take each day on poverty, schools, housing, jobs, crime and racial justice, we will determine our capacity to have a viable and open society for blacks and whites in the decades to come.

I urge that we first focus on the racial injustices of three hundred, two hundred and one hundred years ago because now, with the hindsight of history, it is apparent that even the most esteemed forefathers committed, sanctioned, or at least tolerated grievous racial injustices. If we understand their failures, even though acknowledging that in many if not most respects they were exceptional individuals, maybe we will be more critical of or at least more realistic about our present efforts to deal with racial injustice today. With such a perspective during the decades ahead, we will be able more effectively to narrow the gap generated by past and present racial injustices.

I.

Blacks and the Declaration of Independence

During this Bicentennial era, many will applaud the revolution that was launched in Philadelphia on July 4, 1776. Some will call it the first, and others might suggest it was the greatest, revolution in the history of all mankind. Yet, while the Continental Congress was proclaiming the self-evident truth "that all men are created equal," at that very moment, with the absolute sanction of the legal process, more than half a million Americans were condemned to slavery solely because of their race. The fact that revolutionaries could speak of liberty for all while at the same time they unhesitatingly deprived blacks of any semblance of freedom reflects the ambiguity or hypocrisy which then existed and often still does exist on the issue of race and the American legal process.

In reaction to the Declaration of Independence, Frederick Douglass said:

> This Fourth of July is yours, not mine . . . the sunlight that brought light and healing to you, had brought stripes and death to me.

Abraham Lincoln later commented:

> When we were the political slaves of King George, and wanted to be free, we called the maxim that "all men are created equal" a self-evident truth; but now when we have grown fat, and have lost all dread of being slaves ourselves, we have become so greedy to be *masters* that we call the same maxim "a *self-evident lie.*" The Fourth of July has not quite dwindled away; it is still a great day for burning fire-crackers!

Was the Declaration of Independence a self-evident truth or was it, in the words of Abraham Lincoln, a "self-evident lie"? The answer depends on whose freedom one is concerned with. As Frederick Douglass and Abraham Lincoln noted, the first Revolution was not a victory for most blacks for it did not free the more than one-half million slaves in the colonies. For the mass of black people, the Revolution merely assured the rights of plantation owners to continue the tyranny of slavery.

It is ironic that the first emancipation proclamation involving American slaves was issued by the British during the Revolutionary era. On November 7, 1775, John Murray, Earl of Dunmore and Governor-General of the Colony and Dominion of Virginia, issued a problamation which freed "all indentured servants, Negroes or others . . . able and willing to bear arms . . ." with His Majesty's troops. In contrast to Lord Dunmore's proclamation freeing all slaves who were willing to bear arms for the King, the colonists never announced that they would free blacks who were willing to fight for the colonists' cause. Tragically, what the colonists wanted was both their freedom from the King and the simultaneous right to deny freedom to their slaves.

II.

The White Colonists' Perception of their Enslavement

The historical paradox is perhaps best exemplified by noting how the white colonists described their plight as one of enslavement. The "enslavement" existed because of taxation without representation and because of economic prohibitions such as the Sugar Act of 1764, which had been enacted without their consent. Thus, in voicing his opposition to that Sugar Act, Governor Stephen Hopkins of Rhode Island started his diatribe by asserting that "Liberty is the greatest blessing that men enjoy, and slavery the heaviest curse that human nature is capable of." Of course, Governor Hopkins was not speaking of the enslavement of blacks. Ironically, he argued that white colonists were being enslaved by England because the Sugar Act of 1764 decreased the profits from Rhode Island's involvement in the international slave trade.

In 1768 Pennsylvania's John Dickinson argued that:

> Those who are *taxed* without their own consent expressed by themselves or their representatives are *slaves. We are taxed* without our consent expressed by ourselves or our representatives. *We* are therefore—SLAVES.

Five years later Boston's Josiah Quincy proclaimed:

> I speak it with grief—I speak it with anguish—Britons are our oppressors: I speak it with shame—I speak it with indignation—*we are slaves.*

John Adams agreed that the colonists were ". . . the most abject sort of slaves to the worst sort of masters!"

While today we most often think of slavery as chattel slavery, in the eighteenth century it was often used with a political connotation which was later lost. In the political context of the eighteenth century, "slavery" pertained to concepts of property and of consent of the governed. It did not refer to racial chattel slavery. In almost every statement of political principle and in every discussion of constitutionalism and legal rights, the denial of rights to white colonists was linked to a concept of "slavery" as an absolute evil. "The slave was the man, or community, whose possessions could be taken without consent." Thus, as a term, slavery had bifurcated meanings. For whites it meant any enactment which limited their freedom or reduced the value of their property when they had not previously chosen representatives to vote on such an enactment, but at the same time those arbitrary acts of enslaving blacks, despite the absence of black consent, were not embraced within the definition of slavery whites used in condemning the King's abuses.

Nowhere is this racially bifurcated construction of slavery more manifest than in the July 6, 1775 Declaration of the Causes and Necessities of taking Up Arms. Franklin, Rutledge, Johnson, Livingston, Jay, Jefferson, and Dickinson constituted the committee which drew up this declaration, though the final draft appeared to be primarily the work of Dickinson and Jefferson. They began the Declaration by asking whether it was possible for men "who exercise their reason to believe that the Divine author of our existence intended a part of the human race to hold an absolute power in, and an unbounded power over others . . . as the objects of a legal domination never rightfully resistable, however severe and oppressive." Then they responded that:

> . . . the great Creator ['s] principles of humanity, and the dictates of common sense, must convince all those who reflect upon the subject, that government was instituted to promote the welfare of mankind, and ought to be administered for the attainment of that end.

They condemned the legislature of Great Britain for "enslaving these colonies by violence" which acts ". . . have thereby rendered it necessary for us to close with [our] last appeal from reasons to arms," and thus they were "bound by obligation of respect to the rest of the world to make known the justice of our cause." They emphasized that when "reduced to the alternative of choosing an unconditional submission to the tyranny of irritated ministers, or resistance by force," they must respond by force:

> We have counted the cost of this contest, and find nothing so dreadful as voluntary slavery.—Honour, justice, and humanity, forbid us tamely to surrender that freedom which we re-

ceived from our gallant ancestors, and which our innocent posterity have a right to receive from us. We cannot endure the infamy and guilt of resigning succeeding generations to that wretchedness which inevitably awaits them, if we basely entail hereditary bondage upon them.

In the document, they referred several times to their condition of slavery or enslavement. "With hearts fortified" they pledged "before God and the world" that they would use arms "in defiance of every hazard with unabating firmness and perseverance," and they resolved that "we are of one mind" *determined "to die freemen rather than to live slaves."*

Yet while the revolutionary leaders were resolving "to die freemen rather than to live slaves," they did not perceive that blacks had the same human right "to die as freemen"; by their very statutes the colonists had made it a serious crime, often punishable by death, for blacks who had the temerity to break the shackles of slavery to seek to live as free men.

Prominent Englishmen commented on the contradiction in the colonists' perception of themselves as enslaved. In 1775, in response to the resolution and address of the American Congress, Dr. Samuel Johnson said:

If slavery be thus fatally contagious, how is it that we hear the loudest yelps for liberty among the drivers of negroes.

Johnson summed up the colonists' arguments as "too foolish for buffoonery [and] too wild for madness."

Perhaps an advertisement placed by Thomas Jefferson for one of his runaway slaves more adequately describes the plight of black people in the United States in the eighteenth century than did his moving words in the Declaration of Independence:

[7 September 1769]

Run away from the subscriber in *Albemarle,* a Mulatto slave called Sandy, about 35 years of age, his stature is rather low, inclining to corpulence, and his complexion light; he is a shoemaker by trade, in which he uses his left hand principally, can do coarse carpenters work, and is something of a horse jockey; he is greatly addicted to drink, and when drunk is insolent and disorderly, in his conversation he swears

> much, and his behaviour is artful and knavish. He took with him a white horse, much scarred with traces, of which it is expected he will endeavour to dispose; he also carried his shoemaker tools, and will probably endeavour to get employment that way. Whoever conveys the said slave to me in *Albemarle,* shall have 40 s. reward, if taken up within the county, 4 1. if elsewhere within the colony, and 10 l. if in any other colony, from
>
> THOMAS JEFFERSON

III.

The Human Impact of Slavery

The human impact and tragedy of the slavery system is not adequately revealed by the mere reading of cases, statutes and constitutional provisions. Most of these cases dealt "merely" with distributing the assets of an estate or the rights of plantation owners versus the rights of creditors, or the rights of the state against those evil creatures—runaway slaves, people who dared to challenge the appropriateness of their lifetime imprisonment.

A reading of most of these cases impresses one with the casualness of the judicial process as it dealt with human beings who happened to be slaves. Generally, no more sensitivity was displayed than one would expect of a court decree adjudicating interest on corn, cotton, lumber or horses and dogs. To heighten one's consciousness as to the consequences of the slavery system, the advertisements of that era should be read. The following are typical:

An advertisement in Hamburg, South Carolina, on September 28, 1838 noted:

> One hundred and twenty Negroes for sale—The subscriber has just arrived from Petersburg, Virginia, with one hundred and twenty likely young Negroes of both sexes and every description, which he offers for sale on the most reasonable terms. The lot now on hand consists of plough-boys, several likely and well-qualified house servants of both sexes, several women and children, small girls suitable for nurses, and several small boys without their mothers. Planters and traders are earnestly requested to give the subscriber a call previously to making purchases elsewhere, as he is enabled to sell as cheap or cheaper than can be sold by any other person in the trade.
>
> Benjamin Davis

The advertisement of Benjamin Davis in 1838 was not unique; it was typical of thousands of advertisements posted in newspapers and bulletin boards throughout our land. In the *New Orleans Bee* an advertisement noted:

> Negroes for sale-A Negro woman, 24 years of age, and her two children one eight and the other three years old. Said Negroes will be sold separately or together as desired. The woman is a good seamstress. She will be sold low for cash, or exchange for groceries. For terms apply to Matthew Bliss and Company, 1 Front Levee.

Looking at these tragic, though routine, events of the seventeenth, eighteenth, and nineteenth centuries, one should ask what happened to the rule of law? How could a legal system sanction this cruelty, cruelty which permitted the sale, as Benjamin Davis bragged, of "several small boys without their mothers," cruelty which permitted a mother, twenty- four years of age, to be sold in exchange for groceries and separated from her eight- and three-year old children? Have we often distorted our history to keep from our full consciousness the extraordinary brutality of past racial injustice?

What was the response of our legal system to this institution of slavery which permitted the sale of children from their mother and other gross forms of cruelty? Probably the most typical example of the response of the legal system is found in an opinion by Judge Ruffin of the North Carolina Supreme Court in *State v. Mann,* 13 N.C. 263 (1828). Before the court was the simple issue of whether it was a criminal offense to subject a slave woman to "a cruel and unreasonable battery." Some historians have implied that slavery was a paternalistic institution wherein masters treated their slaves as if they were children. To decide the issue Judge Ruffin said, "We must look to . . . the established habits and uniform practice of the country . . . as the best evidence of the portion of power deemed by the whole community requisite to the preservation of the master's dominion." Counsel had argued that a master's relation to the slave was analogous to the principles which restrain the authority of a parent over the child, the tutor over the pupil, or the master over the apprentice. The court unanimously rejected those analogies by saying:

> There is no likeness between the cases. With slavery . . . [t]he end is the profit of the master, his security and the public safety; the subject, one doomed in his own person and his posterity, to live without knowledge and with the capacity to make anything his own, and to toil that another may reap the fruits.

The court went on to emphasize that a slave was to "labor upon a principle of natural duty," to disregard "his own personal happiness," and that the purpose of the legal system was "to convince slaves they had no will of their own and they must surrender [their] will in implicit obedience to that of another. Such obedience is the consequence only of uncontrolled authority over the body. There is nothing else which can operate to produce the effect. The power of the master must be absolute to render the submission of the slave perfect." The court emphasized that for a slave "there is no remedy," that "we cannot allow the right of the master to be brought into the discussion in the courts of justice. The slave, to remain a slave, must be made sensible that there is no appeal from his master; that his power is in no instance usurped; but is conferred by the laws of man at least, if not by the law of God."

The court noted this unlimited "dominion is essential to the value of slaves as property, and to the security of the master, and the public tranquility." Then finally and most paradoxically the court concluded that the law's impotence in protecting slaves from cruel batteries was designed to "effectively secure the general protection and comfort of the slaves themselves."

Of course, when Judge Ruffin wrote, there had been some acts of partial enlightenment by northern courts and legislatures toward abolishing slavery, but Judge Ruffin's views reflected the then legal status of more than ninety percent of the blacks in America. His attitude toward blacks was echoed in the *Dred Scott* decision by Chief Justice Rober B. Taney, writing for the United States Supreme Court in 1857, when the Court held that a black man "had no rights which the white man was bound to respect; and that the [n]egro might justly and lawfully be reduced to slavery for his benefit. He was bought and sold, and treated as an ordinary article of merchandise and traffic, whenever a profit could be made by it. This opinion was at that time fixed and universal in the civilized portion of the white race."

Representative Summers of the Virginia Legislature stated in 1832 that, "when, in the sublime lessons of christianity, he (the slave holder) is taught to do unto others as he would have others do unto him, he never dreams that the degraded Negro is within the pale of that holy canon."

In reply to some members who had proposed abolition, Mr. Tholson of the Virginia Legislature said in 1831, "Why, I really have been under the impression that I owned my slaves. I lately purchased four women and ten children in whom I thought I obtained a great bargain, for I really supposed they were my property, as were my brood mares." In the United States House of Representatives one Congressman said, "slaves have no more right to be heard than horses and dogs." On February 11, 1837, the House of Representatives of the United States resolved, by a vote of 162 to 18, "that slaves do not possess the right of petition secured to the people of the United States by the Constitution."

The daughter of Judge Grimkey of the Supreme Court in South Carolina said, "Slaveholders regard their slaves as property, the mere instruments of their convenience and pleasure. One who is a slaveholder at heart, never recognizes a human being in a slave."

With generally the notable exception of the Quakers, there appeared to be no difference in the treatment of slaves by men who purported to practice the canons of organized religion. The Charleston Baptist Association addressed a memorial to the Legislature of South Carolina maintaining that "the divine authority of our holy religion adopted the institution of slavery as one of the allowed relations of society." They argued that neither society nor individuals have any authority to demand a relinquishment of slaves and that they would "resist to the ulmost any invasion of this right, come from what quarter and under what pretense it may."

Mr. Al Turner, a regular and respectable member of the Second Presbyterian Church in Springfield, Illinois, said "Slaves are neither considered nor treated as human beings." In the settlement of the estate of the Rev. Doctor Furman of the Charleston Baptist Association, his legal representatives advertised the public sale of his property at an auction as follows: "A plantation or tract of land on and in watery swamp, a tract of the first quality of fine land on the waters of Black River; a lot of land in the town of Camden, a library of miscellaneous character, chiefly theological; 27 Negroes, some of them very prime; two mules, one horse, and an old wagon." Thus as Rev. Furman went to meet his maker, he did not differentiate in his estate between mules, slaves, and books.

IV.

1865 - 1976

Some persons might be incensed by my reference to the brutalities sanctioned by the law in the pre-Civil War era. Some might even assert that this period of our history is now irrelevant; they might ask: "Why doesn't he look at the operation of the rule of law after the Thirteenth, Fourteenth and Fifteenth Amendments to the Constitution were passed?" True, those Amendments were designed to eradicate slavery and in the words of Charles Sumner (the conscience of the United States Senate) were designed so "that hereafter in all of our legislation, there shall be no such words as black or white, but that one shall speak only of citizens." Some might say, "Why don't you look at those constitutional amendments and the related civil rights legislation of 1865 to 1875."

Yet if we reflect on the laws and judicial decisions in the post-reconstruction period, it becomes evident that the rule of law more often than not precluded a truly democratic and open society for blacks. The harsh and disparate impact of the late nineteenth century constitutional doctrine is reflected by the federal birth of the separate but [un]equal doctrine of *Plessy v. Ferguson.* For in 1896, the United States Supreme Court upheld the right of a state to pass a statute providing for separate railway accommodations for the white and colored races. In the opinion, they gave implied approval of the right of a state to legislate separate school facilities for blacks and whites. They said:

> we think the enforced separation of the races, . . . neither abridges the privileges or immunities of the colored man, deprives him of his property without due process of law, nor denies him the equal protection of the laws, within the meaning of the Fourteenth Amendment.

In an eloquent dissent, Mr. Justice Harlan said:

> [I]n view of the Constitution, in the eye of the law, there is in this country no superior, dominant, ruling class of citizens. There is no caste here. Our Constitution is color-blind, and neither knows nor tolerates classes among citizens. In respect of civil rights, all citizens are equal before the law. The humblest is the peer of the most powerful. The law regards man as man, and takes no account of his surroundings or of his color when his civil rights as guaranteed by the supreme law of the land are involved. It is, therefore, to be regretted that this high tribunal, the final expositor of the fundamental law of the land, has reached the conclusion that it is competent for a state to regulate the enjoyment by citizens of their civil rights solely upon the basis of race. In my opinion, the judgment this day rendered will, in time, prove to be quite as pernicious as the decision made by this tribunal in the Dred Scott case.

Finally, he concluded:

> The destinies of the two races, in this country, are indissolubly linked together, and the interests of both require that the common government of all shall not permit the seeds of race hate to be planted under the sanction of law. What can more certainly arouse race hate, what can more certainly create and perpetuate a feeling of distrust between these races, than state enactments, which, in fact, proceed on the ground that colored citizens are so inferior and degraded that they cannot be allowed to sit in public coaches occupied by white citizens?

Think in terms of what type of nation we would now have if in 1896 our leaders had really followed the message of Justice Harlan that ". . . the common government of all shall not permit the seeds of race hate to be planted under the sanction of law." If this message had been implemented, subtle or blatant racism would not be one of the hidden issues in current politics. There would be no problems of busing today; there would not be the extensive racial ghettos which now exist in the inner cities of our nation. The striking racial gaps between black and white economic, health, and educational attainment would be either nonexistent or significantly diminished.

But today we have these tragic gaps because moral leadership was not provided for the concept of an open society. In fact, it was abandoned by the 1877 Hayes-Tilden Compromise, the 1896 capitulation in *Plessy v. Ferguson;* and for decades no moral leadership was provided in this field by the White House, by the courts, by the schools, by the Congresses, by the Legislatures, and often not even by the churches.

The catastrophic backlash in education by the 1896 *Plessy v. Ferguson* doctrine seems almost unbelievable. In 1899 the United States Supreme Court failed to strike down the Richmond County, Georgia school system which used its funds to support a "private" high school for white children without providing a high school for colored children. The Supreme Court sanctioned a state court's finding that the "suspending temporarily, and for economic reasons, the high school for colored children . . . was not a violation of the colored children's rights of . . . equal protection of the laws [Fourteenth Amendment] or of any privileges belonging to them as citizens of the United States."

In *Berea College v. Kentucky* in 1908 the United States Supreme Court upheld the validity of a 1904 Kentucky statute which prohibited a college from teaching white and Negro pupils in the same institution, holding that it was no violation of federal constitutional rights. Tragically, Berea College had been established in 1859 by its founders to establish and maintain an institution of learning "in order to promote the cause of Christ." Yet the United States Supreme Court held that a state could deprive a private institution from promoting the cause of Christ if it did so through integrated education. In Berea College, Justice Harlan wrote another eloquent dissent and tragically, Mr. Justice Oliver Wendell Holmes (the darling of legal liberals) concurred in the majority's repressive opinion.

Harvard Law School's distinguished Professor Derrick A. Bell, Jr., in commenting on this period, has said:

> And as the gains made by blacks—political, legal, and social—were erased in the 1870's the Supreme Court and the lower courts confirmed in their decisions what blacks had feared, that the citizenship they had been granted, which indeed they believed they had earned through the blood of

> thousands of blacks who had died fighting on the Union side during the War, was citizenship in name only.
> . . . In the process, blacks were damaged. But with faith and that grace that some of us still sing about, that Amazing Grace, we survived.

Today, thoroughout the nation, we suffer the backlash of decades of such racial inequality. What hurts most is that many who have profited from the espousal of racial hatred, many who have urged segregation and racial injustice and many who stood aloof while blacks were being debased are now the most strident critics of the blacks and the current racial malaise. It is almost as if one who has fathered a child born out of wedlock now piously condemns the child as immoral.

When examining the issue of racism during the last thirty years, one notes many significant events which repudiate the old racial injustice: The United States Supreme Court's opinions in 1944 in *Smith v. Allwright,* the key primary voting rights case, and in *Brown v. Board of Education* in 1954; the several civil rights acts from the late 1950s; the proliferation of executive orders and fair housing laws and fair employment laws. All of these constituted advances toward creating racial justice.

The legal system's efforts have not been in vain. By any measure, the years following the *Brown* decision and the Civil Rights Acts of 1964, 1965 and 1968 have been years in which the "promise" of racial equality has become more of a reality for blacks and other minorities. Blacks have made substantial gains in almost all crucial facets of American life, including education, employment and housing.

Still, we must face hard reality. Despite the gains in these areas, disparities continue to exist. Despite the EEOC's efforts to ensure equal access to jobs, the unemployment rate among blacks generally remains twice that of whites; and most blacks continue to remain at the bottom of the income ladder. Despite *Brown,* blacks more often than not continue to be educated in de facto segregated schools. Despite the 1968 Fair Housing Act, blacks more often than not continue to live in the worst sections of our cities and suburbs.

The data indicates that black people remain seriously disadvantaged and it demonstrates that the legal system's efforts to ensure the constitutional rights to equal protection and due process under our laws for all of our people have fallen short of the mark.* The courts may have caused a reassembling of some components in American life. But examination of the current status of black Americans in areas such as housing and employment leads to one conclusion: The courts cannot alone restructure American society. Any meaningful and lasting change will result only when all of the institutions which encouraged four hundred years of racial suppression are called upon to destroy the fruits of their malevolent labors.

In short, gaps have been narrowed and progress has been made, but it is nevertheless essential that we assess how much progress has been made, how much is left to be done, and what the role of the courts, the legislators, the legal profession and people in general should be to eliminate the malignant vestiges of that racial dehumanization which pervasively remains.

V.

THE FUTURE

The Role of the Constitution, Courts, Legislature and Executive

Regrettably, in the past, the courts have helped mightily to create the ambiguity and hypocrisy of the American legal process toward the issue of race. Fortunately, during the last three decades, the federal courts have played a major role in eliminating some of the racial injustices which the legal pro-

**The following provide indisputable data as to the serious disparities and deprivations still sustained by blacks:*

Dr. Bernard E. Anderson (Professor, Wharton School, University of Pennsylvania) *The Labor Market Experience of Youth; the Black Worker Today.* Sar A. Levitan, William Johnston, Robert Taggert, *Still a Dream: A Study of Black Progress, Problems and Prospects* (Washington, D.C. Center for Manpower Policy Studies, 1973). John F. Kain, *Housing Market Discrimination and its Implications for Government Housing Policy* (June 29, 1973). U.S. Commission on Civil Right, *Twenty Years After Brown; The Shadows of the Past* (volume 1, June 1974); *Equality of Educational Opportunity* (Volume 2, March 1975); *Equality of Economic Opportunity* (volume 3, July 1975); *Equal Opportunity in Housing* (volume 4 December 1975); U. S. Dept. of Commerce, Bureau of Census: *Current Population Reports, Special Studies Series,* #54, at 23; *General Demographic Trends for Metropolitan Areas,* 1960-1970, 1970 *Census of Population—Series PH; Monthly Labor Review,* November 1974, 30, 31, Tables 4 and 5; *Occupational Characteristics, 1970 Census of Population Series PC(2)-7A,* Table 2; *Occupational Characteristics, 1960 Census, Series* PC(2)-7A, Table 3; Social and Economic Status of the Black Population in the United States (Current Population Repts.) Series P-23 #48 (1973) Table 34, Series P-60 (annual issues) #46, Table F.

cess previously caused. But what can, or should the courts and the Constitution do in the future to narrow the gaps? We know that the Supreme Court can make a mighty difference. If the Supreme Court had followed the course it charted in *Dred Scott v. Sandford, Plessy v. Ferguson,* and *Berea College v. Kentucky,* the ambiguity of the American legal process toward race would have been completely and tragically resolved, for the courts and the legal process would have been solidly aligned against the legitimate aspirations of millions of black Americans.

Happily, the Supreme Court began, a few degrees at a time, to change course, to veer away from the morally and legally bankrupt vision of American society that underlay decisions like *Dred Scott, Plessy* and *Berea College.* In the White Primary and early voting rights cases, it struck down a variety of subterfuges employed by the states in repeated attempts to deny blacks the right to vote. In other cases involving institutions of higher education, the court held that the states could not shelter behind the doctrine of "separate but equal" while they ostracized black students and denied them access to meaningful educational opportunity. In short, the Supreme Court was saying that there were some limits to the disabilities that a state could inflict on American citizens solely because of their race. This demarcation of limits prepared the way for *Brown v. Board of Education,* a case whose significance I have already touched on. Not only did *Brown* hold that segregated education was inherently unequal education, it stripped away the moral pretensions of every such discriminatory arrangement. *Brown* sounded the death knell of officially sanctioned racial separatism in American life. It created the climate of opinion in which the Executive and the Congress, during the 1960's, after nearly a century of virtual inactivity, would at last use their awesome power to redeem the promise of America and secure justice for all American citizens.

The courts had a role to play in this redemption of America's promise. They validated the remedial statutes—principally the Civil Rights Act of 1964 and the Voting Rights Act of 1965—devised by the national legislature to cure the effects of past discimination. Yet when we blend the rationale of past civil rights victories with the economic data which demonstrates both some significant progress during the last two decades and also some stalemating and plateauing, particularly during the last few years, it becomes obvious that there is no certainty that the remaining disparities will be eliminated, even during the next one hundred years. Yet, at the same time, our past history also suggests that, with proper commitment by all major private and public institutions, the major racial disparities could be almost obliterated within the next quarter century. Thus, the issue before this forum becomes what role, if any, can the courts and/or the Constitution play in eliminating the gap.

I submit that in the future, the courts by their very nature, will not be and cannot be as significant an instrument in narrowing these racial disparities as the Supreme Court has been during the last three decades. We are now moving away from the blatant *de jure* type of racist statutes and acts that existed in the pre-*Brown* era to problems where the solutions are less obvious and the remedies more complex. I am not suggesting that the Supreme Court has swung the pendulum as far as it is constitutionally permissible, for I personally would have probably agreed with the dissenting opinions in cases such as *Milliken v. Bradley, Rizzo v. Goode, Moose Lodge No. 107 v. Irvis* and *Rodriguez v. San Antonio Indep. School District.*

Nevertheless, by their nature, courts decide individual cases on their specific facts. As courts progress beyond cases like *Brown,* where clear issues of principle are presented, to suits that challenge de facto segregated housing or schools, not just in a single neighborhood or school district but in an entire metropolitan area, and oblige the courts to make more refined judgments on issues of social educational and economic policy, it is probably naive to expect the courts to speak with a single voice as the Supreme Court did in *Brown.* And it is certainly naive to expect the courts, through the device of constitutional interpretation, to solve all of the problems that are the legacy of the legal process's ambiguity and hypocrisy toward race. There are inherent constraints imposed both by constitutional doctrine and by common sense which preclude the courts from narrowing all of the gaps. Thus, while on occasion the Supreme Court may express the conscience of the nation, the principles of that conscience can often remain unimplemented and may even sometimes be circumvented.

On the other hand, the Executive and the Congress express the will of the nation, and that will, once it is embodied in legislation, can become almost irresistible. When the nation finally came to its moral senses and decided that the last, lingering, state-sanctioned badges and incidents of slavery must be eliminated, Congress passed the Civil Rights Act of 1964. When the nation finally decided that no state or its officials should be able systematically to deny its citizens the right to vote on the basis of race, Congress passed the Voting Rights Act of 1965.

Given the realities of American politics, it is doubtful that these two statutes would ever have been enacted if the courts had not, in case after case, held state-supported segregation unconstitutional, and thus awakened the American people to the inherent injustice of racial separatism in any form. Yet these two statutes, as remedies for the dehumanization and deprivation that centuries of an unresponsive legal process had helped to create, were far more effective than many justly-famed court decisions. I am confident, for example, that the Voting Rights Act of 1965 gave blacks a voice in their own political destiny that was far more meaningful than all of the White Primary Cases combined.

With the passage of these statutes, with the court decisions that sustained them against constitutional challenge, and with their vigorous enforcement by the federal government, most of the obstacles that the legal process had placed in the way of black Americans on the road to genuine equality have been removed. In this country today there is no great clamor for the passage of new civil rights laws, even among the groups and organizations that traditionally have been the strongest supporters of such legislation.

Does this mean then that we have reached a millenium in race relations in this country? I do not believe we have. While many of the legal barriers to full equality for blacks have fallen, the economic effects of the dehumanization inflicted on American blacks in the past still persist. And in this area of economic deprivation, though the root causes of the deprivation may be different, there are millions of white Americans whose lot is very much like that of most blacks. Thus, while there is less need for the nation to focus its attention specifically on the legal disabilities that once burdened blacks, *the nation must continue to focus on the economic disabilities that still restrain tens of millions of Americans, white as well as black.*

For what value ultimately resides in integration if it leads only to integrated proverty, integrated schools that fail to educate any of their students, integrated medical facilities that do not care adequately for any of their patients, integrated neighborhoods that are crumbling around the ears of all their residents, and integrated fear for one's personal safety on the streets of our major cities?

Though the courts can order integration, they cannot implement successfully a pervasive order which will end fear, eliminate urban blight, eradicate inadequate medical care, or abolish unemployment and poverty. The effective solution to these problems will generally remain the province of the Executive and legislature. What I am suggesting then is the need for a new, broadly based national consensus, of whites as well as blacks, of males as well as females, that will impel Congress and the Executive to secure full economic justice for all Americans. Such a consensus, if it led those two branches of government to act—and sometimes they need to be led—would go far toward finally eliminating the effects of the dehumanization visited on blacks throughout their history in this country. More important, it would redeem the promise of America for all of this nation's people.

All too often in the past, unscrupulous politicians, preying frequently on the real though not necessarily justified fears of white people, have pitted blacks and whites against each other, even though their fundamental interests were the same, and thus have sabotaged the consensus that might have been created. Permit me to mention just two examples. The phrase "law and order," which was always both popular and honorable when used in Western movies, came to mean in recent years, for most blacks and a substantial number of whites, the repression of blacks under the rubric of a "get tough" policy on crime. Reacting to what they perceived to be thinly disguised racism, these people were placed in the false position of seeming to oppose "law and order," a concept which in itself is and should be especially precious to blacks, who are so often the victims of crime when law and order does not prevail.

"Quality education" is another phrase that has come to be charged with racial connotations. When it is used as a synonym for continuing racial segregation in the public schools, those who so employ it should be opposed at every turn. But the phrase itself is not only inoffensive, what it stands for is actually desirable, and is just as important to blacks as it is to whites. Quality education is what all parents, of whatever race, want for their children.

In so many urban areas, affluent parents of both races have, in effect, abandoned ship, either by physical relocation to the suburbs or by placing their children in elite private institutions. Quality education is precisely what the children of poor and working parents—of both races—often do not receive in the decaying public school systems that the more affluent have left behind. The parents whose children attend these schools thus have a common interest, a decent education for every child. Sadly, that common interest has often been obscured. Until it is recognized, until parents, both black and white, work together to secure it, their children, both black and white, will be the losers.

"Law and order" and "quality education," once the racist overtones that they have acquired have been peeled away, are two issues among many where blacks and whites possess common interests, and where blacks and whites can and should transcend the artificial dividing lines of race and color to work together for common goals. Indeed, I would go further and say that blacks and whites *must* work together if this nation is to become what I earlier described as a viable and open society in the next one hundred years of its history.

I am not an economist; I am a federal judge. I know something about the Federal Rules of Civil Procedure; I know little about trends in the domestic and world economies. Yet if I had to select the most important of the common goals that blacks and whites together must work toward to insure the openness and viability of this society in the year 2076, that goal would be meaningful employment for every citizen who is able and willing to work. I am not for a moment suggesting that we relax our efforts in any area to secure total justice for all American citizens. I am not suggesting that the role of the courts or the EEOC should be diminished. Of course we ought to support every rational attempt to improve the quality of our schools or our medical care or our housing. Still, one does not have to be another John Maynard Keynes to recognize that millions of Americans, a disproportionately large number of them black, presently lack the economic resources to lead lives of dignity and modest comfort. The available statistical data gives ample evidence of that fact. Nor does one have to be a Keynes to recognize that the major key to redressing the economic imbalances in our society is employment—in a word of one syllable, jobs, in particular jobs for young people, and most especially jobs for young black men. Unemployment among the last group has reached staggering dimensions. Reduce it, and the crime rate, I assure you, will come down. Give youngsters a reasonable hope for a decent job, with the possibility of upward mobility and without the prospect of racial discrimination, and they will, I assure you, become considerably more educable.

I am not competent to comment on the merits of legislation presently before the Congress that is designed, I am told, to assure the kind of employment situation I think is desirable. In any event, it would be highly inappropriate for me to do so. I am sure, however, that Congress and the political arena generally are the forums where the last crucial battles must be fought in the long struggle of American blacks to achieve a total rendezvous with justice. Courts can punish criminals; they can order the integration of schools; but they can seldom create jobs when factories are closing. Court-decreed affirmative action policies for graduate schools are irrelevant to children who do not master in elementary school the rudiments of reading, writing and arithmetic. Thus, I do not believe that in the future the courts will be the decisive forums for the eradication of the remaining effects of the suffering inflicted on American blacks by the ambiguity and hypocrisy of the legal process. Whatever its original causes, the illness is now primarily economic, and its remedy must be economic too. And because the illness is economic, it affects not just blacks, but millions of other Americans as well. All of them, black and white, sharing a common interest, can and should work toward a common goal, the provision of employment for every citizen who is able and willing to work. Once that goal is achieved, it would bring with it a life of dignity and modest comfort for every American family. Once that goal has been achieved, we will be able to say that the poison injected into the nation's bloodstream by racial chattel slavery will at last have been drawn. We will also be able to say that the last malevolent effects of the ambiguity and hypocrisy of the American legal process toward race will finally have been cured.

CIVIL LIBERTIES PROTECTING OLD VALUES IN THE NEW CENTURY

David L. Bazelon*

One advantage—I sometimes think the only advantage—of having been a judge for twenty-six years is the opportunity I've had to forge close friendships with persons in many disciplines. As I often do, I exploited the wisdom and patience of some of these friends in preparing this paper. I quickly discovered they fell into three categories. The pessimists, when told I was to speak about the future of civil liberties, glumly muttered, "That's easy—civil liberties don't have any future." The optimists waxed eloquent predicting changes that would make Eden look like a raw deal. And the realists were brutally honest. They suggested, "Just tell them you don't know about the future—and sit down." This last suggestion was most tempting.

Seeking inspiration, I tried to imagine what predictions a speaker might have ventured at a celebration of the Centennial. But I wonder how many commentators in 1876 would have anticipated things we take for granted—for instance, the electronics, media, or transportation technologies that have revolutionized our world and altered our freedoms. Most thinkers would have rejected any suggestion that by 1976 we would nationalize the Bill of Rights; apply the equal protection clause to sex discrimination; or come to believe that we cannot provide equal justice unless we treat haves and have-nots unequally, providing the poor some things the rich can afford to buy. In 1876, no one envisioned Japanese internment camps. The bete noirs of civil libertarians—*Plessy v. Ferguson*[1] and *Gitlow v. New York,*[2] for example—had not yet been decided, let alone discarded. The history of civil

**Chief Judge, United States Court of Appeals, District of Columbia.*

liberties illustrates the wisdom of the philosopher Heraclitus' teaching: The only constant is change. None of which gave me much confidence in my crystal ball.

What do we mean by civil liberties? Civil liberties define the interface of governmental power and individual freedom. They do so by carving out a sphere of autonomy around each individual. This sphere has been defined in part spatially, as by recognizing the sanctity of the home against unreasonable searches; in part with procedural safeguards, to limit arbitrary actions of government; and to a great extent in terms of protected activities, like worship, expression, or—more recently—travel,[3] child rearing[4] and family planning.[5] In protecting the sphere against various invasions with differing degrees of vigilance, we have approached what Justice Brandeis termed "the most comprehensive of rights," "the right, as against the government . . . to be let alone."[6]

Significant practical benefits flow to both the individual and social groups from recognizing these rights. Individuals are accorded latitude to develop in directions they choose. The resulting diversity facilitates an interplay of ideas that can lead to fruitful innovation. The groundwork is also laid for an order more secure than that imposed by repressive regimes.

While the pragmatic justifications for liberty are indeed impressive, the framers relied mainly on principle when arguing for the rights of persons. They found rights compelling not just as means to an end, but as ends in themselves; not only after calculating costs and benefits, but in recognition of self-evident truths. And just as the framers' decisions to recognize certain rights reflected their moral principles, so, too, court decisions defining the scope of these liberties are necessarily statements of our ethical bearings. This infusion of morality into law need not involve judicial overreaching. To give meaning to words like "cruel and unusual," "reasonable," or "due process," we must consider not just history and precedent, but developing morality as well.

This is not to say that by donning black robes, judges acquire mystical insight into ultimate truths. I recognize relativity as a law of metaphysics as well as physics. But I believe we *can* take note of evolving notions of human decency, and *must* reflect them in our decisions. As Judge Elbert Tuttle has written, "[t]he only way the law has progressed since the days of the rack, the screw, and the wheel is the development of moral concepts. . . ."[7] Unless our law aspires to morality, its justice will not merit the name.

Although moral and pragmatic arguments in the long run may converge on the proper balance between citizen and state, in the short term they often appear at odds. Since the actions of individuals radiate outward, the freedom of each appears to conflict with the interests—especially the security interests—of all. This may be a free country, but I will be much happier in it if your freedom to swing your arms stops short of where my chin begins. Thus, even in tranquil times, groups attempt to constrict the protected spheres of others. And in times of crisis, when passions color perceptions, exaggerated fears lead to overly harsh responses. As Justice Brandeis wrote, "Men feared witches and burned women."[8]

The founders of the nation foresaw such dangers. James Madison wrote to Thomas Jefferson that "The invasion of private rights is chiefly to be apprehended . . . from acts in which Government is the mere instrument of the major number."[9] Indeed, the framers enacted the Bill of Rights to insulate the delicate liberty/security balance from passing emergencies and political might. And they looked to "independent tribunals of justice" to provide, in Madison's words, "an impenetrable bulwark against every assumption of power" by the branches of government closer to the political process.[10]

If the history of our first two centuries fails to justify fully the framers' faith in the judiciary, it certainly vindicates their fears for liberty. Time and again, in passing emergencies, majorities have attacked dissidents' freedom without much hindrance from the courts. The ink on the First Amendment was only seven years dry when a Federalist government, fearing "subversion" by Jeffersonian Republicans, enacted the Alien and Sedition Acts, which outlawed publishing malicious or scandalous statements directed at the government. In our century, government responded to fears of anarchism by passing new Sedition Acts and sponsoring Attorney General Palmer's Red Raids; answered an alleged military necessity by locking over 100,000 Japanese-Americans in concentration camps; and met a communist threat with loyalty oaths, blacklisting, and McCarthyism.[11] Even more recently, intelligence agencies invaded the liberties of anti-war, civil-rights and women's movement activists whose only crimes seem to have been dreaming dreams differing from FBI and CIA versions of revealed truth.[12] During these crises the courts approved some of these responses and failed to face others; too seldom did they say, "No."

Although instituted to preserve rights for all, our government has repeatedly seen its own preservation as its raison d'être, as "the highest value" to quote from the *Dennis* case.[13] But we should remember it is a revolution we celebrate in the Bicentennial. The people who fought it took great risks to overthrow a government destructive of rights, and establish one recognizing a right to change even the form of government itself. The great danger is that individuals who wield the power of government will confuse dissent with insurrection, and preservation of government with preservation of the status quo and their own power. Of course, freedom carries many risks, but we have learned they are seldom as great as they seem when expanded by the heat of the moment.

Although we might wish otherwise, the challenge of protecting freedom is not just a historical curiosity. New threats to security press in on us, and later ones, in unforeseeable forms, will succeed them, providing fresh fuel for the fires of repression.

Today street crime has replaced anarchism and communism as our cause for alarm. That concern is manifest in President Ford's recent warning that our legal system leaves the rights of the majority "sadly out of balance."[14] In the courts, we see an expansion of searches deemed "reasonable" and a contraction of those requiring a warrant[15]; a loosening of the elementary prophylactic rules of *Miranda*[16]; and far-reaching limitations on the opportunity to litigate questions of this sort.[17] And in the legislatures there is a clamor to adopt tougher sentencing provisions. The spirit of our responses to previous demons can be discerned in our reaction to the crime threat.

Of course the crime problem is neither illusory nor easy to solve. And the civil liberties issues are *not* battles pitting forces of light against minions of darkness. To the contrary, the issues are increasingly complex, and libertarians themselves frequently line up on both sides.

Consider, for example, the sentencing issue. Proponents of mandatory minimum prison terms for all persons convicted of violent crimes offer a lofty justification for their proposal: protecting the rights of potential victims.[18] Certain incarceration would do this, they claim, by enhancing whatever deterrent effect punishment has and by removing dangerous persons from the streets. Advocates of determinate sentencing also make an appealing case for their suggestions.[19] They argue that curtailing efforts to tailor sentences to the criminal rather than the crime would, first, reduce the need for probation officers to probe into the private lives of offenders in preparing presentence reports; second, undermine the justification for compelling treatment and prolonging confinement until an offender is "rehabilitated"; and third, limit the unbridled discretion of judges and parole boards that has led to gross disparities in sentences.

But the cost to liberty of such proposals, while perhaps more subtle, is still significant. The great increase in violent behavior which has put us in fear is for the most part only a symptom of the frustration, desperation and rage felt by many living in our rotting inner cities. The response most consistent with our libertarian tradition is *not* to get tough with those who manifest these symptoms, but to get tough instead with the deprivations that cause the disease. It is simply unjust to place people in dehumanizing social conditions, do nothing about those conditions, and command those who suffer, "Behave—or else!" To save our hides, we lose our souls.

Mandatory incarceration, determinate sentencing and the like are thus first steps in a thousand-mile journey, but in precisely the wrong direction: toward repression. Mandatory incarceration means nothing more than locking up those manifesting symptoms of the underlying ill. If it reduces crime, it will only be because repression and fear can be effective. Mandatory incarceration will not cure—or even address—the roots of the disease. Determinate sentencing is also an ostrich-like response. It expressly eliminates from the sentencing process any effort to learn about the circumstances that fostered the behavior of a particular offender, so that we can better know what must be done to prevent him—and others in like circumstances—from committing future offenses.

Our last best hope is to seek out the causes of the criminal act. The criminal process—from arrest to sentencing—is like a postmortem. A postmortem cannot revive the dead, and the criminal process cannot undo a heinous act. But in each case we can learn about the cause of failure. To do that effectively, however, will require (1) a major commitment of resources to produce probing presentence reports that permit critical insights; and (2) an erosion of the obdurate resistance of almost all sentencing judges to systematically spelling out exactly what has been learned about the individual and exactly what facts and reasoning led to their decisions.

Of course, eliciting the information necessary to understand the forces that drive people to crime is not a solution to the crime problem. But it is a prerequisite to a solution. Once we improve our understanding, we will still have to decide whether the costs of grappling with those forces are more than we are willing to pay. But that question must be addressed directly, not swept under the rug. Tackling the causes of crime admittedly will not be easy. But the path of total reliance on punishment is a super highway leading to a cow path. Rather than conceding the inevitability of social injustice and seeking the serenity to accept it, we must recognize its intolerability and search for the strength to change it.

If I have dwelt on the crime crisis, it is because I find it illustrative of the pressures against liberty that have arisen—and will arise—in response to threats. The first challenge to civil liberties in the next century will be to meet these pressures. Our past performance does not give much cause for optimism. But institutional and doctrinal changes are possible to better insulate courts from these forces. For example, statutes creating emergency powers usually are enacted before an emergency actually arises. Questions as to the legality and scope of these statutes also should be resolved before the crunch is on. Similarly, in adjudicating individual cases, courts should articulate *per se* rules defining protected activities and prohibited government conduct, so that in emergencies there would be less need to strike *ad hoc* balances, and less danger that the balancers would have their thumbs on one side of the scales.

I foresee a second challenge to civil liberties in the next century coming from developments in science and technology. By placing new tools at government's disposal, technological advances enhance its power, and raise the question of when, if ever, government may use these tools.

In recent years, we have asked that question with regard to various surveillance technologies, from X-rays and magnetometers to wiretaps and "bugs." I am told it is now possible to intercept conversations through window panes with laser beams, and to eavesdrop on telephone conversations by monitoring microwave radio channels. The uses of these new technologies are so invisible that even if the courts articulate clear-cut rules, enforcing them will be difficult. As our experience with surveillance technology teaches, however, to protect the freedoms the framers sought to guarantee, we must guard against much more than the specific evils they feared.

Although I cannot predict the technological developments of the next century, I foresee intractable issues looming in behavioral and thought control. The emerging wizardries of chemotherapy, psychosurgery, behavior modification, and genetic engineering, with their clockwork orange overtones, might seem an unlikely source of moral dilemmas. To keep George Orwell from looking prophetic, we may decide that these "cures" may never be used, at least without informed consent, itself a complex issue. But these developments—like all technological advances—carry promise as well as peril. The promise here is twofold: alleviating suffering and protecting society from "dangerous" persons. Thus, even if banning these wizardries were the right decision—and it may well be—we should not feel righteous about it. After all, society always has shaped value formation and behavior. And if socialization fails, we employ less subtle means: caging those we find mentally or morally deficient and attempting to "rehabilitate" them with electroshock, psychotherapy and the like.

Thus far I have focused on the need to enforce existing controls on government and develop new ones. Restraining government is a holding action, however; it does not extend the frontiers of the individual's protected sphere. We undoubtedly will extend those frontiers in the future by recognizing new interests as rights. But at the moment I am less concerned with defining new rights than with finding new ways to vitalize old ones. Traditionally, we have guarded civil liberties with a "thou shalt not" strategy, seeking to foster freedom by protecting citizens from the state. Sooner or later we will have to consider whether that strategy alone can make freedom meaningful. Several factors suggest that if it was enough in the rural, open society of 1776—and perhaps it wasn't even then—it is woefully inadequate today.

The first such factor is the increased power of private groups. With the advent of huge corporations, powerful unions, and sophisticated technology, the might to invade liberty on a massive scale is no longer the monopoly of government. Individual scientists, for example, in performing experiments can unleash forces capable of untold destruction. A single television network can limit free speech by denying air time to outsiders or by censoring its own reporters. Unless private power is exercised responsibly, we will either have to suffer private abuse or countenance increased public regulation.

The second factor tending to undermine the sufficiency of our "thou shalt not" approach is the growth of government and our heightened sensitivity to its presence. No wall of separation between government and protected activity can be inviolable in our complex society. Government intermingles with religion, for example, when it taxes or exempts church property. It affects freedom of expression when it creates parks or sidewalks; enforces—or declines to enforce—antitrust laws against networks or newspapers; or simply sets postal rates. And even with respect to the most basic freedom—freedom of thought—government plays an important role, contributing to socialization directly through curriculum and schooling decisions, and indirectly through almost everything else it does.

These twin developments portend the need to complement our traditional "thou shalt nots" with a set of "thou shalts." Requiring government to affirmatively facilitate freedom is not free of costs. Augmenting the power of government always carries risks. But the risks can be minimized by vigilantly seeking the least intrusive strategies of affirmative protection.

Consider, for example, the problem of expression where effective means of communication are seemingly scarce.

Government could simulate a laissez-faire position by randomly allocating radio and television frequencies and allowing the fittest to survive, subject only to tax and regulatory laws applicable to all businesses. This, however, would leave open the possibility of monopolistic suppression by those in control. To avoid that danger, government has compelled those who control the forums to open them up to a diversity of views.[20] But deciding what is a "fair balance" of opinionated programming leads government knee-deep into regulating speech. The Supreme Court has struck down a "fairness doctrine" law for newspapers,[21] and may well reconsider its approval of the FCC's fairness rule.[22] A third alternative would be for government to neutralize the influence of those with access by limiting the amount of speech they can engage in; the Court, however, rejected this approach in its recent *Buckley* decision as "wholly foreign to the First Amendment" when applied to campaign expenses.[23] But the Court approved another approach in *Buckley*: subsidizing speech so as to equalize access.[24] This approach could be supplemented by increasing the number of communication outlets, like UHF, cable TV, or subscriber broadcasting. These latter strategies are fully consistent with our constitutional values.[25]

Treatment of the mentally disturbed provides another example of the need for minimally intrusive affirmative action. Many libertarians, reacting to total institutionalization, would end involuntary commitment altogether. But setting disoriented persons adrift in the back alleys of a hostile world is no more likely to make them free than confining them in the back wards of a public hospital. To provide more freedom, they must receive ample treatment and supportive services in the community. But adequate funding for such programs would be costly indeed, and permitting the mentally handicapped to live in our midst would make many uncomfortable. Once again we confront the inescapable: freedom is never free. And once again we must decide whether these costs are more than we are willing to pay.[26]

Perhaps the most compelling case for a set of "thou shalts" lurks in Anatole France's observation that "The law, in its majestic equality, forbids the rich as well as the poor to sleep under bridges, to beg in the streets, and to steal bread."[27] Our courts have begun—tentatively and hesitantly—to deal with these problems. There was a time not too long ago when we accorded rich and poor an equal opportunity to retain counsel in criminal cases, or to buy their way to the ballot box. We put rights at our own eye level, although the growth of others had been stunted by many circumstances, including the accident of birth. As our moral concepts evolved, however, we began to provide the stunted a box to reach the eye-level of the more fortunate.[28] Unless we choose to tolerate inequality in the exercise of rights, we will have to provide more of a box than just court-appointed counsel, and free trial transcripts and voting.

The freedom of children in Appalachia or Watts can be no more than a meaningless abstraction if government's only action to implement that freedom is the *in*action of leaving them alone. Babies need the chance to become human. This requires minimum income, quality education and adequate medical care as matters of right, not grace. To protect equality, we must ask not only when government *may* take group differences into account, but when it *must*. To foster freedom we must difine not only what the state may *not* do *to* its citizens, but what it *must* do *for* them.

Recognizing basic needs as rights would raise new problems of liberty, as our experience with income redistribution demonstrates. Too often welfare recipients pay for government largesse with their privacy and autonomy—enduring oversight of their shopping lists and searches we euphemistically label "home visits." The intrusion of the IRS—the self-incrimination questions self-reporting raises, the First Amendment problems in deciding which charities are tax-exempt, and the potential for misusing tax returns as a lending library—need no recapitulation here. Such problems are not endemic to income redistribution, however. And I detect a trace of irony in the argument that recognizing basic needs as rights would intrude on the privacy the poor currently enjoy in overcrowded tenements among rats, roaches, junkies and muggers.

Questions of government power and individual freedom have never been easy. In 1788 James Madison wrote to Thomas Jefferson: "[I]t is a melancholy reflection that liberty should be equally exposed to danger whether the government have too much or too little power, and that the line which divides these extremes should be so inaccurately defined by experience."[29] Our subsequent experience has not made that line any easier to find. Continuing to search for it in a changing world, with sensitivity to the enduring values and wisdom of the framers, is the ongoing task that lies before us.

FOOTNOTES

1. 163 U.S. 537 (1896).
2. 268 U.S. 652 (1925).
3. *See, e.g.,* Crandall v. Nevada, 6 Wall. 35 (U.S. 1868).
4. *See, e.g.,* Pierce v. Society of Sisters, 268 U.S. 510 (1925); Meyer v. Nebraska, 262 U.S. 390 (1923).
5. *See e.g.,* Roe v. Wade, 410 U.S. 113 (1973); Griswold v. Connecticut, 381 U.S. 479 (1965).
6. Olmstead v. United States, 277 U.S. 438, 478 (1928) (dissenting opinion).
7. Novak v. Beto, 453 F.2d 661, 672 (5th Cir. 1971) (dissenting opinion), *cert. denied sub nom.* Sellars v. Beto, 409 U.S. 968 (1972).
8. Whitney v. California, 274 U.S. 357, 376 (1927) (concurring opinion).
9. Letter from James Madison to Thomas Jefferson, October 17, 1788, in 1 SCHWARTZ, THE BILL OF RIGHTS: A DOCUMENTARY HISTORY 616 (1971).
10. Address by James Madison to House of Representatives, June 6, 1787, in 2 SCHWARTZ op. cit. *supra* note 9, at 1031.
11. *See generally,* ROCHE, THE QUEST FOR THE DREAM (1968).
12. See, e.g., Ungar, *The Intelligence Tangle,* ATLANTIC MONTHLY, April, 1976.
13. Dennis v. United States, 341 U.S. 494, 519 (1951) (Frankfurter, J., concurring). quoting, Chinese Exclusion Case, 130 U.S. 581, 606 (1889).
14. Address by Gerald Ford, Federal Bar Association Dinner, Miami, Florida, February 14, 1976.
15. *See, e.g.,* United States v. Watson, 96 S.Ct. 820 (1976); Cardwell v. Lewis, 417 U.S. 583 (1974); United States v. Robinson, 414 U.S. 218 (1973).
16. *See, e.g.,* Michigan v. Mosley, 96 S.Ct. 321 (1975); Michigan v. Tucker, 417 U.S. 433 (1974).
17. *See, e.g.,* Francis v. Henderson, 44 U.S.L.W. 4620 (May 3, 1976); Estelle v. Williams, 44 U.S.L.W. 4609 (May 3, 1976); Davis v. United States, 411 U.S. 233 (1973).
18. *See generally* VAN DEN HAAG, PUBLISHING CRIMINALS 153-81 (1975); WILSON, THINKING ABOUR CRIME 162-83 (1975).
19. See generally VON HIRSCH, DOING JUSTICE (1076); TWENTIETH CENTURY FUND TASK FORCE ON CRIMINAL SENTENCING, FAIR AND CERTAIN PUNISHMENT (1976).
20. *See, e.g.,* 47 U.S.C. § 315 (1970), as amended (Supp. IV 1974); Personal Attacks, Political Editorials, 8 FCC 2d 721 (1967).
21. Miami Herald Publishing Co. v. Tornillo, 418 U.S. 221 (1974).
22. *See* Red Lion Broadcasting Co. v. FCC, 395 U.S. 367 (1969).
23. Buckley v. Valeo, 96 S.Ct. 612, 644-54 (1976).
24. *Id.* at 666-77.
25. For a more comprehensive statement of my views regarding regulation of the broadcast media, see Bazelon, *FCC Regulation of the Telecommunications Press,* 1975 DUKE L.J. 213.
26. *See generally* Bazelon, *Institutionalization, Deinstitutionalization and the Adversary Process, 75* COLUM. L. REV. 897 (1975).
27. FRANCE, LE LYS ROUGE ch. 7 (1894).
28. *See, e.g.,* Boddie v. Connecticut, 401 U.S. 371 (1971); Harper v. Virginia State Board of Elections, 383 U.S. 663 (1966); Gideon v. Wainwright, 372 U.S. 335 (1963); Douglas v. California, 372 U.S. 353 (1963); Griffin v. Illinois, 351 U.S. 12 (1946).
29. Letter from James Madison to Thomas Jefferson, loc. cit. *supra* note 9.

INTERNATIONAL LAW

Dean Rusk*

If we are to try to think about the next one hundred years, perhaps we should begin with a confession to our successors in 2076, if there are to be such successors. We do not pretend to be able to pierce the fog of the future with certainty or accuracy. I was born in 1909 in a part of our country where daily life was more like life in the time of Christ than life in 1976. The breathtaking acceleration in the pace of change and increasing complexity can be expected to continue. It is impossible for us to forecast with clarity the next one hundred years. On the other hand, there are some urgent questions now with us or on the near horizon which may determine whether *homo sapiens* will reach the year 2076. We face an overriding necessity to address ourselves to the needs of that future, however inadequate our time-bound vision appears to be. Otherwise, we or our children or their children will become lemmings rushing over the cliff and into the sea because we shall not have checked our compass bearings in time.

When I left government in 1969, I decided to spend such time as remains to me in working with young people in the field of International Law. I shall not detain the reader with a full examination of the question as to whether there is such a thing as International Law. For many years I have been struck by the great gap which exists between the tongue in cheek attitude of most laymen and a great many lawyers about International Law and the pervasive reality of International Law among the governments who live and work in the real world.

As in other fields of law, International Law can not be understood in too simplistic terms. It operates in a variety of

**Professor of Law, Georgia University Law School*

modes and for different purposes. We think of it as norms of conduct among the nations of the world—whether we are talking about piracy, the slave trade, the foundations of treaty law, Article 2 paragraph 4 of the United Nations Charter, or rules for the protection of ambassadors and consular officers abroad. There are important fields of the law which do establish norms of conduct generally supported by the community of nations as well as by the peoples of the world.

If we think of law as a compelling standard of conduct, we must acknowledge a major piece of unfinished business—that of imposing restraints by law upon the use of force among nations. In August, 1945, I was on the General Staff in the Pentagon when we first heard of the use of a nuclear weapon at Hiroshima. A Colonel of our regular Army at the next desk exclaimed, "From this time forward, war is turning upon itself and devouring its own tail. It will make no sense to try to settle disputes henceforth by means of war." We have not yet been able to translate into reality that instinctive insight which he expressed on that occasion.

International Law may also be thought of as prevention. It provides a capability to anticipate problems which might become serious or even violent and remove them from the range of controversy for a substantial period into the future. I have in mind, as one example, the Antarctic Treaty concluded in 1959 during the Eisenhower Administration. Under this Treaty national claims to portions of the Antarctic were suspended for the lifetime of the treaty and that vast area was reserved for scientific research. Provision was made for regular visits by each signatory to all installations and activities in the Antarctic to insure that unlawful activities were not in progress, thereby removing the entire area from military competition among the great powers. I think of the Outer Space treaties which have gone a long way in restraining the use of outer space in the military rivalry between the superpowers. It is already time for us to seek a similar arrangement which puts limits on the art of weather and climate modification before this Pandora's box yields a lethal harvest. In New York City we are engaged at present in another effort—to devise a new Law of the Sea to provide arrangements for new circumstances and needs in order to avoid years, perhaps decades, of controversy and violence over vast ocean spaces.

From another vantage point, International Law has served as the principal instrument for the organization of voluntary international cooperation—a role ably expounded by the late Professor Wolfgang Friedmann. Here we are talking about the safety of life at sea and in the air, the allocation of radio and television frequencies, international postal services, the suppression of epidemics, humanitarian responses to natural disasters, and hundreds of other daily tasks which affect the quality of life for us all. Here reciprocal advantage is a powerful force to promote and sustain cooperation, often despite serious ideological and political differences.

Unfortunately, limited column inches and breathless moments of radio and television journalism tend to concentrate our attention upon the abnormal, the controversial, and the violent. Most of our citizens see very little of that massive, habitual and constructive context of international cooperation from which we could draw elements of hope and confidence.

International Law plays a crucial role in dispute settlement, for most disputes among governments are resolved by mutual undertakings having the force of law. The United States and Panama are now engaged in an effort to resolve the future of the Panama Canal, where differences of interest and aspiration could inflame the western hemisphere and produce an impact in every other continent. The 1903 treaty between the United States and Panama appears to be an anachronism in 1976; it is difficult to imagine that such a treaty could be negotiated with any nation in the modern world; if the validity of the original treaty were put before the community of nations today, the United States might very well find itself in a minority of one. Yet, there are vital interests both of ourselves and other nations involved in the assured operation and protection of this critical waterway. If we and Panama succeed in reaching a mutually tolerable result, it will be reflected through instruments of law.

We can think of International Law as persuasion. Some readers have undoubtedly seen Professor Abram Chayes's study of the role of law in the Cuban missile crisis. Here persuasion is not used in the sense of abusing the very words of law to conceal misconduct by pretense, but to denote the pervasive influence of legal notions upon those who are faced with critical decisions. These notions remind decision makers of the general expectations of the community of nations, of the important element of precedent, of the attitudes of one's own people toward lawfulness.

If we were to look through all the debates and proceedings of the United Nations since it was born in 1945, we would not find cynical or abusive statements about the Charter itself. Whatever one's point of view or whatever one's conduct has been, there is constant pressure to bring one's views into accord with the Charter. One distinguished President of the General Assembly on one occasion referred in the corridors to the United Nations Charter as a "piece of paper." There was such an indignant response around the Assembly that the President was forced to call a press conference and apologize for the remark. Many would say that the persuasive influence of international legal values is thin and insubstantial and there are times when such would seem to be the case. Someone should report, however, that the question, "What does International Law say about it?" is a question asked over and over again in the foreign ministries of the world.

In sum, International Law provides a rich variety of means for dealing with the issues generated by a diverse and turbulent world. It can not provide the ingredient necessary for survival—the will to settle disputes by peaceful means and to bring into being that sense of world community which will now be required to demonstrate that the human race is accurately called *homo sapiens*.

What are the major tasks already perceptible on the horizon of the decades immediately ahead? We can already see most of them.

Perhaps you might agree that it is more than a reflection of my own experience for me to believe that our primary task is to organize a durable peace in a world in which thousands of megatons now lie around in frail human hands. It is not name dropping for me to recall many associations with the so-called famous people of our time; but I have never met a demi-god or a superman—they are all human beings with feet of clay. Yet, far too many of them have at their disposal a destructive power which threatens the very existence of our species.

The nuclear arms race continues with only trivial restraints imposed upon it. Thus far, we have built a dam one eighth of the way across the river. Unless we can do much more, just as much water will flow as heretofore, if in slightly different channels. Meanwhile, the present prospect is that more and more governments will come into possession of these dreadful weapons.

Most of us have long since forgotten that the United States concluded at the very inception of the nuclear age that even one nuclear-weapons power would be too many. For reasons explicated in the famous Acheson-Lilienthal Report, the United States, Great Britain, and Canada submitted the Baruch Plan to the United Nations, a plan under which all fissionable material would be turned over to the United Nations to be used only for peaceful purposes and there would be no nuclear weapons in the hands of any nation, including ourselves. Unhappily, the Soviet Union rejected this proposal. There is little room for sanctimony on our part, however. Had the Soviet Union first developed a nuclear weapon and had made an identical proposal to the United Nations before we ourselves had achieved the "know how," we can not honestly say that our own executive and legislative branches would have accepted it. But we can still regret that a critical opportunity was lost.

There are those who seem to think that our concern about the further proliferation of nuclear weapons is based upon a desire to maintain for ourselves and as few others as possible some sort of elite status as a great power. Those of us who have looked down the silo's mouth in operational terms have a more basic fear. We shall not have a general nuclear war because some nuclear power makes a calm, considered decision to launch a nuclear strike—that would be mutual suicide. We could have a nuclear war, however, if a man or group of men find themselves driven into a corner from which they see no escape, losing all stake in the future, and elect to play the role of Samson and pull the temple down about themselves and everyone else. The greater the number and diversity of nuclear powers, the greater is the chance for the "Samson syndrome."

I have long since concluded that we should go as far with

nuclear disarmament as mutual verification will permit. If we could find the answer to the need for complete verification—and I see none in prospect now—I would favor zero nuclear weapons tomorrow morning. It seems obvious that, in terms of the safety of the American people, we are far less secure today than we were before these weapons became a reality.

The organization of a durable peace, for many centuries a lofty aspiration, has now become a harsh necessity. My generation of students was led down the chute into the catastrophe of a world war which could have been prevented. The Covenant of the League of Nations and the governments of that day were not willing or able to stop the momentum of aggression before World War II become inevitable. We came out of that war committed to the idea that collective security was the key to the prevention of World War III. The idea was written into Article One and Chapter Seven of the United Nations Charter and reinforced by mutual security treaties in this hemisphere and across both the Atlantic and the Pacific.

In 1976 we must acknowledge that the idea of collective security is rapidly eroding. I can understand why that should be so among the American people. We have taken over 600,000 casualties in dead and wounded since the end of World War II and the effort has not been very collective. We furnished ninety percent of the non-Korean forces in Korea and eighty percent of the non-Vietnamese forces in Vietnam. Many of my fellow Americans at the grass roots say that if collective security means fifty thousand American dead every decade and is not even collective, it does not appear to be a very good idea. For that view I have a profound respect. I am deeply concerned, however, by the absence of serious discussion about the alternatives. If not collective security, then what? Those of my age must remain open-minded about the possibility of alternatives. But all of us of any age must address ourselves to the necessity of an organized peace lest our power of self-destruction is unleashed and makes all other questions and answers irrelevant.

Among other major issues snapping at our heels is the environment and the possibility that man himself can inflict irreparable damage upon this fragile biosphere on which we depend. There is some hope, here, that there may be time to take hold of the problem while it is merely serious but not yet disastrous.

We can not avoid the consequences of the population explosion. On the most optimistic basis I have seen, there will be 14-15 billions of us on this limited globe by 2076 unless the truisms of Malthus—war, pestilence and starvation—intervene. While we think about the impact of such numbers upon food, housing, jobs, raw materials and other necessities, we must be soberly mindful of the fact that exploding populations have been a major cause of war since the dawn of human history.

We are much too relaxed these days about the longer range aspects of energy, where demand continues to soar and readily available supplies are likely to level off or even decline in an embarrassingly short time. We have already heard an American Secretary of State say that he could not exclude the possibility of military action to assure oil supplies if there were to be a strangulation of the industrial countries. That would mean that war on a large scale for such an objective could not be achieved by a handful of marines or commandos. Along with supplies of energy we must also think about diminishing raw materials of other types, such as non-renewable key minerals.

Even a summary list of crucial issues must include improvement in relations among peoples of different races, religious and national and cultural traditions. We can no longer afford the tensions between "we" and "they" which have produced so much tragedy and violence in our past.

As we address ourselves to these tasks of the future, we are in some difficulty at the present time in developing a general sense of the importance of International Law because of the revolt of the so-called Third World. The United Nations, which started off with 51 members, now has 144 and there must be 12 or 15 others ready to join in the next very few years. It is understandable that many of these newly independent nations would say to themselves and to others that they were not around when traditional International Law was developed by the Christian community of Europe, or by the trading nations, or by the capital exporting nations. Traditional International Law does not meet their needs, they say, and they did not have a voice in its formulation. Therefore they want to undertake a fresh start.

We find such pressures in the trade field, taking such forms as an assertion of the right to form cartels among producers of primary products, and the assertion that if the industrialized countries take corresponding retaliatory or protective action against such cartels, such action would be impermissible. In the investment field we have many of the developing countries turning away from the capacity of the industrialized countries to provide large sums of capital through private channels, by insisting that large sums be provided through tax channels. A country like the United States can export from $14 to $20 billion a year in private capital rather easily, but it is very difficult for us to get more than $3 or $4 billion of foreign aid through public funds. The reality of the situation is going to produce a shock for a good many of these developing countries who will have to decide whether or not they want substantial capital from the industrialized world; they can get it through private channels but not through public funds on the scale on which they need external capital.

There is a growing demand now, as you know, for what amounts to nothing more than transfer payments from the rich nations to the so-called have-not nations. I see little prospect down this trail because of the sheer mass involved. If we were to add $10 per capita to the developing countries per year, it would cost about $30 billion to do so. That is not within reach. And if that were attempted in any significant scale the result would probably be to share poverty rather than to share wealth. If we consult our own experience in rapid development within the life time of many of us, we can understand the powerful combination of education, public health, nutrition, and increased productivity as the principal explanation for rapid economic and social development. We ought, therefore, to keep our doors wide open in order to assist the developing countries to help themselves along the lines of tested experience in the field of development.

We come to some matters of faith or judgment. I happen to believe that the family of man is at a fork in the road, that we are facing some far-reaching events with greater consequences than at any period since the industrial revolution; that the stakes are not only important, but lethal. Either we are going to put our heads together and act like an organic community to solve some of our major problems in a rational way, or we are going to find that these very problems themselves will once again become a cause of major warfare.

Not since World War II has any government or nation talked about using force in behalf of what Hitler used to call *Lebensraum*, living space. All nations apparently have been relying upon the possibility that science and technology can somehow find the means to give us our minimum requirements. But when we think ahead to the exploding populations on the immediate horizon, then we must wonder whether once again these populations may not themselves become a major cause of war. Are we going to use force to get the energy and the raw materials which we shall need? If not we, will someone else? These are questions to which we cannot have a certain answer. But I must confess that in this Bicentennial Year I am inclined to express a note of optimism. I do not believe that we as a people in this country are of the opinion that somehow, by eating of the fruit of the tree of knowledge, we are to reach out and grasp the very power of the sun itself to burn human life off of this speck of dust in the universe. I do not believe that we are here to let our insatiable appetites turn this beautiful earth into a moonscape. I do not believe that it was intended that we so infest this planet with our own kind as to send us tearing at each other's throats for any scrap or morsel of food to sustain our own lives. There are notions of human dignity, there are notions of value which, it seems to me, will impel the human race to be reasonable at the end of the day, even if in the early morning we are all pretty ridiculous. All these things add up in my mind to the conclusion that the young people of our immediate period, now in our schools and colleges, whether they like it or not, are destined to write a unique chapter in the history of the human race. Many of these problems to which I have alluded are different in kind than any of the problems the human race has ever faced before. Unless we get some reasonably satisfactory solutions to some of them around the turn of this century, then there may not be much point in worrying about the year 2076.

I must confess, without patronizing them, that I am very much impressed with this present group of young people. I do not think we have any choice except to try, because if there is a danger or a problem, it is far more satisfactory to be able to advance upon it and try to remove it, then it is to shiver in a foxhole waiting for extinction.

In conclusion I do earnestly suggest, that International Law has an indispensable role to play in your future because of the very nature of the issues which confront mankind as a whole. Even if you are among those who now have a certain contempt for International Law, it might be well for you to proceed as if it can be a reality—the alternative is too dismal to contemplate.

CRIMINAL LAW—

Some Second Century Problems and Third Century Solutions

Norval Morris*

I approach with confidence the task of reflecting on the criminal law of the third American century. I have been set free to speculate uninhibitedly, to perform what the diplomats call a "tour d'horizon." This is *not* what gives me confidence. My confidence flows from a determination to protect myself from the charge of imprecision by maintaining a high level of generalization. I shall offer broad concepts expressed with sweeping enigmatic freedom. I shall cultivate ambiguity with the fervor of Chairman Mao phrasing a great thought. Another political leader, Mayor Daley, put it precisely at the University of Chicago when he last visited us. He urged us to exercise unremitting effort to achieve new levels of platitude. I shall try.

Confidence also flows from my awareness of the transience of human memory. My Third Century predictions will not survive into the third hour of reading this volume, let alone the third century of America's efforts to achieve liberty under law. They will be supplanted in your recollection by Braucher on Contracts, Casner on Property, and Mentschikoff on the world. It is a privilege to be in such fine company, a privilege I shall not abuse by dwelling on it too long.

Prediction of where we are going requires some assessment of where we are. How then stands the American criminal justice system at the end of its second century? The frequently invoked visitor from Mars often assists in such a survey. Let us summon him. That simplistic chap would, I think, conclude that in our first two centuries we have

*Dean, University of Chicago Law School

achieved remarkable success in encouraging crime in this country. Crime rates, particularly rates of violent crime, stand grossly higher than in countries of otherwise comparable cultures. America *may* by the land of the free but she is *most certainly* the home of the brave.

We have gathered together our minority, ill-educated youths, without employment, in large pockets of desolation in our inner city areas. Our welfare programs have contributed powerfully to the breakdown of the families of the poor and have thus tended to criminalize their children. Governmental action has fostered a drug culture that has increased crime in the ghetto. A plague of hand guns, unchecked by governmental control, escalates the injury flowing both from domestic conflicts and from other pressures towards crime. A multiplicity of police forces has achieved low and declining clearance rates for serious crime. Prosecution and defense services, exiguous in relation to the incidence of crime, help to keep the jails and the courts overcrowded. Continuances flourish, speedy trial is an idealistic dream rather than a constitutional guarantee, and pressures of expediency compel reliance on charge and plea bargaining. Prison, the residual punishment, the ultimate legal threat, is often criminogenic rather than curative of crime, finding its typical expression in cluttered fortresses of fear which impede rather than facilitate the prisoner's self-direction away from crime. I never did like that visitor from Mars, particularly when his depressing assessments seem to me not much exaggerated.

Let us put him aside and try a more cautious, lawyer-like assessment of our own. America enters her Third Century with her criminal justice system in disarray, lacking consensus on purposes and methods, unsure both of what works and what ought to be done. Though her citizens have surely demonstrated their tolerance of crime, their patience wears thin and there is the risk of the invocation of crime control methods which would threaten other more important democratic values. The criminal justice system is at the pivot of that delicate balance between freedom and authority on which a democratic society depends. The contemporary challenge of crime to freedom is not inconsequential.

Insofar as the criminal law is concerned, this time of entry to our Third Century is particularly depressing, following as it does a decade of proclaimed federal effort at better crime control which, by any fair standard, has not been a success. Indices of crime, though unreliable, are certainly not encouraging. We have not learned much about crime control. Priorities are unsettled, resources are misallocated, myths swamp the few efforts at scholarly analysis. Serious students of the criminal justice system remain a small and uncertain band, knowing more what is not true than what is true. The fact is that the promises of the past decade may take much of the ensuing century to achieve. Reform in crime control is not for the shortwinded.

Happily, some of the directions of reform seem reasonably clear to me. So I shall throw off these depressions and turn to the broad paths of reform, as I see them, briefly discussing

1. Trial and Plea Bargaining
2. Sentencing
3. New Crimes and Old: Toward an Administrative Law of Crime
4. The Paradox of Punishment

I can characterize one quality of my predictions on these topics. My view of Third Century criminal law and its implementation is buttressed by the comforting belief, impossible to prove and immune to disproof, protected by the certainty of death, that my present reformist proposals will all come to pass.

1. *Trial and Plea Bargaining*

In the last quarter of the Second Century, under the growing pressure of increased crime on inadequate resources, the criminal trial suffered dramatic change. Until then it had been accepted doctrine, and was in large part true, that guilt and the degree of guilt were determined by jury trials or by bench trials. In the past twenty-five years, charge and plea bargaining—the settlement by prosecutors and defense counsel of both the guilt and degree of guilt issues, only marginally controlled by judicial review—has moved from being an occasionally admitted anachronism of the criminal justice system to become its central dispositive technique, certainly in the crowded urban areas where crime most flourishes.

In our Third Century, the law merchant will surely come to the plea bargaining market-place. And soon thereafter, the common law.

The trial is unlikely to regain its earlier dominance; it is an expensive and usually unnecessary means of settling the issues of punishment and compensation which are outstanding when a suspected offender is caught. But the present inadequately controlled expediencies, the improprieties and inequities of present plea settlement processes, cannot survive any serious effort to bring efficiency and justice to crime control in this country.

I have elsewhere tried to spell out the pattern of a principled pre-trial settlement process in criminal cases which could build both on American practice and practice in certain Western European countries to produce principled plea bargaining, with the traditional trial a reality only in those cases where such pre-trial settlement fails. I shall not inflict the details on you now; just the broadest sketch.

The plan is soon to be tested in three jurisdictions. It involves bringing together the five relevant parties, instead of only two as now: prosecutor, defense counsel, a judge, the accused and, if he or she so wishes, the victim or complainant. Plea discussions other than in that forum will not be permitted. All issues of punishment and compensation may be settled. A veto power over such settlement is to be held only by the judge and the accused. Nothing at the pre-trial settlement discussion is admissible at trial which, if it takes place, will be before a different judge and (possibly) prosecuted by a different prosecutor. The scheme aims to take advantage of the best of European pre-trial inquisitorial procedures, to regulate our present anarchy of plea bargaining, and to preserve the adversary trial for those few cases in which it is an appropriate barrier to tyranny.

It may not be a good scheme but this at least is clear: devising principled pre-trial processes in criminal cases is a major task for our legal system in its Third Century.

2. *Sentencing*

In a short paper, shaping a century of criminal law, one is allowed surely to pick and choose one's topics. So choosing, let me offer some ideas on the central question of the just sentence.

We lack a common law of sentencing to guide us into our Third Century. The purposes to be achieved by sentencing are not agreed, nor are our procedures. A mixture of motives has led us astray. On the one hand an exaggerated belief in the efficacy of deterrent punishments; on the other an excessive faith in the possibility of coercively reforming the criminal. Both deterrence and reform have failed us, deterrence because our limited capacity to catch, convict and sentence the guilty fails to fulfil the threat of punishment, reform because coercive reform is no business of the criminal law and when the criminal law enters that business it tends to corrupt its other legitimate purposes, achieving neither justice nor social protection.

The philosophic foundations for just sentencing will not, it seems to me, long elude us if we pursue them by procedures that have served us well elsewhere. These procedures rely on the traditional balance between the legislature and the judiciary; they have been too long ignored in our criminal law practice. The initiative of the American Law Institute properly framed the legislative duty, defining with reasonable precision in its Model Penal Code the purposes of punishment to be pursued by the judge in imposing sentence. I disagree strongly with some elements of that definition; but such disagreements are not the central issue. What matters is that the Code states its general purposes, moves toward principled sentencing, and thus opens up these areas of disagreement to judicial interpretation, application, and modification, and to legislative reconsideration.

This type of legislative reform will in time bring order to the Statute Book of sentencing and will help to reduce the present irrational disparities of sentences.

The Brown Commission and the several proposals for a Federal Criminal Code, the American Bar Association's Committee on Sentencing in its Standards project, and a number of recently proposed and legislatively accepted state criminal codes are building on the American Law Institute's initiative and will increasingly give a rational frame of reference to the judge in his difficult task of punishing the convicted criminal.

To continue this evolution toward a common law of sentencing it will increasingly be required that the judge give reasons for his choice of sentence and that sentences will be subject, as in other countries, to appellate review. Given the relative rarity of the trial and the judicially defined sentence, once principled pre-trial settlement of criminal charges becomes commonplace, allocation of judicial resources to provide this reasoned frame of reference for sentencing seems to me well worthwhile.

I am tempted to spell out my prejudices concerning the concepts of just desert and parsimony, limiting the deterrent and educative purposes of the criminal law which should shape the purposes of punishment; I shall resist the temptation and submit to you only that philosophic principles of punishment acceptable to the values of our Third Century will emerge from adherence to those procedures which elsewhere in the law have helped us develop reasoned principles, building on the accumulated wisdom of an informed and legislatively guided judiciary.

If the philosophy of sentencing is difficult, the social setting for just sentencing presents intractable problems. How can there be just sentencing absent, for example, full employment? Let me take a simple case. Assume two thieves of equal social threat, equal wickedness, who inflicted equal social harm. One is employed, the other unemployed and indigent. The fine may well be the sentence of choice for the former; it cannot be for the latter for whom, paradoxically, if it is to be given reality by a job being found for him, it is a benefaction.

Pour these simple tensions into the realities of the black, ill-educated, socially deprived, drug tempted, unemployed youths of our inner city areas.

Absenteeism in some Harlem schools is, I am told fifty percent; so it is in Woodlawn, hard by my University. The unemployment figures exceed the truancy figures. It is hopeless to think that the youths from these areas can be sentenced justly for their criminal offenses on scales that equally weigh the white collar offender, the spouse killer, the child beater, the tax criminal and the corrupt public official.

Compensation of victims, restitution, pecuniary penalties, limitations on freedom while at large, and penalties which interfere as little as possible with the working and family life of the criminal are at the heart of a rational sentencing policy. They can be deterrent. They can be denunciatory. They are not mere expressions of sentimentality. They would lead, if criminality recurs, to more severe and possibly segregative or incarcerative punishments. But this sound and graduated hierarchy of penalties depends on a social setting in which fines can be related to income and in which the opportunity to work is available to all who wish lawfully to work.

Here, as in so many other ways, the criminal justice system is a dependent system. More effective policing, reasonably swift trial, fair and even-handed sentencing, an adequate and graded armamentarium of punishments—all are obviously desirable but all will not make much difference to the incidence of crime or juvenile delinquency. Those phenomena respond to deeper social, cultural and political currents beyond the substantial influence of the criminal justice system. Clearly that system cannot itself rectify social inequities; indeed, it does well if it does not exacerbate them.

3. New Crimes and Old: Toward an Administrative Law of Crime

We inherited a morally sound common law of crime. In this country's formative years and as it moved into the industrial era, the content of the criminal law, the definition of what was criminal, caused no great problem. But with industrialization at a rate beyond previous experience, rapid urbanization and an expanding view of the state's duty to provide minimum standards of social welfare for all citizens, the federal and state governments greatly increased the reach of their efforts at social, economic, and industrial control and confronted challenging, still unsolved, problems of the proper role of the criminal law.

The criminal law is reasonably well-principled in relation to crimes of violence and the traditional crimes against property—the old crimes. It is relatively unprincipled, almost archaic and random, in its impact on the new crimes.

I have in mind two broad types of new crime, though the classification is arbitrary. First, the application of the criminal law to the regulation of traffic, pure foods, housing conditions, dangerous drugs and alcohol, industrial safety, discrimination in employment, and the regulation of business practice generally—that range of crimes called by Beale "public welfare offenses." Secondly, as a new crime, though enjoying an ornate and rich parentage, I have in mind corporate criminality, the plunder of the market-place and of the consumer by our contemporary "overmighty subjects," the nation-wide and sometimes multinational corporations. Traditional criminal law doctrine and practice will not assist us to draw and enforce even reasonably clear lines between predation and competition, plunder and sharp business practice.

One sees both the success in defining the old crimes and the failure in framing the new in the Model Penal Code of the American Law Institute. For the old crimes, Herbert Wechsler and his excellent team built on the codification efforts of Sir James Fitzjames Stephen and his fine contemporaries in the last quarter of the nineteenth century, and on commentaries by thoughtful and informed English and American scholars. For the new crimes, they were not so assisted. The sound initiatives of the Model Penal Code in relation to the old crimes heavily influence the statute books of America and the progeny of that Code (with Illinois as the oldest brother) now spread steadily across the land. We may have difficulty in catching, convicting and punishing the murderer, manslaughterer, robber, burglar, and thief, but we are reasonably content that we have fairly stated what are the prohibited acts and the prohibited states of mind which define those crimes. That is not true of our efforts to apply the criminal law to industrial, economic, health, and welfare offenses; even a basis of principled criminal law prohibition is absent. As in plea bargaining, expediency dominates; the pressures of excessive case loads, of a regulatory reach beyond our means have corrupted both practice and principle.

Strict liability, liability without proof of fault, cases like *United States v. Balint*, 258 U.S. 250 (1922), *United States v. Behrman*, 258 U.S. 280 (1922), and *United States v. Dotterweich* 320 U.S. 277 (1943), are defensible only on grounds of expediency; that we cannot take time to allow the accused to prove that he is without fault. The tolerance of such liability in the Model Penal Code, though modulated by its reduction of stigma and penalty for such crimes, was a failure of moral judgment. Nor is a decision like *Morissette v. United States*, 342 U.S. 246 (1952), any cure. Setting aside its weak analytic structure, *Morissette* accepts the morality of strict liability as a social expedient and suggests only vague classificatory practices to minimize its impact. The cure will have to go further than that.

I predict that in our Third Century an Administrative Law of Crime will be devised. Its origins are to be seen in a variety of present practices: in specialized courts and specialized administrative and enforcement practices in the control of traffic; in the work of a growing multiplicity of regulatory agencies controlling transport, communications, housing, employment, the conditions of manufacture, agriculture and trade, and to a likely increasing degree wages, prices, dividends and investments. These origins of a new criminal jurisprudence are also to be seen at a very different level, so far as the prosperity of the fortunately involved attorney is concerned, in contemporary antitrust litigation, with its close and informed attention to the realities of the marketplace and of business practice.

The parturition of such an Administrative Law of Crime is not clear to me; it will not leap full-fashioned from the ear of a legislature. But both Nostradamus and Coleridge under opium have assured me that such a system would more effectively provide the regulatory sanction for all present public welfare offenses, for increasing and further-reaching efforts to regulate truth in advertising, fairness in political funding and canvassing, fair business practices in relation to the proper limits both of competition and of monopoly, and (though it will be vastly more difficult), the proper limits of manipulation of international trade and the transnational movement of investment, dividends and tax liabilities.

The traditional criminal law may well continue to serve as an occasionally invoked fail-safe mechanism for the most flagrant and contumacious breaches of regulated standards of business and political practice—the law of larceny and conspiracy then being of particular value—but in its front-line impact the administrative law of crime requires different investigators, different enforcers, different arbiters and different sanctions from those that serve the criminal law.

Consider the typical price-fixing allegation. Neither the local police nor the FBI are of much use. The issues lie outside the range of interest and training of the local criminal court judge. The local court's punitive armamentarium of prison, jail, fine and probation are ill tuned to the regulatory-punitive task. This is not merely a class point I am making—the difference between no collar and white collar crime. The point is more fundamental. The police and the criminal courts are ill-equipped as investigators, arbiters, and punishment imposers to handle the criminal charges arising from the burgeoning regulatory as distinct from prohibitory reach of the state. And always criminal charges and criminal offenses are implicit in all regulatory processes, since at a certain level of breach of the regulation sanctions must be imposed. This is as true for the mendacious indigent welfare mother as for the prosperous company overconfident of its ability to find the oil without polluting the sea.

At present, these sanctions for regulatory offenses are scattered and diverse, without integrating principles having been developed between a multiplicity of regulatory agencies and the criminal courts of first instance—federal, state or local. It is time that order and principle were brought to this administrative law of crime; it is an important and difficult task for our third century.

The social pressures which lead me to this prediction are obvious enough: the burgeoning range and detail of economic, industrial and social regulation; the increase of licensing practices regulating what used to be the prohibitions of "victimless crime;" the chaos of regulatory agencies, federal and state, captured too often as my colleague George Stigler has demonstrated by the corporations they seek to regulate; the increasing efforts at control of political funding and lobbying; the scope of federal and state efforts to define minimum standards of health, housing, safety and fair competition in post-industrial society; and the inutility of traditional common law concepts of *actus reus, mens rea* and adversary trial to these and similar ends will frame a new regulatory criminal law with our inherited practices of guilt finding and condign punishment functioning only as a back-up system.

Aldous Huxley, having reflected long on the issue, concluded that modern man has invented only one new sin—speed. But we have, by contrast, devised an astonishing range of new crimes; it is time we handled them better and brought order to this chaos.

If you ask me further to define more precisely what I have in mind, to descend from this lyric of academic fantasy and at least to chart the outline of a relevant law and practice, I nervously note that my space is nearly elapsed and hurry on to a finale to these diverse scenes from an opaque crystal ball.

4. *The Paradox of Punishment*

As a concluding topic let me turn back to the traditional crimes, to the crimes which cause fear in America.

In our Third Century we will, I believe, at last reach clarity on why we punish; we will agree on the purposes to be served by the criminal sanction. I certainly lack that knowledge now; nor am I alone. But one hint of understanding relevant to the purposes of punishment does seem to me recently to have become clear. It merits mention here.

Paradoxically, we will both better serve the community and deal more fairly with criminals if we recognize that *au fond* the criminal law, the police, the prosecutors and defense counsel, the courts and the prisons serve predominantly punitive ends. The issue of punishment or treatment, to sanction or to cure, resonates throughout the criminal justice system. But since I have recently been reflecting on the future of imprisonment let me try to suggest the resolution of this issue in the context of the current fruitless public debate between those allegedly hard-nosed, who favor punishment as the purpose of prison, and the supposedly bleeding-hearted, who see the prison as serving rehabilitative purposes.

As to punishment: The intellectual punishers cleave to the position propounded in 1822 by the Reverend Sydney Smith in his essay "On the Management of Prisons." Prison, the Reverend averred, should be "a place of punishment, from which men recoil with horror—a place of real suffering painful to the memory, terrible to the imagination, i.e., a place of sorrow and wailing, which should be entered with horror and quitted with earnest resolution never to return to such misery; with that deep impression, in short, of the evil which breaks out in perpetual warning and exhortation to others." The Reverend Smith would be well content with our larger state prisons and city jails, though the perpetual warnings and exhortations are apparently unheard or inconsequential. The truth is that deterrence flows from the fact of imprisonment apparently unaffected by its duration or by the severity of prison conditions.

As to rehabilitation: The current cry is that rehabilitation has failed; that criminals cannot be reformed; that nothing works. What this means is that compulsory helping programs for convicted criminals in prisons do not overcome the social alienative effects and other disadvantages of conviction and imprisonment. The cage is not a sensible place in which to cure the criminal, even when the medical analogy makes sense, which it rarely does.

Let me abbreviate the argument in order to come directly to the conclusion: "Rehabilitation," whatever it means and whatever the programs that give it meaning, must cease to be the claimed purpose of imprisonment. This does *not* mean that such treatment programs as we now have in prisons should be abandoned; quite the contrary, they urgently need great expansion. No one of any sensitivity can visit any of our mega-prisons without recognizing that they contain, as in all countries, populations which are disproportionately illiterate, unemployed, vocationally untrained, undereducated, psychologically disturbed, and socially isolated. It is both in the prisoner's and the community's best interests to help them to remedy these deficiencies. But rehabilitative programs to that end are not the purpose, or even one purpose, of imprisonment.

We should avoid hypocrisy: we send men to prison sometimes as punishment for what they have done, sometimes to deter those who are like-minded, and sometimes because we do not know what else to do with them. We cage them for what they have done; it is a cruel injustice to cage them also for what they *are* in order to change them, to attempt to cure them coercively. There is a sharp distinction between the purposes of imprisonment and the opportunities for the training and assistance of prisoners that may properly be pursued within those purposes.

Should coercive rehabilitative purposes in prison be rejected on the ground that human behavior is immutable, unchangeable? Certainly not. After all, if we are sufficiently ruthless in the matter, we *can* coercively cure criminals. Capital punishment is a superb remedy against terrestrial recidivism. Protracted imprisonment is a remarkably effective cure for violence. Aging cures all but the most exceptional proclivities to violent crime. Keep all criminals convicted of a crime of violence in prison until their fortieth birthday—few would return to violence. But consider their color, their age on imprisonment, their number; we would have built a different but no less terrible Gulag Archipelago.

The rejection of the model of coercive curing of criminals flows not from lack of power to change human behavior, if human rights and concepts of a just desert limiting punishment are ignored; coercive curing must be rejected as a punishment because of certain centrally important issues concerning the relationship between individual freedom and state authority. We must stay out of the business of forcibly remaking man.

By like analysis I believe it will in time be demonstrated that the criminal law in all its manifestations should avoid all coercive efforts to cure crime. The central point is this: Punishment not cure is the business of the criminal law. The purposes of the criminal law are easy to state, though difficult indeed to achieve: the criminal law should, with justice and mercy, parsimoniously punish those whose punishment is both deserved by their conduct and necessary for the common good.

When the functionaries of the criminal law seek to extend their reach beyond those purposes they imperil fundamental values on which this country was built, not the exuberant bellicosities of the Declaration of Independence but the great and lasting values of the Constitution and the Bill of Rights. So much for the Bicentennial.

TORTS—THE LAW OF THE MIXED SOCIETY

Guido Calabresi*

Losses are best left on the victims. Only if it can clearly be shown that injurers could have cheaply avoided the loss—were at fault—should incentives to avoid injury rest on them.[1] And even where injurers can readily choose the safer path, the victim should frequently still bear the loss and the incentive to avoid it.[2] That this allocation places all unavoidable losses, as well as the cost of avoiding many avoidable losses, on those activities or social classes which give rise to victims, is either irrelevant or beneficial from a wealth distribution standpoint.[3]

These related notions were nearing the high point of acceptance in 1876 and yet the first signs of a reversal were already discernible, though perhaps only to those with hindsight.[4] Typically, for this is common law and not nature, the tide had started to turn even though it had not yet quite reached its high point. Today, one could state the same propositions substituting victims for injurers and injurers for victims throughout and approach the way in which most commentators and many courts would describe tort law.

Given this recent history, it would be foolhardy to predict how the curious mixture of desire to reduce injuries and to favor certain wealth categories which we call tort law, and quickly describe in the language of justice,[5] will develop in the *next* century. Too much depends on the industrial structure of society.[6] And what *that* will be in the next hundred years I happily, but not confidently, leave to the economists. Yet, even if one abstains from attempting that most intriguing of guesses, if one refuses to try to figure out who in what areas will bear unavoidable losses and, hence, the incentive and burden of avoiding most *avoidable* losses, something can

John Thomas Smith Professor of Law, Yale University

still be said about tort law and the next century.

Tort law and more particularly the rule of liability is, I submit, the paradigmatic law of the mixed society. The purely "liberal," *laissez-faire* polity prefers contracts, the truly collective state the criminal sanction; tort law lies in between. That torts has always been present and significant, that it is so today in the so-called "people's democracies," are testimonies to the fact that purely "liberal" and purely collective systems exist solely in the minds of theoreticians and ideologues. The world knows better. That the role of torts has changed testifies to the fact that not all mixtures are the same and in some times and places individual atomistic choices dominate the blend, while at others collective decisions control.

Why do I say that tort law is the law of the mixed society? Let us spend a few minutes examining how injuries would be approached by ideologically pure states. It will help us see why the approach of tort law is, at a minimum, the compromise which the ideologue must make with reality, and at a maximum the preferred choice of the ideologically skeptical and of those whose ideology is skepticism.

A purely collectivistic society would approach each situation or activity which has injury-causing potential in a way which would leave no room for tort law. A judgment would be made as to whether a particular act or activity engaged in at a particular time in a particular way by particular people is too dangerous to be permitted, or alternatively is desirable despite its risks. If an act is deemed too dangerous it would be forbidden and a penalty sufficiently severe to deter it would be imposed whenever it occurred and regardless of whether in the specific instance "harm" to victims occurred. The act—it might be driving by people below a certain age, or driving at all, or driving between certain hours—would have been deemed wrongful and punished accordingly by the criminal law. If instead, the act was not wrong, then, even if harm resulted, there would be no purpose in burdening the doer of the act (whether injurer or victim) with the damages. The act was deemed worth doing, despite its risks, when judged from a collectivistic, societal point of view and the harms, if any, like the benefits, would be borne by the society.[7] If consistent, that is ideologically pure, the collectivistic non-market society would handle damages collectively. These, like all the ills that can befall one, would be socially insured and paid out of the general coffers of the state.

Such a society would handle enterpreneurial activities analogously. No one could start a shoe factory—under penalty of law—unless such a factory were deemed collectively desirable, in which case such a factory would be mandated. If harm to some previously made investment resulted or if the shoe factory turned out to be a mistake, that would be the state's worry. Conversely, if the factory was as, or more, beneficial than expected, the benefit would also be the state's. Risk taking would exist (because the collective society cannot destroy risk any more than can the liberal atomistic society) but the benefits and harms—the profits and losses—of risk taking would accrue to the state to be parcelled out among its citizens according to its prevailing notions of appropriate distribution of wealth.

What we think of as the province of tort law, injury-causing activity, is but one kind of risk taking and would be handled in the same way. Accordingly, risky behavior would either be forbidden and subject to criminal law sanctions, or required and socially insured. Either way civil liability rules and damages would have no place.

That such a purely collective society is unworkable (and would to my way of thinking be extremely undesirable) I will pass over for the moment. The same is true of its converse, the purely atomistic or market society, at which I would now like to look.

The atomistic market society would establish starting points, "entitlements"—based on its views of what wealth distribution is desirable and on its guesses as to what starting points could make contracts and transactions least costly. Once these starting points had been established, it would *forbid* nothing except what I shall call non-contractual behavior. That is: it would *prohibit* the taking of anyone else's entitlements; it would permit, indeed *enforce*, all consensual transfers of entitlements; and except for (a) determining these—unavoidably collective—starting points, (b) requiring agreement by the parties as a pre-condition to the transfer of entitlements, and (c) enforcing all contracts representing such agreements, the state would play no role.[8]

The "entitlements" would establish who would bear a harm if it occurred—that is, who would be the initial risk bearers. Risky behavior would then be handled in one of two ways. If the harm fell on the party whom the starting point had burdened, it would stay there—unless an "indemnity" or "insurance" contract had been entered into with another party who willingly, and presumably for a price, had undertaken to bear the risk. (Such contracts would not, of course, be required.) If instead the harm initially fell on a party, *not* originally burdened with the risk, the other party would be bound to pay damages. But the damages would not be collectively determined; they would be arrived at contractually. The original risk bearer would only be permitted to engage in the dangerous activity if he had either purchased from the victim the right to inflict the loss (an exculpatory agreement) or agreed ahead of time with the victim on the compensation to be paid if harm occurred (contractual compensation schedule), or agreed with him on a procedure to determine, after the event, the damages to be paid (arbitration agreement).[9] Such contracts would be mandatory (a requirement which would be enforced penally), for only through them could the atomistic market society be assured that, within its ideology, a beneficent shifting of the risk had occurred.[10]

To state either of the two "pure approaches" is to deny the possibility of using them *universally*. Can any society, however collectivistic, as a *practical* matter decide whether each and every act is undesirable, and hence forbidden, or worth doing, and hence required? It would be manifestly impossible. Conversely, can any society require that before a person engages in an act he contract with all those potentially harmed by it? One need only think of the automobile driver seeking out and contracting with all possible victims to recognize the impossibility of the approach. Of course, if victims were chosen to bear *all* risk initially, total atomism would be possible. Such a starting point—essentially a might makes right entitlement—is not *logically* impossible. But no atomistic *laissez-faire* society can, in fact, tolerate it. Total risk bearing by victims would neither avoid injuries cheaply (be efficient) nor result in an acceptable wealth distribution (be fair). At its extreme it would entail no property or bodily integrity. Those we now call thieves or murderers or rapists could steal or injure to their hearts' content. The victims could be safe only by buying protection. No, the market society cannot be indifferent to who bears the initial risk of harm resulting from the behavior of others. It cares, both for efficiency and distributional—not to say justice—reasons about the placement of the initial entitlements, and it cares even when contracting before the injury is not feasible; hence it can no more exist in its "pure" form than can its converse, the purely collective society.[11]

But if to describe the two pure approaches is to deny the possibility of their universal application, it is also to recognize how frequently both are in fact used, in their pure forms, in all societies to deal with particular problems or segments of problems. Even a cursory look at traditional situations close to tort law in which behavior is forbidden or—for it is the same thing—is required (driving by infants or without lights after dark) demonstrates that collective approaches have always had their due. When one moves to those areas which have traditionally been "criminal" the spectrum of collective controls, of course, broadens still further. Conversely, even in traditional tort areas, there has always been a place for contracts which shifted the risk onto a party initially protected from it. And again, as one moves away from traditional tort areas to those we think of as governed by contract or sales law, one sees how frequently the pure atomistic approach is used. Theft (non-contractual behavior) is forbidden, but by contract it can become a valid sale.[12]

We can conclude that legal systems generally employ mixed collective and atomistic approaches. We can also see that the simplest mixture involves using both of the pure approaches but limiting their scope. Some acts are forbidden or required (driving by minors, without lights after dark), and neither contractual arrangements nor payment of damages will alter this. Others are permitted without sanction (the taking of property) *but only if* contractual behavior preceeds the action or ratifies it after the event.

This simple mixture does not suffice, however. Too often neither pure approach is acceptable. The atomistic approach is rejected for one of two reasons:

a) Contractual behavior is too expensive to be required before acting;[13] or
b) The society does not trust the parties to contract in their own best interest.[14]

But the collective approach is also rejected for either of two analogous reasons:

a) It costs too much collectively to decide on, and enforce, controls on all behavior; or
b) The society is not sure enough about the desirability of the behavior to wish to require or forbid it.

Where *either* reason for rejecting pure market controls joins with *either* reason for rejecting collective controls, one is apt to find the torts approach in one of its many forms.

It is well to notice that each set of two reasons for rejecting a pure approach contains an *ideological* ground (lack of faith in the ability either of the atomistic contract or of the collective decision to achieve desired results) and a *practical* reason (contractual behavior is costly, but so are collective decisions). Obviously the more a society is *ideologically* pure, the more it will employ torts *only* when using its favored "pure" system is not feasible, *i.e.*, is too costly. The nineteenth century tended to employ torts only when letting losses lie on victims was manifestly inefficient or distributionally intolerable, and when requiring possible injurers to engage in contractual behavior before acting mandated the impossible, and precluded potentially desirable activities. Skepticism as to people's ability to contract in their own best interest was only rarely a basis for torts. Conversely, a truly collective society uses torts only when it wishes to be freed of the *costs* of deciding the desirability of every minute action, not because it wishes to let individuals decide—to some extent—whether an action is worth doing. The ideologically skeptical society, instead, will use torts even when pure approaches are feasible, precisely because it is skeptical of the desirability both of pure contractual behavior and of collective decisions.

What then is this mixture I have been calling torts and which in Europe is more felicitously called "civil responsibility"? *Its essence is the liability rule* which itself mixes individualistic and collective decisions. Behavior is not collectively forbidden merely because it is risky or required despite its risks; individuals are free to choose; but their choice entails civil liability, that is, the payment of *collectively* determined damages if harm occurs.[15] Conversely, contractual behavior to purchase the right to harm those entitled not to be harmed is not required.[16] Again, the payment of collectively determined compensation to those injured takes its place.

The ideology which underlies use of liability rules is a mixed ideology. The party entitled to be free from harm is not compensated to the degree or in the way that he might have chosen. He has not sold his entitlement for a price satisfactory to him; it has been taken from him and he is given damages, which may be greater or less than what he would have negotiated for, but which are, in any event, decided upon collectively.[17] Conversely, decisions on the desirability of engaging in risky activities are not made collectively. They are left up to individuals who will, presumably, be influenced by the damages they may have to pay or bear if harm occurs.[18]

If ideologically mixed, liability rules are also intensely practical. They enable actions to take place where contractual behavior, before harm, would not be feasible. Damages after harm replace such unfeasible agreements. And they permit control of behavior which could only at too great an expense be governed collectively. By varying the size of the applicable damages according to the various circumstances involved, the collective decision makers can go a long way toward enforcing their views without engaging in minutiae of control which would not be worthwhile.

We are now, finally, in a position to talk briefly about the future of torts—about the next hundred years. That future depends fundamentally on the degree to which our society will be relatively pure ideologically—and use torts mainly out of necessity (as a hundred years ago), or will continue to be ideologically skeptical (as it is now)—and opt for the liability rule even when contractual behavior, or collective prohibitions are eminently feasible.

Torts, or the rule of liability, is currently used in many areas in ways which reflect the prevailing ideological skepticism. Skepticism toward pure collectivism—even where collective judgments are feasible—can be seen in all those areas where the fault standard prevails. In these areas the initial entitlement (the right to act without bearing the burden of the injuries one causes) is negated by the fact that the faulty party acted in a way which was collectively judged to be undesirable—wrong.[19] Despite this, the "undesirable" act is not forbidden, and criminal law even if applied is not viewed as sufficient to control it. Rather, the actor is—in effect—given the opportunity to second guess the collective determination and to decide that acting in the faulty manner, or taking the chance of so acting, is worth the—collectively determined—damages he must pay. In other words, the collective decision is subjected to another, atomistic or market review by the faulty party.[20] This skepticism toward collective judgments takes its most dramatic form in the acceptance of insurance for injuries caused by faulty behavior. Insurance is, after all, essentially contractual behavior which permits the insured to buy the right to risk injury to those entitled to be free from risk bearing. The contrast to the criminal sanctions which a "pure" collective society would employ is both obvious and dramatic.

Similarly, torts today also reflects skepticism toward the pure market even where contractual behavior—before action—is feasible. One need only consider the restrictions commonly placed on exculpatory or indemnificatory agreements, and the decline of the doctrine of assumption of risk, to see how far from the "pure" market ideology we have come.[21] An equally significant sign of this skepticism, if one stops to think about it, is the move away from entitlements which placed losses on victims. These entitlements were favored by a pure market ideology because they did not require that unfeasible contracts be made before action could take place. The victim did not need to buy indemnity from the risk of injury from all his potential injurers (who might be hard to identify and pay); he could relatively easily find an insurance company ready to take on the monetary risk. Therefore, the pure market society tended to place risks of loss on the potential victim, unless such an allocation was *clearly* unjust or inefficient, or unless contractual behavior by injurers was clearly feasible before action.[22] The turn away from this allocation inevitably suggests skepticism toward pure market ideology. Moreover, even when the entitlement to be *free* of the risk is given to the potential injurer, and the potential victim is burdened with the risk, the victim is typically *required* to insure himself. We call this first party insurance, but whatever its name, the requirement of insurance represents a deep skepticism of pure market choices. We wish the burden to lie on the victim, but we do not trust his atomistic judgment in evaluating the entity of the burden or the desirability of risking it.[23]

The death of contract has taken many forms, not the least of which has been the movement from a tort law designed to be the minimum necessary to make a pure market feasible, to one which glories in its limited but not unavoidable collective interventions.[24]

What does this suggest about the next hundred years? It is hard to conceive of a return to the ideology of the pure market. Even the nineteenth century found too inflexible the notion that the best we can do with respect to risks is to decide who seems to be able to avoid harm most cheaply[25] and make him act at his criminal peril should he harm others, unless he can induce these others to take on the risks for a price. Nor is it likely that we will return to the compromise with reality that the *laissez-faire* period made—

(a) not to *require* contractual behavior but to allow actors, who have been chosen to bear the risk and have not shifted it contractually, to pay collectively determined damages, and
(b) (in order to keep such collectively determined liability at a minimum) to let the loss lie on the victim unless efficiency and distributional imperatives required burdening the injurer.

This *minimal* use of torts will remain unacceptable because it depends too much on a willingness to believe (1) that victims are frequently the cheapest avoiders of harms, or (2) are distributionally desirable loss bearers *and*, in addition, (3) can intelligently value the risk they are bearing. The decline of faith in the first two propositions has led to more "strict injurer" liability and hence to a greater use of torts and liability rules on feasibility grounds, which must inevitably trouble the true believers in the nineteenth century liberal state. (The defense of ideologically second best positions, and the liability rule is always second best to contractual behavior, rarely appeals to true believers.) The decline of faith in the third proposition represents a direct assault on the market ideology. Together they amount to a skepticism that forecloses a return to a minimal law of torts—to a law of torts limited to being the unavoidable adjunct to a contract based society.

But what of the other ideology? Will the next hundred years bring the decline (if not the death) of torts and liability rules, because there will be no room left for the individualism torts implies? Will the liability rule become that minimal concession which the collectivist state must permit only because it cannot enforce an infinity of judgments collectively? Will damage size increasingly come to depend on the relative undesirability of the payor's behavior instead of on the best estimate of what is needed to compensate for the harm caused?[26] Will, and this is the other side of the coin, compensation itself become increasingly covered out of general taxes? It is possible—for certainly the trend toward greater collectivism in our society is still running strong.

Still, and this may perhaps reflect only my own ideological skepticism, I am inclined to doubt that the trend will go that far. As in 1876 the tide is rising but may at the same time have started to recede. The failure of regulation, as we know it, as a means of furthering safety is too patent. The very advocates of more regulation, like Mr. Nader, base their pleas on the failure of past "regulators"—that is, of regulation. The corruptibility of the "allocating state," of the state which decides too many things which affect too many people, becomes more manifest every day.[27] There is talk, even in societies committed to collectivism, about the utility of incentives as means of enforcement and choice. At the same time, in the United States the many experiments currently being tried with class actions, pollution licenses or taxes (simply another form of liability rule), reverse damages in nuisance suits, and even civil self-enforcement against law violations, suggest an increasing skepticism toward the pure collectivist mode of controlling risk and harm.[28]

Perhaps in this disillusionment with "pure regulation," hindsight will be able to discern the beginning of a trend. It will not be a trend toward the tort law of the nineteenth century. Nor—I suspect—will it even be a trend toward that relatively individualistic, second best market society which I have, at times, been charged with promoting. The object won't simply be to place liability on the cheapest cost avoider, taking into consideration distributional goals, and then letting atomistic decisions determine the extent of safety and harm. Rather, if there is a trend, it is a trend toward an *ideologically self-conscious use of torts as a mixed system*. The possibilities inherent in the liability rule as a device for promoting clearly collective goals and mitigating perceived incapacities of people to decide best for themselves, while still permitting a wide degree of atomistic choice and determination, will under this view be fully exploited. If that is the case, if—as I believe it will—the mixed society prevails, the next century will be the century not of contracts nor of criminal law (though both will remain dominant in limited areas as part of the ideological mixture)[29] but of torts and of the rule of liability.

FOOTNOTES

1. Fault implies not only that injurers can cheaply avoid the loss, but also that they either know or should have known this. For a 20th century definition of fault which attempted to state systematically the relationships involved, *see* Conway v. O'Brien, 111 F.2d 611, 612 (2d Cir. 1940) (L. Hand J.) revd. on other grounds, 312 U.S. 492 (1941); *see also* United States v. Carrol Towing Co., 159 F.2d 169 (2d Cir. 1947), Terry, *Negligence*, 29 Harv. L. Rev. 40 (1915).
2. Diverse, often self-contradictory, reasons were given in the high days of the fault system to explain why in many instances victims should bear losses despite the availability of a "faulty" injurer. Some of these were consistent with the goal of efficient reduction of accident costs; some were not. Perhaps the two most important were contributory negligence (which treated victim fault, and by implication the possibility of injury avoidance by victims, as a different order of things from injurer fault and avoidance) and proximate cause (which had the effect of leaving the burden of avoidance on innocent victims—those of whom it could not be said that they ought to have avoided harm—rather than placing it on injurers who, *by definition*, could and should have avoided the harm). Imputed contributory negligence, intra-family immunities and, most dramatically, assumption of risk went in some ways even further in establishing a system in which, even where injurer precautions were feasible and cheap, the incentive to avoid the harm often rested on the victim. I have expressed this view of the fault system more fully in various recent writings. *See generally*, Calabresi, *Concerning Cause and the Law of Torts*, 43 U. Chi. L. Rev. 69 (1975); Calabresi, *Optimal Deterrence and Accidents*, 84 Yale L. J. 656 (1975); and Calabresi and Hirschoff, *Toward A Test for Strict Liability in Torts*, 81 Yale L. J. 1055 (1972).
3. It would be irrelevant if one believes that efficient accident avoidance, through the placement of the incentive to avoid on the appropriate party, is more important than what categories are made richer or poorer. "Efficiency" might be short run (minimizing the sum of accident costs and safety costs); it might include administrative costs (avoiding unnecessary costs of shifting); and it might even include long run cost avoidance (giving a subsidy to new industries whose development would benefit "injurer" and "victim" categories alike—at least in the long, long run when, unfortunately, all those now present might long since be beyond benefiting). The allocation of losses described in the text might be viewed as beneficial from a purely distributional standpoint if one believes that injurers, as a category, are "worthier" than victims as a category. Oliver Wendell Holmes, Jr. certainly believed in the efficiency reasons for normally burdening victims (even though he accepted some very limited non-fault injurer liability). Whether he believed that such allocations were also distributionally beneficial is less clear. He clothed his undoubted preference for victim loss bearing in language which can be read to rely either on long run efficiency or on worthiness. *See, e.g.*, Holmes, THE COMMON LAW, 76-77 (M. Howe, ed., 1963). *Cf.* Calabresi, THE COSTS OF ACCIDENTS: A LEGAL AND ECONOMIC ANALYSIS (1970). See also

Calabresi and Melamed, *Property Rules, Liability Rules and Inalienability: One View of the Cathedral*, 85 Harv. L. Rev. 1089 (1972).

4. In 1876 Rylands v. Fletcher had already been decided and one can, with hindsight, see at least in Justice Blackburn's opinion, the seeds of ultra-hazardous activity, non-fault, injurer liability. Other opinions, however, make the case seem like a last bastion of a pre-fault approach, preserved for a particular category of victims, the landed gentry. *See* Fletcher v. Rylands, 3 H & C. 744, 159 Eng. Rep. 737 (1865), *rev'd*. Fletcher v. Rylands, L.R. 1 Exch. 265 (1866), *aff'd*. Rylands v. Fletcher, L.R. 3 H.L. 330 (1868). Only with hindsight can we say that Blackburn's approach was to prove more important than Baron Bramwell's or Lord Cairns'.

   Clearer signs of reversal can be seen in some statutes dealing with liability of railroads for fire. *See, e.g.*, §7899 Conn. General Statutes (1949), enacted in 1875 (injury suffices to establish a *prima facie* case of negligence), followed by §5557 Conn. General Statutes, (negligence no longer needed for liability), enacted in 1881, and upheld against a constitutional challenge in Grissell v. Housatonic R. Co., 54 Conn. 447 (1886).

5. This is not the place to go into the relationship between efficiency and distributional desires and justice. That results which can be analyzed with some success in terms of their efficiency and distributional effects are commonly—and often quite properly—described by courts and commentators in justice terms is a commonplace. Sometimes the use of justice language can be helpful (for one brief discussion of why *see* Calabresi, *Concerning Cause, supra* n. 2 at 105-108). At other times justice language can serve mainly to obfuscate; (a particularly egregious example is Ives v. S. Buffalo R.R., 201 N.Y. 271, 94 N.E. 431 [1911]).

   Among recent attempts to explain tort law in terms of justice language, the most interesting have been by Epstein, *Intentional Harms*, 4 J. Legal Stud. 391 (1975); *Defenses and Subsequent Pleas in a System of Strict Liability*, 3 J. Legal Stud. 165 (1974); *A Theory of Strict Liability*, 2 J. Legal Stud. 151 (1973); and *Pleadings and Presumptions*, 40 U. Chi. L. Rev. 556 (1973), and by Fletcher, *Fairness and Utility in Torts Theory*, 85 Harv. L. Rev. 537 (1972).

6. In a society where unions do not exist or are small and disorganized, the placement of industrial accident costs on the employer-injurer, rather than on the employee-victim, is likely to lead to a greater recognition of accident costs and to greater incentives toward accident avoidance. (The individual worker is not as likely to know and evaluate the risk as is the employer for whom such harms are a statistic). In a society in which both unions and employers are large enough to treat industrial accidents as a statistically "known" risk, the legal placement of the cost burden is unlikely to have any great significance. (It will be renegotiated by the parties either openly or through wage rates changes.) In a society where unions are large and employers small and scattered, greater incentives to safety are likely to result from placement of initial losses on the unionized employees—at least absent compulsory employer insurance (The employers are less likely than the unions to know the precise extent of the risk; many may choose to "chance it" and go under.)

7. An "act," as I am using the word, is simply a sub-category of an "activity." For that reason a collective decision to deter an activity only "to some extent" or when done by "some people" or in "certain ways" can be described as a decision fully to deter some acts.

   It does not matter, for these purposes, what the governmental structure of the collectivistic society is. It might be democratic and governed by elected individuals who can be voted out if they do not choose in accordance with popular desires. It might be dictatorial—of the proletariat or otherwise. What is crucial is that the decision makers—however chosen—are expected to decide for the mass of the people which risks are worth taking and which, instead, are not.

8. I have elsewhere said that the market society would (apart from distributional considerations) establish entitlements so as to put the burden of accidents on

that activity which can avoid accidents most cheaply. *See, e.g.*, Calabresi, COSTS OF ACCIDENTS, *supra* n. 3, Calabresi and Melamed, *Property Rules and Liability Rules, supra* n. 3. That statement may seem inconsistent with the one made here. But it is not, for included in the definition of the cheapest cost avoider was the ability to negotiate cheaply and, by implication, to establish contracts which could be enforced cheaply. Conversely, placement of the initial burden on the party who could, *literally*, avoid the harm most cheaply, would also entail that placement which would make contracts and transactions least costly. For such a placement would obviate the need for *any* transactions or contracts with respect to that risk, and hence reduce such costs to zero. Where there is sufficient uncertainty about the identity of the cheapest cost avoider, however, the party which seems most able to alter its behavior cheaply may not be the party which seems most able to negotiate cheaply. In such cases a judgment must be made, based on the particular facts, as to which ability offers the greatest promise of reducing the sum of the costs of accidents and of their avoidance.

The collectively determined starting points are frequently described by advocates of a pure market society as based on a series of essentially utilitarian judgments. These are *collective* judgments of utility, however. Ironically, once such collective utilitarian judgments have been made, the pure market ideology permits changes only on the basis of atomistic, libertarian-contractarian utility judgments, *i.e.*, only free market transactions are permissible means to further utility improvements. *See notes* 10 and 11, *infra. See also* Demsetz, *Toward A Theory of Property Rights*, 157 Am. Econ. Rev. 347 (1967) (Vol. 2—Papers and Proceedings).

9. The analogy to liquidated damages and to resolution of commercial disputes through arbitration is obvious and intended. From this point of view, the limitations placed by contract law in some jurisdictions on liquidated damages and on arbitration agreements "in derogation of law" are deviations from the pure market ideal. They, like all restrictions on the legal ability of one of the parties to take on risks by contract, smack of tort law and represent "mixed society" incursions into the very citadel of the market. The expansion of old, and proliferation of new, constraints on the ability to contract (whether because the result would violate public policy, be unconscionable or what have you) are part of the ascendancy of the liability rule—torts—approach which I am describing in this paper. I do not, however, wish to be taken to suggest that contract *law* ever represented pure market ideology. Specific performance and promissory estoppel are but two examples of contract doctrines whose relationship to pure market ideology is at best uncertain. Because contract law was not as brittle as market ideologues would have had it be, it has been able to survive the decline of that ideology. *Cf.* notes 17 and 24. *infra.*

10. The ideology of the market society is premised on the notion that—absent unanimous societal consent—an improvement from any given starting point can be shown to occur only if an individual or group freely transacts with another individual or group to bring about a change. Such a move leads to what is termed a Pareto-superior position, and the parties are by definition better off; by definition because the pure market ideology premises that individuals always know best for themselves what they want and what will better their state. There is no need to go into the host of practical and theoretical limitations of this approach, many accepted by strong free market advocates. It is enough for us here to note that unless the parties agree *before the accident* on the compensation to be paid for bearing a loss or for bearing its risk, in derogation of the initial entitlement, the free exchange of rights mandated by the market ideology will not exist. A collective determination of the loss—that is, tort damages, or eminent domain compensation for that matter, does not constitute an agreement by the parties to sell and buy an entitlement for the price which suits them. As such it may over or under compensate and hence does not necessarily leave both parties—still presumed to know best for themselves—better off than before.

There will be some losers—*e.g.*, those who would not have sold at the eminent domain price—and the change cannot be shown to constitute a Pareto-superior move. Unlike "legal compensation," an agreement (before an accident) on the procedure to be used for determining damages (after an accident) does meet the requirements of the market ideology. Once again since the parties "knew best for themselves" when they accepted the procedure, they by definition are fully compensated through that procedure. The analogy is to a free sale of a good at a price to be determined later by an expert chosen by the parties.

Any attempt (through "social contract theory" or by implying consent) to convert *state* determination of tort damages into such an "agreed upon procedure" proves too much, however. The same "consent" can be implied for *any* state action, and Pareto-superiority can then be claimed for *any* state-made collective decision. The term, at that point, loses all significance and . . . utility. *Compare* Buchanan and Tullock, THE CALCULUS OF CONSENT: LEGAL FOUNDATIONS OF CONŒ STITUTIONAL DEMOCRACY (1962); Buchanan, *Positive Economics, Welfare Economics, and Political Economy*, 2 J. Law & Econ. 124 (1959); and Buchanan, THE LIMITS OF LIBERTY (1975).

All this emphasizes the—too often ignored—difference between a pure utilitarian ideology and a pure libertarian-contractarian one. The first would have no problems with collectively determined shifts in entitlements and, *a fortiori*, with collectively determined compensation, so long as it appeared that winners gained more than losers lost. The second rejects such shifts unless the gains, losses, and compensation are demonstrated through freely established contractual-market transactions. *See note* 8, *supra*.

11. The tension between the utilitarian bases of free market thinking (whether collective or not), and the libertarian-contractarian aspirations of that ideology are all too rarely recognized explicitly. *But see* Buchanan, THE LIMITS OF LIBERTY (1975).

In the absence of what Professor Coase has called transaction costs, any initial allocation is as efficient as any other. But transaction costs (as the term is used by Coase, to mean *any impediments to bargaining* including absence of information and knowledge) are—like friction—only absent in theoretical models. The question then inevitably becomes how significant in any given situation is "the friction." Where impediments to bargaining (transaction costs) are significant, the initial entitlement can be crucial in terms of efficiency. *See* Coase, *The Problem of Social Cost*, 3 J. Law & Econ. 1 (1960); Calabresi, *Transaction Costs, Resource Allocation and Liability Rules*, 11 J. Law. & Econ. 67 (1968); Calabresi and Melamed, *Property Rules and Liability Rules, supra* n. 3. And a *laissez-faire* society knows this as well as any other. Indeed, the *efficiency* basis of the 19th century's preference for victim loss bearing lay precisely in the existence of transaction costs. Injurers could not seek out and contract with all possible victims. When, nevertheless, injurer avoidance seemed *patently* cheaper, efficiency, given the presence of transaction costs, required that the initial burden be placed on injurers. A simple "always let the loss lie on the victim" was, therefore, unacceptable to these utilitarian 19th century free marketeers and liability for many fault caused injuries followed, *cf.* Demsetz, *When Does the Rule of Liability Matter*, 1 J. of Legal Stud. 13 (1972), Stigler, *The Law and Economics of Public Policy: A Plea to the Scholars*, 1 J. Legal Stud. 1 (1972). *Cf. notes* 8, 10, *supra*.

12. To say that illegitimate non-contractual behavior can become valid through a contract or sale is not to say that a society must always permit all contracts. Rape, by contract, can become prostitution—a very different thing, but not necessarily legal. Murder cannot be made legal through victim consent. All such restrictions on contract are, in a sense, limits on the "pure" market society, though many were recognized even in the high days of that ideology. Some restrictions on alienation can in fact be explained in terms which are, on the whole, consistent with "pure" markets in the "real" world. As such restrictions become more widespread, however, explanations inconsistent with market

ideologies become more plausible. *See* Calabresi and Melamed, *Property Rules and Liability Rules, supra* n. 3.

13. Any time initial injurer liability is appropriate, and finding and contracting with all possible victims is impossible, a clear instance of this first reason exists. Negligent driving is the classic example. Burdening injurers was widely deemed to be appropriate; *ex ante* contractual arrangements with possible victims were prohibitive; fault based tort liability followed. A somewhat more complex example of the first reason is the case in which contractual behavior harms "third" parties with whom contractual arrangements are not feasible.

14. This second reason may be present because the parties do not have adequate knowledge to contract in their own best interests. And making such knowledge available in an *effective* way may not be deemed feasible or may be prohibitively expensive. For a discussion of what is an *adequate* warning or disclaimer, even in contractual situations like those involved in products liability cases, *see, e.g.*, Henningsen v. Bloomfield Motors, Inc., 32 N.J. 358, 161 A.2d 69 (1960), Sills v. Massey-Ferguson, Inc., 296 F. Supp. 776 (N.D. Ind. 1969).

It may also be present because the society believes that the parties, even if informed, will not decide in their best interest since they are incapable as a result of age, poverty, lack of education, or any other "limitation" which seems crucial to that no longer purely individualistic society.

15. The behavior may also be forbidden criminally, as is the case in many automobile negligence situations, but that additional bit of collective intervention is for my present purposes beside the point. To the extent that civil responsibility or liability exists, the actor must take that possible—collectively determined—payment into account in deciding whether the behavior is worth undertaking. It might seem that damages in contract cases are also collectively determined. But if the parties to the contract had the option, at the time the contract was made, of agreeing to liquidated damages or to arbitration and chose not to do so, then judicial damages would be fully consistent with the libertarian ideology. *See* note 10, *supra*. If arbitration and liquidated damages are forbidden, however, the approach is closer to that of the ideology mixture I am here describing. *See* note 9, *supra,* and note 17 *infra*.

16. As a general rule, it is not forbidden. Exculpatory agreements exist, as do agreements to let damages—should harm occur—be determined by arbitrators chosen by the parties. Such "contractual behavior," however, even if permitted is not a prerequisite for acting.

17. Tort law is only one instance of this ideological mixture; it is only one area in which what I call liability rules are used. Eminent domain is another, for in that area too a transfer of an entitlement is imposed at a price which is not negotiated by the parties. Closely analogous are prohibitions on particular means of assessing damages agreed to by the parties. Thus, from the point of view of this paper, restrictions on the use of liquidated damage clauses or of arbitration agreements are examples of the same mixed approach of which torts is my paradigm. Moving a bit further, but still close, is the unenforceability of certain contracts as "against public policy" or as "unconscionable." The analogue here, of course, is to the invalidity of certain exculpatory or indemnificatory agreements and the "inadequacy" of some warnings in torts. In all these instances there is substituted for the "agreement" of the parties a collective determination. But also in these instances, the collective determination does not cover the field; it leaves substantial room for individual decisions and for the play of incentives. *See generally* Calabresi and Melamed, *Property Rules, Liability Rules, supra* n. 3.

18. One could, of course, look at criminal law and criminal penalties analogously. From this viewpoint the penalty becomes the price which the criminal is free to risk and, if caught, pay in order to engage in the criminal behavior. Those who have looked at criminal law this way are, understandably, led to take the next step; in attempting to convert that area of law into a torts-like mixture they fre-

quently urge fines, or victim compensation instead of more traditional criminal sanctions. *See, e.g.*, Becker, *Crime and Punishment: An Economic Approach*, 76 J. Pol. Econ. 169 (1968); Del Vecchio, *Equality and Inequality in Relation to Justice*, 11 Nat. Law Forum 36, 43-45 (1966) *cf*. Posner, ECONOMIC ANALYSIS OF LAW 66-69, 357-73 (1972).

But this approach, to my way of thinking, misperceives the societal judgment involved in criminal law. Leaving aside ambiguous areas like parking tickets and other "administrative" violations (which are in fact normally subject only to fines), the societal intention in criminal law is not to permit individuals to choose whether or not committing the crime is worthwhile. The object, though never fully enforceable, is to keep the crime from happening regardless of the criminal's desire to commit it because a *collective* decision has been made that the criminal conduct is not worthwhile regardless of individual desire to engage in it.

This collective determination is easily reconcilable with a market ideology whenever negotiations between the victim and the criminal are eminently feasible. Indeed, the *criminality* in such cases can be viewed as consisting simply in the willful refusal on the part of the criminal to engage in contractual behavior before acting. Theft is the most obvious case; criminal sanctions are imposed in order to require a negotiated sale rather than a *taking* at a collectively determined "price-penalty" (as Becker would have it). Rape, when prostitution is permitted or in practice tolerated, is another. Ideologically, traditional criminal sanctions in these areas can be justified in order to protect the integrity of a market society and are totally consistent with it.

At times, however, the collective nature of the decision to forbid behavior is more basic. Criminal sanctions are used to prohibit consensual behavior (the fact that victim was willing does not exonerate the killer), or are used where negotiations are not feasible (where a pure marketeer would accept a liability rule, but not a criminal sanction, as the necessary second best). The societal decision in these cases is, typically, *ideologically* collective, because it attempts to make some entitlements inalienable despite the desires of the immediate parties. See generally Calabresi and Melamed, *Property Rules, Liability Rules, supra* n. 3. Those who are devoted to pure market approaches and ideologies are, understandably, likely to chafe at criminal sanctions in such areas. In the consensual cases, where negotiations between all the relevant parties are possible, the pure marketeer would abolish all criminal penalties except those needed to enforce the requirement that such negotiations take place. In the areas where negotiations are not feasible he would also decriminalize, but would require, as a second best, that the injured parties be compensated by the injurers at a collectively determined price.

If one views Becker *et al.* as ideologically committed pure marketeers, one can readily understand their desire to convert the sanctions in these last areas of criminal law to torts-like, liability rule, sanctions. (One cannot, however, understand their desire to apply liability rules to crimes where negotiations are feasible.) But to say that one can *understand* what they are about is very far from saying that they are right from the society's point of view. A society that has chosen (wisely or not) a rule of inalienability (a collective prohibition of some behavior) has rejected in that instance the market ideology, and hence is not likely to be talked into accepting a torts-like sanction in lieu of a traditional criminal penalty, merely because a liability rule would serve as the market's feasible second best.

19. For present purposes it does not matter whether the collective judgment was based solely on an efficiency calculation or on broader grounds.

The initial entitlement to act without bearing the burden of the injuries can be given to the victim or to the injurer. Letting the loss lie where it falls (unless the injurer is at fault) is an example of injurer entitlement. Strict injurer liability (unless the victim is negligent) gives the entitlement to the victim. Calabresi, *Opti-*

mal Deterrence and Accident Law, supra n. 2, and Calabresi and Hirschoff, *Toward A Test for Strict Liability in Torts, supra* n. 2.

20. We can now begin to understand why writers like Richard Posner, who are devoted to a market ideology, support a fault approach in torts law. Use of fault in lieu of a broader collective prohibition (*i.e.*, the employment of a liability rule based on a collective determination that behavior is wrongful, instead of a criminal sanction) manifests deep skepticism toward collective decisions. For a feasible (indeed an *actual*) collective determination of the merits of individual behavior is not enforced criminally but instead is subjected to an atomistic, market review. This skepticism, while it explains a reluctance to use criminal sanctions instead of fault (*cf.* note 18, *supra*), does not, of course, explain why, in the absence of fault, the pure marketeer prefers universal *victim* liability to universal *injurer* liability or, more plausibly, to strict non-fault liability sometimes on one and sometimes on the other party. That preference can, however, also be explained once one understands the fact that liability rules are only a poor second best for the pure contractarian-market ideologue, and that victim liability may render *any* non-contractual behavior unnecessary. (*See* text at *notes* 8-11, *supra*, and *notes* 21-22 *infra*.) Such a preference may, however, be quite costly from both an efficiency and a distributional point of view. Once again, the difference between utilitarian and libertarian-contractarian approaches becomes crucial. *Compare* Posner, *A Theory of Negligence*, 1 J. Legal Stud. 29 (1972); *Strict Liability: A Comment*, 2 J. Legal Stud. 205 (1973); and ECONOMIC ANALYSIS OF LAW, *op. cit. supra* n. 18, *with* Calabresi, *Transaction Costs, supra* n. 11; *Optimal Deterrence and Accident Law, supra* n. 2; Calabresi and Hirschoff, *Toward A Test for Strict Liability in Torts, supra* n. 2; Calabresi and Melamed, *Property Rules, Liability Rules, supra* n. 3, and Calabresi, COSTS OF ACCIDENTS, *op. cit. supra* n. 3. *See also notes* 8, 10, 11, *supra*.
21. *See, e.g.*, Henningsen v. Bloomfield Motors, Inc., 32 N.J. 356, 161 A.2d 69 (1960); Sills v. Massey Ferguson, Inc., 266 F. Supp. 776 (N.D. Ind. 1969); McGrath v. American Cyanamid Co., 41 N.J. 272, 196 A.2d 238 (1963). *See also* Calabresi and Hirschoff, *Towards A Test for Strict Liability in Torts, supra* n. 2, at note 65, 16 and cases there cited.
22. Protection of property through criminal sanctions in pure market societies is readily explained by the feasibility of contractual behavior (purchase rather than theft) before injury, as well as by the efficiency and distributional intuitions of such societies. *Cf.* Demsetz, *Toward A Theory of Property Rights*, 57 Am. Econ. Rev. 347 (1967) (Vol. 2, Papers and Proceedings). Similarly injurer liability for at least some fault caused injuries was generally justified in such societies on efficiency grounds (*see especially* Richard Posner's writings cited at note 20 *supra; see also* Holmes, *Common Law, op. cit. supra* n. 3); the same would be true, *a fortiori*, for intentional or willful torts, where the feasibility of contractual behavior, before the injury, cannot be excluded. *Punitive* damages would seem particularly appropriate in such cases even in pure market societies. *Cf. note* 18, *supra*.
23. Compulsory insurance for at least part of the loss is a common feature of all so-called no-fault or first party automobile insurance plans currently being debated. The insurance is not merely compulsory toward third parties to whom the motorist is held strictly liable (*e.g.*, passengers and pedestrians) but is also compulsory with respect to the motorist's own injuries. *See, e.g.*, Keeton and O'Connell, BASIC PROTECTION FOR THE TRAFFIC VICTIM (1965) from which most such plans derive.
24. *See generally* Gilmore, THE DEATH OF CONTRACT (1974).

One can, from this standpoint, usefully compare the various attempts made by courts to distinguish between contracts limiting liability in the case of a toaster that is defective in the sense that it fails to work and that of a toaster that is defective in the sense that it blows up or sets a house on fire. The most common first try was, of course, in terms of property versus personal damages. *See, e.g.*, Justice Traynor's "defect causing damage to humans" test for strict liability, Es-cola v. Coca Cola Bottling Co., 24 Cal. 2d 453, 150 P.2d 436 (1944) (concurring opinion); Greenman v. Yuba Products, Inc., 59 Cal. 2d 57, 377 P.2d 897 (1963). But such an approach failed because the same society which is sufficiently *laissez-faire* to permit an ordinary contract to determine who bears the risk of a toaster's failure to work (or of other relatively frequent minor damages, whether personal or property) is not willing to permit major, relatively rare victim-property damages (like those following on toaster caused fires) to be so allocated. Where the law of sales ends and the law of torts begins, in other words, tells us a great deal about the ideological makeup of the society, about how far from a pure market it has gone, without, for all of that, becoming ideologically committed to collectivism.

25. This assumes that the pure market ideologue is concerned solely with efficiency and is uninterested in the *distributional* consequences of the allocation of risks. In fact, it seems likely that the initial entitlement always was based on distributional as well as on efficiency grounds. *Cf.* Calabresi and Melamed, *Property Rules, Liability Rules, supra* n. 3. Holmes, *Common Law, op. cit. supra* n. 3.
26. Punitive damages or fines, used *in lieu of criminal law* do not, of course, represent a move toward greater collectivism, quite the contrary. *See* note 18, *supra*. The same kind of damages and fines employed in place of *compensatory* damages, in situations where torts was traditionally used as a substitute for unfeasible contractual transactions, do represent a turning away from relatively atomistic and individualized decisions and an increase in collective decision making.
27. This corruptibility is evident both in "Western" style democracies and in the "People's" republics.
28. *See, e.g.*, Spur Industries, Inc. v. Del E. Webb Development Co., 108 Ariz. 178, 494 P.2d 700 (1972) (the now classic case of reverse damages in nuisance); *International Herald Tribune*, June 3, 1976, p. 3, col. 1, noting a proposed pollution tax which some United States economists and legislators believe will be more effective than regulation. The proponents of the pollution tax emphasized the administrative unworkability of regulation. An official of the National Association of Manufacturers, instead, defended regulation in a Congressional Seminar, saying "It is working well and should not be scrapped for an untried theoretical approach." *Cf.* Wash. *Post*, Feb. 1, 1976, sec. B, p. 1, col. 6, reporting the civil damage suit brought by a rape victim to buttress what were viewed as inadequate criminal law controls in the area. *See also* the debate between Posner & Landes and Stigler on the relative merits of "Private Law Enforcement," 3 J. Leg. Stud. 1 (1974), 4 J. Leg. Stud. 1 (1975.
29. If this view is correct, one can expect that there will be increasing tort-like influences in areas where contracts and criminal law prevail. The concept of contracts of adhesion, for instance, will continue to grow (thus limiting the pure market even in areas nominally governed by contract law), as will the notion of compensation of victims of crimes (thus putting some market type incentives at work in a traditionally collectivist area of law).

My colleague Leon Lipson has pointed out that a disproportionate number of American and English jurisprudes, in the last century, began their careers in contracts law, while a disproportionate number of Russian jurisprudes, since 1917, have been scholars of criminal law. It will be interesting to see if the American legal philosophers of the next years will come from fields in which *liability rules,* as I have here used the term, are dominant.

CONTRACTS

Robert Braucher*

Some of those who are law students today will no doubt be practicing law half a century from now, in the year 2026. I hope they are being taught, as I was some forty years ago, that no one can live in the future, that predictions are hazardous, and that detailed planning for the long run is commonly very unwise. Our vision of the year 2026 is clouded enough, but I am bold enough to predict that in that year it will be even harder to see fifty years ahead than it is now.

It is worth remembering, perhaps, that our vision of the past and the present is also sometimes clouded. Not so long ago, Professor Gilmore favored us with an obituary of Contract.[1] The concept of contract, it seems, was discovered for the first time by Dean Langdell of Harvard about one hundred years ago, and was elaborated in something like an unconscious conspiracy involving Langdell, Holmes, and Williston, all responding instinctively to mysterious and blind historical forces favoring the interests of the rich and powerful. More recently, under the bludgeonings of sociology and "legal realism," the concept of contract has decayed, and Contract is now being reabsorbed into the mainstream of Tort, which for some undisclosed reason is thought to be better suited to the welfare state and a regime of codifying statutes. So says Gilmore.

Others have sufficiently denounced Professor Gilmore's historical method.[2] Here I merely note that about the same time Professor Morton J. Horwitz was reporting that the foundations of modern contract law had been laid by English and American judges nearly a century earlier, soon after the American Revolution, and that the will theory of contract

*Associate Justice, Supreme Judicial Court of Massachusetts.

found its way into the first English treatise on contract, published in 1790.[3] I merely note the hundred-year difference, without taking sides. My own impression is that people all over the world had a generalized, abstract concept of contract many centuries earlier. If there are any people a hundred years from now, I predict that they will still have that concept. Moreover, I predict, the law governing contracts, whatever its form and by whomever it is made, will be thought by some, as it always has, to favor the rich and powerful.

One might think that our perceptions of the present would be more certain. And indeed I do have some confidence in my own understanding of the law of contracts as it has existed over the last forty years, partly because during our work on the Restatement of Contracts Second I have had an unusual opportunity to test my understanding against the views of others.[4] I am not at all shaken by Gilmore's perverse dictum that Contract is dead, or by the fact that he finds a "schizophrenic quality" in our Restatement coexisting magically with what he calls "syncretism," and defines as "the reconciliation or union of conflicting beliefs." When we descend from the clouds of cosmic generalization, or perhaps merely of stylistic elegance, I do not find myself very far apart from Professor Gilmore on matters of substance, although we would be most unlikely to express the same thought in the same way. I am afraid, much as he would like to conceal it, that he is not a radical but a neo-traditionalist in the stream of Corbin and Llewellyn, approving references to whose works adorn his footnotes. I should add that I also number among the neo-traditionalists Fuller,[5] Havighurst,[6] Kessler,[7] and myself.

Let me focus for a moment on the matter of Contract and Tort. I learned the law of contracts, not from Professor Williston, but from Professor Gardner, who sought even more fervently an abstract, generalized theory of Contract as a legal institution.[8] With six classmates I came from Harvard to an apartment on Washington Square North in New York City, later, happily, acquired by New York University. One of those classmates was courting a girl at Barnard College, and he arranged to borrow my car regularly for the purpose. Throughout the court and courting year 1939-1940, to the distress of our roommates, we took every possible opportunity to work out—usually in the bathroom—the legal consequences of our arrangement in hypothetical situations of varying degrees of plausibility. Our imaginations had not even approached exhaustion when he spoiled the game by marrying the girl.

This was possibly the most exhaustive analysis of a transaction in human history, and I can report that our common legal heritage enabled us to work out an agreed solution to each hypothetical case as it was presented, without undue strain. I emphasize that we were not negotiating an agreement, but deducing rationally the consequences of the agreement we had already made. As a matter of hindsight, we were probably discussing the law of torts and the law of property, including bailments, more than the law of contracts, but that was not the spirit of the enterprise. Neither of us, I suspect, referred to the seminal bailment case of *Coggs* v. *Bernard*,[9] and in this and other respects our discussions bore more resemblance to consultations among the members of an appellate court than to some academic discussions of similar issues.

I have two points to make about the non-contractual aspects of this car-borrowing transaction. The first relates to Contract and Tort; the second to the "Contract is Dead" movement. In an entirely traditional and conventional spirit, we knew thirty-five years ago that nature had not divided life or its problems neatly into contracts and torts. To speak of contracts as separating from the mainstream of torts and later rejoining the mainstream is to speak of a world that never was. When I used to teach school, I regularly had to correct law students who, misled by less conceptual teachers, referred to a statute of limitations governing personal injuries as a "tort" statute of limitations. In Massachusetts until recently many actions at law properly bore the label "Contract or Tort."[10]

As for the "Contract is Dead" movement, the point is the open-ended quality of our car-borrowing transaction and the fact that, no matter what happened, neither of us had any intention of starting a lawsuit against the other. Here I must pause to say a little more about the "Contract is Dead" movement. Despite what has been said above, Professor Gilmore is not a leader in that movement, nor even an enthusiastic follower. Professor Stuart Macaulay of Wisconsin, says Professor Gilmore, is entitled to rank as Lord High Executioner.[11] Professor Macaulay has published "a series of highly interesting articles on the irrelevance of traditional contract theory;" he and others conclude that Contract is no longer a fit subject of study for law students, and that legal scholars should turn to sociological analysis. Somewhat reluctantly, Gilmore seems to accept the first step, but he declares himself "completely uninterested" in what the leaders of the movement are doing. The problem seems to be that sociologists count things, and Gilmore doesn't like to count things. I am with Gilmore.

Let me shift now to another open-ended transaction. When I came back from the wars to teach at Harvard in 1946, we became subtenants of a single family house. The house was a little large for a couple with one small child, and we were short of funds. We found a slightly younger couple, both graduate students, and arranged to share the house and the rent. After we had agreed on all the terms we could think of, I said something might come up we had not thought of, and we needed a principle of order. "I have tried to think what it should be," I said, "and the best I can do is to suggest that what I say goes." They thought that sounded fair, and we lived happily together until we went our separate ways at the end of the school year. I never made a decision under the unconscionable clause, and we are still friends.

I did not then, and I do not now, think that either the car-sharing transaction or the house-sharing transaction was in any way out of harmony with traditional contract theory. But apparently Professor Macaulay and his cohorts would regard the conduct I have described as non-contractual behavior in non-contractual relations.[12] Professor Ian Macneil tells us that "the superstructure of traditional contract law" rests on a "presupposition that a contract is a discrete transaction,"[13] and he defines transaction so as to exclude continuing relations.

I adhere to a quite different view: in the words of the Restatement,[14] "Like 'contract,' however, the word 'promise' is commonly and quite properly also used to refer to the complex of human relations which results from the promisor's words or acts of assurance. . . ." Moreover, those words or acts are to be read in context.[15] Again in the words of the Restatement,[16] "connotations depend on the entire past experience and the attitudes and expectations of the person whose understanding is in question." Continuing relations are everywhere, and in my version of traditional orthodox legal theory contracts and continuing relations are in no way incompatible.

One caveat: When I taught a subject called Contracts to a law school class, I did not focus very hard on what Havighurst calls "contract in fact." In a law school course taught by the case method, primarily from opinions of appellate courts, continuing relations, if any, have ordinarily been thoroughly disrupted. Appellate courts rarely give opinions about contracts that have worked out well. Our methods of litigation are not designed to settle disputes among friends. They are inhumane—not to say brutal—and the man who goes to law, even against the Government or a stranger, is commonly not as likable as the man who does not. So contract cases typically involve comparative strangers, or friends who have severed diplomatic relations and do not appear in their best light.

Let me now shift from the generalizations of others to some of my own. Lawyers have a great deal to do with the making and performance of contracts, but they do not think of themselves as practising Contract Law. They are dealing with Corporations, or Collective Bargaining, or Securities, or Insurance, or Banking, or perhaps Franchising or Leasing or Consumer Finance or Collections. As a teacher of Contracts I tried to pull out of all this some problems which shed light on contracts in general. I did not find it hard, but I did not limit my reading of advance sheets to cases bearing a headnote label: "Contracts." I fully recognize that one man's rule is another man's analogy, and I have never been sure there was any difference. I did not recognize jurisdictional limits in class discussion: to the confusion of my students, in the discussion of offer and acceptance in the case of the unsolicited newspaper, I expected them to think of going to the Post Office regulations, to the Federal Trade Commission, or even to the Legislature. In some ways I preferred the course title Commercial Transactions, which brought some emancipation from categorical blinders.

Today I have left the academic halls, and I no longer deal

with contract cases at all. Every civil case is first a case in appellate procedure and then a case in civil procedure. Many cases deal with contracts, but they are land contracts or insurance contracts or arbitration agreements or some other subcategory. Nevertheless, I seek enlightenment wherever I can find it, and often I feel a need to go beyond the briefs. You will not, I think, be surprised if I tell you that I often find the Restatement of Contracts helpful.[17] Or the Uniform Commercial Code, even in cases to which it does not apply.[18]

Where will all this lead us, as the future unfolds? First, I think we can anticipate more and more anti-contract law, limiting the extent to which agreements are effective.[19] Second, more and more of our contract law, designed to facilitate agreement, will be statutory. Third, we can expect continued luxuriant growth of bureaucracy, both public and private, and massive flowering of rules, regulations and standardized practices and forms. I say this, please note, with enthusiasm, as a Llewellyn disciple.[20] I quote again from the Restatement:[21] "Standardization of agreements serves many of the same functions as standardization of goods and services; both are essential to a system of mass production and distribution. . . . Operations are simplified and costs reduced, to the advantage of all concerned."

From these premises, conclusions follow easily. The problems of formation and validity will tend to be resolved separately for different types of contracts, as problems of illegality have been. General principles will continue to have utility for multi-party problems, which are sometimes too complex for resolution in advance.[22] Problems of implication will continue to arise, and recourse will inevitably be had to analogy and to such general concepts as the power of a court to supply a missing term, the obligation of good faith, and the avoidance of unconscionable results.[23] Perhaps the principal developments will be increasing realism in interpretation and increasing efficiency in remedies.

A word should be said here about equal treatment of those similarly situated. We are living through an expansion of the obligation of governments to provide equal protection of the laws, but we have not yet fully recognized a similar obligation on the part of private institutions. Standardized contracts and practices call for standardized treatment of the customers,[24] and may call for some revision of our tradition that two juries can decide the same question of fact two different ways. It is not clear to me how this is to be done: neither the parol evidence rule,[25] the law of res judicata,[26] nor the class action[27] yet does the job.

Our urge for consistency is powerfully invoked by a claim that an airline has the same duty of care to two passengers sitting side by side in the same airplane,[28] or that Carte Blanche has the same duties to all the holders of its credit cards. But it goes further. When discovery before trial became familiar in civil cases, it was predictable that there would be a comparable development in criminal cases, and the development only took one generation.[29] Similarly, formulas painfully worked out for sales of goods and embodied in the Uniform Commercial Code have been extended to other types of contracts.[30] Insurance law gave us the concept of a contract of adhesion, and counsel have not been slow to extrapolate.[31] We will see more of this.

Here I must insert a qualification relating to my enthusiasm for bureaucracy. I have spent a good deal of my life as a rather specialized type of bureaucrat: the channel evader, the inspector general, the ombudsman, the manufacturer of special exceptions for special cases.[32] This is an essential specialty in a bureaucracy. In our drive for consistency, for law and rules, we must leave some room for discretion and common sense, for equity and fairness.

My final prediction is that developments in remedies will be revolutionary. If we let our minds go loose, we can visualize reliable fact-finding, assisted perhaps by the polygraph or similar devices, and videotape records which recreate a trial visually as well as verbally. Perhaps we can end the absurd practice of submitting complex commercial cases to a jury, and resolve disputes less than five years after they arise. If so, and if we can retain confidence in our judges, timely specific relief may become the standard remedy for many breaches of contract, rather than money damages.

I have saved until last what is not a prediction but a hope. In my lifetime I think I have seen a growth of candor in the law, and I hope that will continue. Judges seem to me, more often than they used to, to deal realistically and frankly with facts and law, explaining the real reasons they decide as they do, rather than taking refuge in procedural nicety or other obscure technicality. Future development on these lines rests in hope rather than prediction, because it depends on the judge's sense of security. That sense is a fragile thing; it depends in turn on public confidence in the system and the judges. If too many people throw beer bottles at the umpire, he dare not give an honest explanation of what he is doing. For the time being we are secure enough, but you don't have to shoot the judge in the courtroom to impair his serenity.

Thus I conclude: the law of Contracts is alive and well in Massachusetts, and apparently elsewhere. If there is any law a hundred years from now, it will include a law of Contracts. But if any of us could survive to try to practice that law, I am sure we would need to learn many things we do not now know.

FOOTNOTES

1. G. Gilmore, the Death of Contract (1974).
2. See, e.g., Gordley, Book Review, 89 Harv. L. Rev. 452 (1975).
3. M. Horwitz, The Historical Foundations of Modern Contract Law, 87 Harv. L. Rev. 917 (1974).
4. See Braucher, Offer and Acceptance in the Second Restatement, 74 Yale L.J. 302 (1964); Braucher, Freedom of Contract and the Second Restatement, 78 Yale L.J. 598 (1969); Braucher, The Unconscionable Contract or Term, 31 U. Pitt. L. Rev. 337 (1970).
5. Fuller and Perdue, The Reliance Interest in Contract Damages, 46 Yale L.J. 52, 373 (1936).
6. Havighurst, The Nature of Private Contract (1961).
7. Kessler and Fine, "Culpa in Contrahendo," Bargaining in Good Faith and Freedom of Contract: A Comparative Study, 77 Harv. L. Rev. 401 (1964).
8. Gardner, An Inquiry into the Principles of the Law of Contracts, 46 Harv. L. Rev. 1 (1932).
9. 2 Ld. Raymond 909, 92 Eng. Rep. 107 (K.B. 1702).
10. E.g., Knowles v. Gilchrist Co., 362 Mass. 642 (1972).
11. See, e.g., Macaulay, Non-Contractual Relations in Business: A Preliminary Study, 28 Am. Sociological Rev. 55 (1963); Symposium on the Relevance of Contract Theory, 1967 Wis. L. Rev. 303.
12. See note 11, *supra*.
13. See Macneil, The Many Futures of Contracts, 47 So. Calif. L. Rev. 691, 693 (1974). See also Macneil, Restatement (Second) of Contracts and Presentiation, 60 Va. L. Rev. 589 (1974); Macneil, A Primer of Contract Planning, 48 So. Calif. L. Rev. 627 (1975).
14. Restatement Contracts 2d § 2 Comment *c* (Tent. Drafts 1-7, 1973) (hereafter Restatement).
15. *Id.* § 228 Comment *b*.
16. *Id.* § 227 Comment *b*.
17. See Robert Indus., Inc. v. Spence, 362 Mass. 751, 754-755 (1973).
18. See George v. Coolidge Bank & Trust Co., 360 Mass. 635, 639-640 (1971).

19. See, e.g., Mass. Gen. Laws ch. 183, § 61 (requiring holders of mortgages on dwellings to pay interest to the mortgagor on amounts deposited with the mortgagee for the payment of real estate taxes); 40 Fed. Reg. 53506 (1975) (FTC regulation, effective May 14, 1976, requiring consumer credit contracts to contain a provision subjecting all holders of the contract to the defenses the debtor can assert against the seller).
20. See Llewellyn, Book Review, 52 Harv. L. Rev. 700, 701-702 (1937); Llewellyn, The Common Law Tradition: Deciding Appeals 362 (1960); Llewellyn, Jurisprudence: Realism in Theory and Practice 281 (1962).
21. Restatement § 237 Comment *a*.
22. See, e.g., Canter v. Schlager, 358 Mass. 789, 791-795 (1971).
23. Restatement §§ 230, 231, 234.
24. Restatement § 237(2).
25. Restatement §§ 239-243.
26. Restatement, Judgments 2d § 88 (Tent. Draft No. 2, 1975).
27. See Katz v. Carte Blanche Corp., 496 F.2d 747 (3d Cir. 1974), cert. den. 419 U.S. 885 (1974). Cf. Carpenter v. Suffolk Franklin Sav. Bank, Mass., (1976).
28. But cf. Van Dusen v. Barrack, 376 U.S. 612, 639 (1964).
29. See Fed. R. Crim. P. 16; 1 Wright, Federal Practice and Procedure § 251 (1969).
30. George v. Coolidge Bank & Trust Co., *supra* note 18, at 639-640; Murray, Under the Spreading Analogy of Article 2 of the Uniform Commercial Code, 39 Fordham L. Rev. 447 (1971); Annot., 48 ALR3d 668 (1973).
31. Compare Koshland v. Columbia Ins. Co., 237 Mass. 467, 471-472 (1921), with Lechmere Tire & Sales Co. v. Burwick, 360 Mass. 718, 720-721 (1972).
32. For an unsuccessful effort, see Braucher, J., dissenting in Boston Safe Deposit & Trust Co. v. Fleming, 361 Mass. 172, 183 (1972).

PROPERTY

A. James Casner*

Introduction

Property law is not noted for its rapidity of change. There is a long tradition of making changes long after they should have been made. When Lord Mansfield in the eighteenth century undertook to loosen up the old rules in the name of practicality and common sense, he evoked two statements which epitomized the temper of the English courts and the conveyancing bar. Mr. Justice Blackstone, severely reproving Lord Mansfield, announced the conveyancer's creed when he said:

> "The law of real property in this country is now formed into a fine artificial system, full of unseen connections and nice dependencies, and he that breaks one link of the chain, endangers the dissolution of the whole."[1]

And Junius, a controversialist, uninhibited by the limitations of the Bench, added:

> "Instead of these certain positive rules by which the judgments of a court of law should invariably be determined, you [Lord Mansfield] have fondly introduced your own unsettled notions of equity and substantial justice. . . . By such treacherous arts the noble simplicity and free spirit of our Saxon laws were first corrupted."[2]

The common law doctrine of destructibility of contingent remainders rested firmly on the rule that the seisin could not be in abeyance and hence if the remainderman was not ready to take the seisin when the prior supporting estate came to an end, the seisin would have to return to the grantor, and once back in him, it could not move out again without a

**Austin Wakeman Scott Professor of Law, Harvard Law School*

fresh livery of seisin. Adherence to this ancient doctrine was so firmly entrenched, as late as 1695, that a judge who acquiesced in a minor exception to the rule brought down upon himself the severe censure of his brethren. The minor exception is illustrated by a conveyance to "A for life and on A's death to his first born child." On A's death no child has been born to him but his wife is then pregnant. The seisin could not go to the child in gestation. If it went back to the grantor it could not come out again if the child in gestation is born alive. The decision in which the judge in question acquiesced allowed the seisin to be in abeyance pending the birth of the child and then to pass to the child if he is born alive. The judge involved was Baron Turton of the Court of Exchequer who was present in the House of Lords when that memorable decision was made. The Reporter of the decision notes that "all the judges . . . very much blamed Baron Turton for permitting it to be found specially where the law was so clear and certain." This stimulated a Harvard Law School student some years ago, after reading this case and the appropriate passages in Charles Fearne's great work on Contingent Remainders, to respond poetically:

> "Let's fill the cups to Baron Turton
> who, though the law was clear and certain,
> would rather help a little foetus
> than round out Charlie Fearne's dull treatise."[3]

This background has made it difficult to bring about changes in the field of property law. Nevertheless, as we will see, many notable changes and developments in this field have taken place, surprisingly, through judicial channels. Frequently, the legislative route to change has been difficult to achieve because of the political influence of those interested in maintaining the status quo. Some significant legislative changes, however, have found their way into the property law picture, such as the Statute of Uses,[4] the Statute of Wills,[5] and the Statute of Frauds.[6]

What is Included in Property Law?

In a broad sense, law affects either property or persons. Obviously, if property law is to include all aspects of the law that in some way affect the ownership and use of property, I have not received an appropriate allocation of space.

The property law package as I visualize it for the purposes of this presentation has three components. They are, first, the law applicable to donative arrangements with respect to both real and personal property; second, the law applicable to commercial transactions in land, including landlord and tenant; and third, the law applicable to land use and development. Each of these components is fairly wide-ranging in what it encompasses.

When we look at donative arrangements with respect to real and personal property, we move from the simple transaction that everyone from childhood on has engaged in of delivering by hand an item of little intrinsic worth, but of great sentimental value, to a person for whom he has affection, to the multipage inter vivos or testamentary document that sets up an array of successive interests in the transferred property that will control the devolution of beneficial rights in such property for the period of the rule against perpetuities. The common law has given us an extremely flexible system which permits an almost infinite variety of arrangements of donative transactions.

I can divide the ownership of property among multiple beneficiaries who succeed one after the other to the current beneficial enjoyment of the property, or I can provide for multiple beneficiaries to enjoy the property concurrently with each having an undivided share in the whole, or I can give perpetual ownership in severalty limited in enjoyment in possession to a specified portion of each year. I can make these arrangements through inter vivos transactions or by testamentary dispositions. I can confer these benefits directly in the legal title or I can employ a trust which places the legal title in the trustee and the equitable beneficial title in the beneficiaries of the trust. Through what we now call estate planning, the accumulated wealth of individuals moves in these donative transactions.

This aspect of property law touches everyone either on the giving side or on the receiving side, and will continue to do so until we find some way that enables you to take your accumulated wealth with you when you leave this earth, or until the state decides that the only donee of property can be the state. Some people think that our system of taxation already comes close to naming the state the universal donee.

The second component of the property law package, as I see it, is the commercial transaction in land. I exclude the commercial transaction in personal property because it has developed out of a different background and under different influences. The historical comments I made earlier relate to land. Donative transactions in personal property remain in the property law package because the influences on their development are generally the same as those applicable to donative transactions in land.

The commercial transaction in land covers a number of easily recognized topics. It begins with the negotiations that bring the parties together, frequently through a broker, which lead to the contract of sale. The consummation of the transaction is then held up until the title search is completed and the financing arranged. The performance of the contract then leads to the execution of the deed. The final step is the recording of the instruments relating to the commercial land transaction.

In recent times, the commercial transaction in land has had new life breathed into it by the development of so-called cooperatives, condominiums, and a growing variety of other arrangements involving purchasers of permanent interests in the same piece of property, each to have exclusive possession for some portion of each year.

In regard to the commercial transaction in land I have been referring so far to the sales transaction. The lease transaction that leads to the establishment of a landlord-tenant relationship is a commercial transaction in land and is more pervasive than the sales transaction in the number of people that it touches in one way or another.

In the commercial transaction in land, two or more people are bargaining for the best personal position with respect to the transaction. The one in the superior bargaining position may be able to impose on the other rather harsh terms. This has been particularly true with respect to residential rental property where, because of the shortage of adequate housing, the landlord has had a superior bargaining position.

The third component of property law relates to the use and development of land. The private law aspects of this body of property law have developed under the labels of waste, covenants running with the land, easements, licenses, lateral and subjacent support, water rights, and airspace. In recently modern times, however, the public law aspect of land use and development has taken a dominant position. I refer, of course, to zoning which was in a sense legitimated in its so-called Euclidean form by the *Euclid* case decided by the Supreme Court of the United States in 1926.[7] The more recent widespread interest in the three E's—Energy, Ecology, and Environment—has given great impetus to restrictions on the use of land through a widening variety of public laws. The continuing role of private law devices in regard to the use and development of land in the light of the surging public law interest is not clear at this time.

A word may be appropriate at this time as to what I mean by public law in this context. I refer not only to legislative enactments which restrict the uses that may be made of land by an exercise of the police power but also to the utilization of eminent domain to convert land from a current use to one more in keeping with the public interest. A significant aspect of the public law controls is the role of the courts in determining whether constitutional limits have been exceeded by governmental action relating to the use and development of land.

Before leaving this sketch of the area covered by property law, I should like to mention the problem of racial discrimination in property transactions. Private covenants running with the land were utilized for many years to keep certain racial groups out of residential developments. This practice came to a well deserved end in 1948 when the Supreme Court of the United States[8] held that the judicial enforcement of these private racial restrictions was state action and such state action denied the racial group excluded under the covenant the equal protection of the laws in violation of the Fourteenth Amendment. Since then, of course, there has been the revitalization of the Civil Rights Act of 1866 by a 1968 decision of the Supreme Court[9] and the enactment of the Civil Rights Act of 1968,[10] an act concerned not only with racial discrimination in housing but also with discrimination on the basis of color, national origin, religion, or sex.

Reform in the Property Area–How Accomplished?

I mentioned earlier that reform in the property area has been difficult to attain through the courts, but that there have been significant instances where the courts have played a dominant role.

The fee simple estate as we know it today probably had its birth to a significant extent as a result of a judicial decision in 1225 which established that the heir was bound by a conveyance made by his ancestor.[11] Prior to that time apparently an ancestor could not alienate his land without the consent of his heir apparent. This was an opening wedge in the battle fought by the courts down through the centuries for freedom of alienability of land.

It was a judicial decision rendered in 1472[12] that broke the shackles placed on the alienability of the fee simple title in land by the Statute of De Donis Conditionalibus enacted in 1285[13]—the statute which brought into existence the fee tail estate. This new estate forced the passage of title by descent from generation to generation as long as there were lineal descendants of the original owner. The Common Recovery, a judicial remedy, was the vehicle that was utilized to enable the owner of the fee tail estate to make a disentailing conveyance and move the fee simple title back into the channels of commerce.[14]

The enactment of the Statutes of Uses in 1536 opened the door to the creation of remotely vesting legal future interests in land, with the resultant fettering of the alienability of the fee simple title. One of the most remarkable judicial achievements in history was the development in the courts of the common law rule against perpetuities to meet this new challenge to the alienability of the fee simple title. This judicial development took place over a century and a half beginning with the famous *Duke of Norfolk's Case* in 1682[15] and ending in 1833 with the initial formulation of the rule completed.[16]

The most recent judicial breakthrough of an established property doctrine has been the overthrow of the doctrine of caveat lessee in the field of residential housing. This breakthrough has produced the implied warranty of habitability with various accompanying remedies in the tenant for its breach by the landlord.[17]

This brief and incomplete review of judicial action in the property field makes it clear that the courts can and have and will continue to play an important part in shaping the future of property law.

The *Restatement of the Law, Second, Property*, is now in the process of development. This work can be a significant supporting arm for judicial change in the property field by offering a critical analysis of existing doctrines where appropriate. The initial two volumes of the *Property Restatement Second*, which covers landlord-tenant law, will be published in the near future.

A considerable effort is now in process to bring about improvements in the property field through legislation. The Uniform Probate Code which relates to donative transactions has been adopted in some states and is under consideration in many others. The Uniform Land Transaction Act and the Uniform Simplification of Land Transactions Act, both concerned with commercial transactions in land, are before us for consideration. The Model Land Use Development Code which deals with land use is now available. The Uniform Residential Landlord and Tenant Act is in the picture.

As we attempt to formulate the major issues that are ahead of us in the property field, history teaches us that all available legal mechanisms must be employed to solve them and at best, progress is often painfully slow.

The Futute of Donative Transactions

In regard to Donative Transactions in real and personal property, I think that the major issue for the future is whether we can continue to afford the luxury of the common law period of the rule against perpetuities for the vesting of property interests. The period for vesting allowed by the common law rule against perpetuities is twenty-one years after lives in being when the donative transaction takes effect. As a practical matter, this means that uncertainity as to the determination of the person in whom the full ownership of the beneficial rights in property will come to rest can continue for over one hundred years. This is accomplished by providing for a succession of beneficial interests in the property disposed of in a donative transaction which succession will continue until twenty one years after the death of the survivor of ten or twelve named persons who are very young who come from families noted for their longevity.[18] The measuring lives thus selected need have no connection with the beneficiaries under the donative transaction. If only one of the persons selected to be a measuring life attains the age of eighty, and he or she was one year old when selected, the identity of the ultimate taker under the disposition is postponed for one hundred years after the donative transaction takes effect.

If most of the wealth of individuals should become tied up in donative arrangements which continue from generation to generation for one hundred years, a conservative management policy of such wealth is very likely to eventuate with possible serious economic repercussions. When you add to the amount of the wealth of individuals that may be tied up in personal donative transactions, the billions of dollars that are similarly tied up in various kinds of employee benefit plans under conservative management policies, the potential economic effect is even more startling.

Why do donors of accumulated wealth adopt donative transactions that control the movement of current beneficial enjoyment of their accumulated wealth from generation to generation without freedom in any one generation to take over the complete ownership of such wealth? I think there are two principal answers to the question. One is that there is a natural human instinct that causes a person who has accumulated wealth to want to build some kind of family memorial to his achievement. The other answer is that the Government, through its current tax policies, encourages donors to make such long-lasting donative arrangements.

The second answer to the question needs some explanation. If I have accumulated some wealth and I give it outright to my son, I must pay a federal gift tax, if the gift is made in my lifetime, and a federal estate tax, if the gift is made on my death. My son is subjected to the same taxes as he moves the wealth I give him, and what he adds to it through his own efforts, on to his children. If, however, I give my accumulated wealth to my son for life and provide that on his death it will go to his children, he can enjoy the income from the wealth as long as he lives, and then the ownership can move to his children with no death tax being imposed on his death. The federal gift and estate tax laws permit me to insert in the life estate and remainder arrangement various powers which make it possible for my son to pull down annually limited amounts of the underlying wealth if he so desires, and to control within limits, where the property will go on his death, without causing him to be treated as the owner of the tied up property for federal gift or estate tax purposes. This so-called generation skipping arrangement can be extended to my son's children, and on and on until the rule against perpetuities requires that the wealth come out into the complete and unfettered control of some of my descendants. The federal gift and estate tax policies in effect tell me that I have a choice in setting up donative arrangements, either to subject my descendants to federal gift and estate taxation as my wealth moves from generation to generation or not to subject them to such taxation. Is it any wonder that more and more people, when given a choice whether to bring their family under a system of taxation or not bring their family under it, choose the latter course?[18a]

The common law rule against perpetuities was judicially developed to prevent the undue fettering of the alienability of property through the creation of remotely vesting future interests. I suggest that an examination may be overdue as to whether what is now regarded by the rule against perpetuities as not undue fettering has become undue fettering. The examination of this issue at the state level in recent years, largely encouraged by the fact that a finding of invalidity under the rule against perpetuities will bring the wealth back into the tax arena earlier, has been to adopt legislation that in effect preserves the tie-up for the maximum period possible. I refer of course to the widespread adoption in recent years of so-called wait-and-see statutes under which invalidity under the rule against perpetuities depends on whether in fact an interest vests too remotely, and then if it does, many of these statutes provide for some kind of reformation of the instrument of transfer at that time to avoid the invalidity.[19]

I predict that in the future we will see first a change in the tax laws that will take away or cut down significantly on the present tax advantage of utilizing a succession of contingent future interests in donative transactions. Proposals to accomplish this are now before Congress.[19a] Sooner or later, in some form or other, a change will be made in regard to the tax benefits of generation-skipping donative transactions. When the change in the tax laws occurs, but not until then, an atmosphere will be created at the state level that will enable some serious consideration to be given to a shortening of the period of the rule against perpetuities. The period of the rule against perpetuities will always be long enough to give local citizens the full tax benefits that the tax laws give to delay in vesting under donative transactions. Political considerations make that statement inevitably true. Aside from that qualification, the period of the Rule, on reexamination, should be set in the light of the probable adverse economic effect of the fettering of the alienability of property through the use of contingent future interests, which was the primary consideration in the original formulation of the period of the Rule.

The Future of Commercial Transactions in Land

In regard to commercial transactions in land there is only one matter I should like to refer to. It relates to the assurance that can be given to the buyer and to the lender as to the state of the title of the land that is being bought. The present system of the retrieval of information as to the title to land, on the basis of which the state of the title is determined, is archaic, out-of-date, and unnecessarily cumbersome and expensive. When all is done that can be done under the present system, title assurance cannot be given because of the many things outside the land records that theoretically could upset the buyer's expectations with respect to his purchase. It does not take much imagination or ingenuity to see that land title information that is to be relevant should be collected in one place and that such information as to any particular piece of land should be easily obtainable by one who is called upon to evaluate its significance in relation to the title to land.

Work is going forward in connection with the computerization of information relating to land titles.[20] Other technological advances may have a bearing on retrieval of land title information. Where computerization is too expensive in relation to the volume of information, other methods such as indexing by land description rather than by grantors and grantees, should be more widely used, and the required period of backward search to retrieve relevant information must be drastically shortened, so that a land description index that is started will quickly become the only place where one has to look to find all the information that has to be evaluated. I cannot predict the exact form that reform in the retrieval and evaluation of land title information will take, but I do predict that the public interest requires a change and that the public interest will have to be served. Almost everyone at one time or another in his life engages in a commercial transaction in land. Consumers who are so widespread have a voice that sooner or later will be heard and heeded.

The Future of Land Use and Development

In regard to private law relating to the use and development of land, I suggest that the directions which it may take in the future depend to a large extent on the job that is done by public law in this area. The more adequately public interest in Energy, Ecology, and Environment are fulfilled by the public law sector in the controls placed on the use and development of land, the less need there will be for private law to play a significant role in this area.

There are two important private law property doctrines that conceivably could play an important contributing role to help achieve energy, ecological and environmental goals that are in the public interest. I refer to the law of waste and to the law of promises running with the land.

The law of waste, as it has developed over the years, has endeavored to work out a reasonable allocation of the benefits of the use of land between the current user and one who has an interest in the same land which will entitle him to a current use at a later date. The current use that one makes of his land increasingly affects others from the standpoint of Energy, Ecology and Environment. An expansion of the doctrine of waste, which heretofore has protected the interest of other persons in the same land, to protect the energy, ecological and environmental concerns of others may conceivably be a development for the future that will contribute from a private law standpoint to the interest of all of us in Energy, Ecology and the Environment. Such expansion would go beyond the present law of nuisances that now, to some extent, curtails the use a neighbor may make of his land.

Promises between adjoining landowners that relate to Energy, Ecology and Environment and which run with the land to succeeding owners, could influence land use and development significantly. If the public law does not do what ought to be done, a wider use of promises to achieve goals in regard to land use and development might come into the picture. The wider use of such promises, however, is not likely to occur on a voluntary basis. If land transactions generally carried implied obligations on the buyer as to use and development of land, which implied obligations were treated as promises running with the land, a wider and more uniform set of rules would be operative. We have as an example to lead us down this road the recent judicial development referred to previously of the implied warranty of habitability in the landlord-tenant area which could be a springboard to other and more far-reaching implied obligations accompanying the ownership of land.

As I said at the beginning of the comments on land use and development, the developments in the future as to private law in the area depend on the adequacy of the job done by public law in regard to Energy, Ecology and Environment where land is involved.

It should be noted, however, that promises between adjoining landowners as to the use and development of land may work against the improvement of the living conditions of persons at lower or middle economic levels. This may also be true of exclusionary zoning that sets up single family use zones that practically are only available to persons of wealth. Due to the fact that a large percentage of the persons at lower economic levels are usually members of various minority racial groups, enclaves of residential land developments that achieve maximum environmental benefits for the persons who occupy them by limiting lot size to large lots and by restricting the area to single family homes tend to force large segments of underprivileged racial groups to reside in undesirable environmental surroundings. Exclusionary zoning that produces such result should be unconstitutional as a denial of equal protection of the law.[21] If this constitutional development takes place with respect to zoning laws, the judicial enforcement of private restrictions that are designed to achieve the same ends should be equally unconstitutional or little will be accomplished in opening up desirable residential areas to low-income housing.[22]

The preservation of open areas and historical and artistic landmarks is in the public interest and the cost of doing this may be prohibitive if this process of preservation has to be accomplished through the payment of compensation in eminent domain proceedings. The imposition of restrictions on private owners by public laws that preserve certain open areas and historical or artistic landmarks in exchange for saleable development rights as to other land is a significant development for the future that is already under way.[23] Its constitutional boundaries are not yet clearly defined.

CONCLUSION

In conclusion, I can only say that I predict with certainty that property law in all of its aspects has an exciting future.

FOOTNOTES

1. Perrin v. Blake, reported in Hargrave, Tracts Relative to the Law of England 489 (1787).
2. Campbell, Lives of the Chief Justices 337.
3. See Casner and Leach, Cases and Text on Property, 332, n. 14 (2d ed. 1969).
4. 27 Hen. VIII, c. 10 (1536).
5. 32 Hen. VIII, c. 1 (1540).
6. 29 Car. II, c. 3 (1677).
7. Euclid v. Ambler Realty Company, 272 U.S. 365 (1926).
8. Shelly v. Kraemer, 334 U.S. 1 (1948).
9. Jones v. Alfred H. Mayer Co., 392 U.S. 409 (1968).
10. Pub. L. 90-284, 82 Stat. 73.
11. D'Arundel's Case, Bracton's Note Book, Pl. 1054.
12. Taltarum's Case, Y.B. 12 Edw. IV, 19.
13. 13 Edw. 1, c. 1.
14. See the explanation of the Common Recovery in Casner and Leach, op. cit. supra note 3, at 256, n. 13.
15. 3 Ch. Cas. 1, 26. Affirmed by the House of Lords in 1685 (3 Ch. Case. 53).
16. See Cadell v. Palmer, 1 Cl. & F. 372 (H. L. 1833).
17. See Restatement of the Law, Second, Property, Tentative Draft No. 2, §5.1-5.6, in regard to the implied warranty of Liability.
18. American Law of Property (Casner ed.) §24.13.

18a. The Tax Reform Act of 1976 which passed Congress subsequent to the prepera-tion of this paper eliminates to some extent the avoidance of taxes through the use of so-called generation-skipping arrangements.

19. See Casner, Estate Planning 655 (3d ed., 1961, with annual Supp.)

19a. See note 18a supra.

20. See Land Parcel Identifiers for Information Systems, 1973, published by the American Bar Foundation, in cooperation with various other groups.
21. To this effect so far as a state court is concerned, see Southern Burlington County N.A.C.P. v. Township of Mount Laurel, 67 N.J. 151, 336 A. 2d 713 (1974).
22. See Metropolitan Housing Development Corporation v. Village of Arlington Heights, 517 F. 2d 409 (1975); Hills v. Gautreaux, 96 S. Ct. 1538 (1976).
23. See Costonis, The Chicago Plan: Incentive Zoning and the Preservation of Urban Landmarks, 85 Harv. L. Rev. 574 (1972); Costonis, Development Rights Transfer: An Exploratory Essay, 83 Yale L.J. 75 (1973).

CODIFICATION

Soia Mentschikoff*

The question of codification and what should or should not be codified is a very different question from the question of what legislative actions should or should not be taken in connection with particular types of problems. To put the matter into somewhat better perspective I should take you back to some fundamentals on what law is about because what law is about greatly conditions what codification is about.

The basic function of law, is to settle disputes well enough so that the society does not disintegrate, and so that the people whose law it is, are not alienated too much.

The second function of law is what I will call the aspirational function about which we hear a lot. In a sense a great many constitutional decisions are decisions dealing with aspirational aspects of our law, and aspirational aspects are in a sense a luxury item. When you get to the question of the direction in which they are, that of course is the area in which we have conflicting values. It is perfectly clear the more generally one states values, truth, freedom, justice, et cetera, the more you have general agreement on that; the more one gets into what is truth, freedom, justice in a particular context, the more disagreement results. This is an area which is of peculiar difficulty. It is an area which allows for a great deal of disagreement, hopefully on a rational basis. It is also unfortunately an area in which much emotion and much heat is generated.

I think that Edmond Cahn in his book on *The Sense of Injustice* put a finger on one very important aspect: people have a sense of injustice. If you say to somebody, "Give me two instances of injustice which you have personally experienced

**Dean, Miami University School of Law.*

or personally seen," they don't have much trouble giving you that. If you say to them "Give me two instances of when you have seen justice," they have a great deal of difficulty with that.

The truth of the matter is that, in terms of claims which have a fairly legitimate base, that is to say, an arguable morality, an arguable need, an arguable desirability, they can not all be satisfied. They never will be. There isn't enough justice to go around in the sense of satisfying everybody's felt need for some kind of satisfaction. That is why it is easy, much easier for us to identify what we believe is unjust, and almost impossible for us to think too conclusively on what is justice in the same sense.

So basically the aspirational aspects deal with trying to work out a system which creates a kind of fairness, recognizing that reasonable men are going to differ in terms of the allocations, and the fact that they differ is an aspirational aspect of law.

The third thing that law does, which I think we tend to overlook, is that it allocates who has the final power of decision. I want to point out that the power to decide, finally, is the power to decide wrongly as well as rightly. I think this is something that has to be faced. You have to know who it is that you are going to give the power to decide wrongly to, as well as who it is that you are going to give the power to decide rightly to.

The second thing I want to say about the allocation of the final power of decision is that the discussion tends to center on whether it shall be the Supreme Court, the Congress, the President, some administrative agency, or some other organ.

The truth of the matter is there is another very viable alternative. It can be the people involved in the transaction, private people. It doesn't have to rest with Government. The Government can give the final power of decision to be wrong as well as to be right to private parties. This is something which we have overlooked for quite a long time. It is something which we ought to start taking a look at.

Americans are funny people in that respect. They believe in law and the power of law to right wrongs. Not to do right, but to right wrongs. And the general tendency is whenever something occurs, some situation develops which gets people upset, the first popular response is "Let's pass a law about it." Whether we know anything about it or not, let's pass a law about it. That has rather terrible consequences for us. I think in point of fact those terrible consequences have resulted from the amount of legislation which has occurred in the last forty or fifty years.

When the demand is "Let's pass a law about it," two things are really occurring: first, false hopes are being raised. False expectations arise that the passage of a law will remedy the evil and produce a better result. This was the case with the civil rights legislation of the sixties. The expectations rose. There was absolutely no reason on God's green earth to have those expectations. They were there, they were a disappointment, created a kind of state of chaos, riot, what you will. The reality penetrated, that the passage of the legislation in and of itself didn't solve the problem. The expectations fell apart. This myth that we have developed in the United States that the law can take care of it if we pass a law—this had this kind of unfortunate consequence.

The other unfortunate consequence that it has had, which is of the same nature, is that we have forgotten that men enforce law, implement law, and are responsible for carrying it out. And we have developed in the bureaucracies a very interesting phenomenon. If the men whose job it is to implement and enforce the law are not doing it well, our typical response has been "Let's put a control on it. If that control doesn't produce action put a second control on it. If that doesn't work, put a third control on it." The obvious solution is to fire the man. We don't need all these bureaucracies. A related technique is that of control by committees—a method used in university administrations; it happens in Government, it happens in the Congress. Let's form a committee, let that committee look at that committee. If we don't like the way this committee looks at that committee, let's have that committee look at this committee.

The second set of major problems that arises out of this popular notion that if we have a problem, let's pass a law, is that the law that is passed is usually very bad because it is piecemeal; it does not deal with the total problem that is involved in the situation, whether it be the total life situation or transaction. A good illustration has to do with laws relating to business crimes. Is making something criminal the most desirable way to control business behavior? You feel deeply about it, you make it a crime. If you don't feel deeply about it, give a cause of action. Take your choice.

So we have a great deal of piecemeal not thought-through partial sets of legislation, though sometimes they are called codes. Now, if you have piecemeal stuff, if you enact legislation without really knowing what you are doing, what is the second thing that happens? We are going to pass a law about it, and we don't know what kind of law to pass, but nobody knows anything, so we set up an administrative agency and say do what you like in the public interest. They pass regulations. They change the regulations steadily, because they don't know what they are doing either. So what you have is proliferation in that direction. Those are the two common responses which have been made in many, many instances over the last forty or fifty years. I think that they are very unfortunate.

In the process, we have lost sight of the importance of trying to see something whole. Not one person ever sees anything really whole, is able to walk around it. We all see through the lenses of our own prior experience and our own prior training. We don't come down from Olympus and say "I understand the totality." One of the important things is to see how we can magnify the seeing of a situation so as to see more and more of it, to get closer and closer to the whole. We have a number of deflecting factors apart from the emotional response of "Let's pass a law," that interferes with the seeing of it all. One is in the drive towards specialization.

Specialization puts the blinders up. Specialization makes the specialists peculiarly incompetent to deal with legislation that affects all of us. Because all they see is their line of specialization.

Take, for example, the property area. Professor Casner's paper talks about the private law of property and the public law of property. One of the fascinating points he makes is that the private law of property is moving toward a situation where some kind of agency is going to enforce it. How can you deal with land development or land use without knowing who? Are you going to be a specialist in the private law, in the public law?

One of the curious dichotomies we have evolved in the law school world, not as much in practice as in the law school world, is that God came down and said let there be private law and let there be public law, and never the twain shall meet. That is obvious nonsense. The twain meets in life. It meets when you are setting up the transaction. It meets when you are trying to decide what you want to do with it. You can't have that kind of dichotomy.

This drive that has arisen in the bars of a great many states towards specialization is a detriment to the ability of the bar to see things as a whole. You don't see things whole by calling in two experts, each of whom is biased.

The second deflecting factor to seeing things whole is that in addition to the legislative response we have the court response. Things go up to the courts. They are going to take care of something and they go up with the advocates on one side saying "Truth, light, and justice lie here."

Courts do not and should not sit down and think about all the possible situations which may arise and then have a principle which they are applying. That is not the way a common law court operates. It is fine if they think two cases ahead or three cases ahead.

What the contrary view presupposes is that the court knows enough to know what the situations are. I suggest to you that our courts do not know enough to be able to make that kind of analysis, and in the context of a particular case do not have that kind of information. I can state that without hesitation, with respect to commercial transactions.

There is no doubt that they don't know. They don't understand the personal transactions or the problems of commercial litigation. You have to educate the courts first as to what a commercial transaction is. I have grave doubts that they know much about correctional institutions. Maybe they know more in criminal areas as a result of what has been happening, which is that case after case after case has been coming with variations of the facts. This has been the history of our courts and our courts' attempt to solve problems.

A case comes up, they solve it, they state a cause, a doctrinal cause which is a "principle." The next case comes up and we either distinguish the first case or expand it.

The whole history of the common law has been the bringing of cases up and up and up until the court finally works out a solution which is satisfactory to whoever the law consumer is. When that happens, cases don't come any more. Then all you have left are issues of fact. They don't get to the highest court in the state, to the Supreme Court. It is only when you have changes, either in technology or in value structure that the cases start coming again.

Any time you have got a situation in which the cases keep coming, by definition you have a situation in which the court has not made a satisfactory solution. But what the court is doing is developing a body of special experience that might ultimately allow it to make a satisfactory solution.

On the remedial side people talk about the civil law—contracts, commercial law and the like—as being subject to the same difficulty that arises from improper functioning of the adversary system. That really isn't true, at least in the commercial cases.

In the commercial cases, the truly commercial cases, they never have gone to courts, because merchants aren't crazy. They have gone to arbitration. They have gone to the Lord Mayor of London courts. There have always been courts where merchants have been sitting. They have not always been called courts. It doesn't make any difference.

The second area which has successfully evaded the courts from its inception has been the area of labor relations. It went to arbitration immediately. The continuing relationship of the labor relations contract or agreement, if you prefer that term, was one which was steadily, constantly and perennially adjudicated. That law of contract clearly is not only not dead, but never showed any signs. It has been going on forever.

The final thing is the expense of remedy in the simple transaction, particularly in the field of consumer law. One of the most idiotic things that has happened is the proliferation of law in that area by people who don't know anything about what the existing law was when they started proliferating the law. There is a hodge-podge there now, most of which gives less protection to the consumer than they have under the Uniform Commercial Code which exists in all states except Louisiana. The other thing is you can't enforce the code. What is involved is a TV set versus the cost of the adversary system.

On the other hand, consumers have a great self-help remedy when they really buy a "lemon." They revoke acceptance; they acquire interests in the goods to the extent the price has been paid or obligated. They can resell the goods in a reasonably commercial way and recover the difference between the resale price and contract price, thus the reasonable value of the use of the goods. Self-help is not a nasty word that deals only with security lenders. Every consumer who revokes acceptance or has paid part of the price and rejects part, has precisely the same remedy.

The final thing is the complexity which is involved in finding the law. We have complexity at really two levels. One is the very existence of libraries. For those of you who practice in New York, it is hard to envisage areas of the country where there are no libraries. How do you find law? You are in a county made up of small towns. If you have a county library, it could be one hundred miles away. Are you going to dash one hundred miles to look up a point? No.

You may say that we have the answer to that in computer services. The cost of a Lexis terminal for a year is $18,000. That is a lot of money for a small city practitioner.

Maybe they could all get together if there are eighteen of them. Suppose there are only three or four. One of the nice things about codification is that it helps solve this problem.

The code is what you need now to find the law. All you need in the future is this one book. That is one of the great advantages of codification, if people will treat a code as a code. It simplifies the finding of the law.

The second thing about codification is that it is possible to enter the material across fields so that the code is then built on a financial or transactional level. So when you have a problem you can find it that way.

You can even have the appropriate references to the fact that there is a tax problem. You can't give him a tax code in the same volume, but you can tell him there is a tax problem at X point and he should hire somebody to look it up for him.

The integration of material, I suggest, omits at two levels. There have been a lot of uniformity attempt as far as state law is concerned. There has been no uniformity attempts as far as I know of federal law. To take an illustration already discussed, that of federal business crimes. Who has ever looked at them until now? Who has ever made a decision as to what should be or should not be a crime?

When they say crimes, what do they mean by sanctions? Are we going to fine them, going to give double damages? I get in trouble with damages.

Finally, it should be noted that when you draft a code you really deal with two kinds of problems. You cannot draft a code the way a conveyance is drafted. You cannot draft a code in the English manner because that is essentially a conveyancing manner. You cannot draft a code in the manner of the tax code, because that too is a conveyancing manner. A code drafted that way will be amended, amended, and amended, every time there is any change, if anything changes at all.

The only way in which a code can be drafted is, first, to try to get the needed knowledge as to the transaction or the live situation in as functional and broad a context as you can, really by walking through rather than by sending out armies of questionnaires which usually are not very good, because to have a good questionnaire and response you have to know what the questions are, and if you know what the questions are, you really know the answer. It is kind of silly.

To get the good questionnaire you have to know a lot about the subject matter. The real problem with empirical research is that too many questionnaires get sent out by people who don't know what it is about. You get garbage in and garbage out.

Then you have to differentiate between the existing recurrent problems where there has been a division of opinion. You have to settle one way or another. They have been coming up and up and up. People are divided on them. For better or worse you have to take a deep breath and say that this seems the fairer way.

When they come up and courts split, you know you are in an area where there is justice on both sides. I refer to the problem of unequal justice. Sometimes you can slant it a little differently, cut it differently, get more justice for both sides. But frequently enough on the recurrent problem this is it. And that ends it.

And then you have to leave room for growth. I call that the planning of provisions which creates seeds for future growth. Today nobody is startled when somebody says unconscionable. If you could have heard them in the 1940's, when that provision first went into the Uniform Commercial Code, you would have thought that God was dead, not just contracts. Now, it is a familiar term.

The growth bud is there to be used by analogy or directly. Either way. Unless you have that kind of growth, you cannot have anything that will endure for any length of time.

Now, the method of drafting has an additional component. You cannot merely state a number of principles, like I am against sin, I am for the good, and so on. When you do that you have created a mammoth problem of constant litigation. What you really have to do is to state the rule so that the reason for it appears on its face as much as possible. That allows the court to say, "the situation before me does not fit into the reason, I am not going to apply the rule." Then you have got leeway that way.

TRIALS AND PROCEDURE—FROM PRIVATE FIGHTS TOWARD PUBLIC JUSTICE

Marvin E. Frankel*

I. The Adam Smith System of Adjudication

Many observers have noted in our Bicentennial year that 1776 is also memorable for the publication of *The Wealth of Nations*. It is more than a random coincidence that our national Declaration of Independence and Adam Smith's "declaration of independence of modern capitalism"[1] should have been thus simultaneously proclaimed. Our political manifesto and Smith's heavier tome may be taken together, without too much oversimplification, as a compendious account of the American Ideology for most or all of the intervening two centuries. Indeed, if one had to choose, it would probably be correct to say that Smith's ideas were the more prevalent and important. Our leaders and leading ideologues have been faithful, at least until very recently, to the fundamental premise that the social good is best pursued by competitive pursuit of individual self-interest. We have not been as enthusiastic about the idea that "all men are created equal."

The principle of competitive struggle as the road to social order has been the brightest star in our legal firmament. Smith's "obvious and simple system of natural liberty"[2]—a system in which seekers after selfish advantage were to be freed to vie with each other, though under rules designed to keep the warfare bounded and putatively fair—has been the essence of our professional creed. In the law courts as in the market place, the "State was to be reduced to the position of umpire between competitors."[3] It was to be expected that our institutions for administering justice would embody and

**District Judge, United States District Court for the Southern District of New York.*

reflect our fundamental axioms as a community. It could scarcely have failed to be the case that our basic forms of adjudication would have the central qualities of free private enterprise.

In the ideal as it is stated, when parties have disputes thought to be legally cognizable, we do not pretend first to quell the contentiousness and then seek out the rights and the wrongs of the matter. Instead, we continue the battle, but by transferring it to a public arena and transmuting its forms. As said by a lively lawyer-writer, we "set the parties fighting."[4] The legal combat is not a malady to be managed resignedly. It is extolled rather as an ideal, the ultimate method of reason for achieving the ends of truth and justice. This is The Adversary System.

The familiar theory is that the interests of justice will be best served if each side seeks its private advantage by conquest, by striving to establish its own version of the facts as well as the law. In a close legal analogue of Adam Smith's reliance upon "private interests and passions" to produce results "most agreeable to the interest of the whole society",[5] "[t]he very premise of our adversary system . . . is that partisan advocacy on both sides of a case will best promote" the ascertainment of truth and right results.[6]

Implementing the adversarial scheme, the parties are in main charge of the litigation process. They frame the issues, investigate the evidence, select what they respectively choose to present. Private people, not bureaucrats, run the show. The private parties are strong, active, creative; the adjudicators are passive, receptive, reactive. The parties are equipped and knowledgable; the decision-makers work with what they are given. The court is a setting, a forum, the place to which the combatants bring their skills and weapons for the fight. To make the contest fair and acceptable for the achievement of justice, each side has its independent lawyer-champions. These gladiators, by the Canons of their profession, owe their most solemn duties "to a Client" and "to the Adversary System of Justice."[7] Just results are expected to emerge because there is an unreservedly zealous advocate on one side, matched by a counterpart on the other side with "an impartial judge over both."[8]

Such at any rate is the outline of the professed ideal. The reality is something else again.

Like Adam Smith's economic model, the adversary justice model is simpler and lovelier than the facts of life. A deeply inherent flaw is the mismatching of the contestants. The unequal resources of clients and (frequently corresponding) inequalities in the skills of their lawyers blight the vision of a fairly balanced contest.[9] All of us wondered sometimes in law school whether results meant to embody justice should depend upon the relative talents of partisan advocates. Though we managed to put the worry behind us, it may be we were more nearly on the mark in the first place.[10]

Apart from the defect of inequality, the adversary conflict is discovered most of the time to be too costly, risky, and unpredictable to be pursued fully or, frequently, to any extent at all. Jerome Frank wrote cogently about the harrowing uncertainty as to how facts will be "found" after the contestants have struggled, respectively, to advance the desired version and block or destroy or distort the hostile version.[11] The resulting unpredictability of the law has been noted ruefully by observers with widely varying perspectives.[12] The reluctance to gamble over serious concerns becomes a steady pressure to forego the supposed benefits of our trial process in favor of settlement before or during litigation.

As for expense, the elaboration of adversary procedures has reached a point where the game is scarcely worth playing or capable of being played except for high stakes and with substantial investments of time and money. Civil claims in modest amounts are less and less susceptible of effective prosecution.[13] Larger claims, though their proponents may be capable of supporting lawsuits, are similarly foregone or are compromised because full adjudication is uneconomic. It is scarcely less accurate today than it was 70 years ago to note, as Roscoe Pound did then, "a deep-seated desire to keep out of court, right or wrong, on the part of every sensible business man in the community."[14]

The pressure of criminal business seems even heavier, and is a source of more strident expressions of dissatisfaction. Metropolitan courts sag under enormous dockets. Unbailed defendants wait too long for trials in foul jails. The refinements of protective procedures are seen by proponents of Law and Order—the followers of Herbert Packer's "Crime Control Model"[15]—as intolerable obstacles. The criminal prosecution becomes a kind of "obstacle course"—a "struggle from start to finish."[16] For those more solicitous about defendants—attentive primarily to Packer's "Due Process Model"[17]—the time-consuming protections are minimal concessions to a civilized concern that innocence be protected and the decencies observed even if this means expense and the escape from punishment of some who are guilty.

Taken all together, our techniques for trying criminal cases are such that it is more difficult here than in just about any place else in the world to achieve a full-scale conviction after trial. As a seeming corollary, if there is such a conviction, we impose probably the most severe sanctions of any country in the so-called civilized world. It is as if we said to a defendant:

> "You may have the most elaborate form of trial in the world. Your chances of getting off, even if you are guilty, will be better here than they would be elsewhere. But if you lose in the end, look out!"[18]

Whether or not that is the consciously intended doctrine, the participants behave to a considerable degree as if it is. Most criminal cases expose the fear of, or aversion to, trials. They are bargained or pled away, with guilty pleas exchanged for the promise or hope of lighter sentences. Our trial procedures are too cumbersome, too threatening, and too chancy to employ in more than a slim minority of the matters for which they supposedly exist. While our ideals about the criminal justice system have the jury trial as the centerpiece, it is a precious ornament, displayed on a small fraction of its possible occasions. Exercising the options of free competitive enterprisers, the contestants in a criminal proceeding mostly avoid the trial process that the nonintrusive state makes available but does not prescribe. Indeed, far from prescribing, the state discourages use of the model. If more than a few demanded trials, the system would collapse more entirely than it has. The catastrophe is limited or postponed by the threat of an imposing price.

And so, while the adversary trial is employed in a few of the cases, most are concluded by the adversaries themselves, through the best bargain their competitive skills, their undisclosed secrets, and justice market conditions may combine to fashion.[19]

The conflicts between self-interest and public justice include a nastier aspect that we have been driven of late to confront: the interests of the individualist lawyer are not in inevitable harmony with those of the client.[20] The client poorly served or, worse, betrayed is, unfortunately, a known phenomenon. Perhaps the most poignant cases are those of criminal defendants whose fates are neglected or dealt away in dubious bargains. These are said sometimes to be perversions or betrayals of "the adversary system," which is thought to epitomize due process.[21] In fact, however, the disease is endemic. It is not realistic to expect that lawyers will take the brunt of the competitive struggle and entirely disregard themselves in the process.

The point of all this is important, but it is not new, and it need not be labored. In 1976, resting still upon the cultural heritage of Thomas Jefferson and Adam Smith,[22] our system continues to entrust the resolution of legal disputes, criminal as well as civil, primarily to the results of competitive, individualist, combative actions by the litigants and lawyers rather than the authoritative guidance of the tribunal and its officials. The choice rests upon profound commitments—to *laissez-faire* generally, to individual liberty, to private initiative as a preference over bureaucratic control.[23] But the costs are high. They, together with public dissatisfaction, appear to be mounting. The lawyer as advocate, never revered, is far from the highest point he has reached in public esteem. The courts fare no better. Our reputation for truth-seeking and truth-telling is not good. The unequal, happenstantial results of trial by combat promote festering dissatisfactions among litigants, from the parties in civil cases to defendants prosecuted for crimes. The regime of privately managed justice has produced far too much of congested, unregulated, primitively administered facilities.

Although the preceding paragraph tells only of negative things, the picture is, of course, not totally bad. The role of the courts in fashioning and implementing human rights has been a momentous good, especially in recent decades. The wide respect for the rule of law, above all for the towering authority of the Supreme Court, remains a national miracle. The law as a vocation enlists increasingly talented and devoted young people. The many achievements, and the attractions of the profession to thoughtful new students, are owed in substantial measure to the creative exertions of advocates championing people and causes in the traditional adversary ways.

You will think of still more things to celebrate. The fact remains that on my assigned topic of "trials and procedure" the Bicentennial is a time better used for reformist criticism than for congratulatory retrospective. A prime need, I wish to suggest, is to recognize that the interest in justice is too vital and too public to be left as dependent as it has been upon the outcome of essentially individualist contention. It is necessary that the agencies of the public, the agencies charged with the impartial administration of justice, take a stronger hand than they have thus far. The need has been recognized before now. In the following sections of this essay, I propose to mention steps already taken or in process, then to suggest illustrative measures of the kind that I think must be considered.

II. Changes in Administration

In one important respect, which is familiar to and considerably identified with the Law School of New York University, the need for the exercise of leadership by the public agencies of justice has recently come to be recognized and implemented. I refer, of course, to the *administration* of lawsuits by the courts.

Under the leadership of N.Y.U.'s notable Dean, later New Jersey's Chief Justice, Arthur T. Vanderbilt, we have ceased in the last generation or so to leave the procedural management of lawsuits exclusively to the private initiative of the parties.[24] Court management has become a profession. Court managers are being trained, and are taking posts of leadership, in increasing numbers. The timing of motions, the framing of issues, the scheduling of trials—all such steps, which formerly awaited instigation by one side or the other, tend more and more to be determined and directed by the court on its own motion. Manuals of judicial administration advise the judge to take charge (often through managerial aides) of the litigation from its inception and stay in command until there has been a disposition. The judges themselves have become more managed, less individualist, more bureaucratic. From the regulation of court hours and opinion-writing, for which Justice Vanderbilt was loved and not loved, to the wide proliferation of statistics and computers, the managerial revolution proceeds apace through the judicial establishment. The scene becomes less romantic, but, it is hoped, more efficient. The older judges, among some others, may resist the change in the image of the unique, autonomous, self-propelling jurist.[25] The lawyer-gladiator may rue and oppose the lessening of private control. But the trend seems necessary and inexorable.

It is a trend largely confined, however, to the problems of managerial efficiency as such. The concern is with easing congestion, lightening dockets, "moving" cases. This is not irrelevant, surely, to the ends of justice. But it is not centered upon the substance of fair, sound, accurate results as such. The focus is not the ascertainment of factual truth and the thorough exploration of legal issues; it is, rather, the speedier, higher-volume dispatch of the business.

This is not to suggest any inconsistency between effective management and the quest for justice. Quite the contrary. My point is simply that thus far the courthouse modifications of Adam Smith's principles—the enhancement of public as against private control—have emphasized efficiency and volume rather than the quality of justice. The emphasis has not been accidental. Choices are made. The Chief Justice of the United States was explicit a few years ago:

> ". . . The challenges to our system of justice are colossal and immediate and we must assign priorities. I would begin by giving priority to methods and machinery, to procedure and techniques, management and administration of judicial resources."[26]

I have no quarrel with the interest in "methods and machinery" and all that. In the end, methods and machinery, properly understood, are a main hope. My thought is, however, that the emphasis must shift to—or, at least, that there must be an emphasis upon—a public, less purely adversarial, less privately determined goal of substantive justice in adjudication. The Chief Justice merits citation again. For he has lately taken this Bicentennial time to urge that "we should take a searching look at some of the basic aspects and underlying assumptions of our legal and judicial institutions and try to determine, not merely how to tighten the 'nuts and bolts' of the existing mechanisms of the judicial system but whether fundamental changes need be made."[27]

III. Illustrative Proposals for Further Change

If, as I have suggested, the determinative effects of individualist warfare before a passive tribunal are not the sufficient conditions for just results, the direction of reform must be to limit or mitigate those effects. I have no revolution to propose. I work at a job that is rarely open to revolutionists and not much calculated to breed revolutionists. I mean only to mention some partial, piecemeal, experimental kinds of change. It is my hope that you will be persuaded to think about these illustrative suggestions and, more importantly, to formulate other, improved measures that might more closely approach the shared goals.

Let me recall in a few words the evils or defects I have associated with the Adam Smith system of adjudication. Private or party control leaves decisions to turn too much upon competitive skills, the accidents, planned or not, of hostile maneuvers, the relative resources of the contestants, and the familiar congeries of advocates' tricks, devices, dodges, and stratagems. The proposed objective must be, then, to minimize these forces or substitute other means for reaching truth and sound rulings. My suggestions for change are meant to answer aspects of this need in one way or another.

A. A Lawyerless but Effective Tribunal for Civil Cases

Much is written these days about the need to expand small claims courts, create "neighborhood courts," and otherwise cope with the problems of the relatively modest claim that tends to be barred by expense from effective judicial enforcement. The first suggestion which follows expands upon this idea.[28]

Consider schematically the existing system as it deals with a civil claim of up to $10,000 or so.[29] The prospective plaintiff, after whatever preliminaries, arrives at his lawyer's office. After learning "the facts"—i.e., the client's account, which is, more or less, but sympathetically, tested—the lawyer may seek a settlement. The opposing party is soon equipped with a lawyer, who likewise learns the (probably different) "facts." If there is no settlement, the quarrel goes to court, where a third legal professional, a judge, is enlisted in the enterprise. Assuming all the while the effort is affordable at all, the contending advocates, the judge, and sundry supporting personnel work through the familiar steps to a decision.

Now consider a species of court intended normally to function without lawyers. The aggrieved party comes again to a legal professional, but this one is a magistrate. The magistrate, like the prospective plaintiff's (or defendant's) lawyer, inquires about the facts. He is, however, at least in theory, desirous of learning them, not seeing how they may be cooked, exploited, tailored, or otherwise manipulated. The magistrate may decide, or persuade the complainant, ex parte that there is no case. Or he may go forward, summon the defendant, and interrogate the latter. As the case proceeds, all under the aegis of the magistrate, he may discover, as any lawyer might, a need to investigate beyond the mere summoning of parties and witnesses. He has a staff of investigators for this purpose. He has junior colleagues, like law clerks or associates, to assist in legal research. Thus equipped, he "tries" the case, or otherwise pursues it to a final disposition.

Whatever the final disposition—from ex parte determination at the outset to a complete trial and adjudication—our magistrate will file a full account of what he has done, with copies to the parties, as a permanent, reviewable record. Suitable forms of appellate review will exist. Granting these are matters of first importance, I omit them here in the interest of brevity, to avoid undue multiplication of enemies, and to leave as much as possible to more fertile imaginations that may be drawn to this subject.

Bypassing a host of things, let me focus upon only one difficulty before pleading grounds favoring the proposed tribunal. Its quality of diminished adversariness is found, of course, in the presumptive absence of lawyers.[30] What if people surreptitously consulted counsel? This danger would require an apparatus of oaths and detection. A party would be made to state if he was proceeding, as presumed, without a lawyer. If he so stated—and was then heard to say something like *"res ipsa loquitur"* or "the document speaks for itself" or some other awkward and unlikely thing—measures would have to be taken. On the other hand, if either side openly insists upon having an attorney, the agencies of a free society ought not to forbid that. The counter, however, would be the supplying of counsel at state expense to the other side.

Such details are negotiable. Granting, further, that the things airily dismissed as "details" may amount to fatal objections, I note here, in ascending order of importance, three arguments for the proposed form of tribunal:

(1) It would be economical; one legal professional or team would normally do the work now calling for three—not necessarily one-third the work, but less by far than is now done.[31]
(2) Cases would tend to be decided more quickly and more often finally at the first level.
(3) The only legal professionals in the usual case would be pursuing what we have sometimes thought to be our main objective—truth and a just decision.

Having tested the idea briefly in a law school seminar, I know some of the immediate (and passionate) arguments against it. E.g.:

(1) The facts would not be fully developed (prejudicing which side?)
(2) Our magistrate, designated only to do right, would lack incentive (a point I have trouble accepting).
(3) "Errors by the magistrate would go unnoticed (leaving, of course, the open question how much more or less net injustice would result as against the products of the existing system).

I tender the thought in this partisan and partial fashion in the hope that some may see fit to pursue it and with the plan, in any event, to work at it some more on my own.[32]

B. Another look at Miranda

Nobody, "liberal" or "conservative," is happy with *Miranda* v. *Arizona*.[33] Nobody should be. It is at best a tense, temporary, ragged kind of truce between combatants. The police-prosecution team declares itself "handcuffed" by the rule that an arrested person may not incriminate or effectively convict himself in the police station unless he has first been advised of his rights to keep quiet, to have a lawyer, etc., and has decided to waive those rights. The defense team finds it a travesty that so many people are discovered to give such waivers, stupidly and unaccountably, getting nothing in return except an increased likelihood of conviction.

By the narrowest of majorities, the fragile rules of *Miranda* were fashioned to implement "the privilege against self-incrimination—the essential mainstay of our adversary system. . . ."[34] Designed in the end to govern an adversary game, those rules, not surprisingly, have effects that vary with the skills, the accidental conduct, the stratagems, and the persuasive powers of the multifarious adversaries. There is no thoroughgoing attempt to put all defendants upon a genuinely equal footing with respect to the occasions when, and the safeguards under which, they may be heard to give evidence against themselves. Individual initiative and fortune, on either side, may make all the difference in determining what self-incriminatory statements may be employed against any particular defendant. The only assured uniformity is in the application of the privilege at the trial itself, in the fraction of cases that go to trial; there the privilege does apply equally to all. Viewed in its broader aspect, however, *Miranda* allows defendants to be tricked, cajoled, and perjured into incriminating themselves outside the courthouse while we forbid any "orderly inquiry"[35] of a defendant, duly counseled and visibly protected, in the courtroom.

The result is exquisitely ironic since the decision was so strongly undergirded by the desire to achieve equal treatment for the poor and the rich, the ignorant and the sophisticated.[36] That compelling objective, given principled respect, and given the explicit recognition by the Court that unknowable "pressures" and "devices"[37] must account for many admissions by the dazed suspect, could have led to only one conclusion: that nobody's confession in the police station may be received in evidence over objection. Rational people do not condemn themselves advisedly in the stationhouse.[38] Knowing how people improvidently and imprudently err in far slighter matters under far slighter pressure, we have come finally to allow the targets of door-to-door salesmen a few days of tranquil reconsideration before committing them to the purchase of a vacuum cleaner.[39] But *Miranda*, proclaiming that by its force illicit means of procuring confessions were being "eradicated,"[40] went on to declare that a suspect, informed of his rights by his pursuers, could then proceed, "voluntarily, knowingly and intelligently"[41]—and irrevocably—to waive his right to refrain from incriminating himself.

Mr. Justice Harlan, dissenting, noted that dishonest policemen could be expected "to lie as skillfully about warnings and waivers" as they had about "brutality or other unmistakably banned forms of coercion."[42] An eminent critic commented wryly that the former "swearing contests" about voluntariness would be altered mostly in form, that *Miranda* "just moves the battleground from the voluntariness of the confession to the voluntariness of the waiver."[43] Those predictions have proved sound. There are divergences of sorts in the lower courts, but the general state of *Miranda* doctrine amounts very nearly to a rule that if an arrestee (1) is warned of his rights, (2) then confesses, (3) understands the language and is *compos mentis*, he will (4) be found to have made a "knowing, intelligent and voluntary" waiver. On approximately such reasoning, despite the fact that any intelligent person who knows what he is doing ought to volunteer nothing, multitudes of waivers are found each year to have happened.[44]

Why did the Court, having verged upon a different conclusion following the principles stated to that point, end with such an anomaly as the *Miranda* waiver doctrine? The explanation, partly visible, must be partly speculative. The main point, I presume to venture, is that the total denial of access to an accused in custody as a source of evidence, given the net of Fifth Amendment prohibitions the Court had already woven, was totally unsalable to a majority, probably unbearable after all to everyone. The majority gave reassurance that its decision "should not constitute an undue interference with a proper system of law enforcement."[45] The Court had already cut off almost totally the opportunity to question an accused in a civilized and uniform fashion, or even to comment upon his silence, devices that could apply alike to every defendant.[46] So it was driven largely to stultify itself by leaving an opening that predictably meant the naive, the confused, the unintelligent, and the careless defendant would confess to the police while others would not.[47] Reflecting the style of the adversary system its opinion extolled, the majority assigned a broad place for losers. The upshot is a denial of the first principle of justice.

It would be infinitely preferable to make the *Miranda* protection complete and meaningful—not waivable—and, at the same time, to allow open, fully recorded questioning of suspects and defendants before trial, with a judicial officer presiding, with the assistance of counsel, with a right of silence, but with a concomitant right on the other side to make explicit what exists now furtively and all the time, namely, a right to comment on the arguable inferences from the refusals to answer. The proposal is not original. It tracks largely the cogent analysis of Justice Walter V. Schaefer,[48] as elaborated and endorsed by Judge Henry J. Friendly,[49] both building upon a brilliant essay by Paul G. Kauper almost a half-century ago,[50] and all lately extended in a cogent commentary by Yale Kamisar on "the Kauper-Schaefer-Friendly model. . . ."[51] The idea remains to be pressed in the "serious debate"[52] to which those jurists have contributed so much. What is of special interest just here is that the idea describes a regime of publicly administered, uniformly applied, rational and non-coercive questioning as the alternative to the explicitly adversarial game plan of *Miranda*, with its arbitrary and treacherous implications.

Among its chief virtues, the proposal is candid. As things stand now, we satisfy the powerful need for evidence from those under suspicion by a multitude of absurd "waivers" from haplessly selected people in custody. The State, for all the denunciations of "compelled" self-incrimination, is not effectively neutral. It affords rich opportunities for law enforcement maneuvers to extract "voluntary" confessions. Effectively joining in the course of trickery, it demands only formal regularity, then declares piously that it is "not at all offended when a guilty man stubs his toe."[53]

A State taking more responsibility upon itself to pursue the truth, but fairly and by civilized means, and leaving less to the wiles of the parties, would not permit uncounseled waivers of constitutional rights by overreached citizens in custody. It would stop treating law enforcement as a game of cops and robbers, giving handicaps to one side or the other as the tides of the times happen to change. It would outlaw as evidence all confessions or statements given without counsel in station-house interrogations.[54] At the same time, it would, as do most countries elsewhere, claim the commonsense right to question the best of all witnesses to the defendant's guilt or innocence, exerting the unquestionably considerable pressure of adverse inferences from silence, but otherwise ensuring courtesy, safety, and an entire absence of trickery.

Copying some more from other models, we might outlaw altogether evidence of a defendant's prior criminal record for impeachment.[55] This would strip away another of our hypocrisies—that such evidence is received only to assail credibility. It would also eliminate one of the overworked grounds of our professed belief that innocent people in numbers have estimable reasons (nervousness, lack of public presence, etc.) for preferring silence to protestations of their innocence.[56]

The case for questioning a defendant in a public and safeguarded place, without punishing refusals to answer, but allowing elementary inferences from the refusals, has been made often and compellingly.[57] The ostensibly contrary rule of our Constitution has been maintained only at the cost of baleful fictions like the *Miranda* waiver doctrine. There remains the considerable question whether the reordering urged here could be accomplished without a constitutional amendment. Eminent authority suggests that it probably cannot.[58] On the other hand, only one decision, of recent vintage, seems to stand squarely in the way.[59] That ruling, by a divided vote, that comment upon defendant's silence is forbidden, should not be deemed so central and inevitable as to defy restudy in an altered context.[60] If custodial admissions in the absence of either counsel or a presiding magistrate were totally excluded, protecting the luckless or entrapped multitudes who currently "waive" along with those who do not, we may be certain that the amount of truly "compelled" self-incrimination in our society would be sharply diminished. The suggested *quid pro quo*, allowing comment upon silence in the courthouse, "compels" testimony only in a strained, ahistorical, unrealistic sense of compulsion.[61] It is at least within the realm of permissible hope that constitutional statesmanship would sustain the resulting rearrangements as more thoroughly consistent with the Fifth Amendment privilege—less productive of genuinely unacceptable coercion—than is the existing situation.[62]

In any event, again offering a sketch and a provocation rather than a full thesis, I suggest the broad change as desirable. The exact character and means of its implementation are matters left for further pursuit and more wisdom later on.

C. Breaking the mold of the "live," continuous trial–videotape

The trial as a contest, featuring active litigants and a passive public referee, implies familiar qualities of pace, timing, and rhythm. Girding for the event, the parties collect the evidence and fashion their strategies with maximum possible secrecy. Discovery in recent years is designed to limit the secrets and the surprises. But litigants wrestle with each other and with the court, more or less successfully, to defeat such invasions. Much of the tension along the preparatory route arises from the struggle for advantage in the drama of the trial, where sudden turns, unexpected challenges, and vivid incidents may assume disproportionate significance. Because the play is to run steadily once the curtain rises, episodic happenings may generate advantages or harms that are not effectively reversible before the inexorable ending.

The format works its negative effects in sundry ways prior to the trial, probably even more than during the trial. The technique of pretrial discovery, once hailed as a major revision of the sporting practices of surprise and concealment, has been much warped to adversary uses. In civil cases it has become too often a means for crushing a weaker, poorer opponent. Nobody with experience defending rich corporate clients has failed thus to employ for oppression a device fashioned for truth-seeking.

Discovery in criminal cases is a subject for steady dissatisfaction on both sides. The prosecution knows that most discovery sought by defendants is not to learn about things unknown, but to learn how much of things known are known to the prosecution. Indeed, one of the "liberal" arguments for broad discovery is that it pays off in guilty pleas when defendants learn the strength of the case against them.[63] Still not averse to withholding surprises when possible, many prosecutors give the least they can get away with.

In Europe, on the other hand, where the dread system is "inquisitorial," the standard practice is to disclose to the defense everything the prosecution has.[64] How can that be? How, especially, in the face of the fear, so often heard among us, that a defendant may destroy evidence, including witnesses, when he learns of them well in advance of trial?

A major part of the answer is in the less rigid format of a European trial. The results of pretrial investigations—susceptible of sufficient analogy to our "discovery" for instant purposes—are substantially available later on at the trial. A corresponding practice here would be enormously useful, not least because it could erase much of our existing strains about criminal discovery. As things stand, when the prosecution expresses fears that its witnesses will be killed if their identities are revealed, those favoring liberal discovery tend not to be impressed. They would order the discovery anyhow. The illiberals are too impressed, too prone to deny discovery on what turns out frequently to be paranoid or ulterior worries. Usually the prospective witnesses would not be killed no matter what discovery was allowed. Sometimes, however, they are killed.

The dilemma could be largely resolved if we adopted the simple device of discovery depositions videotaped as promptly as possible after a criminal case begins. The evidence thus "frozen" should be available for use at trial. Beyond its virtue of relative closeness to the disputed events, the videotape would obviate the asserted fear for witnesses' safety as grounds to oppose discovery.

Reverting to a prior topic, I would favor similar use of videotape to record pretrial interrogations of a defendant.[65] Whether these could be shown at trial might present a variety of questions variously answered. Presumably the tape of the defendant refusing to answer would not be shown (because it would resemble too closely an involuntary appearance on the witness stand) though, on my submission, the refusal could be reported and argued. The defendant who did answer would be exposed to the usual rules concerning admissions. In addition, though it might depart from Wigmore, strong arguments could be made for a rule allowing the defendant's use of such recorded evidence in his own behalf at the trial. At least the idea seems prima facie fair to me, subject to responses and complications I leave for later study.

There are many more possibilities in the new technology. Videotaped depositions have become familiar for at least some witnesses on tight schedules—from busy medical doctors to the President of the United States.[66] A far broader vista, already opened, embraces the full-scale trial packaged on videotape for presentation to a jury. Substantial experiments in Ohio and Michigan have revealed the potential of this device for rational, efficient, orderly, and economical presentation of the evidence in a trial.[67] Of course, the changed form does not accomplish a revolutionary departure from the traditional adversary mode. Indeed, it is fair to say that its proponents have not urged it primarily for any such reason. In fact, however, some of the combative aspects we need least may be erased, or sharply curtailed, by videotaped trials. In this category would be the admixture of lawyers' theatrics in posing objections and the putting of questions known in advance to be dubious but used anyhow for effect. The added time for thought between witnesses, and even during the testimony of a single witness, would lessen the effect of instant decisions on the spot, a necessity we choose to accept but never deem good in the existing system. Benefits like these are in addition to the economies and efficiencies commentators have noted—all interesting enough to mention here, but assigned for organizational strictness to the margin.[68]

Also, of course, there are objections and problems. What I have called dispensable "theatrics" will be for many a lawyer his lost opportunity to commune effectively with a jury while arguing or asking questions. The witness on the screen is two-dimensional, less "real." The tension of the courtroom may be thought more productive of truth-telling than the comparative relaxation of a videotaping session. The expected differences will merit close study and analysis. Changes from the tried and familiar are not automatically attractive. On the other hand, the tried and the familiar has not been critically tested or objectively evaluated. In any event, the suggested questions, an undoubted number of others, plus problems of technology must be confronted.[69] The outcome, I think, or, at least, hope—must be increasing, and increasingly salutary, use of the videotape wonder. The prospect is of special moment and attraction from the standpoint of this essay. For it is likely that the videotaped preparation of a whole trial before the jury's arrival must lead to a wholesome increase of concern, responsibility, and authority in the judicial director of the enterprise, discharging, it is hoped, the commission to seek justice rather than partisan advantage.

Caveats and Conclusions

In appraising and provocatively characterizing the Adam Smith style of adjudicative procedure, I have probably invited attacks broader than my submission. Perhaps too tardily, let me say that none of this has been meant to question the high value of partisan advocacy in the quest by free people for justice. Nobody could have spent three decades as student, advocate, and judge without coming profoundly to cherish this value. The assurance of loyal champions for causes and claimants has demonstrated its worth in the vindication of great human values, the rescue of oppressed people too long ignored, and even the protection of our highest temples against betrayal and destruction. There is a continued need, at least as great as it ever was, to preserve the values of tireless and unstinting, but honest, advocacy for the unorthodox, the unpopular, and those otherwise disadvantaged.

What I have critically in view is not the techniques by which our advocates seek to lead, but those available indifferently, and commonly employed, to mislead. The heart of the concern is in the effort to find factual truth—an effort counsel are likely much of the time to obstruct, not to assist, by seeking to block full revelations, to further false positions and to make honest witnesses seem dishonest.[70]

Finding individualist combat an insufficient means today for seeking truth (and just decisions grounded in truth), I have suggested that one approach to improvement is in the devising of procedures that enhance the public responsibility for this objective. There are, of course, other ways and other approaches. Among such things, I have heretofore suggested the possibility of changed rules to govern the contestants, including as incidents alterations in the attorney-client relationship and in the kinds of adversarial weapons to be deemed acceptable.[71] My specific suggestions, however, are not more than illustrative and not the essence of the thesis. The basic proposition throughout has been to mitigate combat and enhance the public duty of impartial inquiry as the route to just decisions.

Put this way, as it should be, the thrust of the argument must still reach sensitive nerves in all of us committed to government by the people. The idea of individualism, far from being dead, remains in intimate kinship with our cares for freedom and self-fulfillment. Reforms of the kind I have suggested amount to the enhancement of social ordering as against individualist initiatives. The proposals contemplate at least some transfers of power from private to public hands, not wholly unlike the transfers that have marked and effected our departures from Adam Smith economics.

By no means all modifications of the kind here contemplated would enhance the power of government over individuals. The revision of the *Miranda* regime would diminish the secret powers of police and prosecutors while enlarging the power of courts as agencies of orderly inquiry. The uses of videotape would tend more to modulate the adversary contest than to eliminate it. Nevertheless, it is to be recognized that in law as in economics, departures from Adam Smith generate deep issues of social policy and could pose dangers to our liberties. I believe, without urging the analogy as decisive, that our revisions of the philosophy of rugged individualism have been on the whole necessary and beneficial in the economic sphere. I believe a comparable enhancement of the public concern for the public good must be sought in our methods of adjudication, both civil and criminal. It is necessary to know the risks. Not to prevent change altogether, but to stimulate prudence. Keeping the risks always in view, I invite your attention to the possibility that we may find procedures ahead that are less governed by "private interests and passions" and more effectively managed in the interests of truly equal and public justice.

FOOTNOTES

1. 1 Parrington, Main Currents in American Thought 271 (1927).
2. Smith, The Wealth of Nations 651 (Modern Library, E. Cannan ed.).
3. V. Parrington, op. cit. *supra* note 1, at 271.
4. Curtis, It's Your Law 1 (1954).
5. Smith, op. cit. *supra* note 2, at 594-5.
6. Herring v. New York, 422 U.S. 853,862 (1975); see also Tehan v. Shott, 382 U.S. 406, 416 (1966).
7. The quoted words are from italicized headings preceding Ethical Considerations 7-4 and 7-19, respectively, in the Code of Professional Responsibility.
8. Freedman, Lawyers' Ethics in an Adversary System 9 (1975).
9. See Auerbach, Unequal Justice 12-13, 281-82, and *passim* (1976).
   Writing about the problem of inadequate representation for criminal defendants, Chief Judge David L. Bazelon has said: "I have often been told that if my court were to reverse every case in which there was inadequate counsel, we would have to send back half the convictions in my jurisdiction." The Defective Assistance of Counsel, 42 U. Cin. L. Rev. 1, 22-23 (1973). A remarkably similar statement was reported by a Committee which recently proposed revised rules (imposing law school curriculum requirements) for admission to the district court bar. It said:

   > "the most startling testimony came from a former U.S. Attorney for Connecticut who stated that of the last twelve cases he tried as U.S. Attorney he was of the opinion that one-half of the defendants were convicted because of the incompetency of their counsel. This so shocked him that he resigned his office to become the first head of the Connecticut Criminal Defense Committee."

   Qualifications for Practice before the United States Courts in the Second Circuit, Final Report of the Advisory Committee, 67 F.R.D. 159, 166 (1975). Neither Chief Judge Bazelon nor the former U.S. Attorney nor the Advisory (Clare) Committee indicated any doubts about the acceptability of a system *qua* system in a supposedly civilized jurisprudence that may be reported so responsibly to entail a disaster rate so high.
10. In what may be a slightly (but understandably) erroneous account of the "ideal," two students have said:
    "In an ideal adversary system, the less skillful antagonist is expected to lose the dispute, which under the laissez-faire notion is the proper outcome."
    Neef & Nagel, The Adversary Nature of the American Legal System from a Historical Perspective, 20 N.Y. Law Forum 123, 162 (1974).
11. See Frank, Courts on Trial 80-102 (1949), and Law and the Modern Mind 100-117 (1930).
12. See, e.g., Bailey with Aronson, The Defense Never Rests 11, 38, 255-6, 257, 260 (1971); Fleming, The Price of Perfect Justice chs. 1-10, 14, 17, and 20 (1974). These books are cited as illustrative of viewpoints which are prevalent, not as positions in the particulars of which I would join.
13. See Johnson, Justice and Reform 245-246 (1974); Fox, Settlement: Helping the Lawyers to Fulfill Their Responsibility, 53 F.R.D. 129 (1971); Burger, Deferred Maintenance, 57 A.B.A.J. 425 (1971).
14. Pound, The Causes of Popular Dissatisfaction with the Administration of Justice, 57 A.B.A.J. 348, 351 (1971) (reprint of a famous 1906 address, also to be found in 29 A.B.A. Reports 395 (1906)).
15. Packer, The Limits of the Criminal Sanction 158-163 (1968).
16. Id. at 163, 149.
17. Id. at 163-173.
18. The full set of actual reasons for our leadership in harsh prison sentences lies

deep in history, social psychology, and other domains yet to be adequately explored. The approach suggested here is not meant to be anything like a full or empirically documented account. It is meant, however, to reflect an aspect of how key actors in the process are believed to think, if not always consciously, and to behave. The belief rests upon years of informal and "unscientific" reading, talk, and introspection.

19. The secrets may include in criminal cases the prosecutor's knowledge that a key witness is missing or defense counsel's inability to collect a fee making a trial worth his while, the fact that defense counsel fears trial generally, patterns of relationships between prosecutors and defense lawyers, and other matters Plato might not have perceived as essentials of justice. On these and a far wider array of pertinent thoughts, see the extensive studies by Professor Albert W. Alschuler: The Prosecutor's Role in Plea Bargaining, 36 U. Chi. L. Rev. 50 (1968), and The Defense Attorney's Role in Plea Bargaining, 84 Yale L.J. 1179 (1975). See also Skolnick, Social Control in the Adversary System, 11 J. Conflict Resolution 52 (1967). "Justice market conditions" include the state of court calendars, the prosecutor's docket, the jail population, the court's receptivity to trials rather than pleas. I should add here, in fairness to many people and agencies, that this mention of plea bargaining reflects almost entirely, at least for the time being, conditions in state rather than federal courts. Until now plea bargaining, though known, see, e.g., Hoffman, Plea Bargaining and the Role of the Judge, 53 F.R.D. 499 (1972); Lambros, Plea Bargaining and the Sentencing Process, id. at 509, has not been a major activity in the relatively uncongested, leisurely, and luxurious federal courts. That this may be changing, for an array of reasons, is reflected in the recently enacted express sanction for plea agreements. Fed. R. Crim. P. 11 (e).
20. See Rosenthal, Lawyer and Client: Who's in Charge? 96-99 (1974).
21. See, e.g., Blumberg, Criminal Justice 4-5, 6, 26, *and passim*. (1967).
22. It is not important or possible here to recall the substantial points of divergence between Jefferson and Smith. Both agreed sufficiently for our purposes on the paramount value of individualism.
23. Cf. Frank, Courts on Trial 92 (1949); Eggleston, What is Wrong with the Adversary System? 49 Australian L.J. 428 (1975); Verkuil, The Ombudsman and the Limits of the Adversary System, 75 Colum L. Rev. 845, 852-3 (1975).
24. Illustrating the germinal contributions of Vanderbilt to the business of judicial administration, see 2 Klein and Lee eds., Selected Writings of Arthur T. Vanderbilt 37-250 (1965).
25. See Cook, Perceptions of the Independent Trial Judge Role in the Seventh Circuit, 6 Law & Society Rev. 615 (1972); cf. Battisti, An Independent Judiciary or an Evanescent Dream, 25 Case West. Res. L. Rev. 711 (1975).
26. Quotation of remarks in November 1972 as given in Note, Right to Defend Pro Se, 1973 Wash. U. L. Q. 679, 707 (1973).
27. 1976 Annual Report on the State of the Judiciary, 96 S. Ct. No. 9 (advance sheets) 3, 10 (Yellow Pages 1976).
28. The proposal now sketched elaborates upon, and varies somewhat, an idea put forth by Judge Shirley M. Hufstedler in her valuable Charles Evans Hughes Address to the New York County Lawyers Association on March 18, 1971, New Blocks for Old Pyramids: Reshaping the Judicial System, 44 So. Calif. L. Rev. 901, 908 (1971). For an interesting and detailed account of a proposed form of "activist" small claims court, see Ison, Small Claims, 35 Mod. L. Rev. 18, 27-37 (1972).
29. The use of a jurisdictional amount to define jurisdiction is admittedly open to grave question. Among the improvements needed in the present sketch of a suggestion would be some better, more sophisticated definition of the tribunal's competence.
30. In the Orient today, in this country during its infancy, in Biblical and Talmudic injunctions, in song and in story, lawyers have been substantially outlawed or

reviled for stirring up contentiousness, promoting falsehood, and other sins. See, e.g., Cohn, Attorney, in 3 Encyclopedia Judaica 837-838 (1972). A lawyer, numbering lawyers as best friends, could scarcely join that tradition. Nevertheless . . .

31. A wise magistrate, like any wise decision-maker, might build a measure of adversariness into his own organization, demanding that the opposed possibilities be discovered and argued. But there would be no incentive to distort, conceal, or otherwise mislead.
32. The description of illustrative alternatives to our standard adversary proceeding could fill a paper longer than this one. Among the possibilities neglected here are familiar and emerging forms, here and abroad, of mediation, arbitration, fact-finding, and counseling. A valuable discussion of the subject is in Sander, Varieties of Dispute Processing, a paper delivered at the National Conference on The Causes of Popular Dissatisfaction with the Administration of Justice, April 8, 1976, and soon to be published in a volume of papers from that Conference by the West Publishing Company.
33. 384 U.S. 436 (1966)
34. Id. at 460. See also Garner v. United States, 96 S. Ct. 1178 (1976); Baxter v. Palmigiano, 96 S. Ct. 1151 (1976).
35. Palko v. Connecticut, 302 U.S. 319, 326 (Cardozo, J.).
36. See 384 U.S. at 472-473; Friendly, The Fifth Amendment Tomorrow: The Case for Constitutional Change, 37 U. Cin. L. Rev. 671, 698 (1968).
37. See, e.g., 384 U.S. at 449-50, 455, 457, 458.
38. See Watts v. Indiana, 338 U.S. 49, 59 (1949) (Jackson, J., concurring and dissenting).
39. See Uniform Consumer Credit Code §2.502 ("the buyer has the right to cancel a home solicitation sale until midnight of the third business day after the day on which the buyer signs an agreement or offer to purchase . . ."). "An underlying consideration [for this cooling-off period] is the belief that in a significant proportion of such sales the consumer is induced to sign a sales contract by high pressure techniques." 7 National Conference of Commissioners on Uniform State Laws, U.L.A. §2.501, at 168 (1970) ("Official Comment"). See Jordan and Warren, The Uniform Consumer Credit Code, 68 Colum. L. Rev. 387, 441-43 (1968); Sher, The "Cooling Off" Period in Door-to-Door Sales, 15 U.C.L.A. Rev. 717 (1968).
40. 384 U.S. at 447.
41. Id. at 444; see also 475, 478, 479.
42. 384 U.S. at 505.
43. Prof. James Vorenberg, quoted in Graham, The Self-Inflicted Wound 183 (1970).
44. See, e.g., United States v. Gardner, 516 F.2d 334, 340-42 (7th Cir. 1975); United States v. Rodriguez, 523 F.2d 738, 740 (5th Cir. 1975); United States v. Cox, 509 F.2d 390, 392-93 (D.C. Cir. 1974); United States v. Moreno-Lopez, 466 F.2d 1205, 1206 (9th Cir. 1972); United States v. Glasgow, 451 F.2d 557 (9th Cir. 1971); United States v. Hayes, 385 F.2d 375 (4th Cir. 1967), cert. denied, 390 U.S. 1006 (1968); United States v. Choice, 392 F. Supp. 460, 466 (E.D. Pa. 1975); United States v. Tuggles, 334 F. Supp. 383, 387 (E.D. Pa. 1971); People v. McIntyre, 299 N.Y.S.2d 88, 31 A.D.2d 964 (2d Dept. 1969). See Note, Waiver of Rights in Police Interrogation: Miranda in the Lower Courts, 36 U. Chi. L. Rev. 413, 422 (1969). But see Williams v. Brewer, 509 F.2d 227 (8th Cir. 1974), cert. granted, 423 U.S. 1031 (1975).
45. 384 U.S. at 481
46. Griffin v. California, 380 U.S. 609 (1965).
47. Cf. Kauper, Judicial Examination of the Accused—A Remedy for the Third Degree, 30 Mich. L. Rev. 1224, 1238-39 (1932); Kamisar, Kauper's "Judicial Examination of the Accused" Forty Years Later—Some Comments on a Remarkable Article, 73 Mich. L. Rev. 15, 30 (1974).
48. The Suspect and Society 76-81 (1967).

49. The Fifth Amendment Tomorrow: The Case for Constitutional Change, 37 U. Cin. L. Rev. 671, 708-16 (1968).
50. Kauper, *supra* note 47.
51. Kamisar, *supra* note 47 at 33.
52. Friendly, *supra* note 49, at 672.
53. State v. McKnight, 52 N.J. 35, 52, 243 A.2d 240, 250 (1968). Like more major things, the quotation is owed to Judge Friendly, *supra* note 49, at 716, though I respond to it somewhat differently than he does.
54. Among the many places where such a restriction, or its substance, is said to be borne by the police are Scotland and Yugoslavia. See Kilbrandon, Scotland: Pre-Trial Procedure, in Coutts ed., The Accused: A Comparative Study 56, 73-74 (1966); Hrones, Interrogation Abuses by the Police in France—A Comparative Solution, 12 Crim. L. Q. 68, 88 (1970).
55. See, e.g., 3A Wigmore, Evidence 862 (Chadbourn rev. 1970); Israeli Criminal Procedure Law §146 (American Series of Foreign Penal Codes, 1967).
56. See Wilson v. United States, 149 U.S. 60, 66 (1893).
57. For a brief review of the key writings, see Friendly, *supra* note 49, at 673-4.
58. See id. at 714, 716; but see also id at 726.
59. Griffin v. California, 380 U.S. 609 (1965).
60. The proposals supported in this paper would require for federal purposes some modification of 18 U.S.C. §3481, which provides:

    "Competency of accused

    "In trial of all persons charged with the commission of offenses against the United States and in all proceedings in courts martial and courts of inquiry in any State, District, Possession or Territory, the person charged shall, at his own request, be a competent witness. His failure to make such request shall not create any presumption against him."

    That is not a major subject in the context of what is at a minimum a plea for legislative reform.
61. See Griffin v. California, *supra*, 380 U.S. at 620-21 (Stewart, J., dissenting).
62. See Kamisar, *supra* note 47, at 33-35. It is arguable that *Griffin* v. *California*, *supra*, has been weakened by Baxter v. Palmigiano, 96 S. Ct. 1551 (1976), allowing adverse inferences from silence in a prison discipline proceeding. Of at least passing interest for present purposes is Justice Brennan's dissenting observation that the majority's ruling in the latter case disserved "one of the fundamental purposes of the Fifth Amendment: to preserve our adversary system of criminal justice by preventing *the government* from circumventing that system by abusing its powers." *Id.* at 1565 (emphasis in original).
63. See, e.g., Brennan, The Criminal Prosecution: Sporting Event or Quest for Truth, 1963 Wash. U. L.Q. 279, 287 (1963); ABA Project on Standards for Criminal Justice, Discovery and Procedure before Trial, Standard 1.1(a)(ii) (Approved Draft 1970).
64. Schlesinger, Comparative Law 342 (3d ed. 1970); Damaska, Evidentiary Barriers to Conviction and Two Models of Criminal Procedure, 121 U. Pa. L. Rev. 506, 535 (1973).
65. See Kamisar, *supra* note 47, at 27-29.
66. On November 1, 1975, the deposition of President Ford was taken in a case involving his attempted assassination, United States v. Lynette Fromme, Dkt. No. Cr. S75 451 (E. D. Calif., verdict November 26, 1975). It was shown to the jury as part of the trial two weeks later.
67. See McCrystal and Young, Pre-Recorded Videotape Trials—An Ohio Innovation, 39 Bklyn L. Rev. 560 (1973); Brennan, Videotape—The Michigan Experience, 24 Hastings L.J. 1 (1972). There have been experiments elsewhere. See, e.g., N.Y. Times Sept. 23, 1973, p. 64, col. 6, concerning one in San Francisco.
68. Judge James L. McCrystal of Ohio has been an enthusiastic student and user of the videotape technique. With co-author James L. Young, he enumerates the advantages: "(1) the trial flows without interruption from objections, bench con-

ferences, delays for witnesses, counsel's pauses, client conferences and chamber retreats; (2) maximum utilization of juror time is achieved; (3) the time required for a given trial is shortened considerably; (4) the trial can be scheduled, with certainty, for a specific day; (5) the witnesses can be presented in the desired order, obviating the need for adjustment to availability at the last moment; (6) the chance of mistrial is greatly reduced; (7) there is no need to recess for the preparation of instructions; (8) directed verdict motions are decided when the tapes are previewed and do not infringe on courtroom time; (9) opening statements should be more effective with knowledge of precisely what the evidence will show; (10) the judge need not be present during the viewing of the tape, freeing him for other duties; (11) the presence of the lawyers is not required during the viewing of the tape; (12) it is possible for judge and counsel to conduct simultaneous trials; (13) trial preparation can be more effectively scheduled and the taping may be in the most convenient order of witness availability; (14) last-minute preparation is eliminated; (15) time is afforded for study of evidentiary questions; (16) testimony on location is facilitated; (17) elimination of live trial impediments give [*sic*] the jury a comprehensive related view of the entirety of the case; (18) the tape can serve as the transcript of proceedings on appeal; (19) retrial is facilitated; (20) extrajudicial judge influence through reaction to witnesses and comments to counsel is reduced; (21) the court need no longer resort to the fiction that a juror can disregard what he has heard in accordance with the judge's instructions."

69. One subject of some magnitude merits specific mention at least in passing. The right to a public criminal trial creates obvious difficulties for the videotape technique. I have not explored the adaptations or inescapable limitations entailed in this sixth amendment requirement. Dout, Trial by Videotape—Can Justice Be Seen to be Done? 47 Temple L.Q. 228, 259-61 (1974); Note, Video-Tape Trials: A Practical Evaluation and a Legal Analysis, 26 Stan. L. Rev. 619, 642 (1974); Note, Videotape Trials: Legal and Practical Implications, 9 Col. J. of Law & Soc. Prob. 363, 383-85 (1973).
70. See generally Frankel, The Search for Truth: An Umpireal View, 123 U. Penna. L. Rev. 1031 (1975), and The Adversary Judge, 54 Texas L. Rev. 465 (1976).
71. See The Search for Truth, *supra* note 70, at 1052-59.

The Legal Profession

LAWRENCE E. WALSH*

I shall begin with an anecdote about George III, without whom we probably would not be commemorating the Bicentennial. He happened to see a regiment of lawyers who had been raised for a possible defense of England against a Napoleonic invasion. As individuals they could not keep step and were not a very impressive parade. The king asked whoever was next to him, "What is that?" He was told that this was a regiment of lawyers who volunteered in the defense against the invasion. He asked "What do you call them?" The answer, "they don't have a name yet." George said, "call them the devil's own." The problem of predicting what the "devil's own" will do in the next century is something that I hesitate to enter upon.

I can only say that the profession is looking at itself very much in an attitude of reformist criticism. It is a very introspective period for us. We are very proud of our traditions but concerned that we are not using them fully in the service of the public.

As I try to outline the more specific trends which I see, I thought I would start first with somewhat of a background picture of a polarization which is tugging at our profession in a very gradual way, but nevertheless is there.

Toward one pole the more routine, the mechanical, the administrative, albeit very important functions which we perform are being drawn toward other groups, whether subprofessionals or others who may serve the public without as heavy recourse to the courts or as heavy use of lawyers. In California, our largest state, the bar has seriously debated whether uncontested divorce and uncontested probate

**President, American Bar Association, 1975-1976*

should be eliminated from court supervision and left to some administrator. The proposition lost, but it was a very significantly divided bar that conducted the debate.

Similar suggestions are made with respect to bankruptcy. We are all aware of the interest in no-fault accident determination. Medical malpractice is now also under consideration for finding some other method of dispute resolution other than courts and a lesser reliance on lawyers and concern with the size of their fee.

Judge Frankel's paper mentions minor disputes. The bar recognizes that it isn't doing a very good job on minor disputes. Our methodology is too expensive for them and yet they are important; they are minor only in terms of the amounts involved. They are important to someone. A task force has been set up by the American Bar Association for the development of better alternative methods of resolving these disputes.

Finally, among other things which I don't think we are doing well is our handling of criminal justice. There are large areas of conduct which are dealt with by our elaborate, expensive, time-consuming criminal sanctions which could be dealt with in other fashions. And the ABA plans to look into this.

There are areas here where the profession may find a loss of activity as we look into the next century. But because controversy can be depended upon in this society of ours, I don't think that we should regard this as the end of our activity. At the other end of the pole there are areas waiting that are complex, sophisticated, and which require great originality and ingenuity. Our economy is now very largely regulated.

The American Bar Association's Commission on Law and the Economy, twenty excellent lawyers and economists, has started consideration of what we can do as lawyers to try to bring a more orderly quality to economic decision making in this country. Proprietors and managers of large organizations can't plan their future without an understanding of what the Government is going to do and at times it seems unpredictable and in conflict with itself. This is an area which in the coming century is going to be far more acute, far more grave, and far more challenging than it has been in the past.

Our regulatory agencies are still largely in the model of the 1880's. The Interstate Commerce Commission was the first one. It has been forty years since the New Deal agencies were created. We have largely failed in our effort to reduce the complex judgment requirement problems of economic regulation to simple rules which can be administered by a second-rate mind, and we are going to be challenged. Although the lawyers may not have the substantive answers that are called for by our economic problems, it is they who will probably be called upon to devise the procedures and the structures by which these problems can be resolved.

Secretary Rusk refers to the shortages that we anticipate. These are very real. Energy is one, natural gas is another which was artificially aided by our system of regulation, which in its pricing practices has sharply decreased the supply that we need.

In addition to our economic problems, science is ready to hand us a good package. With scientific thought and technological developments outdistancing the work of lawyers and political scientists, our problems with dealing with these great forces have not even begun to show themselves. As we learn what our attitude is going to be about abortion, then we have the problem of when somebody is dead, and as we begin to deal with that, we learn that the next step is going to be genetic manipulation. We have dealt with prenatal injuries, but nothing of this subtlety and difficulty, or this profound possibility.

Environmental problems are just beginning. We have been hearing about the SST and possible atmospheric damage. We have weather manipulation equally in our hands. What this is going to do is a problem for lawyers as well as scientists. Again, we can take Secretary Rusk's reference to shortages. The sea as a source of solving those shortages is a matter that has to be dealt with in a civilized way. There has to be a forum and a method of adjudicating the conflicts which are going to arise as we attempt to meet our needs which are no longer capable of being met in some other fashion.

He refers to nuclear power and nuclear arms. We all shudder as each new nation gains capability in the use of this destructive force. But the time is going to come when private groups will have this power, when terroristic groups will have it. We have not even begun to think of how to deal with these problems.

As I think of our profession, and of the great advances that have been made by our law schools and the higher selectivity of our law students, I take great assurance, because the demands upon the young people who are now coming out of law school are going to be far greater than they were on us.

I become concerned as I view this polarization as it is beginning, because I don't know what is going to happen to the general practioner. Lawyers have always been something more than persons capable of giving treatment. I think of a lawyer whom I knew as a youngster, handling some of my family's problems; he was a family counselor. I think of Mr. Davis who was the head of my firm. Persons came to him not just because they wanted the treatment capability of his partners; they wanted his wisdom, his personal interest, and his personal advice. I don't know what is going to happen. Are these highly refined skills which are going to be called upon to solve these terribly difficult public problems going to still reside in someone who is willing and capable of giving that same kind of general advice, willing to stay in a small city or a small town and serve a community which has many simpler problems to deal with too? With all of this I am concerned with the loss of independence, just as Judge Frankel is concerned with the loss of judicial independence.

As scientific demands and economic demands intensify the depth of interest that we must take and the amount of time that we must devote to each of them, we will become more and more specialized not in terms of our particular capability as between trial and office work, but specialized in the service of particular kinds of clients. Will one client have so many difficult problems for a lawyer that it will take all of his time or of a firm's time, and as he becomes more narrowly interested will he lose the breadth of judgment that has been traditional with our system?

Let me run through quickly some of the specific areas for which the profession has responsibility.

Beginning with the selection of lawyers for law school; I

don't see any problem there. They are being selected in an objective fashion on the basis of their skill and capability. I am concerned only that as we select a much more elite group, some of the more menial functions of the profession will be less interesting to them. I will come back to that in connection with public interest law.

With education the organized bar has only a remote concern, in accreditation of law schools. There are 163 that have been accredited and 40 that have not been. There is a development, particularly in California, for unaccredited proprietary law schools which are interested in making a profit, therefore in reducing the cost, and serving as large a number as they can effectively. This is going to pose a problem in the coming years. I think that our law school structure is so strong that it will persevere, but with increased expense we are going to have to look in time at the length of our academic education. This will simply increase the importance of post-graduate education which I will come to shortly.

The question of admission to the bar is the profession's responsibility and I am happy to report a decreasing provinciality in this area. It wasn't too long ago that in Pennsylvania lawyers were admitted county by county, not even statewide. Now I don't think there is any of that narrowness left. Forty-two states are now using a multistate bar examination, at least in part. This means that in the common substantive areas one examination is used for all these states. There may be problems in community property states, there may be problems of peculiarities of practice, but since the adoption of the federal rules forty years ago, there has been a happy movement toward harmony, even on the procedural side. This means that the picture of a possible nation-wide bar will become real during the next century.

There will be greater interest in specialization. Because of the exacting demands which I have already referred to, I think it is obvious that there is going to be a need to specialize in fact. We are experimenting now with two models. One is in California which requires special experience, special training, special courses, and an examination. This has been in effect for a couple of years. Not too many have taken advantage of it, in comparison with the size of the bar. I think there have been less than 2,000 out of over 40,000, who have become certified for specializations. Only three areas are available on this experimental trial.

In New Mexico there is a different system. There anybody can become a specialist by picking his area of concentration and committing himself to spend sixty percent of his time in that area. The Yellow Pages which carry the listing indicate that the state does not insure the expertness of any of the specialists. This is simply an indication of area of interest.

The American Bar Association is starting now—with the help of five sections, all of which are in areas of specialists—to generalize standards, looking toward ultimate specialization. This will take a while but will come clearly during the next century.

This type of specialization is simply the permission to hold one's self out as an expert. It doesn't keep anyone else out of the field. Anyone can practice taxation in California without being a specialist. A second type of specialization is proposed in the Second Circuit which would have excluded from the trial courts persons who had not had certain types of training, certain courses, and certain experience. This provoked considerable controversy and has never gone into effect. So we are without experimental experience in this area. But this will, I am sure, recur. Sooner or later we will have a model like this to educate us and that certainly will be in this coming century.

With all of this the burden on post-admission education will go up tremendously. Specialization will require it and the expense of academic education will add pressure to shortening the law school term and compensating by post-graduate education. Three states have already made it compulsory, Minnesota, Iowa and Wisconsin, both for judges and for lawyers, requiring fifteen hours per year. This may be a token, but it is the beginning. In other states, like the State of Washington, almost one hundred percent of the lawyers take some form of post-graduate education on a voluntary basis. The American Bar Association is going to fund a very large program here, because it is obvious there is going to be heavy demand which can't be met by existing educational groups. I believe that the universities will find themselves doing the same.

The profession also has a problem in seeing that computer technologies are developed in a way which will be the most useful and most economic to the public, to avoid duplication where we can. A new ABA section is attempting to do this and I think it is really barely started in its task. It is obvious that in the next century we are going to be as concerned with the development of computer systems as we were in the last century in the development of libraries.

All of the educational requirements are going to make very real the possibility of recertification as a requirement for lawyers. The demands upon lawyer competence are going to increase. Along with this is going to come a much more meaningful disciplinary system. Five years ago Justice Clark analyzed our disciplinary system and found it not very good. Since then there has been a great improvement, but only in terms of what we had then, not in terms of what we need. The number of sanctions against lawyers has doubled in this period. The number of states which have set up state-wide systems and gotten away from the problems of small county disciplinary problems has greatly increased. Moneys appropriated for this purpose have all increased very substantially. But they have a great way to go.

I can say that there is no committee in the American Bar Association more important than its committee on professional discipline, even though we don't ourselves have any disciplinary powers. We simply urge and plot an adequate development by states and localities.

Turning to the delivery of legal services, we again are faced with recognition that we have not adequately served the poor, or the lower or middle income groups of our society. But in addition to legal aid which we have been supporting for many decades, we now have the Legal Services Corporation which is a government agency created with the strong support of the organized bar, and it is now, by its estimate, serving one out of seven indigents who are entitled to and require its service. Obviously it is going to require more funding and more help, but it is a program in motion.

Prepaid legal service plans now serve 800,000 lower middle income families in this country. It was begun with an experimental system that showed it could be done on a self-supporting basis. There was a great dispute between those who wanted closed panels and open panels, great concern that this would have an impact upon practice that might lead to the domination of practice in a particular city by one union or one particular company. All of these things, notwithstanding, the bar has gone ahead. These experiments are going ahead. There are four state bar associations which now have plans ready to start on a statewide system. The New York County Lawyers Association has a plan developed in New York. Even acknowledging the defects, I think that we have hit upon a system that will offer a solution in the future and in the coming century this will be a broadly used system.

Clinics also have been subsidized and developed. We have one now, an experimental system just starting. If it can handle the problems of the less wealthy, and still support itself, this again will be a pattern which we will see in the coming century.

I think the role of the lawyer in the next hundred years as a civic leader is going to be just as important as it always has been. There are more learned professions now perhaps than there were when we only recognized three. But lawyers with their understanding of government and political science and their ability to deal with disputes in a very highly contentious society, have a purpose beyond that of any other profession, except perhaps the press, in seeing that those who are not organized, who are not members of groups, are protected. And the lawyers are capable enough, are able enough, and in the past have been dedicated enough to see that this has been done. I am sure that in the pattern of the future, in public interest activities, civic activities, and political activities, the profession in the next hundred years will be an articulate center in the preservation of our ideals.

LEGAL SERVICES

Jacob D. Fuchsberg*

It is a great time to be a lawyer. It is a great time to be a judge. To some, I suppose it is the worst of times; to others, the best. In the nature of such things, probably both are right. And, anytime when it is some of both, it is indeed very exciting to be alive.

For me 1976 marks forty years at the Bar. A lot of things have happened in that time. I would like to go back with you, if I may, a little longer than that, not all the way to 1776, but just to 1906. In that year, Roscoe Pound delivered a talk which has become part of American legal history. Entitled "The Causes of Popular Dissatisfaction with the Administration of Justice", it is somewhat sad to reflect that, a full Biblical seventy years later, that address is still only pointing the way to badly needed—and largely unaccomplished—law reform. Nevertheless, if I had a title to choose for a visionary view of the law in 1976 as we look to the century ahead, I would use the paraphrase "The Beginning of Popular *Satisfaction* with the Administration of Justice". And I would stress the word "justice" rather than "administration", which connotes the operational and procedural ways in which our courts work. For it is the substantive satisfaction of its craving for justice with which our people and, hopefully our judges and our lawyers and our law schools, are becoming increasingly concerned.

That concern is an acute one. It dominates our times. In fact, today, in 1976, just as Americans did in 1776, we find ourselves in a time of revolution. True, the chief characteristic of today's revolution is not military; but the goals of all revolutions are not achieved by force of arms. Nor is it essentially an economic revolution as, for example, was the Great

**Judge, New York Court of Appeals*

Depression of the late twenties and thirties. It is certainly not a political revolution; broadly speaking, there could hardly be a greater sameness of political philosophy than exists among the many candidates vying for the presidency this year. Contrast that with how the election of Andrew Jackson as president of the United States over a century ago, as then expected, ushered in an age of populism; that was a very meaningful political revolution.

I would suggest that the revolution of today is a legal revolution. It is a legal revolution that has taken place in the main since the end of World War II. Its pace has been escalating ever since. While, roughly speaking, it has now spanned thirty years, it has become most evident in the last decade.

It is no exaggeration that the average lawyer engaged in practice twenty to thirty years ago and the average judge engaged in the decisional processes at the time, and even the average legal philosopher or teacher of that day, would have found himself as comfortably at home in the courtroom, classroom and legal milieu of, say, a hundred years earlier. Surely, in that span of time, things had not stood still; nothing is ever exactly the same in the social world. But what movement there had been was relatively minimal, perhaps affecting style but not substance.

In the last two decades or so, however, change has clearly become the order of the day. It has dealt—or had to deal—with criminal justice; violence; the mounting impact of the drug scene; the proliferation of pollution—by land, by sea and by air; consumer rights; the rights of the young; the rights of women; the rights of the mentally ill; the rights of prisoners; the rights of students; the rights of privacy—of mind and of body, not the least of which currently involves the sensitive issue of abortion; one man-one vote; the right to welfare; the right to an equal opportunity in education, employment, housing, and so on without end. Wherever we turn, our problems are legal problems. It appears to me that they cannot be confronted adequately without equality before the law, and equality before the law cannot be trusted to exist without equality in representation.

The complexity of today's society, the inundating intrusion of governmental bureaucracy into our lives, the growth of bigness with its concomitant dependence on computerization—these are among the forces which have made modern man more dependent on others than ever before, if he is to maintain his integrity as an individual midst the endless numbers of transactions and confrontations which face him at every level. Who is to provide this help if not the lawyer? Unlike the situation in totalitarian countries, the outcome of these confrontations is not inevitably against the citizen. Therefore, since the very nature of our legal process is not only to defend rights but to create them, at stake for the individual citizen is no less than a choice between a State which serves and one which swallows him.

So, you see, I find no reason to feel overwhelmed by the fact that our country now has about 400,000 lawyers, or that there are in the neighborhood of 110,000 students attending the law schools of this country at this time, or that, as a consequence, a decade from now our lawyer population is likely to have reached 800,000. If the job before us is to be done, we will need all of them. The spectre of lawyer overpopulation, of long lines of unemployed lawyers, only looms for those who do not carry the vision of the essential and pervasive role of the lawyer in evolving the evolving society. Yes, we need them all. And I am optimistic enough to believe we are going to use them all. At one time England's greatness was attributed to the fact that it was a nation of shopkeepers. I feel no uneasiness at all at having us thought of as a nation of lawyers.

My views are no doubt conditioned by the fact that my own college and professional education spanned the Depression. Gloom had "busted out all over". The breadlines were pathetic. The American "dream" appeared to have ended. I received my law degree not too long after the New Deal and Franklin Delano Roosevelt offered the magic wand of hope to replace our despair. You had to come out of that experience completely flattened or very optimistic. For me, it was the latter.

While engaged in a debate on disarmament, I remember one of my fellow debaters, with great insight, argued that soldiers find war. Just think of that for a moment. Isn't it likewise true that lawyers find causes? I am not talking about champerty; I am not talking about maintainance. I speak especially about citizen causes that need rectification, most often possible only by operation of law. Lawyers, as a practical matter, have a monopoly grant on access to the courts. For successful advocacy in our legal forums, almost invariably, there is need for a trained representative, and we require that he be a licensed representative as well. Does the fact that a layperson cannot really effectively plead his case without a lawyer mean that the right to one is assured? Hardly.

As I see it, there are three layers to the right to counsel. Let us take a quick accounting of where we stand on each of those levels.

From the day it was first inscribed as part of our Sixth Amendment, we have, at least in theory, recognized a right to counsel. But, as it was long read, the qualifying phrase "if you have one" or "if you can afford one" might just as well have been appended. For nothing was said about how counsel was to be obtained or afforded.

That brings us to the second level of right to counsel. That is the right to *a* counsel. In other words, are our people only to have a right to counsel when they choose one, find one, afford one, pay one, or because one volunteers, or are they to be entitled to one irrespective of whether they can meet these conditions or not? In theory at least, it is fundamental to justice that the enforcement of a person's rights not hang by the happenstance of that person's articulateness, his education, his wisdom, his personality, or the extent to which he has the capacity of subordinating his tensions so that they do not interfere with his ability to plead for himself, indeed on even the basic knowledge of what his rights are in the first place. But the gap between the right to counsel and the right to *a* counsel is still great.

We are beginning to close that gap, particularly in the last 10-15-20 years, but thus far mostly in criminal cases only. *Gideon, Powell, Miranda, Argersinger*, the cases begin to trip off one's tongue. Yes, indigent defendants now have a right to a lawyer, not only at trial but at earlier stages of the criminal process as well. And we are providing counsel for juveniles in cases that reach beyond the criminal law.

But we are a long way from doing so for indigents in other cases. For instance, with all the dislocations that now abound in family life, a person without means has no assurance of legal guidance in a matrimonial case. My own court considered the subject intensively and extensively just this past year. Our decision was a close vote. Three judges were ready to compel provision for counsel; but the majority of four, while recognizing the problem, thought it best to leave the matter for the Legislature. Still that was a lot of movement. I doubt whether it would have taken place five years ago, ten years ago, certainly not twenty years ago. And I venture the prediction that, whether legislatively or judicially, the matter will not long remain static.

Needless to say, the surface has not yet been scratched in assuring the right to a lawyer in civil cases generally. One cannot help but ponder why it is more important that one charged with a minor drug offense, such as the possession of marijuana in New York, be entitled to the assistance of a lawyer for his defense than one whose livelihood is jeopardized by discrimination in employment or by the suspension of a license necessary to carry on his vocational calling. Once poverty is established, should it make any difference simply because the quest for justice is in a criminal rather than a non-criminal legal arena?

So we move to the third level—the right to adequate counsel, not just right to counsel generally nor the right to *a* counsel, but the right to a competent lawyer, one who knows his business. Such a qualitative standard is almost entirely for the future.

It would be naive to expect our adversary system to ever yield exact equality of counsel. But who would gainsay that, realistically, there should be an entitlement to adequacy of representation? I have been dismayed, therefore, upon surveying hundreds and hundreds of cases in the course of my service as an appellate judge, to note the frequency with which the result at trial appears to have been determined by the inadequacy of counsel. Important rights and penalties, imprisonment for some, shattered lives for others, fortunes wiped out or recouped, all too often come about because of the accident of legal representation. I have compiled no exact statistics which I can quote for you, but I have noted that my observations accord with those of Judge David Bazelon and other students of the appellate process. Judge Bazelon, from his long experience as a jurist, estimates that defective assistance of counsel is evident in two-thirds of appeals from trials. Hardly a reason for optimism but what a challenge it nevertheless presents to us! Many of our increasing coterie of lawyers are deployable to meet it.

Response to all these needs will also bring a shift in the predominant nature of law practice. Today the private practice of the law is still dominant and its tremendous importance is not to be gainsaid now or in the future; the rights of those who can afford lawyers are, of course, of equal importance with those who cannot. In the century to come, however, I believe we are going to find that the felt need and expectations of our people for availability of legal services to all who require them are going to be met, and they are going to be met by the lawyers. Because of the large numbers of people of limited means who will thus come for the first time to have access to the channels of justice, the private practice of the law will become, quantitatively at least, the secondary practice.

The beginnings of this trend are already visible. On the criminal law side, over 2500 lawyers are now engaged as public defenders. There were practically none twenty years ago. The growth, taken in the abstract, is most impressive. But the National Legal Aid and Defenders Association tells us that the current minimum need is already for 17,500, not 2500. In the past, the vacuum was partially filled by volunteers from the private sector. The need for that will disappear.

Of course, the Legal Aid and Defenders Association does not talk of the civil side of things, including the need of poor people for counsel in meeting their everyday legal problems. The experience in the development of the OEO national legal services program during President Johnson's administration tells us a great deal. I had the good fortune to watch it develop from the inside. Though having to create an entirely new organization where none had previously existed, within a period of three years, on a far too limited budget, nearly one and a half million people a year were receiving legal aid on meaningful matters involving their family rights, their jobs, their governmental benefits, their housing and their other concerns running the gamut of everyday living. Interestingly and excitingly, as tested in an adversarial setting, the vast majority of these matters turned out to be meritorious. Yet they had not previously been serviced by the private law sector, simply being ignored. In many cases the inability to secure justice in our courts had thus not only led to alienation from society, but to recourse to riots in the streets. The law for many had become a suspect instrument of oppression, to counter which the OEO Legal Services Program, when it did come into being, had to undertake major educational efforts.

Even today, despite the fact that the Program suffered a serious setback, being besieged by budgetary reduction and attacks on its independence during the Nixon administration, there are some 2,000 lawyers engineering a program in hundreds and hundreds of neighborhood and rural law offices across the nation for poor people who could never have found their way to conventional law offices. Regrettably, though the participation and support of major bar associations, such as the American Bar Association, the Association of Trial Lawyers of America, and the National Bar Association made this outstandingly successful program possible, in some areas of the country the program was vigorously resisted by local bar groups, either out of insecurity or lack of vision and sensitivity to the people's awakening yearning and desire for justice.

My figures have to be loose, but instead of 2,000 OEO (now National Legal Services Corporation) lawyers, we need many times that number and, instead of the present budget of about seventy million dollars, which works out to only some thirty cents per citizen each year, it should be several times that much. On a sound scale of national priorities, these would probably be conservative figures.

Meeting, if possible, even a greater related need, at long last, our society is also just starting to provide legal services for people of modest means above the poverty level. The extent of the unavailability of legal services to this largest of all segments of our population, except of course in some contingent fee areas, is scandalous. The economic barrier has not been unlike that associated with medical and hospital care. It may not matter to the wealthy that semi-private hospital accommodations in the metropolitan New York City area now approach $180 per day and that a three day hospitalization, inclusive of X-rays, laboratory tests and other incidental services, can hardly be managed for $1,000, not including doctors' fees. Or to the poor insofar as public programs are available to them without charge. But, absent generous insurance, things are utterly unmanageable for the citizen of average means. In like manner, OEO and Legal Aid may take up some of the slack for the indigent in meeting legal services needs, but the cost alone is enough to turn the average person from law and lawyers like the plague.

Prepaid legal service plans projected as a possible answer to that problem are more than just a hope. Between one and two million people have already secured some coverage for legal services needs under more than seventy-five responsible plans which have come into existence on the heels of a series of experiments undertaken in the last several years. In our own court, last year we reviewed holdings of one of our own intermediate appellate courts, which had interdicted two proposed plans, one for a closed panel plan sponsored by a labor union and the other for an open panel plan put forward by a county bar association. We reversed and permitted both to go ahead.

Group plans, sponsored by labor unions and others, are also beginning to proliferate. The Taft-Hartley Act permits their negotiation as a collective bargaining provision. Our most populous state, California, is said to now have over eight hundred of them, again covering an estimated million or more people. And the ABA Committee on the Delivery of Legal Services has been commissioned to work out an ethically acceptable way to overcome resistance to the establishment of legal clinics.

In sum, I see more and more lawyers serving the public in such directions, incidentally thereby heightening the skills of those at the traditional private bar who, often for the first time, now will have to deal with the legal representatives of the large segments of the population who, for all practical purposes, had come to see the law as though it were always an enemy and never a friend. Young, eager and idealistic lawyers are readying to help the unrepresented. Training in our law schools is getting better and more relevant to felt societal needs all the time. Participatory government provides the vehicle for growing support and encouragement. These forces are irresistible. For, as Benjamin N. Cardozo pointed out, the law is cast into the mold of life and not the other way round.

With all this will come other changes. Some are already underway. Thus, proscriptions against professional advertising, whatever recently decided or currently pending Supreme Court cases may bode, will have to yield to methods of informing people, firstly, as to their rights and, secondly, as to how they can secure the assistance of counsel whose skills are required for the vindication of the rights involved. A carefully conceived and managed system of specialization, balanced by the continuing efforts of generalists, is bound to raise standards, identify qualifications, and draw talented lawyers to the places of their greatest need and personal fulfillment.

None of these developments need alarm us. If some of the existing mystique in the layman's conception of the law goes by the board, replacement by added respect would make every lawyer—and society—the gainer. As a free society is indispensable for an independent bar, so is an independent bar indispensable to a free society. Individual rights require both.

In this Bicentennial Year, in this Bicentennial volume, it is difficult to avoid thinking of the framers of our Constitution. They well understood this role of the lawyer in the nation they planned. So they provided an express guarantee of the right to counsel. They did not impose an obligation on the State to provide religious or spiritual guidance to its people; to the contrary, they forbade it. They did not compel the State to provide physicians for those ravaged by disease. But they gave formal recognition to the fact that the right to counsel was fundamental to the country they envisaged. Today, as we enter upon an age when I believe we will see a vast extension of that right, I am persuaded that there will follow a corresponding extension of the universality of freedom for all Americans.

THE FEDERAL COURTS

Henry J. Friendly*

I.

It would be hard to sustain the thesis that 1776 is a momentous date in the history of the federal courts. The authors of the Declaration of Independence had more immediate concerns. It cannot even be claimed with confidence that but for the assertion of independence two hundred years ago, there would be no federal courts today. Severance of the direct cord to London was inevitable, as wise men in England already recognized and as the Canadian experience was later to prove. It cannot be said what transmutations would have occurred before total independence was achieved, or what form the American federation would have taken, but no one can believe that, save for the Declaration of Independence, British magistrates would today be sitting in Foley Square.

The dates deserving commemoration from the standpoint of the federal courts are rather 1787 or 1789, and also 1875. The two first dates, those of the framing of the Constitution and of the First Judiciary Act, can be considered together. Madison records that, as early as June 4, 1787, the Committee of the Whole resolved "that a national Judiciary be established . . . nem. con."[1] There was similar unanimity on the establishment of a Supreme Court. In contrast, "The proposal for inferior federal courts . . . aroused opposition in the Convention and major controversy in the ratification debates."[2] The Committee of the Whole considered various proposals—mandatory establishment of inferior federal courts, no inferior federal courts, inferior federal courts for

Senior Judge, United States Court of Appeals, for the Second Circuit; Presiding Judge, Special Court Under the Regional Rail Reorganization Act.

admiralty cases only—before Madison and Wilson successfully moved "that the National Legislature be empowered to institute inferior tribunals,"[3] and although there was some disagreement at the Committee stage, the Convention later adopted the compromise unanimously.[4] The battle, however, was not ended. As a result of debates in the Virginia ratifying convention, there was introduced in the Senate of the First Congress a proposal for an amendment which would have vested the judicial power of the United States "in one supreme court, and in such courts of admiralty as Congress may, from time to time, ordain and establish. . . ."[5] But Congress was proceeding, although not without opposition,[6] in the contrary direction. Disappointing the expectation voiced by Pendleton in the Virginia convention that its "first experiment will be, to appoint the state courts to have the inferior federal jurisdiction,"[7] Congress moved swiftly to use its authority to create federal courts throughout the land; this was "the transcendent achievement of the First Judiciary Act."[8]

The unanswered, probably unanswerable, question about that Act is why Congress made no use of its power to vest the inferior federal courts with general civil jurisdiction over "cases, in Law and Equity, arising under this Constitution, the Laws of the United States, and Treaties made or which shall be made, under their Authority." Was this an oversight? Was it a compromise with the Virginians, also taking into account Hamilton's view that the state courts "will of course be natural auxiliaries in the execution of the laws of the Union?"[9] Was it a belief that what now seems the rather curious composition of the inferior federal tribunals, with Supreme Court Justices being members of the circuit courts which had both original and appellate jurisdiction, made it undesirable for these courts to pass on the kind of questions that were peculiarly likely to raise serious issues for the Supreme Court as a whole? When, in 1801, the Federalists woke up to their omission and sought to plug the gap, it was too late.[10]

The inferior federal courts continued without what today is their most important head of jurisdiction until the Reconstruction period. The various Civil Rights Acts were the beginnings of this.[11] The culmination was the vesting of the lower federal courts with general federal question jurisdiction (although limited by a jurisdictional amount) by the Act of March 3, 1875.[12] The conferring of the jurisdiction is almost as mysterious as the initial omission; today's leading scholars tell us that the bill "passed almost unnoticed inside or outside the halls of Congress."[13] Since then, "The history of federal question jurisdiction . . . revolves largely around the creation by Congress of myriad new federal rights and its provision for their enforcement in the national courts without regard to jurisdictional amount,"[14] as had been true from the beginning under the Civil Rights Acts. Important among these statutes are those providing for jurisdiction under federal laws that regulate commerce, the specialized ones for judicial review of administrative action, and the more general Mandamus and Venue Act of 1962.[15]

The history of the inferior federal courts is thus neatly divided into two centuries—one in which they were primarily occupied with matters not of true federal concern[16] and another in which various types of jurisdiction concerning the federal constitution, laws and treaties have increasingly occupied the stage. In 1928, at midpoint of the second century, I wrote:

> The steady expansion of the jurisdictions of the federal courts, especially since Reconstruction days, has been but a reflex of the general growth of federal political power. That growth will not abate, since it is responsive to deep social and economic causes.[17]

I cite this not out of pride in the authorship of long ago but in the hope that the correctness of that prediction may lend some credence to those I am about to make.

II.

My first prediction is that before the year 2000 the federal courts will be rid of the incubus of diversity jurisdiction and thus be able to concentrate on their proper tasks. While the relative share of the caseload represented by diversity cases has slightly diminished, their absolute number has increased by 67% since 1962, and they constitute 26% of the civil filings in the district courts.[18]

I canvassed the reasons for abolishing diversity jurisdiction in The Carpentier Lectures at the Columbia Law School three years ago[19] and shall not repeat them here. As a federal judge has wittily said, this is an idea whose time has passed.[20] Talks with practicing lawyers in many parts of the country who oppose the abolition of diversity jurisdiction convince me that the opposition is not based on any of the sophisticated grounds urged by academic and other defenders of the jurisdiction[21] but primarily for a reason I do not like to mention but which must be squarely faced. Baldly put, these lawyers do not trust the judges in the lower courts of the states.[22] They believe that many of them are incompetent, indolent, or subject to influence—the three i's; in consequence they cherish any opportunity, however small, to get away from the state courts and into the federal ones. I cannot assess whether this appraisal of state judges is true; certainly it is not of those whom I now know, although I recall that, as a practicing lawyer, I entertained views about particular state trial judges not altogether different from those just mentioned. State bar associations should be devoting their energies to improving their own judicial systems for the benefit of all litigants rather than seeking to preserve for a few a head of federal jurisdiction that has become an outmoded excrescence.

What may need a word of justification is my confidence that, despite this opposition of the bar and the long record of failure, the fight against diversity jurisdiction will be won in the next quarter-century. A committee containing such now legendary figures as Charles William Eliot, Louis D. Brandeis and Roscoe Pound questioned the jurisdiction as long ago as 1914.[23] Felix Frankfurter joined the attack as a professor in 1928[24] and, as a Justice, was not slow to record his views in the United States Reports.[25] Professor Herbert Wechsler raised serious questions about the jurisdiction in 1948.[26] Contenting myself with a query when a callow youth in 1928, I engaged in all-out assault as Chief Judge of the Second Circuit in 1973.[27] Chief Justice Burger has been sounding the tocsin for several years.[28] Yet even a bill based on the more modest proposal, made some eight years ago by the American Law Institute, to curtail diversity litigation by ending the anomaly wherein a head of jurisdiction apparently intended to protect non-residents against local discrimination can be invoked by a resident against a non-resident, has not even been reported out of a subcommittee.

What then is the source of my faith? Although not generally an optimist, I do believe that, while it may take a long time, good sense ultimately prevails. Congress will realize some day that it cannot continue to impose new duties on the federal courts and still expect to see all the old jobs done. Even if more judges are appointed, something must give, and diversity jurisdiction is the obvious candidate. Some day a member of the Senate or House Judiciary Committees—or, perhaps more realistically, an important member of their staffs—will leaf through the Federal Second or Federal Supplement Reports and see opinions dealing with school desegregation, discrimination in employment on the basis of race or sex, the federal labor, securities and antitrust laws, and the federal criminal law interrupted by a lengthy discussion of the amount of damages suffered by a housewife who slipped on a banana peel in a store in the city of her residence operated by a national chain rather than the local grocer. Some day someone will wonder why a federal court, faced with staggering problems of federal law, must struggle with what a distinguished appellate judge has called "the repetitive task of untangling another web of confusion created by the inarticulate language of two automobile liability policies."[29] Some day a district court, or a district judge, hard pressed by the Speedy Trial Act for criminal cases and by a heavy load of urgent federal civil litigations will direct that henceforth diversity cases brought initially in the federal courts be placed at the bottom of the calendar—or a circuit council will order the same. Perhaps such developments will even affect state bar associations; more likely they will lead members of the Judiciary Committees to realize how few votes or even how few campaign contributions hang on a decision to abolish diversity jurisdiction. I am not sure I will see that happy day but I am certain it will come.

III.

Freed from the weight of diversity jurisdiction, the federal courts will be able to absorb the expanding volume of federal question litigation. This will include the increase that will come from the quantity of new legislation pouring out of Congress, from the increasing litigiousness of our citizenry, and from the elimination of irrational jurisdictional restrictions on suits challenging the acts of state and federal officials as contrary to the Constitution or laws of the United States.

Federal courts can now entertain such suits where the amount in controversy exceeds $10,000. When it does not, the situation is chaotic. A state official can be sued, under the Civil Rights Act of 1871,[30] if the complaint asserts the deprivation "of any right, privilege, or immunity secured by the Constitution of the United States or by any Act of Congress providing for equal rights of citizens or of all persons within the jurisdiction of the United States."[31] A claim that a state official acted inconsistently with any federal law can be annexed to a constitutional claim; if the constitutional claim is substantial, this gives the federal court jurisdiction and it should first consider the non-constitutional claim, although the jurisdictional amount requirement would have prevented this if the latter claim stood alone.[32] Against federal officers, suits not involving more than $10,000 cannot be brought—unless there is a special review statute, of which there are many; unless the case falls under a section of the Judicial Code not requiring a jurisdictional amount of which there are several;[33] unless, which has not been authoritatively decided, the Administrative Procedure Act of 1946 constitutes a grant of jurisdiction; or unless the action is "in the nature of mandamus to compel an officer or employee of the United States or any agency thereof to perform a duty owed to the plaintiff." As if that degree of confusion were not enough, the practical rule for construing the phrase "in the nature of mandamus" seems to be that it covers all cases which an appellate court would like to see covered but not those it does not want to see covered[34]—a difficult rule for anyone but appellate courts to apply, and likely to cause some disagreements within them.

These "witty diversities" with respect to suits against state or federal officers provide opportunities for fascinating exercise by federal jurisdiction buffs. But they make little sense in terms of justice to the citizen. The Administrative Conference of the United States recommended eight years ago that the district courts should be opened to "any action in which the plaintiff alleges that he has been injured or threatened with injury by an officer or employee of the United States or any agency thereof, acting under color of Federal law."[35] I predict that long before the year 2000 Congress will adopt this and a similar provision with respect to suits alleging that state officers acting under color of state law have violated the Constitution, laws or treaties of the United States.[36]

This broadening of federal jurisdiction with respect to actions against state and federal officers must, however, be accompanied by a reaffirmation of the rule requiring prior exhaustion of adequate administrative remedies. The Supreme Court now insists on this in suits challenging federal administrative action, at least where there is a factual dispute or a need for the application of administrative expertise.[37] A requirement of administrative exhaustion also was long the established rule in suits against state officers.[38] However, in recent years the Court, without reasoned explanation, has seemingly undercut this salutary rule in actions under the Civil Rights Act.[39] The decisions do not purport to rest on constitutional grounds and should be overruled by statute if the Court does not do the job itself.

Indeed the future will see increased use of the models provided in Title VII of the Civil Rights Act of 1964 and Title VIII of the Civil Rights Act of 1968.[40] Complaints over discrimination and other unfair practices in employment, housing, and use of public facilities will have to be presented in the first instance to state or federal administrative agencies and resort to the courts will be permitted only when satisfaction has not been obtained there.[41] The agencies will provide a winnowing process whereby many cases, hopefully most cases, will be settled or one of the parties will accept an adverse ruling, thus removing them altogether from the courts. They will provide a fact-finding process in others, thereby diminishing the judicial burden. When administrative remedies have been established and have demonstrated their efficiency, which unhappily has not yet occurred, it will be time to consider whether appropriate modifications of the general civil rights statutes of the Reconstruction Era[42] may not be in order.

The most important role I see for the federal courts in the Third Century thus is the control of governmental action—state and federal—so that it does not infringe the Constitution or federal law. But, of course, these courts will have many other important tasks. There will continue to be suits by the United States to enforce its laws, civil and criminal, although I would hope the efflorescence of the Federal criminal law might be diminished both by decriminalization of certain acts and by leaving to the states more crimes in which there is no real federal interest.[43] There will be disputes between private interests over the meaning and application of the expanding federal statute book; securities law, labor law, consumer protection and environmental law are sufficient examples. There will be the traditional "federal specialties"—admiralty, antitrust, bankruptcy, copyright, patents, and federal tax litigation, although I would urge that the two last should be handled by special courts, at least at the appellate level.[44] Federal judges thus will not suffer from lack of variety even if they are shorn of power to hear personal injury cases and actions on insurance policies and take as their primary task the umpiring of disputes between the citizen and his government.

IV.

In discharging these tasks the federal courts will face many problems. I will devote my remaining time to two which are just beginning to surface.

One is the federal decree, usually but not always in civil rights cases, which imposes expensive and detailed requirements on state and city governments. As Professor Archibald Cox has recently pointed out in his valuable Chichele Lectures at Oxford, whereas constitutional adjudication had typically taken the form "of rendering judgments which did little more than validate or veto allegedly unconstitutional action by other branches of government: by the President, by the President and Congress, by the States and the State legislatures, governors and courts, and by other minor officials"[45] now the federal courts "often require affirmative action" which can be secured "only through voluntary co-operation of the political branches or by the courts embarking upon programmes having typically administrative, executive and even legislative characteristics heretofore thought to make the activity unsuited to judicial undertaking."[46] Examples are the Detroit desegregation decree which the Supreme Court reversed ostensibly on other grounds[47] and the attempt, again rejected by a narrow majority avowedly for other reasons, to alter the pattern of school financing throughout the nation.[48] Perhaps a better illustration for our purposes is the decree entered by Judge Frank Johnson with respect to two state mental hospitals in Alabama.[49] This not merely laid down the general principle that patients committed to such a hospital "have a constitutional right to receive such individual treatment as will give each of them a realistic opportunity to be cured or to improve his or her mental condition" but prescribed precise details for physical alteration and patient care. For example, the patients must have water heated to 110°F at the fixture, and the water used for mechanical dishwashing and laundry must be heated to 180° at the equipment. Heating and air conditioning must insure that the temperature never falls below 68°F nor rises above 83°F—a degree of comfort most of the patients probably had not enjoyed in their homes. The decree prescribed the exact number of medical and other personnel for each 250 patients, how plans for individualized treatment should be developed, and what medical records should be kept. The court appointed a human rights committee, with the right to engage consultants to be compensated by the State.

Is a federal judge, even after being informed by expert testimony, really so omniscient as to freeze a state mental hospital into such a mould?[50] Does not such a decree involve some trivialization of the due process clause; would it be really consequential if the water at the faucet were heated to only 100°F or at the dishwasher to 175°F? If the machinery purchased by the State does not achieve the warranted water and air temperatures, is the mental health commissioner in contempt unless he can persuade the judge to modify the decree? What administrative burdens is the court assuming? Worst of all, what if the State legislature simply refuses to make the appropriations which the court demands—a possibility that has become very real, even for well-intentioned states and cities, in these times of financial stringency and impaired credit? Is it a realistic answer for the court to say, as it did, that in that event "it will be necessary for the Court to take affirmative steps, including appointing a master, to ensure that proper funding is realized. . ."?[51] If the court levies taxes throughout the state, who will collect them?[52] Similarly detailed decrees have been entered with respect to state prisons.[53]

Of course, there is another side of the coin. Conditions in the Alabama mental hospitals were hair-raising, and the state may have ignored or trifled with earlier more general pronouncements.[54] If the court had decreed only that the water must be hot, the judge might have to entertain repeated complaints that it was not hot enough—better make it 110°F at the sink and everyone will know just how hot is hot. Indeed, in the particular case the parties stipulated on many of the details in the event the court was held entitled to enter a decree at all; I cite the case by way of illustration more than in criticism. If the legislature refused to appropriate the needed money, the court would not have to impose taxes or direct curtailment of other expenditures; it could simply direct that the hospital for the mentally ill or the institution for the retarded be closed until funds were provided and hope that public opinion would furnish the necessary prod. But, as Judge Johnson noted, bad as the hospitals were, the alternatives to commitment might well be worse;[55] and even if a shut-down of a mental hospital were a possibility, would a court dare take the risk if the institution were a maximum security prison? It is an unhappy fact of life that prisoners, the mentally ill and the institutionalized aged do not rank high on a state's list of financial priorities as compared with schools, highways, or other public improvements. If federal courts do not protect these people, who will?

Yet the risks of collision and the consequences of it seem great. If a judge were to carry out the threat to order the state treasurer not to pay out moneys for functions the judge considered less essential,[56] who is to say that the treasurer would obey? Would the federal judge or the recalcitrant treasurer languishing in jail for contempt emerge as the hero? Courts must be careful not to erode "the respect and trust of the people—which in the end is what sustained and must sustain the remarkable institution of a supreme judiciary in American life."[57] Is the supply of water heated to 110°F worth the risk?

I have no ready solution to offer. One can only hope for greater responsiveness by the states and for patience and moderation by the judges. I wish I were more sanguine that these qualities will be exhibited in the Third Century.

A related, although somewhat less grave, concern is the growing number of instances in which federal judges are being asked to pass on technological issues they cannot really understand. Until recently this problem existed primarily in patent law. As I wrote a few years ago, while it was not hard for ordinary judges to comprehend a patent which substituted porcelain or clay for wood or metals in doorknobs,[58] the courts must "deal today with a great number of patents in the higher reaches of electronics, chemistry, biochemistry, pharmacology, optics, harmonics and nuclear physics, which are quite beyond the ability of the usual judge to understand. . . ."[59] For that reason I proposed the centralization of patent litigation in a Patent Court, staffed by judges having a scientific bent and hearing commissioners and other personnel with specialized expertise.[60] With my usual confidence that good sense will ultimately prevail, I think we will see such a court created in the Third Century, at least at the appellate level, although the prospect is now clouded a bit by the ill-advised proposal to establish a National Court of Appeals.

Complex technological questions are now arising in an area of still greater public concern—environmental litigation. The problem was not great in the first few years of applying federal environmental legislation, for the courts initially were faced primarily with questions as to the procedural requirements imposed on various governmental bodies by the National Environmental Policy Act's mandate that Environmental Impact Statements be issued.[61] Shortly thereafter, however, the federal courts became increasingly involved in the substantive review of decisions made by administrative agencies to see if sufficient regard had been paid to environmental considerations,[62] and meanwhile further legislation had been put on the books. I commend to you, as an illustration of the problems we now face, a recent opinion of the Fifth Circuit[63] which granted in part and denied in part Texas' petition to review the EPA's disapproval of the state's "air quality implementation plan for control of photochemical oxidant pollution,"[64] under the Clean Air Act. The mind boggles at the labor involved in endeavoring to master the problems of technology and statistical theory dealt with in Judge Griffin Bell's opinion which stretches over 28 pages of the Federal 2d Reports. The difficulties were compounded by the fact that the case came to the court of appeals without the agency's having conducted any formal hearing. Judge Clark tells us, in a concurring opinion, that

> The writing judge was required to hold both pre- and post-argument conferences with counsel for the parties to enable the three of us as a court to comprehend the substance of the issues and conduct a minimally meaningful review.[65]

There must be a better way. Presumably the court could have appointed an expert to assist it, but this might not be acceptable in an area where expert position is so polarized. The whole field of environmental litigation itself needs cleaning up. The number of required approvals, each affording opportunity for litigation, and the inordinate expense and delay in preparing Environmental Impact Statements and in reviewing first their adequacy and ultimately the action taken upon them, must somehow be reduced. A project can be killed not only when it is in fact an undue threat to the environment, as it should be, but by the mere expense and delay of litigation.[66] Unhappily I have no pat solution. While I fear that the subject is too politicized to make it possible to centralize review in an environmental court, at least it would seem possible to devise a method whereby experts could find the scientific facts or at least the parameters of difference.[67] Here too a decree is likely to entail much in the way of affirmative action, by industry or even by government, with the potential of exceedingly serious effects on the economy and the environment. There should be ways to insure that courts do not unwittingly fall into errors having grave and often irreversible consequences.

V.

These are the major problems I foresee for the federal courts in the years ahead. For solution they require a combination of resourcefulness, good judgment, greater speed by Congress in considering and enacting sound judiciary laws, and a determination to resist unsound ones, such as the current proposal to interpose a mini-Supreme Court between the courts of appeals and the "one Supreme Court" which was one of the great visions of the Framers.

FOOTNOTES

1. Madison's Journal 108 (Scott ed. 1895).
2. Hart & Wechsler, The Federal Courts and the Federal System 11 (2d ed. 1973) [H&W].
3. 1 Farrand, The Records of the Federal Convention of 1787, 124-25 (1911) (June 5).
4. 2 *Id.* 45-46 (July 18).
5. H&W 22-23 & n.120. The amendment would also have limited federal question jurisdiction to cases arising under treaties.
6. See Warren, *New Light on the History of the Federal Judiciary Act of 1789,* 37 Harv. L. Rev. 49, 65-68 (1923).
7. 3 Eliot's Debates 517.
8. Frankfurter & Landis, The Business of the Supreme Court 4 (1927) [F&L].
9. The Federalist No. 82 at 517 (B. Wright ed. 1961).
10. Act of Feb. 13, 1801, § 11, 2 Stat. 89, 92, repealed by Act of March 8, 1802, 2 Stat. 132. See F&L 25-30. It is interesting to speculate whether the victorious Republicans would have repealed federal question jurisdiction in 1802 if this had been conferred by the Act of 1789 or even if it had not been accompanied by the appointment of the "Midnight Judges." And, of course, the Federalists might not have conferred the jurisdiction but for the latter!
11. See H&W 845-46.
12. 18 Stat. 470.
13. H&W 846-47. The provision was introduced by Senator Matthew Carpenter of Wisconsin, on behalf of the Judiciary Committee, 2 Cong. Rec. 4979. The meagre history is recounted in F&L 65-69. Those authors agree that "This development in the federal judiciary, which in the retrospect seems revolutionary, received hardly a contemporary comment." *Id.* at 65.
14. H&W 847.
15. 76 Stat. 744, 28 U.S.C. §§ 1361 and 1391 (e).
16. This was thrue even of the Supreme Court; Professor Fairman's study of the Court under the chief justiceship of Chase records the tedium of the diversity cases which then constituted the bulk of the Court's business. History of the Supreme Court of the United States, Vol. VI, Reconstruction and Reunion 1864-88, Part One, at 32-35 (1971).
17. Friendly, *The Historic Basis of Diversity Jurisdiction,* 41 Harv. L. Rev. 483, 510 (1928).
18. Of the 61,836 civil filings in the district courts in 1962, 18,359 or 30% were diversity cases; by 1975 the figure was 30,631 out of 117,320, or 26%. Report of Director of the Administrative Office of the United States Courts, Table C2 (1962) [AO Ann. Rep.]; AO Ann. Rep. Table C2 (1975). If state and federal prisoner petitions (collateral attack on convictions and complaints concerning prison conditions) are eliminated from the "civil" filings, today's proportion of diversity cases is 31%. The figures of total filings are, of course, exclusive of the very large number of bankruptcy filings.
19. Friendly, *Federal Jurisdiction: A General View* 139-52 (1973).
20. Bratton, *Diversity Jurisdiction--An Idea Whose Whose Time Has Passed,* 51 Ind. L.J. 347 (1976).
21. Notably Professor Moore, Judge J. Skelly Wright and John P. Frank. See Friendly, *supra* note 19, at 144-46.
22. There is also the trial lawyer's natural desire to keep all options open, but I am convinced that public spirited attorneys would not insist on this if the factor of distrust were removed.
23. Preliminary Report on Efficiency in the Administration of Justice 28 (1914), cited in Friendly, *supra* note 17, at 483 n.2.
24. Frankfurter, *Distribution of Judicial Power between United States and State Courts,* 13 Corn. L.Q. 499, 520-30 (1928).

25. *Indianapolis* v. *Chase Nat'l Bank,* 314 U.S. 63, 76-7 (1941); *National Mut. Ins. Co.* v. *Tidewater Transfer Co.,* 337 U.S. 582, 650-51 (1949) (dissenting opinion).
26. Wechsler, *Federal Jurisdiction and the Revision of the Judicial Code,* 13 Law & Contemp. Problems 216, 234-40 (1948).
27. See notes 17 and 19 *supra.*
28. E.g., Burger, *Report on the Federal Judicial Branch—1973,* 59 A.B.A.J. 1125, 1126; Burger, *The State of the Judiciary—1975*, 61 A.B.A.J. 439, 441; *Annual Report on the State of the Judiciary,* 62 A.B.A.J. 443, 444 (1976).
29. *Miller* v. *Nat'l Farmers Union Property & Cas. Co.,* 470 F.2d 700, 701 (8 Cir. 1972) (Lay, J.).
30. 42 U.S.C. § 1983 and 28 U.S.C. § 1343(3).
31. While the latter phrase has not been authoritatively construed, see H&W 961, similar language in another context has been given a restricted meaning. See *Georgia* v. *Rachel,* 384 U.S. 780, 792 (1966); *City of Greenwood* v. *Peacock,* 384 U.S. 808, 831 (1966).
32. *Hagans* v. *Lavine,* 415 U.S. 528 (1974).
33. Such sections could also afford jurisdiction in actions against state officers.
34. See *Economic Opportunity Comm'n of Nassau County* v. *Weinberger,* 524 F.2d 393, 404 (2 Cir. 1975) (concurring opinion).
35. 1 Recommendations and Reports of the Administrative Conference of the United States 169 (1970) (adopted in December, 1968).
36. I should make clear that, in advocating elimination of restrictions on suits against federal and state officers, I am speaking purely of jurisdictional requirements. What forms of relief should be available—particularly the availability of damages—is quite another issue. This raises serious policy questions which Mr. Justice Powell recently canvassed in *Imbler* v. *Pachtman,* 424 U.S. 409 (1976). *Cf. Wood* v. *Strickland,* 420 U.S. 308 (1975).
37. See. e.g., *McGee* v. *United States,* 402 U.S. 479 (1971); compare *McKart* v. *United States,* 395 U.S. 185 (1969).
38. See *Prentis* v. *Atlantic Coast Line Co.,* 211 U.S. 210 (1908), and later cases cited in H&W at 983, (5).
39. The starting point in the "Court's casual eroding of the requirement of exhaustion in Civil Rights Act cases," H&W at 985, was Justice Douglas' opinion in *McNeese* v. *Board of Education,* 373 U.S. 668 (1963), although this could be read as resting on the inadequacy of the state administrative remedies. The cornerstone of the presently held view (whatever its exact dimensions) is a *per curiam* opinion on a summary reversal, *Wilwording* v. *Swenson,* 404 U.S. 249, 251-52 (1971). See also *Ellis* v. *Dyson,* 421 U.S. 426, 432-33 (1975); *Steffel* v. *Thompson,* 415 U.S. 452, 472-73 (1974). Professor Kenneth Culp Davis has condemned this result with his usual acuity, Administrative Law Treatise § 20.01 at 646 (1970 Supp.). See also Note, Exhaustion of State Remedies Under the Civil Rights Act, 68 Colum. L. Rev. 1201, 1208 (1968); *Moreno* v. *Henckel,* 431 F.2d 1299, 1306-07 (5 Cir. 1970) (Wisdom, J.). Confusion has now been further compounded by *Burrell* v. *McCray,* — U.S. —, 44 U.S.L.W. 4860 (U.S. June 14, 1976) (certiorari dismissed as improvidently granted). Exhaustion of state judicial remedies is quite another matter. See Friendly, *supra* note 19 at 101-07.
40. 42 U.S.C. §§ 2000e to 2000e-15 and §§ 3601-19.
41. See Friendly, *supra* note 19 at 76-8.
42. 42 U.S.C. §§ 1981, 1982 and 1983.
43. See Friendly, *supra* note 19, at 58-61.
44. See *id.* at 153-71.
45. Cox, The Role of the Supreme Court in American Government 76 (1976).
46. *Id.* at 77.
47. *Milliken* v. *Bradley,* 418 U.S. 717 (1974). The decree is described in Cox, *supra* note 45, at 82-83.
48. *San Antonio Independent School District* v. *Rodriguez,* 411 U.S. 1 (1973).

49. *Wyatt* v. *Stickney,* 344 F. Supp. 373 (M.D. Ala. 1972), discussed in Cox, *supra* note 45, at 96-98. A companion case, *Wyatt* v. *Stickney,* 344 F. Supp. 387 (M.D. Ala. 1972), dealt similarly with a state institution for the mentally retarded. Both decisions were affirmed, as somewhat modified, in *Wyatt* v. *Aderholt,* 503 F.2d 1305 (5 Cir. 1974) (Wisdom, J.).
50. As has been written:
Unfortunately in many of these areas of social policy there is no clear knowledge of what the root of the problem is, though an expert can always be found who will oblige a judge with an appropriate program. Glazer, *Towards an Imperial Judiciary?,* the Public Interest 118 (Fall 1975).
51. 344 F. Supp. at 378.
52. The court reserved ruling on the plaintiffs' requests that the Mental Health Board be "directed to sell or encumber portions of its land holdings in order to raise funds" and for an injunction "against the treasurer and the comptroller of the State authorizing expenditures for nonessential State functions," 344 F. Supp. at 377. In the companion case dealing with a state institution for the mentally retarded, the judge characterized a similar reservation as part of the "long-standing policy of deferring to state organizations and officials charged by law with specified responsibilities," 344 F. Supp. at 393. The Fifth Circuit clearly wanted to make sure that this "policy" was fact, not form, and issued a strong "go-slow" warning as part of its otherwise affirming opinion. It said, *inter alia,* that any federal decree reallocating appropriations, or selling lands, would in any case have to be entered by a three-judge district court, *Wyatt* v. *Aderholt, supra* note 49, 503 F.2d at 1318.
53. For an example of the complex remedial problems that can arise in the prison context, see *Rhem* v. *Malcolm,* 371 F. Supp. 594 (S.D.N.Y. 1974), *supplemented,* 377 F. Supp. 995 (S.D.N.Y. 1974), *affirmed in part, remanded in part,* 507 F.2d 333 (2 Cir. 1974), *on remand,* 389 F. Supp. 964 (S.D.N.Y. 1975), *amended,* 396 F. Supp. 1195 (S.D.N.Y. 1975).
54. Judge Johnson thought Alabama had done so. See 344 F. Supp. at 374-75.
55. 344 F. Supp. at 378.
56. See note 52 *supra.*
57. Glazer, *supra* note 50, at 122.
58. *Hotchkiss* v. *Greenwood,* 52 U.S. (11 How.) 248 (1851).
59. Friendly, *supra* note 19, at 156-57.
60. *Id.* at 157-59.
61. See, e.g., *Calvert Cliffs' Coord. Comm.* v. *A.E.C.,* 449 F.2d 1109 (D.C. Cir. 1971).
62. See *Environmental Defense Fund* v. *Corps of Engineers* (Gillham Dam), 470 F.2d 289, 297-301 (8 Cir. 1972), *cert. denied,* 412 U.S. 931 (1973), and cases there cited.
63. *Texas* v. *E.P.A.,* 499 F.2d 289 (1974).
64. *Id.* at 293.
65. *Id.* at 322.
66. See Friendly, *"Some Kind of Hearing,"* 123 U. of Pa. L. Rev. 1267, 1312 n.228 (1975).
67. See Kantrowitz, Controlling Technology Democratically, 63 American Scientist 505-09 (1975), proposing a scientific court before which scientists would appear as advocates.

THE STATE COURTS

Stanley Mosk*

It is healthy for a Westerner to come to the effete East and to demonstrate that occasionally the twain do meet. A good many miles separate us geographically, yet only one meal and one movie by jet plane. But it is a vast historical distance from that speech about the West that Daniel Webster once made in the Senate of the United States. "What," he thundered, "do we want with this vast worthless area, this region of savages and wild beasts, of shifting sands and whirlpools of dust, of cactus and prairie dogs? To what use could we ever hope to put these great deserts or those mountain ranges, impenetrable and covered to their base with eternal snow? Mr. President, I will never vote one cent from the public treasury to place the Pacific Coast one inch nearer Boston than it is now!"

My task is to discuss the Third Century of American law in state courts. A hieromancer can read the entrails of a sacrificial animal for portents of the future. Those of us not skilled at reading entrails must look to other sources to divine the likely course of the Third Century of our republic. My principal source, a vagrant mind, reveals a number of significant trends in the states during the forthcoming century. Space permits me to ruminate over a mere random potpourri.

At the outset, I note a growing sensitivity to the exorbitant expense of litigation in state courts. In response thereto, the bench and bar will be compelled to reduce substantially the public and private costs inherent in the present system of judicial dispute resolutions, and, indeed, to remove from the courts entirely matters the judicial process is not handling effectively or that can be resolved more appropriately by other means.

**Justice, Supreme Court, California*

Justice, like chastity, must be an absolute. On that theory critics assail the judiciary from a variety of fronts. Permeating many of the complaints is the insinuation that appellate judges, insulated in their ivory tower, are unable to comprehend the daily agonies of contemporary society as reflected in trial court proceedings. I suggest the possibility of adapting the old federal circuit system, so that each state appellate judge spends some time each year on a trial bench, appreciating the dilemmas of the trial judges in coping with the real world of crime and criminals, civil disputes, evidentiary problems, and administrative burdens.[1] There are a number of pragmatic problems, but I believe a workable program can be devised.

It would seem elementary that jury instructions should be comprehensible to jurors. You and I know that they seldom are. While serving as a trial judge I invariably cringed when advising a jury on the definition of reasonable doubt. Under compulsion of high court decisions I recited the phrase Chief Justice Lemuel Shaw employed in 1850:[2] "It is not a mere possible doubt, because everything relating to human affairs, and depending on moral evidence, is open to some possible or imaginary doubt." What lawyer, let alone a lay juror, can describe "moral evidence"? Nevertheless courts blithely give that instruction hundreds of times every day. One can be equally uncomfortable about instructing a jury on proximate cause. What is an "efficient intervening cause"? Is it the converse of an "inefficient intervening cause"?

Steteotyped jury instructions will be jettisoned in the future, and in their stead judges will discuss in a conversational tone the broad legal principles which are to guide the jurors in their deliberations. Trial judges' orthodoxy, born out of fear of reversal for failing to dot an "i" or cross a "t", will no longer replace the primary objective of making the law comprehensible to the laymen who must act upon it.

In the criminal law field I foresee greater judicial concern with sentencing. There is virtue in the prevailing indeterminate sentence system, under which the term fits the criminal, not the crime. Nevertheless disenchantment has emerged in the public, which doubts the ability of political appointees on parole boards to perform their role of dispassionately assessing prisoners in order to set terms and parole dates and to discourage recidivism. And the prison population itself is evidencing a marked preference for the old-fashioned system of a determinate sentence; it seems that the cartoonists' version of the prisoner in his cell marking off days on the calendar is not exaggerated. Thus there is a likelihood of a return to the theory of equal deprivation of liberty for equal offenses. The result will be restoration of sentencing responsibility to trial judges, and concomitantly, reviewing of sentences will be vested in appellate courts.

The current demands for consideration of the rights of crime victims—while often political and sometimes demagogic—may lead to more frequent use of restitution as a sentencing tool in the future. In this sense restitution refers to payments, in money or services, by the offender to the victim of his crime. It could conceivably serve three purposes: to the public, satisfy its demand for a penalty; to the victim, a chance to be made whole; to the offender, rehabilitation and future deterrence.

Another aspect of criminal proceedings that will attract future attention is referral of convicted misdemeanants in lieu of penal confinement. This program results in the diversion to useful community service work, through nonprofit publicly-supported agencies, of those who are convicted of minor offenses, and who would otherwise be a public burden by languishing in jail. The agency benefits, the public saves money, and the defendant undertakes constructive work instead of remaining in tax-supported idleness. Though such a program is limited to those convicted of less serious offenses, its use experimentally in Oakland and in a number of other communities has been encouraging.

I forecast drastic revisions of our grand jury system. It has seemed evident to me that prosecution by indictment under the presently accepted scheme denies an accused fundamental rights at a critical stage of the criminal process. While grand juries historically served as a neutral buffer between the crown and the citizens, in practice today we have come full circle to the pre-Runnymede era when "le graunde inquest" was merely an agency of the crown.

In most states there are two widely disparate methods of initiating a felony prosecution: indictment and information. The choice is subject to the whims or strategy of the prosecuting attorney. If prosecution is begun by information the accused immediately becomes entitled to an impressive array of procedural rights, including presence, a preliminary hearing before a neutral magistrate, representation by counsel, confrontation of witnesses and the opportunity to present exculpatory evidence.[3] But if the prosecutor takes his case to the grand jury, the accused has no right to be present and is deprived of his entire panoply of fundamental rights.

It is no answer to point out that the grand jury is mentioned in the Constitution—it is, as an institution, but its procedure is not described; or that it is a venerable agency—antiquity alone is not an antidote for constitutional infirmity.

There are a number of devices through which the due process and equal protection problems can be solved without destroying the grand jury as an institution,[4] and I am confident one or more of them will be adopted in the states in the years ahead.

Finally, and most significantly, I detect a phoenix-like resurrection of federalism, or, if you prefer, states' rights, evidenced by state courts' reliance upon provisions of state constitutions.

For 173 of the 200 years of this republic a relentless tide of judicial authority has flowed from the states to the federal government. From John Marshall's opinion in *Marbury v. Madison* in 1803 to very recent days, the highest courts in the several states were often reduced to the status of intermediate appellate tribunals, mere wayside stations on the route from trial courts to the Supreme Court.

I do not for one moment suggest that this was entirely unnecessary or undesirable. Back in 1951 one learned commentator reviewed the somewhat dismal performance of state courts in enforcing provisions of their own constitutions and observed that "if our liberties are not protected in Des Moines the only hope is in Washington."[5]

That observation turned out to be a prophecy. The Warren Court, from its inception in 1953, served as the midwife to a new design of constitutional law. The previous era had been characterized by a benign acceptance of racism, political rotten boroughs, disability of the poor, an Anthony Comstock approach to sexual matters, denial of universal suffrage, egregious imposition upon the rights of the criminally accused.

Under Chief Justice Warren and his colleagues, the court abandoned its apathetic approach to overt injustice in society and elected to employ the Federal Constitution to achieve a liberating and egalitarian impact in the areas of political opportunity, criminal justice, and racial equality.

As a result, the states were compelled to fall in line. Despite the furor over many of the decisions, notably in the areas of reapportionment[6] and protection of the rights of criminal defendants,[7] state courts swallowed their own prejudices, abandoned the dictates of stare decisis and obediently embarked upon the new course. Between *Mapp v. Ohio*[8] in 1961 and *Benton v. Maryland*[9] in 1969 the nation underwent what one commentator described as a "a criminal procedure revolution."[10]

A few prescient state courts, like California's Supreme Court under Chief Justice Roger Traynor, had anticipated the trend. California adopted the exclusionary rule[11] six years before the United States Supreme Court applied the *Wolf v. Colorado*[12] rule to the states in *Mapp v. Ohio.* Back in 1903 Iowa had anticipated *Weeks v. United States*[13] by 11 years in *State v. Sheridan.*[14] But most states had been apathetic; they took their cue from the 1833 case of *Barron v. Baltimore*[15] which declared: "The constitution was ordained and established by the people of the United States for themselves, for their own government, and not for the government of the individual states."[16]

Although there were a few state court evasions of the Warren court reforms,[17] ultimately the states adapted their criminal techniques to the High Court's requirements. Some results were labored, as, e.g., a conservative justice applying the Fourth Amendment to a back-alley trash can,[18] but in general a satisfactory accommodation was achieved. Police officers were taught how to lawfully enforce the law; trial judges became reconciled to admitting only legally obtained evidence.

Just as an era of peaceful coexistence seemed imminent, the post-Warren counterrevolution began. Few will gainsay the observation of Prof. Wilkes that the current Supreme Court "is no longer a bold, innovative institution and has abandoned, for the moment at least, the role of keeper of the nation's conscience."[19] I do not intend to venture a judgment on that course; perhaps it is wise and inevitable that we follow a period of hypertension with years of lowered expectations.

But what can reasonably be expected of state courts? Are they to alternately create and then abandon doctrines of state authority as the tides in Washington ebb and flow? At a minimum the new circumstances have "introduced complexity into the lives of both litigants and state court judges."[20]

Consider as an example the requirement that counsel be present at lineups. This rule was adopted by the Supreme Court in 1967 in *United States v. Wade*[21] and *Gilbert v. California*[22] under the frequently articulated theory that adversary criminal proceedings begin not in the courtroom but at the police station.[23]

Justice Brennan, writing for the court in *Wade,* emphasized the importance of the presence of counsel at "criticial confrontations" and firmly declared that "we scrutizine *any* pretrial confrontation of the accused."[24] And in *Stovall v. Denno*[25] the court added unequivocally that "counsel is required at *all* confrontations" for identification.

I candidly admit to having expressed misgivings about the role of an attorney at a lineup.[26] But in a series of cases[27] involving all types of lineups our state court obediently followed directions from above. Manifestly, it seemed to us, "any" pretrial confrontation and "all" confrontations for identification implied no limitation to merely post-indictment proceedings.

But along came *Kirby v. Illinois* in 1972,[28] and mirabile dictu the High Court found it to be "firmly established" that the right to counsel attaches only at the time judicial proceedings have been initiated. "Any" and "all" have been translated to mean "very few," for as Judge Sobel points out, post-indictment lineups are rarely held, and when they are, it is merely for the purpose of refreshing identifications previously made. Now the right to counsel "is afforded the defendant where he least needs it."[29]

The right to privacy is another area of concern. In 1927 Justice Brandeis wrote that "the makers of our Constitution undertook to secure conditions favorable to the pursuit of happiness. . . . They conferred, as against the government, the right to be left alone—the most comprehensive of rights and the right most valued by civilized man."[30] In 1967 the High Court began to read into the Fourth Amendment a guarantee of privacy as an essential aspect of human liberty. As Alan Barth wrote, "If the Constitution says nothing about privacy, it says a great deal about liberty."

Consider, in that context, the result of the Supreme Court refusal in March, 1976, to review a three-judge decision in *Doe v. Commonwealth's Attorney, City of Richmond*[31] denying the right of privacy to consenting homosexuals. Apparently upon warrant or probable cause law enforcement officers may now begin nocturnal sweeps into bedrooms in search of sexual scofflaws.

Thus the only hope of preserving this seemingly clear right of privacy remains with the more benign states which, some by court action and some by legislative enactment, have curbed local zealots who suspect Sodom and Gomorrah behind every keyhole.

That leads to the murky field of obscenity. Everyone can agree that the term obscenity refers generically to speech, writing, cinematography and stage performances which deal with sex in such a manner as to put such forms of expression beyond protection of the First Amendment. But the appropriate test to apply creates the dilemma.

For years federal and state courts grappled with the *Roth* rule.[32] To some the problem was simple. The Wisconsin Supreme Court declared "obscenity is not so elusive a concept as to require expert testimony."[33] South Carolina agreed.[34] An Ohio judge adopted a simpler test: "That the material acts as an aphrodisiac can almost be determined physically . . . a judge or juror should be able to estimate that rather closely by the reaction he himself has to the material."[35] I can hear his jury instruction now: "Ladies and gentlemen of the jury: in the final analysis what is obscene is whatever turns you on."

Other courts were less self-confident; they required expert testimony on the concepts of prurient appeal,[36] customary limits of candor,[37] and the *Roth* test in general,[38] which one state referred to in terms of its "exquisite vagueness."[39]

Just as the states, one way or another, were adjusting to

Roth, in 1973 the rules of the game were changed in *Miller v. California*.[40] Whereas previously the High Court declared in *Roth* and reaffirmed in *Jacobellis v. Ohio*,[41] that "the constitutional status of an allegedly obscene work must be determined on the basis of a *national* Constitution we are expounding," in the new *Miller* test courts are to apply "contemporary *community* standards." (Italics added.)

Our court has trouble squaring the *Williams v. Florida*[42] approval of the requirement to reveal alibi witnesses with the constitutional freedom from self-incrimination. Most state courts recognize that a criminal defendant has a right to remain totally mute—he need not even speak to enter a plea; if he is silent, the court enters a not guilty plea on his behalf. Thus how can he be compelled to reveal his defense or his witnesses, and if he persists in remaining mute, how can sanctions be invoked?

Most recently the decision in *Hudgens v. National Labor Relations Board*[43]—a case one commentator declared had been rendered with "invincible myopia"[44]—overruled the eight-year-old decision in *Logan Valley Plaza*[45] and thus catapulted into doubt and confusion the validity of hundreds of state court decisions in the field of labor relations.

As the Supreme Court has careened from one end of the constitutional spectrum to the other[46] state courts have two alternatives. They can shift gears and once again change directions, thus resuming the course upon which they were embarked in the pre-Warren era. Or they can retain existing individual rights by reliance upon the independent nonfederal grounds found in the several state constitutions. A growing number of states have adopted the latter course.

Indeed, in December, 1975, Justice Brennan cordially invited the states to do so. In his dissent in *Michigan v. Mosley*[47] he reminded us that each "state has power to impose higher standards governing police practices under state law than is required by the Federal Constitution," citing *Oregon v. Hass*,[48] *Lego v. Twomey*,[49] *and Cooper v. California*[50] and he enumerated several courts which have done so.

I can supply a more exhaustive list, though undoubtedly still incomplete.

New Jersey[51] rejected *Schneckloth v. Bustamonte*[52] and the "totality of circumstances" test in determining the voluntariness of consent to search. The court interpreted the New Jersey constitution to require a waiver of rights standard, i.e., a knowing consent.

Michigan[53] rejected the "subjective predisposition" test for the entrapment defense, approved in *United States v. Russell,*[54] and selected instead a "government conduct" or objective test. Similar decisions have been made in Iowa,[55] New Mexico,[56] and Alaska.[57]

Michigan employed its constitution[58] to reject *United States v. White*[59] in finding a warrantless electronic surveillance invalid. And in another case[60] Michigan imposed a higher standard for double jeopardy than that required by the U.S. Supreme Court.

Oregon, too, has interpreted the double jeopardy clause of its state constitution independently of the similar provisions of the federal charter.[61]

Pennsylvania also rejected the double jeopardy approach of *Ashe v. Swenson*[62] but based its decision on its inherent supervisory power over criminal proceedings.[63]

Pennsylvania,[64] Hawaii,[65] and California[66] have refused to allow the impeachment exception to the *Miranda* exclusionary rule permitted by the Supreme Court in *Harris v. New York.*[67]

United States v. Robinson[68] and *Gustafson v. Florida*[69] permit law enforcement officers to make full body searches of the person incident to custodial arrests for traffic offenses and other minor violations which involve no tangible evidence. Hawaii[70] and California[71] directly rejected the *Robinson-Gustafson* rule and relied upon state constitutions to afford greater protection for their citizens.

I previously mentioned *Kirby v. Illinois*[72] which limited the right to counsel at lineups. Nevada[73] Oklahoma,[74] and Michigan[75] have declined to follow *Kirby* and have steadfastly clung to the *Wade*[76] principles pursuant to state charters.

The *Williams* rule on a notice of alibi requirement[77] has been discarded by Alaska, which found that "in accordance with our own unique legal background" a defendant need not so incriminate himself.[78]

Missouri refused to follow *California v. Green*[79] and will not permit prior inconsistent statements of a witness to be used as substantive evidence in a criminal case.[80]

The use of state grounds for state court decisions is not confined to criminal cases. There is a marked tendency to resolve novel civil issues on provisions of state constitutions.[81] For example, despite *Silver v. Silver,* an old Supreme Court case,[82] three states—North Dakota,[83] Wisconsin,[84] and California[85]—found guest statutes violative of state constitutions.

An interesting question arises if one of the parties to civil litigation raises a federal question, and the court deliberately ignores the issue while deciding the case on nonfederal grounds. This occurred in *Indiana Civil Liberties Union, Inc. v. Indiana War Memorials Commn.*[86] Claiming that the Indiana court had "attempted to preclude review of its decision in the case giving rise to this petition by failing to rule upon the Federal constitutional questions," the state Attorney General sought certiorari. His petition was denied.[87]

If I may be permitted a certain collegial immodesty, I must observe that California has a long record of reliance upon its own constitution.[88] Its bilingual charter, originally adopted in 1849, a year after the Treaty of Guadalupe Hidalgo, was clearly meant to be an independent source of individual rights. As presently constituted, the bill of rights in our state constitution[89] contains more specific individual guarantees than those enumerated in the Federal Constitution's first ten, plus the Fourteenth, Amendments. Indeed our charter specifically declares: "Rights guaranteed by this Constitution are not dependent on those guaranteed by the United States Constitution."[90]

Before the Supreme Court's decision in *Furman v. Georgia*[91] the California Supreme Court invoked the state cruel or unusual punishment prohibition to hold the death penalty invalid.[92] In virtually every area of constitutional law there are California cases resting squarely upon the state's own constitution.[93] Need I remind you: these are the folks who brought you *Serrano v. Priest.*[94] Two law review commentators have gone so far as to suggest that the "California Supreme Court may be likened, in these years of equal-protection gloom on the national scene, to those monks who kept classical learning alive so that it might be rediscovered in the Renaissance."[95]

At least two relevant questions arise regarding this recycled federalism. Is it historically tenable? Is it permitted by the Supreme Court? I respond affirmatively to both queries.

A reading of the *Federalist Papers* clearly reveals an intent by the Founding Fathers to leave the states as a repository of individual rights. Hamilton and Madison so declared over and over. Madison put it this way: "The powers delegated by the proposed Constitution to the federal government are few and defined. Those which are to remain in the State governments are numerous and indefinite. The former will be exercised principally on external objects, as war, peace, negotiation, and foreign commerce; with which last the power of taxation will for the most part, be connected. The powers reserved to the several States will extend to all the objects which, in the ordinary course of affairs, concern the lives, liberties, and properties of the people, and the internal order, improvement, and prosperity of the State."[96]

It is urged that most state constitutions derive universally in inspiration and often in text from provisions of the Federal Constitution. This is said to be particularly so with reference to bills of individual rights.

However, it may be noted with equal relevance that our Founding Fathers obtained their inspiration and texts for the first ten amendments from the predecessors of the states, the colonies and their declarations of rights. According to Professor Schwartz, the "Virginia Declaration of Rights set the example for eight of the 12 states which framed new Constitutions during the Revolutionary period,"[97] and it was the Pennsylvania Declaration of Rights of 1776 that, with regard to freedom of speech and press, was "the direct precurser of perhaps the most significant guarantee of the federal Bill of Rights."[98] Delaware's Declaration of Rights, 1776, inspired federal provisions against quartering of soldiers and ex post facto laws;[99] Maryland that same year prohibited bills of attainder,[100] and North Carolina's Declaration, 1776, "contains a compendium of most of the fundamental rights which had come to be recognized by American Constitution-makers: trial by jury, right to accusation and confrontation, privilege against self-incrimination, right against excessive bail or fines, cruel and unusual punishment, and general warrants, that not to be deprived of life, liberty, or property 'but by the law of the land,' freedom of the press, right to bear arms, freedom of conscience, and prohibition of ex post facto laws."[101]

As to contemporary authority, the Supreme Court has consistently held that states may impose higher standards than those required by the United States Constitution.[102] Justice Harlan in particular was a consistent advocate of decentralizing criminal justice, urging that state criminal procedure should be uninhibited by federal restraints as long as there is adherence to fundamental standards of fairness.[103] Chief Justice Burger has expressed a similar viewpoint.[104]

The most recent encouragement for this new attitude toward and by state courts can be traced to *Younger v. Harris,*[105] argued in 1969, reargued twice in 1970 and decided in early 1971. The opinion by Justice Black declared, "Since the beginning of this country's history Congress has, subject to few exceptions manifested a desire to permit state courts to try state cases free from interference by federal courts." The underlying reason for federal courts to abstain from interfering with state prosecution is "the notion of 'comity,' that is, a proper respect for state functions, a recognition of the fact that the entire country is made up of a Union of separate state governments, and a continuance of the belief that the National Government will fare best if the States and their institutions are left free to perform their separate functions in their separate ways."[106] This, said Justice Black, is the essence of federalism, to the ideal of which we must remain loyal.

To avoid any misunderstanding, let me emphasize that I am not advocating the right of state courts to differ with the United States Supreme Court on federal constitutional interpretations. Obviously if state courts unduly restrict individual rights under the Federal Constitution, the Supreme Court will take appropriate action.[107] And when state courts have presumed to extend individual rights under the United States Constitution more broadly than has the High Court, state decisions have also been reversed.[108]

What I am forecasting for the coming century is that more state courts will recognize that under our system of federalism the American constitutional scheme neither requires nor necessarily prefers that state judges conform their interpretation of state constitutions to the United States Supreme Court's interpretation of the Federal Constitution. Thus most jurisdictions will agree with Professor Linde that state courts *must* reach and resolve claims in state constitutional terms before proceeding to a consideration of any federal questions that lurk beneath the surface. He concludes that "only if the state constitution does not offer protection does it become appropriate for a state court to consider the case in federal constitutional terms."[109]

The use of state constitutions is no sport designed to thwart federal review, although much can be said for hastening the finality of court decisions. Nor is there anything inappropriate in deliberately seeking adequate nonfederal grounds upon which to base opinions, as implied by some critics.[110] There is not the slightest impropriety when the highest court of a *state* evaluates *state* legislation, *state* administrative action, or the conviction of a defendant in a *state* prosecution, pursuant to the provisions of the *state* constitution. Indeed logic would seem to compel that course. If the result is fragmentation of a national consciousness, it is justified in furtherance of an expanded liberty.

Why do we have two sets of constitutions—federal and state—in this one nation? Perhaps an answer can be found in this mythical quotation from Alice in Wonderland:[111]

Alice skwooched up her forehead and ventured quietly, "If he writes the same thing, why does he do it twice?"

"Because," said the White Rabbit, "he may write the same thing, but it's read differently."

The United States has learned much in two hundred years. But federal institutions still do not have all the solutions. Encouraging the fifty states to experiment, to retain their historic individuality, to seek innovative responses to problems of protecting individual liberty, may ultimately produce more of the answers in the century ahead.

FOOTNOTES

1. Mosk, Recycling the Old Circuit System, 27 So.Car.L.Rev. 633 (1976).
2. Commonwealth v. Webster, 59 Mass. 295 (1850).
3. Jennings v. Superior Court, 66 Cal.2d 867, 428 P.2d 304 (1967).
4. Johnson v. Superior Court, 15 Cal.3d 248, 255, 539 P.2d 792 (1975).

5. Paulsen, State Constitutions, State Courts and First Amendment Freedoms, 4 Vand.L.Rev. 620, 642 (1951).
6. Baker v. Carr, 369 U.S. 186 (1962); Reynolds v. Sims, 377 U.S. 533 (1964).
7. Graham, The Self-Inflicted Wound (1970).
8. 367 U.S. 643.
9. 395 U.S. 784.
10. Wilkes, The New Federalism in Criminal Procedure, (1974) 62 Ky.L.J. 421, 422.
11. People v. Cahan, 44 Cal.2d 434 (1955).
12. 388 U.S. 25.
13. 232 U.S. 383.
14. 96 N.W. 730 (Iowa 1903).
15. 7 Pet. 242 (U.S. 1833).
16. *Id.* at 247.
17. Beatty, State Court Evasion of United States Supreme Court Mandates During the Last Decade of the Warren Court, 6 Vand.L.Rev. 260 (1972).
18. People v. Krivda, 5 Cal.3d 357 (1971); 409 U.S. 33 (1972); 8 Cal.3d 623 (1973).
19. Wilkes, The New Federalism in Criminal Procedure, 62 Ky. L.J. 421 (1974).
20. Project Report, 8 Harv.Civil Rights-Civil Liberties Review 271, 272 (1973).
21. 388 U.S. 218 (1967).
22. 388 U.S. 263 (1967).
23. See, e.g., Escobedo v. Illinois, 378 U.S. 478 (1964).
24. 388 U.S. at p. 227 (italics in original).
25. 388 U.S. 293, 298 (1967) (italics added).
26. People v. Williams, 3 Cal.3d 853, 858 (1971), dissent by Mosk, J.
27. Beginning with People v. Forler, 1 Cal. 3d 335 (1969).
28. 406 U.S. 682 (1972).
29. Sobel, Eye-Witness Identification 33 (1972).
30. Olmstead v. United States, 277 U.S. 438 (1927), Brandeis, J., dissenting at p. 478.
31. 96 S. Ct. 1208 (1976).
32. Roth v. United States, 354 U.S. 476 (1957).
33. State v. Simpson, 201 N.W.2d 558 (Wis. 1972).
34. State v. Watkins, 191 S.E.2d 135 (S.C. 1972).
35. City of Cincinnati v. Walton, 145 N.E.2d 407 (Ohio 1957).
36. Ramirez v. State, 43 P.2d 826 (Okla.Crim.App. 1967).
37. G. P. Putnam's Sons v. Calissi, 205 A.2d 913 (N.J. 1964).
38. Sanza v. Maryland State Board of Censors, 226 A.2d 317 (Md. 1967); Keuper v. Wilson, 268 A.2d 753 (N.J. 1970).
39. Commonwealth v. La Londe, 288 A.2d 782 (Pa. 1972).
40. 413 U.S. 15 (1973).
41. 378 U.S. 184 (1964).
42. 399 U.S. 78 (1970).
43. 424 U.S. 507 (1976).
44. Prof. Arthur J. Miller writing in The Nation, April 10, 1976, p. 422.
45. Amalgamated Food Employees Union v. Logan Valley Plaza, 391 U.S. 308 (1968).
46. Levy, Against the Law 87 (1974).
47. 423 U.S. 96, 120 (1975).
48. 420 U.S. 714, 719 (1975).
49. 404 U.S. 477, 489 (1972).
50. 386 U.S. 58, 62 (1967).
51. State v. Johnson, 346 A.2d 66 (N.J. 1975); also see Robinson v. Cahill, 303 A.2d 273 (N.J. 1973).
52. 412 U.S. 218 (1973).
53. People v. Turner, 210 N.W. 2d 336 (Mich. 1973).
54. 411 U.S. 423 (1973).
55. State v. Mullen, 216 N.W.2d 375 (Iowa 1974).

56. 501 P.2d 1247, 1249 (N.M. 1972).
57. Grossman v. State, 457 P.2d 226 229 (Alaska 1969).
58. People v. Beavers, 227 N.W.2d 511 (Mich. 1975).
59. 401 U.S. 745 (1971).
60. People v. White, 212 N.W.2d 222 (Mich. 1973).
61. State v. Brown, 497 P.2d 1191 (Ore. 1972).
62. 397 U.S. 436 (1970).
63. Commonwealth v. Campana, 314 A.2d 854 (Pa. 1974), cert. den. 417 U.S. 969 (1974).
64. Commonwealth v. Triplet, 341 A.2d 62 (Pa. 1975).
65. State v. Santiago, 492 P.2d 657, 664 (Hawaii 1971).
66. People v. Disbrow, 16 Cal.3d 101, 545 P.2d 272 (Cal. 1976).
67. 401 U.S. 222 (1971).
68. 414 U.S. 218 (1973).
69. 414 U.S. 260 (1973).
70. State v. Kaluna, 520 P.2d 51 (Haw. 1974).
71. People v. Brisendine, 531 P.2d 1099 (Cal. 1975); People v. Longwill, 538 P.2d 753 (Cal. 1975).
72. 406 U.S. 682 (1972).
73. Baker v. State, 498 P.2d 1311. (Nev. 1972).
74. Chandler v. State, 501 P.2d 512 (Okla. 1972).
75. People v. Anderson, 205 N.W.2d 461 (Mich. 1973).
76. 388 U.S. 218 (1967).
77. Williams v. Florida, supra, 399 U.S. 78 (1970).
78. Scott v. State (Alaska 1974) 519 P.2d 774; also see the California case of Reynolds v. Superior Court, 528 P.2d 45 (Cal. 1974).
79. 399 U.S. 149 (1970).
80. State v. Granberry, 491 S.W.2d 528 (Mo. 1973).
81. Wilkes, The New Federalism in Criminal Procedure: State Court Evasion of the Burger Court, 62 Ky.L.J. 421, 450 (1974); Bush v. Reid, 516 P.2d 1215 (Alaska 1973); Brown v. Merlo, 506 P.2d 212 (Cal. 1973); Radone v. Superior Court, 488 P.2d 13 (Cal. 1971); Jolicoer v. Mihaly, 488 P.2d 1 (Cal. 1971); Serrano v. Priest, 487 P.2d 1241 (Cal. 1971); Blair v. Pitchess, 486 P.2d 1242 (Cal. 1971); Blocker v. Blackburn, 185 S.E.2d 56 (Ga. 1971); Corley v. Lewless, 182 S.E.2d 766 (Ga. 1971); Haas v. South Bend School Corp., 289 N.E.2d 499 (Ind. 1972); Milliken v. Green, 203 N.W.2d 457 (Mich. 1972); State ex rel. Payne v. Walden, 190 S.E.2d 770 (W.Va. 1972).
82. 280 U.S. 117 (1929).
83. John v. Hassett, 217 N.W.2d 771 (N.D. 1974).
84. McConville v. State Farm Automobile Insurance Co., 113 N.W.2d 14 (Wis. 1972).
85. Brown v. Merlo, 8 Cal.3d 855 (1973).
86. 291 N.E.2d 888 (Ind. 1973).
87. 414 U.S. 859 (1973).
88. In 1955 California adopted the exclusionary rule, six years before the United States Supreme Court applied Wolf v. Colorado, 338 U.S. 25 (1948) to the states in Mapp v. Ohio, 367 U.S. 643 (1961). The Supreme Court of California adopted the position deliberately in People v. Cahan, 44 Cal.2d 434 (1955), when Chief Justice Roger Traynor wrote that provisions of the Constitution "contemplate that it is preferable that some criminals go free than that the right of privacy of all the people be set at naught." (*Id.* at p. 449.) In taking that step, Justice Traynor declared that "In developing a rule of evidence applicable in the state courts, this court is not bound by the decisions that have applied the federal rule, and if it appears that those decisions have developed needless refinements and distinctions, this court need not follow them." (*Id.*, p. 450.)
89. Article I, sections 1-28.

90. Article I. section 24.
91. 408 U.S. 238 (1972).
92. People v. Anderson, 493 P.2d 880 (Cal. 1972).
93. For a compilation see Falk, The State Constitution: A More Than "Adequate" Nonfederal Ground, 61 Cal.L.Rev. 273, 277-278, fns. 17 & 18 (1973); for a most flattering analysis of "California's example" see the extensive list of state bill of rights cases discussed in 8 Harvard Civil Rights-Civil Liberties Review 324-326 (1973); also Wright, The Role of the Judiciary: From Marbury to Anderson, 60 Cal.L.Rev. 1262, 1269-1272 (1972).
94. Serrano v. Priest, 5 Cal.3d 581 (1971).
95. Horowitz and Karst, The California Supreme Court and State Action Under the Fourteenth Amendment, 21 UCLA L.Rev. 1421 (1974).
96. Federalist Papers, No. 45; also see Numbers 14, 23, 32, 39, 43, 82, 83. The following excerpt from Number 17, Hamilton, is particularly significant on the role of the state judiciary:

    "There is one transcendent advantage belonging to the province of the State governments, which alone suffices to place the matter in a clear and satisfactory light—I mean the ordinary administration of criminal and civil justice. This, of all others, is the most powerful, most universal, and most attractive source of popular obedience and attachment. It is this which, being the immediate and visible guardian of life and property, having its benefits and its terrors in constant activity before the public eye, regulating all those personal interests and familiar concerns to which the sensibility of individuals is more immediately awake, contributes more than any other circumstance to impressing upon the minds of the people affection, esteem, and reverence towards the government. This great cement of society, which will diffuse itself almost wholly through the channels of the particular governments, independent of all other causes of influence, would insure them so decided an empire over their respective citizens as to render them at all times a complete counterpoise, and, not unfrequently, dangerous rivals to the power of the Union."
97. 1 Schwartz, The Bill of Rights: A Documentary History 256 (1971).
98. *Id.* at p. 262.
99. *Id.* at p. 276.
100. *Id.* at p. 279.
101. *Id.* at p. 286.
102. See Jankovich v. Indiana Toll Road Commn., 379 U.S. 487, 491-492 (1965); Cooper v. California, 386 U.S. 58, 62 (1967); Sibron v. New York, 392 U.S. 40, 60-61 (1968); Lego v. Twomey, 404 U.S. 477, 489 (1972); Oregon v. Hass, 420 U.S. 714, 719, fn. 4, (1975).
103. Griffin v. California, 380 U.S. 609 (1965) (conc. opn.); Malloy v. Hogan, 378 U.S. 1 (1964) (dissenting opn.); Cicenia v. Lagay, 357 U.S. 504 (1958).
104. California v. Green, 399 U.S. 149 (1970).
105. 401 U.S. 37 (1971); also see Carey v. Sugar, 96 S.Ct. 1208 (1976).
106. 401 U.S. at 44.
107. See, e.g., Morrissey v. Brewer, 408 U.S. 471 (1972); Argersinger v. Hamlin, 407 U.S. 25 (1972); Dickey v. Florida, 398 U.S. 30 (1970); Roe v. Wade, 410 U.S. 113 (1973).
108. See, e.g. California v. Green, 399 U.S. 149 (1970); California v. Byers, 402 U.S. 424 (1971); Michigan v. Payne, 412 U.S. 47 (1973).
109. Linde, Without Due Process, 49 Ore.L.Rev. 125 (1970).
110. See, e.g., Bice, Anderson and the Adequate State Ground, 45 So.Cal.L.Rev. 750 (1972).
111. This delightful creation can be found in the fine new publication of the young members of the American Bar Association: 2 A.B.A. Barrister, p. 49.

JUDICIAL REFORM IN THE NEXT CENTURY: A JUDGE GAZES INTO THE CRYSTAL BALL

Irving R. Kaufman*

The writer on judicial administration is no longer the *rara avis* he once was. Thus, I can understand Learned Hand's response when called upon to deliver the Holmes Lectures on the Bill of Rights. He said: "My subject is well-worn; it is not likely that I shall have new light to throw on it; but it is always fresh, and particularly at the present time it is important enough to excuse renewed examination."

Neither prophecy nor the problems confronting us are made easier or more certain of solution by repetition. It is, therefore, with some trepidation that I have undertaken the task of addressing those reforms in our methods of judicial administration which the next century may see. The task is, it seems to me, one that would give pause to the Delphic oracle. I should perhaps find some small solace in Justice Frankfurter's assurance, that a judge must be able "to pierce the curtain of the future—give shape and visage to mysteries still in the womb of time." But while I am, after all, a judge, I am not omniscient. I must, therefore, rely upon doubt and scrutiny, as man's most serviceable tools, in summoning whatever prophetic powers I may have.

I. *INTRODUCTION*

A. The Goal in Utopia: No Litigant should be Deterred By Cost and Delay from Trial

At a time when our state and federal courts can barely stay afloat in a latter-day deluge of litigation, the thesis I would offer for consideration will, I fear, sound like a prayer for

*Chief Judge, United States Court of Appeals, Second Circuit.

more rain. Nevertheless I would suggest that too few of the lawsuits filed today are resolved by trial and too many prospective litigants with sound cases are being deterred from bringing suit. Presently, in the federal district courts, more than 90% of all civil cases, and almost 90% of all criminal cases, are terminated short of trial. Many judges view this high proportion of settlements as a necessary and desirable safety valve without which the courts would founder. I perceive such an extraordinarily high proportion of settlements, however, as an index of injustice that mirrors the malevolent workings of the twin demons that plague our judicial system: cost and delay.

Of course, some settlements will occur before trial even in a healthy court system, for there are many grievances far better settled by amicable compromise than by a court of law. Trial of meritless suits squanders our precious—and limited—judicial resources and we should implement procedures to eliminate such suits from court dockets. But a judicial system merely churning out dispositions in all cases through settlement and plea-bargaining cannot be regarded as adequately fulfilling its role, particularly if the judge consumes time in securing the settlement at the expense of presiding over a trial. And a settlement ratio as high as that currently found in our nation's courts is certain evidence that some plaintiffs who have "legal rights" to plenary relief are being coerced by the cost of justice into accepting far less than their due while some defendants are yielding to opportunistic litigants who unabashedly wield the expenses of litigation as a weapon to extort undeserved settlements.

I therefore suggest that the lodestar by which we steer our course into the next century be this simple, yet far-reaching proposition: No civil litigant or criminal defendant or prosecutor should be bludgeoned into a settlement or a bargained-plea, nor, indeed, should any individual be deterred from seeking judicial resolution of a meritorious grievance, by the cost and delay of proceeding to trial. As we celebrate the Bicentennial, we are charged with avoiding trials like the plague, and running our courts as assembly-line operations. This is the very antithesis of the fair hearing and considered judgment that the framers of our Constitution sought to guarantee.

Let me elaborate upon the reasons for my view that the trial should be the primary desideratum of a properly functioning judicial system. Every private civil case involves a plaintiff whose motive falls somewhere between spite or blackmail and an earnest desire to remedy a justifiable and uncompensated grievance. Human nature being what it is, resolution of the dispute by a neutral decision-maker with authority to enforce its judgment will in many cases be the only real alternative to correcting some form of deviant behavior. In the criminal field the importance of courts and trials is even more pronounced: the courts provide the only assurance of the just, consistent and sure enforcement of norms of social behavior. In short, although some may view my omnibus trial proposal as unduly idealistic and impractical, I believe it to be the necessary and proper goal of a judicial system which will not breed cynicism and distrust.

At the risk of destroying your suspense by disclosing the plot in advance, I will, at this point, give a very brief preview of the scope and impact of this key axiom. No one can fail to be aware that perhaps the principal defect of our system of justice is its cost. Yet, it is all too easy for the scholar or would-be reformer to adopt the stance of Professor Pangloss: to ignore the full extent of the problem or to conclude that there is no remedy. It will therefore be profitable to trace briefly both the pervasive extent of cost and delay, and their corrosive impact upon our judicial system. I will then detail steps we must—and, I believe, shall—take to secure speedy, just, and inexpensive resolution of every dispute.

I shall identify three paths which reform may follow: (1) increasing the courts' efficiency; (2) streamlining the litigation process; and (3) diverting certain classes of disputes from the courts. I shall, within this framework, make three major proposals for change, one for each category: (1) the courts must be adequately financed and staffed, and they should make increased use of parajudges and specialized court staff to increase their efficiency and productivity; (2) we must design radically simplified procedures for the small case to streamline the litigation process where appropriate; and (3) the current trend toward diversion of controversies to nonjudicial dispute resolution must be accelerated, to divert from the crowded court dockets those types of disputes that can better be resolved elsewhere.

B. Barriers to Utopia: The Costs of Justice

Let me now begin my examination of the expense and delay which pervades our system. Learned Hand's stinging indictment of our courts is, if anything, more true today than it was in 1921: "As a litigant I should dread a lawsuit beyond almost anything short of sickness and death." Delay in the resolution of disputes is the most visible, although perhaps not the most serious, symptom of this judicial malady. Although protracted litigation, of course, is hardly a new phenomenon, our backlogs are nevertheless grave enough to warrant serious attention. Magellan's crew sailed around the world in an old wooden ship in three years; yet today the resolution, or even the commencement of the trial of many serious cases takes a far longer period. In criminal litigation the problems caused by inadequate judicial resources are multiplied by the inability of understaffed prosecutors' and public defenders' offices to grow at the same speed as an exponentially increasing crime rate.

Delay is, however, but one reason why so many cases which really should be resolved by a trial are settled long before—or never filed at all. The sheer monetary cost of seeking judicial relief may well be the greatest barrier to court access. For example, discovery under the liberalized Federal Rules of Civil Procedure has become for many a game of harassment, with the process little more than an ordeal for parties subjected, in effect, to two trials instead of one. It is a customary, and often successful tactic to disable the other party both by burdensome requests for discovery and by release of only the most limited information. Indeed, in one recent case, 1265 depositions comprising 144,000 pages of transcript were generated *before* trial. My point is not that we should expect litigants to act out an *Alice in Wonderland* script and come forward graciously saying "here is damaging information you may use against me." But, let us not overlook that the process of extraction of the facts has become a very expensive exercise, requiring the services of an attorney or even a corps of counsel, who may be quite well paid.

A second costly undertaking is that of transforming facts into judicially acceptable forms of proof and bringing them to the courthouse. Dented fenders and broken windows are not viewed *in situ*; the litigant must arrange to tell his story through witnesses, authenticated documents, color photographs, scale models, and so on.

Still a third element in the equation of cost is the transformation of the dispute into the language of the law. Skilled craftsmen must be employed to draft and file pleadings, motions and briefs, and to introduce evidence at trial. The costs attendant upon adversary discovery, judicial forms of proof, and use of the language of the law, moreover, are built into our criminal justice system by constitutional rights which are the steel undergirding of the criminal process. They concern themselves with self-incrimination or discovery for the prosecutor, confrontation of witnesses and the need for trials or proof of the case, and notice and representation by counsel, i.e. transformation into legal language.

C. *The Corrosive Impact of Expense and Delay*

The effects which the twin demons—delay and expense—have on the utopian "friction-free" judicial system I earlier posited are startling. The primary impact in private civil litigation is felt by the blameless defendant or plaintiff. Before deciding to submit all the facts at trial to an admittedly fair and detached decision-maker, each party would first be forced to consider an externality, the cost of justice itself. With distressing frequency the expense of a coerced settlement, even after paying court and counsel fees, may be far less than the price of justice. We long ago eliminated trial by ordeal—but some charge it has been replaced with ordeal by trial. Delay, moreover, has a deleterious effect on the outcome of those cases that do come to trial. For example, few witnesses can recall with precision an accident that occurred four or five years before. And compensation is deferred far past the time when the injured plaintiff was plagued by medical and other expenses and most urgently needed the money.

Perhaps even more serious are the secondary effects on the future behavior of the offending party. The disabling effect which resort to the judicial process may have on a putative defendant or plaintiff is the modern American Ring of Gyges for the unscrupulous litigant. The strike suit by a shareholder against his corporation is a frequently cited example. But one can with equal justification point to the Chicago slumlord who turns off his tenants' heat several days each month to save fuel costs, secure in the knowledge that his tenants will be deterred from asserting their rights by the expense they would incur.

The failings in our criminal justice system produce societal consequences of a most serious nature. Having long since passed the point where we can simply leave the question of guilt or innocence in every case to twelve good and true men and women of the vicinage, we must now place enormous reliance upon plea-bargaining, where the defendant pits his relative guilt and the gravity of his offense against the present strength of the prosecutor's case, and the other demands made on the time of the judge, prosecutor, and defense counsel. We must not overlook that defendants also suffer the consequences of hazy memories and stale evidence against which the speedy trial clause was designed to protect. And, if it should come to pass that a case goes to trial and a verdict of guilty eventually is returned, much of the deterrent effect that might have resulted from swift judgment and punishment is lost.

II. *MOVING TOWARDS UTOPIA*

Having hopefully clarified the evils whose eradication must be sought by those of us concerned with sound and effective judicial administration, I would now like to elucidate a few steps which we might, in the next century, take toward that goal's realization.

Preliminarily, we must recognize that no efforts by the courts to slay the twin dragons—cost and delay—can succeed if legislatures continue to enact laws without providing the resources to cope with the increase in litigation these statutes spawn. In the last Congress alone, 26,000 bills were introduced, and hundreds of those were enacted into law, without more than *en passant* regard to their impact on the federal judicial system. Even while the Judicial Conference of the United States, required by law to undertake detailed studies of court needs quadrennially, is now preparing its recommendations for 1980, the Congress has failed to meet the request for needed judgeships submitted in 1972 for the ensuing four years.

This observation is strikingly illustrated by mere mention of a few among the thousands of laws passed within the past few years: the Freedom of Information Act, the Occupational Safety and Health Act, the Black Lung Benefits Act, the Speedy Trial Act. Sometimes, the litigation by-products of Congressional handiwork are amusing rather than overwhelming. Thus, a Federal district court was recently called upon to decide whether a Boy Scout who removed the talons from the partially decomposed carcass of a bald eagle had violated the criminal provisions of the Bald Eagle Protection Act. The court, perhaps fearful of being deluged with thousands of prosecutions of Eagle Scouts, held that he had not. Of course, the humorous aspects of the situation should not blind us to the ominous.

The courts are, in short, flattered by Congress's confidence in the judicial branch but are, nevertheless, being smothered by it. Congress can no longer be blind to the effects its statutes have upon the requirements of the judicial system. Just as state and local governments are beginning to pay for their binges of past years, so too is our society paying the price for the legislators' legal "binge" and their failure to provide sufficient judicial resources to cope with what they have spawned. As ever-increasing resort is made to the judiciary as the arbiters of all possible problems that befall man, without providing the wherewithal to deal with those demands, the courts now suffer the inevitable hangover.

The review Congress must undertake cannot adequately be accomplished on an ad hoc, informal basis. In this regard it is instructive to note that the Congressional Budget Office has assumed the difficult but important task of analyzing effects proposed legislation may have on national spending, prices, and employment. A parallel office, embracing similar professional procedures, should be established within the Congress to assess the impact on the judiciary of every significant piece of federal legislation that may affect the courts. Moreover, committee reports should be required to include analyses of the likely effects of the legislation on such factors as the volume of litigation, possible delays and costs, jury needs, as well as the consequent need for more federal judges.

It is essential, therefore, that legislators adopt methods by which they may estimate the impact of their enactments on the courts. It is equally important that court reformers do likewise, and project the effects of their changes, whether by rules or otherwise, in advance. But we cannot afford to forget that predictions tend to be inaccurate; indeed, totally accurate predictions are impossible. I am told that one otherwise reputable criminologist recently extrapolated from current statistics in the State of Georgia to predict the likely prison population in the future. He concluded, I am sure with tongue in cheek, that by the year 2014 *everyone* living in the state will be in prison. In addition to the dangers of the improper use of statistics, we should be aware that most administrative modifications may have unexpected and significant side effects on the outcome of litigation as well as on trial quality. To complicate the problem still further, since the types of controversy brought to court change over a period of time, so will the effect of any given procedural device.

For these reasons, the only realistic approach to reform is a flexible one. Each proposal for change, once adopted, must not be sanctified after it has outlived its purpose, but rather must be the subject of periodic reexamination.

I should, at this point, note one suggested path for reform that would, in my opinion, be a step in the wrong direction. I refer, of course, to the National Court of Appeals proposed by the Hruska Commission. It would seem elementary that delay and expense are likely to be exacerbated by the erection of yet another layer of review in the federal courts. And there are other costs less apparent yet equally likely. One principal effect of the new court, for example, would be to downgrade the authority of the Courts of Appeals at a time when the need to attract lawyers of the highest caliber to the federal bench is, perhaps, greater than ever.

One would think it obvious that only an overriding necessity could counterbalance these sizeable costs. Yet, as I have noted in the past, the showing of need is, to say the least, "rather unconvincing". The principal *raison d'etre* advanced for a National Court is the resolution of inter-circuit conflicts that an overloaded Supreme Court is seen as currently unable to handle. The Commission's own statistics, however, suggest that there are only about fifty such conflicts a year—hardly a hefty enough caseload to warrant the heavy cost of creating an entirely new court of seven judges. In addition, a significant reduction in the Supreme Court's workload could be achieved through less radical measures, such as the elimination of mandatory direct appeals to the Supreme Court from every decision of three-judge constitutional courts.* The National Court's benefits, in sum, appear trivial and uncertain, and its costs and impact on the federal judicial system too substantial, to warrant its creation.

Although I am virtually certain that my efforts at divining the future will within a decade prove far wide of the mark, I would like now to launch at least a few suggestions concerning the direction meaningful reform might take. If concrete proposals fail to win general acceptance, it is at least possible to indicate the course that future efforts are likely to take. As I have indicated, I believe that in our general framework for discussion we must recognize that any remedies for delay and costs in trial courts must either (1) increase the courts' efficiency, (2) shorten the litigation process, or (3) where appropriate, divert disputes from the courts.

A. *Enhancing the Efficiency of the Courts*

An encyclopedia would likely prove insufficient even to catalogue the numerous suggestions and the voluminous literature which each of these three seemingly simple categories has spawned. Were a bibliography prepared for the first group—increasing efficiency—most of its space would doubtless be devoted to the numerous studies and proposals aimed at curing defective caseflow management. I do not gainsay that caseflow reform is important, for differences in caseflow administration procedures do have a significant effect on delay. But I wish to focus on an approach to increasing efficiency at once more radical and more attractive: the increased use of parajudges and specialized staff. Parajudges who may conduct pre-trial hearings, deal with discovery, assist with motions, calendars and other preliminary matters will go far to free the judge to turn his skills and training to trying more cases and thus clearing the dockets. Eighteen years ago, when I first proposed the increased use of special masters in discovery proceedings, reference of such matters to masters was the very rare exception rather than the rule. Masters were not considered a legitimate

* *On August 12, 1976, President Ford signed S.537, a bill restricting the use of three-judge courts to apportionment cases and instances where specifically provided by statute (i.e. Civil Rights Act of 1964 and Voting Rights Act of 1976).*

means for easing crowded dockets, but rather were viewed as a device for lazy judges. But the use of "parajudges" to streamline the judicial process has, since that time, come to be viewed as an increasingly attractive option.

In characterizing the use of specialists as a radical suggestion, however, I was considering a potential utilization which goes far beyond such obvious and mundane tasks as assisting with pre-trial hearings and motions. I foresee that, in the very near future, the courts may request, in complicated, specialized or unusually important cases, the disinterested expert opinion of legal scholars. The tax law has grown so hopelessly complex, for example, that few of us—even those of us who are judges called upon to decide tax cases—would choose to fill out our own tax returns without expert assistance. It is even less defensible for the courts to be denied expert assistance in complicated tax cases, assistance rarely provided by busy, generalist private practitioners. The state or federal government could provide for the printing of the experts' amicus briefs, and for some modest compensation. Indeed, we might well develop a tradition of regarding such public service as one of the most honorable responsibilities of the profession.

A related procedure would be for court units of appropriate size (e.g., an entire federal circuit, or a large district court) to retain the services of experts who have mastered certain legal specialties. Without supplanting the judge's personal "elbow" law clerk, the circuit staff specialist in a given field could prepare bench memoranda for all judges hearing cases in his field of expertise. These memoranda would be designed to point out any important cases or issues overlooked by the parties in their briefs.

The use of such staff specialists may advance additional goals as well. Litigants could be saved most of the costs associated with use of the "language of the law," without any diminution in the quality of legal analysis presented to the courts, if these staff memoranda were prepared as a matter of course in every appropriate case. These analyses should be required to state both sides of a question without indicating a firm preference for either one. Copies could be furnished to the parties (who would have identified the issues contested), and they could then be permitted to forego the filing of their own briefs. If they believed the staff memo was somehow incomplete or inadequate, they could file briefs covering only those points requiring further elaboration or exposition.

An alternative to specialized staff law clerks employed by individual districts or circuits could be a national resource center, along the lines of the "back-up centers" utilized by the Legal Services Offices to prepare comprehensive memoranda (and, indeed, in preparing pleadings and other papers) in specialized areas. These centers would not signal the demise of private attorneys. Rather, we might anticipate that they could improve judicial decision-making while simultaneously permitting persons of modest means to avoid the disparity in the quality of justice which in too many instances only money currently can cure.

Nor should this specialized, expert assistance be restricted to matters of law. Many cases now or potentially before the courts involve complex questions of science and technology that judges and lawyers are ill-equipped to answer without aid. For example, are nuclear power plants too dangerous? What shall we do with nuclear waste material? What bodily functions should define the cessation of human life? What are the environmental effects of supersonic transport aircraft?

At present, the judge is placed in the uneasy position of umpiring a battle of experts serving as "hired guns" to the litigants. Would it not make sense in light of these serious scientific questions which do and will confront judges, to establish an Office of Science Advisor to the Courts, in which scientific claims can be *objectively* screened, tested, and evaluated?

Indeed, the areas in which the courts could profit from the aid of a nationally-based expert group extend beyond the realm of the purely scientific. The courts, for example, sorely require guidance on what is currently the most capricious phase of criminal proceedings: sentencing. Studies of sentencing procedures—for example, the Second Circuit's proposed sentencing rules—have deplored the inadequacy of the information provided the judge, as well as the lack of any substantive criteria to guide him. The Second Circuit's Sentencing Committee is currently considering sentencing guidelines or "benchmarks"—i.e., recommended terms for different types of offenses—to remove much of the arbitrariness from the sentencing process. A nationally-based group could undertake empirical sentencing studies both to determine the efficacy of these guidelines and the rehabilitative impact of different sentences upon different defendants. These studies could be used periodically to update the benchmarks, and thus make sentencing procedures something more than the lottery they currently are.

Let me hasten to add that I am not unmindful of the financial burden these proposals may place on the state and federal governments—although one suspects that the cost will be somewhat less than that of a single advanced air force plane. But even acknowledging the dollar costs to federal or state governments, I believe my suggestions will provide cost *savings* for our society *as a whole.* I speak not only of savings to those litigants who will find no need to file briefs to supplement those prepared by the courts' scholar-experts. These proposals will have even more important and far-reaching effects: they will enable poor and middle-class litigants, currently barred by high legal fees, to bring their meritorious legal claims to the courts. And, these staff services should also induce a marked improvement in the quality of judicial decisions, by providing the expert assistance judges have needed. Although we tend to overlook the *social* costs of insufficient access to the courts and sub-optimal resolution of disputes, they are *real* costs nonetheless, and they are of staggering magnitude. These costs must not be ignored simply because they do not appear in official governmental budget documents or because they tend to be borne in silence. Moreover, because of the vitality of the important doctrine of stare decisis, all consumers may suffer, for example, if a poor-quality decision is rendered in a case involving a single consumer whose attorney failed to make the best factual and legal presentation to the court.

The expenses of staff experts and other court personnel should properly be absorbed by the Government. I find it distressing that our country, which prides itself on respect for law and free access to its courts, currently devotes roughly 1/50th of 1% of its national income—only $304 million out of our $1.4 trillion annual gross national product—to the entire federal judicial system.

In addition to reducing total societal costs, my proposals

would serve to lessen delay in the courts. A staff *specialist* can prepare high quality memoranda faster than most *generalist* litigators can furnish even mediocre ones, a fact well illustrated by the excellent performance of the staff law clerks who furnish memoranda to the judges of the Second Circuit in *pro se* matters. I would require twice my allotted space to expound fully on this proposal. I believe, however, that I would be remiss if I did not at least pose the question.

B. Sreamlining the Trial

Increasing the courts' efficiency is, of course, but one way of reducing the litigants' cost and delay. Another approach which has received equal attention of late is the modification and modernizing of trial procedures. The features of our judicial system which I enumerated at the outset—adversary discovery, judicial forms of proof, and the use of the language of the law—are in many cases unduly cumbersome and costly, all too readily abused by lawyers to harass their opponents. There is, therefore, much room for procedural reform, limited only by the imagination and courage of the reformers. Future procedural changes may attempt to drive the parties to clarify the issues and streamline the trial. Much discovery and trial time could be saved, for example, by strict enforcement of rules requiring the parties to stipulate all facts not fairly in dispute and perhaps imposing the costs of proof on a litigant who obstinately refuses to stipulate. And the courts might begin to fine or penalize the dilatory attorney himself, rather than his often blameless client.

Much time and expense might be saved if we could nip in the bud those frivolous cases where discovery would have encompassed millions of documents and man-hours. But, this proposal should not be adopted until it has been tested experimentally and evaluated. I offer no "final judgment" on this particular proposal. As with many of my recommendations today, what is most important is *not* that we reach a quick decision on their merits, but that we avoid both inertia and over-reaction. We must seek out new ideas, but also pre-test and then re-evaluate them carefully lest we jump from one fad or supposed panacea to another and in the process do great mischief.

Although much will be gained by promulgating such general procedural reforms as these, an even more promising possibility, in my opinion, would be to provide variegated procedures for different types of cases; in other words, to tailor the trial to the case. While much attention has been given to development of special procedural devices for the "big" case, far too little thought has been devoted to the small case. Yet the costly panoply of discovery, motions, briefs, and trial is wholly unwarranted in most small cases. Where the amount in controversy falls below a specified sum, rules mandating a drastically curtailed procedure might be appropriate. Of course, any such rules should be mindful that there are cases involving small sums but, nevertheless, important legal rights or principles. Some screening procedure might be desirable, to ensure that while we make the judicial system swift, it remains just. The parties to small cases simply cannot afford the application of the full-blown adversary process, at least as it is presently structured. It is a luxury we may have to forego. Perhaps in the future we may even be forced to reconsider the accepted learning that arming the court itself with some investigative powers would impermissibly bias a neutral decision-maker. Where the result would be to deny all redress whatsoever, such concern for passive impartiality might appear to some observers misplaced.

Similarly, we might begin to investigate alternatives to the now-hallowed practice of transforming all evidence into judicially acceptable forms of proof, and bringing it into court. Where the cost of collecting and introducing evidence through witnesses, authenticated documents, photographs, and X-rays is prohibitive, the obvious short-cut may be to dispense with courtrooms altogether. Perhaps it would be sufficient in some instances to have judges, in effect, "ride circuit" to view the evidence *in situ*.

In the small case the use of formal legal terminology and procedures that require the services of a lawyer must be overhauled. Although it would be impossible to dispense with legal research, the cumbersome procedure by which legal ideas are conveyed, and the expense of typing, printing and reproduction, might, where appropriate, be modified. For all its imprecision, there is still no cheaper medium than oral communication.

C. *Diversion from the Courts*

Both approaches to reform which I have now discussed—increasing the courts' efficiency, and shortening the litigation process—concentrate on improvement within the courtroom. But today some, indeed many, disputes, are best resolved outside the courthouse walls. As Dean Cramton of Cornell, the Chairman of the new National Legal Services Corporation, recently observed, a society where the adversary system creeps into normal parts of life is an unhappy one. A person who works out his problems with his neighbor and retailer is happier. The proper bounds for diversion to a non-judicial means of dispute resolution in a society plagued by cost and delay, moreover, may be even broader than Dean Cramton's comment might suggest. In our imperfect world, there are two quite different species of cases for which diversion will prove useful. First are those controversies the removal of which from the judicial system should only be, hopefully, for the nonce. As we approach the ideal of inexpensive and prompt justice the resolution of those matters will gradually be reincorporated. The second variety consists of cases about which we might consider changing our notions of justiciability. Bluntly, I refer to instances where the adversary process may in fact be of little worth.

The distinguishing characteristic of the former group is, not surprisingly, the cost which their resolution imposes on both the judicial system and the litigants. Unhappily it is true that, for some time to come, neither parties nor public will be able to afford processing many cases which in the best of all possible worlds would be decided at trial. The area most widely discussed is automobile accident litigation. The total failure of the tort liability compensation system has become painfully apparent. Less than half the cost of liability insurance goes to compensate victims, and the long litigation process delays recovery for years beyond the time it is most urgently needed. Moreover, the goals of the system are questionable: the party at "fault" is as much in need of compensation for medical expenses as is the "innocent" victim. Indeed, the system is so infected with delay that it has become inefficient even in detecting who is at fault; its determination depends on a jury's evaluation of witnesses' fading recollections of events that happened several years before.

And, there is the cost to the courts: 17% of state judges' time is consumed by automobile accident litigation.

The approach of recent "no fault" statutes holds promise, as they effectively remove a great number of small claims from the courts. But even these systems could be improved. An automobile compensation system modelled after the workmen's compensation acts, and administered by a special agency would be both efficient and inexpensive. Compulsory arbitration for no-fault claims might also be considered. In any event, it is difficult to believe that our tort liability system, so profligate with litigants' time and money, as well as with the courts' resources, will be allowed to continue much longer in its present form.

Small claims—particularly, consumer claims for defective merchandise or services—are perfect candidates for court diversion. Too often the wronged consumer may find that bearing his relatively minor losses in silence is far preferable to costly, time-consuming, and uncertain litigation. The result is that, at least for the unscrupulous merchant, crime does pay.

In response to this problem, small claims courts, with radically simplified procedures, have been created in most states and have become the subject of a large body of literature, including many empirical studies. Indeed, the American Bar Association is about to engage in an in-depth study of these courts. Several reports at hand have informed us that such courts, in some jurisdictions at least, are little more than collection agencies for ghetto merchants. This, however, does not mean that the concept of a court with informal, inexpensive procedures should be abandoned. Rather, it emphasizes that reforms are needed. For example, excessively litigious or corporate plaintiffs should not have easy access to the small claims court. Indeed, even more flexible approaches to consumer grievance resolution may prove fruitful. Some commentators have suggested a no-fault approach to consumer law: a government agency would reimburse defrauded consumers immediately, and would then proceed against the merchant. Consumer dishonesty would be curbed by spot checks buttressed by criminal sanctions.

We should not lose sight of the fact that the reason for shunting such cases aside does not lie in any inherent defect in the court or the trial as a method of dispute resolution. Quite the contrary: if delay and cost were not insuperable obstacles, I insist that there is no fairer or more sensitive method of determining whether an alleged lumbo-sacral sprain is in fact only a feigned whiplash, or whether the manufacturer or the retailer was responsible for a child's defective bicycle brakes. The fault lies rather with the administration of justice, and until we are able to process cases more quickly and cheaply, it is the litigant who must suffer.

But there is another species of controversy which, even under more felicitous conditions, may well have no place in the courts. Within this category fall those cases in which the interest in governmental regulation is minimal, or which for a variety of reasons might *better* be handled outside the judicial system.

Too often we have indulged the fiction that the mere enactment of a statute or promulgation of a regulation will cure some persistent problem that has not proven amenable to other solution. Like the physician frustrated by the slow recovery of a patient, doses of "law" are administered as a "wonder-drug" with little regard for its possible deleterious side-effects or, indeed, for its lack of *any* effect. The question has been asked by some commentators whether we have in fact become "overformalized and oversupplied with legal machinery."

Apart from the familiar catch-phrase, "victimless crimes," perhaps the classic example of an area in which court intervention is destructive as well as time-consuming is the amorphous "persons in need of supervision" jurisdiction of the juvenile courts. To curtail the freedom of individuals who have broken no law is an anomaly in our legal system. And, ironically, PINS programs are as likely to breed crime as to prevent it. Even at their best, they have not been shown to benefit significant numbers of children. And at their worst, they become little more than a device for shunting an unruly or unpopular child off to training school. For these reasons, the Institute of Judicial Administration-American Bar Association Juvenile Justice Standards Project, of which I am privileged to serve as chairman, has recommended that the controversial PINS jurisdiction in the courts be abolished entirely, and taken over by an effective outside agency.

I should add one concluding note. My own jurisdiction today extended to the amorphous and almost infinite entirety of "judicial administration". I confess to having undergone a degree of shock upon learning that the 1976 supplement prepared by my dear friend Professor Fannie Klein to her monumental 1963 bibliography on judicial administration ran some 1100 pages. Accordingly, selectivity has been a necessity, and I have had to treat gingerly many areas of fascinating promise for the 21st century.

I have, instead, concentrated principally upon several promising methods of reducing the cost and delay of litigation. I have discussed, for example, increased use of parajudges and staff "scholar-experts," the development of simplified procedures for small cases, and the removal and diversion of many classes of disputes from the courts. The ultimate goal envisioned by my proposals is a system in which expense and delay will no longer curtail a meritorious lawsuit short of trial. And, we must be guided at all times by the maxim that no litigant should be forced to forego his or her day in court by methods of disposition which serve expediency but not justice. Since my focus has been upon judicial efficiency, I have also truncated my discussion of methods for improving the quality of the judicial output, although, of course, I do not slight the importance of these problems. I have also been forced to omit entirely any mention of possible technological advances that may one day alter the very manner in which the courts go about their business. These developments are rapidly moving from the once-exclusive province of science-fiction writers to that of judicial administrators. Examples that quickly come to mind include the use of videotape to prerecord entire trials, with excludable testimony removed before the tape is played to the jury. We are likely to see more widespread application of computer technology to such routine but time-consuming tasks as calendaring or the preparation of statistics. Computers might also be utilized for longitudinal studies of convicted defendants to determine the possible effects of varying sentencing alternatives on similarly situated individuals. And in our efforts to improve the quality of judicial decision-making, it is not beyond the realm of possibility that we may one day, in the perhaps distant future, witness the use of sophisticated behavioral and natural science approaches in the selection of juries and in assessing facts at trial, or even the application of statistical decision theory to aid judges in their deliberations.

I do not pretend that my brief observations provide a comprehensive survey of all possible reforms, and I recognize the futility of attempting to make all-inclusive predictions about the future. In one sense, therefore, my remarks will not be completed for another century. How could I have made this address in 1876, for example, unaware that the automobile would be invented? Not only would I be unable to consider the pervasive impact of the auto on the very nature and structure of our society—I would also have failed to predict that parking and traffic violations would provide the bulk of the public's contact with the courts, that automobile personal injury cases would constitute a large portion of all civil suits, and that auto thefts and thefts of property from autos would provide a large percentage of the nation's serious crimes.

Thus my conclusions can be no more than tentative until vindicated or discredited in the course of the next century. Yet as we continue our efforts to promote the fair and efficient administration of justice, efficiency should never be considered the only end in itself. After all is said and written, I must confess that a certain degree of inefficiency "may be a price worth paying if it buys or helps to buy individual liberty." Remember also Learned Hand's admonition that "Time's womb may be full of monsters." Life is so inscrutable that it is terribly foolish for any man to think he can forecast the future, or that he knows the only right way to arrive there.

PUBLIC INTEREST LAW

Ralph Nader*

I would like to recall an episode that occurred when I was at law school at Harvard by way of introducing my paper. Back in the fifties when Professor Schwartz had just finished his celebrated experience with the federal regulatory agencies in Washington as a Counsel to a Congressional Committee, he came up to Harvard to tell us about his experience. Austin Hall was packed with students and a sprinkling of career faculty and he delivered a statement which I still remember in its essential points, namely, that the federal regulatory agencies are studied in law schools on the basis that they are independent, impartial, and expert. And he then proceeded to tell us in detail that they were not independent, not impartial, and demonstrably not expert. This led to a number of reversed aspirations among the students and some outraged responses among at least one of the faculty. But the lesson it taught some of us was the danger of restricting our observation and study of the federal regulatory process to those cases which (a) are appealed, and (b) find their way into West Publishing Company's volumes.

The difference between what we study and the broader political reality of these agencies escaped many of us because we were insulated from experience. We were operating on a very high abstraction level dealing with appellate cases which by themselves had gone through a highly political and economic screening process, thereby reducing very much the effectiveness of their significance and increasing the narrowness of their empirical base.

One of the functions of public interest law is to redefine the constituencies of administrative agencies, as well as other legal forums, and represent a number of interests which the legal system does not deal with.

**Consumer advocate.*

It is, I think, necessary to define public interest law. Even though it is a very difficult definition I will define it by two criteria. One, a public interest lawyer is a lawyer who represents cases that are completely compatible with his or her conscience. That can come from the conservative, liberal, progressive, or radical perspective. They still come under that kind of definition, recalling Professor Charles Reich's point, in one of his articles, that lawyers should try to become primary human beings, not only secondary human beings acting on behalf ot clients.

Public interest law, secondly, is an activity which advocates the interest of generally unrepresented groups, minority groups, industrial workers on issues of health and safety, for example, or that recommends procedural reforms that may benefit a whole variety of interests from impoverished people to corporate institutions, just as the Fifth Amendment does.

Public interest lawyers seek to help redistribute power and wealth as a means to further justice in a society. Public interest lawyers are, in effect, organizers of new civic institutions that would defend interests in society that have long been ignored, as well as to reform existing ones in a number of ways that ordinarily would not attract clients. Very often they are lawyers without clients because they are operating in congressional or other legislative forums as advocates, or they are operating to generate constituencies or popular support for reforms. The client's interest is purely a technical one, to test an issue or to bring a particular conflict to judicial or administrative resolution.

Lawyers without clients can be seen in the following context of means: First of all, we have seen the enormous injustice due to contrived complexity. We have to move increasingly toward simplification of legal processes, simplification of statutes, simplification of procedures. The function of complexity is very similar to that of economics. It is a barrier to entry on the part of millions of people to legal forums.

There is also a need to focus very clearly on the new forms of access which are required. Access is not simply a matter of having enough money to obtain a lawyer; it is more fundamental. It is knowing when one's rights exist and when one's rights are violated. That is primary to trying to find the lawyer. And the antiquated doctrines that prevent lawyers from seeking out and informing people of their rights are now coming under severe attack and rightfully so, because the fact of the matter is that many people are being severely injured without knowing they have rights, and rights which can be prosecuted.

This is a very interesting empirical question, Nobody really knows how deep or far it goes, but I suppose that at least a quarter of the population would not be sensitive to their First Amendment rights, which includes about the most basic right, the right to sound off. It has great colloquial connotations. Of course, when you get into more refined rights, health and safety, and many other rights which are not in the Bill of Rights, people are just not aware that they have any basis for redress.

For example, if they go into a real estate office and the real estate agent says we all take six percent, how many people would realize that could be a possible price-fixing situation which violates the consumer rights of the potential homeowner? It is a major example, compared to many examples that could be given, but what is involved is tens of millions of dollars a year and a lack of competition in the servicing of these transactions.

Can you imagine what kind of rights people think they have in a banking or insurance context? If you ask a citizen what rights he has vis-à-vis a bank, you draw a blank. So there is a whole range of sensitivity to rights that is an important function of public interest law which must try to penetrate or reshape communications systems on a mass basis to millions of people which are now sort of off-limits to this kind of informational transfer.

There is also the great challenge of the modern corporation, quasi-governmental, merging government and corporate functions, in how the corporation impacts on its various constituencies. You see how many potential clients in the traditional context of legal practice are willing to challenge the various adverse impacts on various constituencies by these corporations.

Then there are enough kinds of phenomena, perhaps because there have been more disclosures, which are very disturbing. We have all heard, of course, of crimes without victims. Have we heard about victims without crimes? That is a very widespread phenomenon, because the crimes of corporate behavior often require quite a lag time before the law even defines the activities as a crime. For instance, the definition of violence in our legal tradition has been heavily primitive, covering A versus B street attacks, homicides, rape, burglaries, arson, and the like. But the legal definition of crimes as that form of silent and deadly pervasive violence that comes from industrial pollutants and other impacts has only been relatively recent, particularly in terms of judicial consciousness. This has been true though, as you know, there have been a number of laws, such as the Anti-Refuse Act of 1899, on the books for decades. So we have the phenomenon of victims without crimes, which reflects a terribly deep maldistribution of power that has its consequential and predictable effects on the legal system.

There is also another phenomenon which can be described as crimes without criminals. That is the phenomenon we have now been reading about dealing with the FBI and CIA disclosures, where you have admitted pervasive, widespread overt crime by government agencies with condoning or direction at very high levels. These are not charges or indictments, these are admissions, but somehow there are no criminals around. The Attorney General has still not made up his mind as to whether he is even going to start any prosecution of what must have been literally thousands of deliberate violations of the criminal laws here in this country by at least hundreds of government officials and employees over the last twenty-odd years.

Now, you see, these types of issues, victims without crimes and crimes without criminals, are not the kinds of cases that flow into the traditional law office. They do not structure themselves in the typical economics of the legal profession. They require completely different legal roles, which we here call the public interest role.

Of course, the challenges to discernible and elaborated legal rights and interests from new technologies is proceeding at a very rapid velocity indeed. Look at the consequences of, for example, computers, artificial antigens, new kinds of drugs, and electric funds transfer systems that the banking industry is now pushing. Again you see that there are certain conflicts in these areas between litigants who are able to retain lawyers and different companies that contest each other, but in the overall public interest, the way it impacts on consumers, for example, or future generations, these are normally client interests without lawyers, and again, beckon a new dimensional elaboration of the legal profession.

So far as the structure of public interest law is concerned, there needs to be a much more fundamental appraisal of just what the roots of public interest law should be. It is nice to say that we need in our country lawyers without clients, lawyers who pursue causes that are in accordance with their conscience. I certainly hope that that is always the case. But that is only one wing of what we might call the public interest law dimension.

The other is to develop an infrastructure for public interest law that is rooted in new enabling procedures within the legal system as well as new substantive rights for people who are now aggrieved without any redress potential, even if they had a lawyer. And still a third, the building of civic institutions which are the root and fiber of public interest advocacy.

An example of needed procedural changes are class action rights. They have been wholly undermined by a number of recent high court decisions. This is a procedural right. It doesn't debate the merits of the issue. The plaintiffs still have to prove their case on the merits. Class actions have been severely restricted by the Supreme Court, leading to the need for Congressional legislation to clarify and amplify that scope of rights.

By the same token, standing to sue has been severely undermined by about half a dozen major decisions, such as the *Richardson* case, and the upshot of these cases is that the right, for example, to have standing to sue, against government illegality, is denied not only for the plaintiffs who brought the case, but for 215 million Americans.

No citizen under the Supreme Court's determination has the right to file a suit requesting the Treasury of the United States to recover the moneys, public moneys, converted by the Committee to Reelect the President in 1972. No standing to sue. That leaves only one party with the standing to sue, the Attorney General of the United States, appointed by the

President, with allegiance to the President, hardly about to sue the White House on such a matter.

So 215 million Americans, in effect, have no standing. They have no standing to challenge the constitutionality of the secrecy of the CIA budget; the *Richardson* case over a year ago took care of that issue. If we look at the restrictions on standing to sue as they have developed in the last three or four years, and probe for a philosophic description, it is a tyranny. You don't have to be any more philosophic than that. When you have a whole spectrum of government illegality that cannot be challenged in the court by any one of 215 million citizens, then the courts do not exist for those citizens to review government action. I define that as a rather serious form of tyranny, even though it comes with the velvet glove rather than the mailed boot.

The third procedural change that I think is coming and is very necessary is the reduction of economic barriers to participation in administrative proceedings and in all civil proceedings in the court. Already there are nibbles here with the Federal Trade Commission having half a million dollar budget to provide the wherewithal to permit groups who represent generally unrepresented interests like consumers to participate in specific Federal Trade Commission proceedings, and that is going to spread. There is an Attorney's Fee Bill up now before Congress with substantial support, not enough yet to override a veto, but moving with a deeper base of support than ever before.

As far as substantive rights are concerned, I see two major areas that are going to have to be very thoroughly explored in at least the next decade. One is the area of government civil service accountability, making the civil service accountable horizontally to the citizens that are affected by it. There are bills now pending in Congress with a good deal of empirical material built up to support that kind of challenge. Disciplinary proceedings, for example, with due process, against government officials or employees who abuse their trust, or violate the law, or refuse to enforce the law, et cetera. This will go far beyond the present law and develop a direct right of action in a clearly defined form, starting with an administrative forum to decide the dispute, such as a kind of Government Accountability Board, as an example.

The second major area is constitutionalizing our large corporations. The United States Constitution was not expected to extend to such organizations as corporations, but arbitrary power has been seen to not only come from Government. It can come from these corporations, vis-à-vis five constituency groups: one, the shareholders; two, the workers; three, the consumers; four, community residents, taking in pesticides or other deadly pollutants; and fifth, the taxpayer. These are five distinct constituencies whose participation role in well-defined corporate deliberations needs to be accorded a whole new constitutional-corporate reform.

There will be hearings very shortly on federal chartering of corporations. I rather think that a kind of national debate-dialogue will be launched unlike other attempts starting with the early twentieth century. I think this one will end up in a definite resolution for federal chartering. That these large corporations operating multi-nationally throughout the world, are able to charter exclusively and so permissively in the state of Delaware, has to be one of the most egregious atavisms in human history.

As far as civic institutions being built to undergird the public interest lawyer, the reasons here are quite clear, I believe. To the extent that the public interest lawyer operates on legislatures, it is a political dimension. There has to be a constituency for that lobbying to be effective.

To the extent funding is needed to sustain large numbers of public interest lawyers, there needs to be these kinds of new civic institutions. To the extent where perhaps the best mission of the public interest lawyer would be to gradually develop the self-reliance or preventive policymaking or forseeing and forestalling by these civic institutions and their members, neighborhoods, and communities, there needs to be civic institutions.

There is often a tendency to see the public interest lawyer's mission as a kind of climax to a whole process of injustice without a closed loop sequence. The real mission is not only winning the cases and getting the laws passed and reshaping government and corporate institutions, but developing a new kind of civic culture, a new kind of civic obligation, a new kind of community fiber, that can plan and forestall and foresee these risks, conflicts, crises and the like, into the future.

What do I mean by these civic institutions? Prepaid legal services, for example, is one of the more traditional ones that is on the horizon. Another is the rapid elaboration of an alternative economic system at the retail level, that is, consumer-owned businesses, consumer cooperatives to establish both economic bargaining power, self determination in terms of what they want to sell to each other, the political power that flows from these kinds of institutions, and the ability to set up their own communications system.

For example, if you had 2,000 food markets in the United States owned by consumers, they would have political power, they would have their own communications systems, publications and the like. They could develop cash flow, could develop other services, including prepaid legal services, as well as cooperative housing, cooperative communications systems, health services, repair services. They could develop the kind of critical self-reliance that gives people a level of civic confidence that perhaps is the fundamental reform—at least in any secular sense that a democracy can aspire to.

Given these procedural, substantive and civic constitutional changes, the dimensional role of public interest law assumes significant numerical proportions. The students who are coming out of our law schools will no longer have to battle for the few opportunities that are available; it would become 10, 20, 30 percent of the profession in terms of new career development.

And with it will come perhaps a new broader role called the full-time citizen—a full-time citizen being, for example, a lawyer, scientist, engineer, organizer, writer, people with any of the skills that we are witness to in our society, only working to apply their analytic ability and their value system at the same time on their task as their daily work. It is very important because we have just the opposite situation for most of the other job and career opportunities, where the employer hires the skill, and asks the potential employee in effect to leave the value system at home.

There is a bifurcation of human personality here which leads to a reduction in individual potential and accountability as well as what is now routinely called job enrichment. The development of the full-time citizen career would not only enhance the part-time citizen, people would more likely put a few hours on various community or national causes if they know they are linking up with full-time citizen groups. Such a career may also help redefine the nature of work. There is always a lag behind any kind of political and economic development and the definition of work.

If you ask 100,000 engineers in a stadium what is their definition of work, they will define it largely as servicing the industrial side of the economy or the commercial or the governmental side of the economy. Very few will define work as directly servicing the consumer side of the economy. They will define work as building new bridges, and building new buildings, but not cleaning the water under the bridges or cleaning the area around the buildings.

Recently the environmental movement has tried to redefine work through a redefinition of values which then raises opportunities for these kinds of career outlets. But by and large it is a kind of a dispensation from the top which depends upon who is in the White House, the mood of Congress at the present time; it is not a building process from a model, where people in the community realize that their children are being poisoned by lead contamination, they realize XYZ has to be done, they realize this requires full-time career commitment and they know how to build the institutions which will ferment these kinds of opportunities.

It is really foolhardy to try to predict a whole century ahead, but I think the reason why a century was designated was more than a symmetrical one. It is because of the likelihood that some of these changes would require a century of deliberation. Let us hope that this is not the case. One, of course, is always tempted to confuse hope with what is going to happen. I don't want to confuse that. What I am saying is what I would like to see happen, not necessarily that it is going to happen.

There are different levels of hope. I don't think this is a pie in the sky level. I think that given some relatively modest changes, likely in the next few years, that a number of these situations can develop into practice. Procedural reforms, attorney's fees, class actions, standing to sue, civil service accountability, cooperatives, these are not low-probability occurrences. They are relatively high-probability occurrences.

Of course, there is always the connection between the will to see this achieved and the likelihood of its being achieved. But there is a note of caution in conclusion, and I would like to share this with you. Very often when criminal activities in, say, governmental or corporate institutions occur, those who are perpetrating these activities have one major restraint on them, and that is the restraint that they should not go too far because it might be disclosed.

In recent years they both went too far and it was disclosed. It was disclosed in a manner quite unlike other disclosed abuses in our history, in terms of the extent to which the disclosure was one of admission. It did not require the long exodus between exposure, charge, indictment, conviction. These are admissions. There is a great amount of government and corporate illegality. The depth of criminality of some of these institutions is far more serious than in past decades, if only because it is so institutionalized and does not reflect a particular elected political figure at a point in history.

Some disclosures did occur and there was probably a suspenseful period on the part of many people in Government and the corporations to see what the public was going to do about it. The public has done virtually nothing about it. Whether it is weary from Watergate, whether it is excessively saturated, whether people have lowered their expectations to a point where they simply don't have any standard that they can anchor to and transform into some kind of resolution, that is the reality of politics. Even Governor Jerry Brown has pursued the following strategy. He rigorously lowered the public expectation of California citizens in what the State Government can do for them, and then just slightly exceeded those expectations.

One may well ask, what is the real reason? I think the most important reason is that our people do not see any instruments that they can link to in order to respond for change and reform. So they are just left with grumblings and cynicism and turn-off and alienation. This leaves of course an excessive burden on a few people in the society known as members of the legal profession.

If you look around you say, "Where is there hope and time combined?" It is largely in the law school area. You have 100,000 or more law students going through the nitty-gritty, and you have thousands of law professors. And many of these frontiers can be broached and overcome by simply a deep redirection of the formal process of legal education. You have numbers, you have time, you have incentive, you have inducements, you have discipline, you have the faculty who have had outside experience, and you put them all together and it can become truly the major innovative force in society.

It is an awesome constituency; but few think of it awesomely; in terms of geographic spread, many of the law schools are right across the street from the state capitol, and courthouse, the greatest legal classrooms of them all; in terms of access to information, in terms of time, discipline, a school of law can teach you how to shape and understand power in the society; and in being a member of the catalytic profession, the catalytic profession that can draw in members of other professions to pursue the public interest. So I think we need to recognize that the principal asset we can start with is where you have a combination of knowledge, of access, and of time and that is what you have at the law schools.

This is going to take a rather severe jolt or a rather severe brand of leadership among numbers of students and faculty and administrators. In the sixties the jolt was the illumination of urban fires which illuminated the conscience of law students and law professors, and I hope it doesn't take that kind of tragic stimulus. Simply the observation of the health scene and where it is going and what it is not doing should be a sufficient stimulus for action. Perhaps the first stage in reclaiming this potential is to be able to step back from the immediate rigors of the daily burdens at the law school and look at the broader horizons. There is such a thing as being so close to the next day's task, that you don't see precisely how you are misshaping your career potentials, even by your own definition, and precluding opportunities that you can have a role in creating while you are at law school.

Clearly the next century is going to see a decisive struggle between law and power. There is always tension between the two, and, in the last few years around the world, power has won again, and again, and again. The sooner we realize that law will begin to prevail when it is reflected upward by a recognition among the citizenry of its utility and its role in the pursuit of happiness, to that extent we will get the prevalence of law. It cannot be expected to withstand the assaults of institutional power and technology simply by keeping it on a high level of abstraction, with a heritage of written precedents and traditions to work from.

We can end with a paraphrase of Learned Hand's comment that the real safeguard of the law is in the citizenry, and not in the statute books.

LEGAL EDUCATION

Robert B. McKay*

Lawyers in the United States have claimed for themselves a monopoly on the instrumentalities of the law and the right to practice in the courts. Assertion has become fact. Lawyers have secured a near monopoly—some would say stranglehold—on the administration of justice. Lawyers sit astride all the avenues for access to justice.

Similarly, law schools have a near monopoly on the training of lawyers. As gatekeepers for those who seek entry to the legal profession, the law schools cannot deny their part in shaping the quality of justice available to the American public. If the training is technically deficient or if it is not responsive to contemporary social needs, the educational failings are reflected in social disarray.

So much is generally understood. But the legal education community has not explicitly accepted—perhaps has not even fully recognized—the implications of this heavy responsibility. More common is the view expressed by Oliver Wendell Holmes that "When we study law we are not studying a mystery but a well-known profession."

That mechanistic view of the legal profession is now generally rejected. But there is no general agreement on a more expansive view of law as dispenser of justice and of legal education as preparation for the delivery of justice.

A beginning can be had in Karl Llewellyn's observation that lawyering, whether in school or in practice, is "trade, culture and profession all in one." He said of the materials of law: "I say in these things there is poetry, in these things

Director, Program on Justice, Society and the Individual of the Aspen Institute for Humanistic Studies; Dean, New York University School of Law, 1967-75.

there is life, in these things there is beauty. If this be not culture, I do not know where to find it."

The more common perception within the legal profession is that the study of law is an intensely cerebral pursuit. Opinions of even the ablest judges are dissected and criticized; students are trained to think with cool analytic skills; and passions are stilled.

Professor Curtis Berger put the issue strongly:

> I do not assert that legal education makes our graduates evil, but I do believe that legal education makes our graduates less feeling, less caring, less sensitive to the needs of others, less tolerant of the frailties of their fellow creatures, even less alarmed about the injustices of our society, than they were when they entered law school.

Lawyers talk much of professional responsibility, and the law schools teach the conventional wisdom. But we seem not to have thought much, or taught much, beyond those lawyer-devised standards that deal more with conflicts of interest than with conflicts in society, more with the integrity of the adversary system than with the integrity of the pursuit of justice. As Professor Geoffrey Hazard observed, "Morality is not the same thing as law, but it is an indispensable resource in evaluating legal norms and adapting them to changed conditions." And he added: "Possibly the greatest challenge for legal education therefore is that it undertake to be rather more intensely concerned with political and social morality than it has been in times more assured, and perhaps more innocent."

Without question legal education in the United States has met the test of technical proficiency. The law faculties are superb; the law students are at least as good; the libraries are generally excellent; and the structures that house the law schools are often magnificent. In all these respects the law schools are stronger than ever before and better than their counterparts in any other part of the world. That is not good enough—at least in terms of what might have been.

Now that I am squarely confronted with what I had thought would be the pleasant task of praising legal education, I find it difficult to capture the "upbeat" Bicentennial mood. To speak of legal education is, I fear, to speak of missed opportunities, of leadership relinquished, of professional responsibility forsworn.

Let me recount the measures of my disappointment.

First. The law schools have remained almost exclusively professional in tone, rejecting repeated attempts for the infusion of the social sciences and the humanities. In defense it is said that law is a "true science" which should not be diluted with the softness of the social sciences and the humanities.

The perception is scarcely new that law and the social sciences have much in common. The need for lawyers to comprehend the teachings of economics, anthropology, political science, and sociology is recognized—but too little acted on. It may be less commonly recognized, but surely no less true, that law is itself a social science. Law can be, and has been, studied as a social phenomenon. Techniques for dispute resolution, the designing of remedies in extended-impact cases, the effect of sentencing and parole procedures on the incidence of crime, and the impact of evidentiary rules upon human conduct all require that legal judgments be informed with behavioral knowledge from the social sciences.

The need of law for the humanities is equally pervasive, although law schools once did not clearly recognize the close relationship that must exist among law, justice, and humanity. There is, for example, the story of the law student long ago who asked in class, "But, sir, is that just?" The professor replied, "If it's justice you're interested in, you should have gone to divinity school." That attitude is long gone from the law schools and from the profession. It is now recognized that law requires the enrichment and compassion of the humanities. Indeed, I will assert that law itself is a humanity, concerned as it must be with history, philosophy, language, and the moral instincts of man.

Law is, as Edward Levi has observed, "a mediating discipline." Law can succeed—and legal education can succeed—only to the extent that law is made comprehensible through the teachings of the social sciences and the humanities.

Second. The proud claim to professionalism has been more facade than solid structure. If the interest in professional training had been the sole motivating force, we should long ago have required clinical training of all law students or at least have continued the apprentice programs that were long ago abandoned in nearly all jurisdictions. Law schools have always denied that they are "trade schools." In the effort to be considered academic, law school training has tended to abstraction without the leavening of the humanities.

Why else the emphasis on the Socratic method except, as is so often said, to make each student "think like a lawyer"? When that most circular bit of reasoning is examined, it collapses of its own round weight. The Socratic method is useful, to be sure, in the hands of the truly skillful teacher, but scarcely to the extent once imposed by each instructor in each subject on every student. Belatedly, we have come to the wisdom that there are other ways: the problem method, research seminars, simulation, clinical training, and even guided study.

Third. Law schools and law teachers alike have ridden too comfortably on the tide of contemporary legal morality. Legal educators should have led the way to new and higher levels of professional responsibility, which in turn they should have inculcated in their student charges. But law teachers have in general been content to share the easy virtue of the profession. They have trained students to keep open a wary eye for the main chance and a cynical readiness to move with the current moods of casual acquiescence in client wrongdoing, whether corporate nondisclosure, income tax cheating, or corruption of government at the highest level.

Fourth. Legal education has been a willing partner to the elitism of the legal profession as a whole. Most law teachers accept the notion that private practice is the natural and proper goal of all rational law students, and many believe that biggest is best among the law firms. Accordingly, law school training has been principally aimed at the kind of specialized practice peculiar to that institution known as the Wall Street firm, which is now found in every major city in the nation. Indeed, it is only within the last decade that the law schools began to be disquieted that their recruitment and selection process had become so structured that only a few women and almost no blacks, Chicanos, Puerto Ricans, or Native Americans were entering the profession.

These complaints are designedly exaggerated; much has

been done in recent years to limit the elitism, to broaden the student base of legal education, to democratize the thrust of the training, and to emphasize the true nature of the professional responsibility that must be accepted by each law school graduate as he or she moves into the profession. But much remains to be done. In some ways, the profession as a whole has moved more rapidly to correct past errors of omission and commission than the law schools. The present challenge is for legal education and the legal profession to move together into the Third Century of American law to serve the needs of justice and democracy. The tools are at hand. They must be grasped, shaped to the necessary tasks, and put to work.

If legal education has made mistakes of emphasis, as I believe it has, there are reasons that make those errors understandable. Lawyers may not be loved—and we have much evidence that they are not; but there is equally convincing evidence that lawyers are increasingly thought to be necessary for nearly every endeavor, public or private, large or small. The legal profession has defined the perimeters of the practice of law and carefully excluded all who cannot utter the password of bar membership.

Consider the lockstep of the profession as it now operates. The process begins no later than college where the performance of the aspiring lawyer is carefully measured by more or less standard grading processes, as further refined by the Law School Admission Test. In recent years only the strongest, as measured by those two criteria, have been allowed to enter the portals of legal education. There the refining process is continued with study and examinations designed to test the same qualities that were measured on the LSAT. Finally, at the end of law school—again a graded performance—there is for nearly all a bar examination, which reviews fitness to practice by testing for the same qualities as did the LSAT and the law school examinations.

Once admitted to the bar the happy practitioner can rest confident that no one who has not gone a similar route can challenge his or her right to secure as large a share of the monopoly pie as other practitioners will permit. The license to practice, once awarded, is rarely taken away, and then only upon the judgment of other lawyers passing upon the wrongoing of one of their own. Thus the monopoly of the profession by the lawyers is complete, from admission to law school through the entire cycle of a life at the bar. The controls may not quite work from cradle to grave, but certainly from entrance to law school to the end of active practice. In the case of most lawyers that does indeed mean until death.

I do not want to be misunderstood. Protection of the public requires that the practice of law be limited to those who meet professionally exacting standards. The law schools are an essential part of that process, and they have become increasingly skillful at selecting students with high potential for the law and turning them into excellent lawyers. What I do wish to emphasize is that law schools, because they control entry to the profession, have a special responsibility to remember that law, separated from justice, cannot long survive—and would not deserve to survive. If law schools become so impressed with their unique opportunity that they select only the elite and train them only for an elitist profession, they will have failed to meet their high obligation to work toward the responsible administration of justice.

Thus far I speak largely of the immediate past, the present, and a future that might, at least for a time, continue unless changed by external forces. But it has not always been so. Legal education in the United States has been subject to periods of ebb and flow. At the moment we ride a crest higher than every before experienced in legal education, although less than a quarter of a century removed from the twentieth century nadir of demand for legal education. In the early 1950s some law schools went out of business, and many were regarded by their parent institutions as precarious and costly appendages. Those times may come again. If the widely predicted oversupply of lawyers is allowed to become a reality, the quality of legal education will again be in jeopardy.

The possibility of a decline in the prestige of legal education is not advanced as a prediction, but as a reminder of what could happen if legal educators and members of the organized bar do not take the necessary steps to make legal services broadly available to those who cannot now afford—or believe they cannot afford—the services of a lawyer even for genuinely needed legal assistance.

There is a very real risk that the legal profession will not satisfy the demand for more readily available and less costly legal services. It is not clear that lawyers as a whole recognize the intimate relationship between the delivery of legal services to *all* who need them and the health of the legal profession. Manifestly, if the economic health of the legal profession becomes less than robust, legal education will suffer. If the applicant pool dwindles significantly, scramble for minimally qualified students will intensify in the marginal schools. Some of the recent entrants to the law school scene would in that event fail, as would some of the not so recent entrants.

The fate of a few law schools may not be a matter of much concern to society in general, which has larger worries. But there would be cause for social alarm if the law schools should continue to put forth an increasing flood of lawyers for whom there is no apparent market. History reminds of the dangers of an oversupply of lawyers. We need look back no further than the 1920s and 1930s to find underemployed lawyers whose ethical standards were shocking even to a more relaxed notion of morality than I hope and believe is the standard today.

It is true that the circumstances are not entirely comparable. Many, perhaps most, of the ethically delinquent lawyers were graduates of law schools with minimal admission standards and low educational standards. Meanwhile, the elite of the bar continued to represent the rich and, we may assume, continued to flourish while the members of the underside of the bar gave the entire profession a bad name.

The situation is not the same today. The 167 American Bar Association-approved schools have vastly higher admission requirements and offer an enormously better legal education than was true in the earlier period. Their graduates are well trained for the law, and we may hope their ethical instincts are better. Nevertheless, experience tells us that even a well trained lawyer might become careless or even indifferent to moral prescriptions if underemployed—or unemployed.

In most jurisdictions the procedures for uncovering and disciplining lawyers who transgress the Code of Professional Responsibility range from the barely acceptable to the downright primitive. If meaningful employment is not found for the large number of lawyers now emerging each year, I fear that the Code of Professional Responsibility and present enforcement procedures will not be adequate to the pressures that would then be placed upon them.

It is not my present purpose to review two centuries of American legal education. That has been done and done well, beginning with such competent observers of the American scene as Alexis de Tocqueville and Lord Bryce. Their admiring comments about law and lawyers, which have understandably caught the fancy of the profession, do not need repetition here. There was, however, no full study of legal education until 1921 when A.Z. Reed published his useful volume, *Training for the Public Profession of Law.* Other significant contributions have been made by A.H. Chroust in *The Rise of the Legal Profession in America;* by Robert Stevens, in "Two Cheers for 1870: the American Law School," published as a long chapter in *Law in American History,* edited by Messrs. Fleming and Bailyn; and by Gordon Gee and Donald Jackson in a soon-to-be-published volume, *Legal Education and Competency Training: An Historical Perspective.*

Even though it may not be useful to retrace those steps here, the broad lessons of history must be recalled. During most of the two hundred years of United States history we now celebrate, two kinds of legal education alternated and sometimes competed: the apprentice method of training by doing and the law school method of training by study. After the Revolution legal education was most often secured through an apprenticeship. Ever since that time the apprentice system has had a wide appeal. Then, as always in apprentice programs, the apprentice most commonly gained his education more through emulation then direct instruction; if the model was good, the education may have been passable. Moreover, apprentices, then as now, were required to perform a variety of tasks, some of which provided useful training, but some of which served no educational purpose.

Only in recent years have the last vestiges of formal apprentice training been abandoned as a requirement for admission to the bar. A few states, including New York, still allow the taking of the bar examination after supervised study in a law office. In response to the demand for clinical training, suggestions have been renewed that a form of apprentice training should be required. Until the problems that have always plagued office supervision are overcome, these proposals should not dominate discussions about legal education.

Thomas Jefferson was one of the first to critize the apprentice system, observing that often "the services expected in return have been more than the instructions have been worth." Partly in reaction to these and other inadequacies of the system, and partly in an effort to make sure that "the Body of the People [were] well instructed in their Laws, Rights, and Liberties," law lectures were established, beginning with a professorship at William and Mary College in 1779, first held by George Wythe. (Thomas Jefferson had been his apprentice student.) Similar beginnings were made at Yale, Columbia, Harvard, and the University of Maryland.

These early efforts to develop law faculties within universities were in general unsuccessful. The bar felt that the apprentice system was good enough. Moreover, there began about the same time the rise of non-university-related private law schools such as the Litchfield School founded in 1784 by Tapping Reeve. Instruction was by lecture, and the curriculum does not sound very different from more modern versions. In the one-year program there were lectures on property, contracts, procedure, commercial law, agency, and master and servant, among others. The curriculum was based on Blackstone with some American overlay. Interestingly, more copies of Blackstone's treatise were sold in America than in England, causing Edmund Burke to react with mixed concern and awe for this new breed of Englishmen.

The university-based law school could not be indefinitely held off. Harvard established its law school in 1817, and Yale followed soon after with the absorption of a private school. But development was slow, particularly during the Jacksonian period when admission to the bar became available in many states without the necessity of apprentice training or training in any law school, whether proprietary or university.

By 1850, there were only 15 university schools, 21 by 1860, and 31 by 1870. The history of the modern law school is generally acknowledged to begin about 1870. The changes since that time have been less dramatic than one might expect.

Standards for admission to the bar have been an important complement to legal education. Despite some early efforts in the colonies to prohibit the practice of law, bar associations and standards of admission have been with us from nearly the beginning of American life. The bar organizations have thus exercised considerable control over legal education and admission to practice. Although not uniform, these admission standards were strict and tended to assure that members of the bar were drawn from the better educated class.

This regulatory power suffered temporary eclipse with the advent of Jacksonian Democracy. By the 1860s only nine states had a formal apprentice requirement, and even in those states the length of required service was reduced. While some sort of examination had been required in most jurisdictions before 1830, this requirement was also weakened or abolished during the Jacksonian surge. Messrs. Gee and Jackson have described one such bar examination.

> In California two "law students," who clerked in the same building, had applied for admission to the bar. One day a member of the Supreme Court of California called upon one of the students and announced that he had come to ascertain his professional qualifications. The whole examination consisted of the question: "Is the Legal Tender Act constitutional?" The student replied: "It is!" Whereupon the judge observed: "I have just examined your friend in the other office and he says that the Act is unconstitutional, but we need lawyers who are able to answer great constitutional questions so quickly, right or wrong. You are both admitted."

The course of modern legal education was set with the appointment of Christopher Columbus Langdell as dean of the Harvard Law School in 1870. He is widely remembered for his introduction of the case method of instruction (and the soon-to-follow Socratic method, which many believed to be a necessary adjunct of the case method). But even more important may have been the establishment of the tradition that has since prevailed in this country that the best legal education is to be secured in the university setting. Never mind that apprentice training continued and that proprietary schools continue to this day. Those who could afford the time and price of university law school training went that route; and the leaders of the bar came almost invariably from the university-based schools. The pattern that Harvard established a century ago continues to dominate legal education today. Critics were few, and their voices were largely unheeded. More than half a century ago even as perceptive a critic as Alfred Z. Reed made little impression with his complaint about "the failure of the modern American law school to make any adequate provision in its curriculum for practical training." Fifty years later clinical training was still greeted with some suspicion that it was not academic because based on the realities of practice. Resistance to change of the pattern continues to be stubborn, perhaps less so at Harvard than at other institutions that continue to follow mindlessly without looking to see if the leader has moved on.

It is scarcely too strong to say that the most important changes in legal education between 1870 and 1976 have been statistical. The number of law schools approved by the American Bar Association has risen from 31 to 167. In addition, there are several dozen unapproved schools. (The exact count is never quite sure because some open and close without the usual amenities.) The number of students has fluctuated somewhat, but the overall trend has been markedly up. In 1953, the low point of law student enrollment after the post-World War II bulge, there were only 34,423 students in ABA-approved schools. Within twenty years the figure tripled, and further increases were recorded in 1974 and 1975. In 1976 the enrollment in ABA-approved schools is 116,991. First-year registrations have also continued to rise (39,038 in 1976). The proportion of those who complete the law program with a degree and are admitted to the bar has risen even more dramatically as the number of dropouts for academic and other reasons decreases and as the percentage of those who pass the bar increases. In brief it is easy to understand the concern often expressed about what to do with all those lawyers. Putting aside the indelicate suggestions sometimes offered for disposition of lawyers, the comment that received the most attention was that of an ABA Task Force on Professional Utilization that speculated there would be about 30,000 new admissions to the bar by 1975 (in fact, an understatement), but only about 15,000 traditional legal jobs. Questions naturally arise whether the law schools are working to find new placements for their graduates and whether they are advising applicants and new students of the potential job crunch at the end of the line.

It is not enough for some schools in a strong competitive position to strengthen their own placement efforts, although of course they will, as they must. Individual efforts do no more than push the bodies around, helping some and hurting others. The solution, which must be national in scope, requires careful consideration of the interests of present practitioners and future law students. Most of all, though, the needs of the public must be given first priority. What, we must ask, can lawyers do better than others? How extensive should be their training? What is the most effective means for the delivery of legal services to those who now get none, or not enough, or not the kind they need?

One other statistical observation should be made. The color and sex balance of legal education has changed more in the last ten years than in all its previous history. After the battle against religious discrimination was finally won (and not so long ago at that), law schools remained too long content to fill their places with white males. Until the second half of the twentieth century some of the finest law schools admitted no women, and at most other schools women were so few that the suspicion was winkingly expressed that they must have come in search of husbands. Even as late as the mid-1960s a number of schools approved by the American Bar Association and members in good standing of the Association of American Law Schools did not admit blacks (and probably would not have admitted Chicanos, Puerto Ricans, or Native Americans if any had been so bold as to apply).

All that has changed. The shameful record has been largely corrected. Women are admitted to the law schools without restriction and without special preference (nearly 25 per cent of the total in the current year). They have more than held their own in academic performance and have proved themselves the serious students we should always have known would be the case.

Attraction of blacks and members of other minority groups to the law schools has been more difficult, but has been assisted by special recruitment efforts, financial assistance for those needing help, and even preferential consideration in terms of admission policy. But the number of minority group law students is still disappointingly low, only about 8 percent of the total enrollment; and there are discouraging indications that this is the group most likely to drop in numbers as the total registration slackens or even declines. Whatever the Supreme Court finally does on the issue of preferential admissions, the need for further creative effort is all too clear, if we are not to revert once more to an almost entirely white bar.

As I have already suggested, the most striking thing about legal education is its resistance to change. It is clearly not all bad to withstand transient and faddish demands for change; and it is a positive virtue to resist ill-considered proposals for change. There is so much that is good about legal education that it is tempting to say that all is well. It is my judgment, admittedly biased in favor of my old friend legal education, that the training provided by today's law schools is the best it has ever been. The law teachers are superbly qualified in terms of training, intellectual capacity, and research and writing abilities. Many of them are even good class room teachers, and quite a few devote a fair measure of their time to *pro bono* activities designed to strengthen the profession or improve the quality of justice in our society.

Contemporary law students are similarly better trained than ever before and have demonstrated their potential for the study of law in ways both measurable and subjective. They are capable of phenomenal intellectual feats of legal analysis, and they are highly skilled in the myriad interconnecting disciplines mostly denied to us, their seniors.

Law libraries have become in many instances truly excellent research laboratories.

Even the curriculum has showed some give. The most notable single addition to the law school scene is a genuine commitment to clinical training, not yet up to what is available in medical schools, but at least open to enterprising students who want a real-life introduction to the profession. In addition, the curriculum in most law schools has been opened up to new electives, not only specialties peculiar to the profession, but as well interdisciplinary courses that introduce law students to economics, psychology, and sociology along with courses in the humanities such as law and philosophy, law and religion, and law and literature.

Look for a moment at the other side of the ledger. Despite much talk of curricular movement, the basic curriculum has emerged almost unscathed, particularly now that law students are becoming again fiercely competitive as they see shrinkage in the job market. The bar examination is not just an additional test. It is a very specific hurdle that is not surmounted by all law students on the first try. It thus becomes a very specific shaper of curriculum. Although many law schools have reduced the number of required courses, Messrs. Gee and Jackson, after an extensive study of law school programs and registrations, observed that "it is probably erroneous to conclude that . . . the courses actually taken by law students have changed." Moreover,

> for those students who are primarily concerned with preparation for the bar examination, there is only one year of real election of courses. Innovations in law school programs that are elective in nature will have to be filled within that one year, short of more extensive curricular and bar examination reforms. Specific reforms like the introduction of clinical programs will either have to be introduced as a new method of instruction in already required courses, or they will have to be fitted into the largely elective third year.

From this scarcely surprising data we can better understand why fewer than one third of all law graduates have any clinical training and why so many of the new electives are underpopulated. The striving in law school by students is for success, as measured by graded performance in traditional subject matter that leads to a traditional bar examination and traditional hiring practices in the law firms. Recall the straight-line theory of legal education, beginning with selection of a college, graded performance there and on the LSAT, selection of a law school, graded performance there, and a bar examination as the final stage of an essentially unitary process.

Once these propositions are understood, it is easier to comprehend how the law schools withstood so nearly completely the winters of student discontent in the late 1960s and early 1970s. Whatever may have been the impact at the time, it has mostly disappeared without a trace. Is the assertion too strong? Perhaps. But consider the record. Admission policies are still based largely on college record and LSAT. The curriculum is not much changed—except for clinical training, which did not come in response to student demands. The poverty studies and urban courses are mostly gone or underpopulated; and the courses on civil rights and individual liberties are back to the relatively few who were always interested. Grades are back at the old stand, and the competition for them is intense. The emphasis is on the individual, not the rights of individuals in the abstract, but on self interest.

The picture I draw is of course too dark. Many law students are unselfishly motivated to work for prison reform, urban improvement, environmental issues, and other *pro bono* causes. My concern is that for many the excitement of law as a justice enterprise seems diminished.

There has been no lack of considered thought about the needs of legal education. But somehow nothing much has come of any of the proposals—again excepting clinical training. The plans of the 1920s for true interdisciplinary training, although periodically revived with new flourishes, have never had a major impact on the law schools. Similarly, the efforts to infuse the humanities into law have not yet succeeded to any significant extent. Able legal educators have reviewed the past, studied the present, and offered suggestions for an uncertain future;* but legal education has remained essentially impervious to change. Proposals for a lowered threshold of college attendance as a requirement for admission to law school have made no greater impact than the proposals to reduce law school to a two-year program.

The one thing on which there is general agreement is that law schools are underfinanced and that their parent universities too often try to tap law schools for some imagined pool of new resources. I join in the chorus that law schools need more funds, but insist as a condition that legal education decide where it is going.

Law schools, law teachers, bar examiners, and the legal profession as a whole have become so engrossed in the pursuit of professional excellence that we sometimes forget that justice is what it should be all about. There is no absence of

**Among the most useful are Packer and Ehrlich,* New Directions in Legal Education *(1973); Association of American Law Schools,* Training for the Public Professions of the Law: 1971 *(Carrington ed. 1971); and Boyer and Cramton, American Legal Education: An Agenda for Research and Reform, 59* Cornell L. Rev. *221 (1974).*

ringing statements in behalf of virtue; but sometimes we do not pay serious enough attention to the principles to which we are committed. For example, we should take to heart the commands of the Code of Professional Responsibility.

Canon 1: "A lawyer should assist in maintaining the integrity and competence of the legal profession."

Canon 2: "A lawyer should assist the legal profession in fulfilling its duty to make counsel available."

Canon 8: "A lawyer should assist in improving the legal profession."

We accept those mandates, and each of us in his or her own way works at meeting the obligation there specified. But I assert strongly that we have failed to satisfy those standards. At least nonlawyers do not believe that lawyers are fully committed to those concepts.

If law schools are to continue to expand—or even to stay constant—in numbers of schools and of graduates, legal educators must share the responsibility with the organized bar for determining what use is to be made of this magnificent resource.

For the first time in the history of this or I believe any other nation there is an opportunity to provide adequate legal services of high quality to all. The lawyers now coming out of American law schools are the most talented we have ever known. But the mechanism for the delivery of legal services does not work well. The organized bar is beginning to examine these questions, including better care for the indigent, prepaid legal services, lawyer fees and lawyer advertising, public interest practice, specialization, certification for competence, heightened standards of professional responsibility, and more effective discipline procedures. The law schools are not enough involved, although in my judgement they have much to contribute to a properly disinterested inquiry into how best to advance the cause of justice for all.

In this Bicentennial year, and for the next century as well, we can settle for no less.

THE ENDS OF LAW

Bernard Schwartz*

That law is best which governs least. That law is also best which provides most. The first is a truth which belongs to the nineteenth century; the second to the twentieth.[1] American law's task in its Third Century will be to reconcile these two truths.

The truths themselves summarize the development of American law during the past two centuries. The ends which the law has sought to attain have undergone substantial evolution since the United States became an independent nation. In this the law has inevitably reflected the changing society that it has served. Each society has its own values which are mirrored in the ends that the legal order seeks to further. At the time of Independence the paramount place in the scale of legal values was held by property rights. "The moment," said John Adams, "the idea is admitted into society that property is not as sacred as the laws of God . . . anarchy and tyranny commence."[2]

Yet if the principal end of law was the protection of property rights, the emphasis was placed more upon the right to acquire property than on the right to secure existing property. This was accomplished by a virtual marriage of property and contract law. Insofar as possible, limits on private freedom of decision were removed. Property itself was defined in terms of a legally assured measure of autonomy for private decision makers. Natural rights came to be thought of as the rights of individuals who had entered into a contract, and it was these rights that the law sought to maintain. The market became the key legal, as it became the key social, institution—with the role of law confined (in theory at least) to securing its untrammeled functioning.

*Edwin D. Webb Professor of Law, New York University School of Law.

Fredom of contract became the dominant characteristic of American law. The emphasis on contract marked the transition from law as a system designed to maintain the social status quo to law intended to secure a maximum of individual self-assertion. It was through contract that the individual could be given the fullest opportunity to exercise his faculties and to employ his substance. Contract was the primary legal tool for increasing the scope of individual discretion in the utilization of resources.

During the nineteenth century property and contract became the all-important institutions by which the free competition necessary for economic and social progress was to be otained. But the emphasis on property and contract rights and their virtually unlimited freedom from public interference went too far. By the end of the century, V. L. Parrington tells us, "Freedom had become individualism, and individualism had become the inalienable right to preempt, to exploit, to squander."[3] In the law as elsewhere, unrestrained individualism becomes self-devouring. If unlimited freedom of contract alone is to prevail, the individual may, in practical reality, be forced to part, by the very contract he is allowed to make, with real freedom. "One law for the Lion and Ox", said William Blake, "is oppression."

All this has changed during the present century. That law which governs least has increasingly been replaced by that law which provides most. The evolving legal order is taking as its watchword the satisfaction of human wants. A maximum of abstract free self-assertion, as the measure of values, has been replaced by the task of adjusting or harmonizing conflicting human wants and satisfying as many of them as possible. The law is becoming a social siphon, its essential function that of ensuring an equitable apportionment of the society's resources.

Even a generation ago, Walter Lippmann could write, "It has, I think, been clearly established that government must henceforth hold itself consciously responsible for the maintenance of the standard of life prevailing among the people."[4] Today we can go further and assume a distributive role that increasingly requires the law to ensure that the individual will be afforded at least the minimum requirements of a standard human life.

How far will this distributive role be pushed during the coming century? The landmark encyclical *Pacem in Terris* affirms "that every man has the right to . . . the means which are necessary and suitable for the proper development of life."[5] By now the law has recognized a responsibility for realization of this end. This recognition of responsibility for ensuring the minimum requirements of life is, however, being questioned as inadequate. Instead the claim is coming to be one for conditions comparable to those enjoyed by others.

A conception of equality is emerging that goes far beyond any previous notion of equality before the law. The classical distinction used to be between egalité de droit and egalité de fait—between formal or legal equality and practical or factual equality. Until the present day the primary aim of reformers was the achievement of the first, since once that was established, the second (insofar as was desirable) would, it was thought, establish itself.[6] Now, it is said, this approach is too narrow. The end of law is seen to be, not only vindication of legal equality, but also provision of equality in fact with regard to more and more of the elements that make life meaningful. The postulate that people may assume that a standard human life will be assured them may give way to a broader assumption that they are entitled to equal conditions of life as compared with their fellows.[7]

The contemporary thrust for equality is one from the long-standing tenet of equality of opportunity to the new demand for equality of result—what has been termed the New Equality.[8] The extent to which this demand is to be accepted by the legal order has become a central value problem of the evolving law.

It is difficult to speak with assurance on the legal future of the New Equality. It certainly bears witness to the continuing truth of de Tocqueville's conclusion that democratic communities may "have a natural taste for freedom. . . . But for equality their passion is ardent, insatiable, incessant, invincible."[9] It is also true that legal rules, unlike those in the physical sciences, do not have fixed areas of strains and stresses. There is a tendency to stretch legal rules to the breaking point. Will this prove true of rules vindicating equality if equality of opportunity is replaced by equality of result as a leading end of the law?

Equality of condition or result is one thing when it is set in the utopian community or the monastery.[10] However, as Macaulay put it in a famous passage, "An acre in Middlesex is better than a principality in Utopia."[11] The Benedictine Rule is scarcely the foundation upon which a secular legal order can be based.

Karl Jaspers tells us, "There can only be equality of opportunity within the external possibilities, no actual equality of all. . . .in fact [men's] equalization beyond equality of opportunity would be the height of injustice."[12] The New Equality tends toward a bloc view of life rather than an individual one; it reverses the historic movement toward respect for the individual and substitutes proportionate representation of groups in all aspects of society. The price of equality of result is a merging of individual rights into group rights. Alexander Bickel summed it up just before his death: " 'all men have equal rights but not to equal things,' since a levelling egalitarianism which does not reward merit and ability is harmful to all and is unjust as well."[13]

The law runs the danger of becoming quixotic if it seeks to equalize all the effects of individual disparities. As Justice Frankfurter once put it, "Those are contingencies of life which are hardly within the power, let alone the duty, of a State to correct or cushion."[14] This is particularly true in the kind of world that appears to be evolving today. The underlying assumption of the New Equality is an escalating level of human wants which should be met by the law. Is such a model appropriate in the nonaffluent society that seems in prospect during the next century?

Edwin W. Tucker raises a number of provocative questions in a review of the present writer's exposition of the law's movement from a regulatory role to a distributive one: "As one discerns what appears to be, at best, a short period of economic distress or, at worst, a long period of grave economic disturbance, one wonders if Professor Schwartz would qualify some aspects of his model if he were writing at this moment. Would he add the variable of individual contribution to society in time of shortages? Is humanistic jurisprudence, unrestricted by limiting factors, consistent with a society which is obliged to combat the rigors inherent in a retreat from affluence? Should there not be a contributive factor linked to the distributive element? Is it necessarily in the best interests of a post-affluent, or momentarily nonaffluent, society to pay close heed to distributing that which is available rather than generating more to distribute?"[15]

It is even more difficult at present than usual to speak with any confidence about the future. That is as true of the ends of law as it is of other things and it is true for two principal reasons: the accelerating pace of change and the perceived relativity of values.

"The pace of change in human affairs. . . ," says Arnold Toynbee, "has been accelerating constantly since the earliest date from which any record of human affairs has survived."[16] During this century the rate of acceleration took a quantum leap forward. Never before has there been a period of such fundamental change in society. This has been true not only with regard to the quantity, but also the quality, of change. At the turn of the century, far-reaching proposals were met with the comment that they were as impossible as flying. Yet the changes go deeper than the awful gifts of applied science. Like Alice through her looking glass, we may still see the old safe world behind it—that other room in which everything was as solid as it seemed, where chairs were actually chairs and tables, tables.[17] But the century of stability and order has become a lost world.

The legal universe, like the physical one, no longer has a center. The world of law, like that of physics, is now perceived only as the relativity of one value compared with another. Relativism has become the basic philosophy of a much-divided civilization. "It packs our hearts," said Alexander Solzhenitsyn in his Nobel Lecture, "with the notion that there are no fixed universal human concepts called good and justice, that they are fluid, changing." The absolutes of an earlier day appear increasingly out of place in the century of Einstein and Freud.

In a relativist world that is changing so rapidly, it may no longer be as meaningful to talk about the ends of law. The present civilization differs so from the civilization of our fathers that our fathers' law has in many respects become a sorry guide—and in none more than in the values it sought to maintain. Has a law without values become the secular reflection of contemporary society?

We can, however, no more eliminate teleology in law then

in religion. The law today is in a groping state—"Wrapt in the old miasmal mist," to use T. S. Eliot's phrase—because we no longer agree on the values to be served by the legal order.

The law's value judgments are reflected in the interests protected by it. The task of the legal order is to reconcile the interests which press for recognition in the society and to choose which among them shall be recognized as rights to be enforced by the law. Until this century that task was thought of in negative terms, in accordance with Justinian's celebrated definition at the beginning of his *Institutes*: "Justice is the set and constant purpose which gives to everyone his own." Two centuries ago such "own" was thought of essentially in terms of private property. The primary function of law was conceived in terms of protecting that system of external "mine and thine" of which Kant wrote.

In twentieth-century society, the "own" that the law must secure has become broader than the physical possessions to which the individual has a title of right. The legal role has become the positive one of securing the conditions necessary to proper human existence. A society in which the legal order finds its ultimate justification in realization of this goal has inevitably been characterized by a veritable rights explosion. New interests have pressed upon the law, as almost never before, seeking recognition in the form of legal rights. The egalitarian revolution, already discussed, has been but the most striking phase of an era of expanding rights.

Now, however, that revolution may have reached its apogee—if it has not already seen its Thermidor. In a finite world of limited resources, the coming century may see a narrowing of the goals which we seek to attain through the legal order.

The ends of law may now come full circle. Popular dissatisfaction has already led to increasing emphasis upon the public interest in the general security and the need to make the law an effective instrument for securing that interest. This is going back to the end of law in the origins of the legal order. In its beginnings law has for its end, and its sole end, to keep the peace.[18] As it grows mature, the law acquires broader purposes, leading in our day to ends far beyond those traditionally associated with the legal order. Now these more-inclusive ends are called into question by what people see as the ineptitude of our legal institutions in fulfilling the elementary end of any legal order: to keep the peace.

If that elementary end is not attained, the legal order is bound to be a failure, regardless of how worthwhile may be the broader goals it has set for itself.

All around us there is a growing malaise that is intimately related to the unprecedented expansion in the ends of law during the present century. Our statute books are cluttered with laws that represent society's good intentions. Accomplishment of the ends deemed appropriate in our day has required the law and its institutions to expand their role in the society at an accelerating rate. The nation has turned to the courts and the law to cure deep-seated ills in the society. But there is only so much that can be accomplished by legal rules and institutions:

"How small of all that human hearts endure,

"That part which laws or kings can cause or cure."[19]

Those who believe that, if only this or that law were enacted, the millennium would arrive, are bound to be disappointed by the success of their efforts.[20] "Law," Walter Lippmann tells us, "is not a method of making us perfect. Perfection cannot be legislated at Albany or Washington. . . .the law . . . sets the standard below which civilization should not sink, but it cannot pretend to say how the best of men should live.[21]

In his *1976 Annual Report on the State of the Judiciary,* Chief Justice Burger declared that "The increase of litigation, the complexity and fantastic growth of government, the changes in society and interpersonal relationships and transactions, and the essential intervention of government into these relationships have placed an enormous strain on the structure of both substantive law and on the institutions we provide to implement it."[22] Are we asking more of the law than it can reasonably do for us? And are our unreasonable expectations in that respect preventing it from accomplishing those ends which it can effectively attain?

If the law has a fundamental end, besides the elementary one of giving effect to the public interest in general security, it is that of vindicating basic rights and liberties. Has this century's unprecedented expansion of the law's role really made it more effective in attaining that essential end?

It is true that we enjoy routinely liberties that would have been unthinkable a century ago. As Robert Nisbet recently put it, "We enjoy the feeling of great freedom, of protection of our civil liberties, when we attend the theater, watch television, or buy paperbacks. But all the while we find ourselves living in circumstances of a spread of military, police, and bureaucratic power that cannot help but have, that manifestly does have, profoundly erosive effect upon those economic, local, and associative liberties which are by far the most vital to any free society."[23] As the joyless reaches of the Welfare State grow more uniform and dreary, more drably food-franchised and supermarketed, and box-architectured, can we truly believe we have gained more real freedom? The law's indulgence in one kind of liberties has had as its correlative a diminution of all the other kinds.[24]

A Bicentennial celebration is not, however, the time for an overly pessimistic appraisal. Our legal system has always proved able to mold its premises and basic goals to meet the felt needs of each period in the nation's history. With Roscoe Pound, we may express the faith that, when once the currents of juristic thought and decision are turned into their new course, our Anglo-American method of judicial empiricism will, as always, prove adequate.[25]

"The life of the law," according to Holmes's most famous statement, "has not been logic; it has been experience."[26] The life of American law has revolved around the effort to mold legal institutions and doctrines to serve societal requirements. The effort has not always succeeded; at times there has been an all too large gap between the law and public necessities. Yet the gap has always ultimately been narrowed as judges, legislators, and lawyers have worked out new principles and doctrines better adapted to the changed conditions of the day.

Gilbert and Sullivan's *Iolanthe* notwithstanding, the law is neither the true embodiment of everything that is excellent, nor is it without fault or flaw. American law has been no more a perfect product than other aspects of American life. The test of perfection is, however, scarcely the proper one by which to judge any institution. The observer of the American legal system may well invoke the pragmatist criterion: the system has worked to served the nation's needs—to adapt the answer of Diogenes, *solvitur gubernando.* A legal system that thus works to serve the community is better than the academic conceptions of a bevy of Platonic guardians unresponsive to public needs.

FOOTNOTES

1. Compare The Essential Lippmann 323 (Rossiter and Lare eds. 1963).
2. The John Adams Papers 185 (Donovan ed. 1965).
3. 3 Parrington, Main Currents in American Thought 17 (1930).
4. Op. cit. supra note 1, at 336.
5. Quoted in Locke, Gibson, and Arms, Readings for Liberal Education 690 (5th ed. 1967).
6. Compare Tawney, Equality 125 (1931).
7. Compare 3 Pound, Jurisprudence 321 (1959).
8. Nisbet, The Twilight of Authority 198 (1975).
9. 2 Tocqueville, Democracy in American 102 (Bradley ed., 1954).
10. Nisbet, op. cit. supra note 8, at 199.
11. Macaulay, Essay on Bacon.
12. Jaspers, The Future of Mankind 19 (1961).
13. Bickel, The Morality of Consent 20 (1975).
14. Concurring, in Griffin v. Illinois, 351 U.S. 12, 23 (1956).
15. Tucker, Book Review, 1974 Wash. U.L.Q. 973, 980 (1974).
16. Toynbee, Experiences 182 (1969).
17. Compare MacLeish, There Was Something about the Twenties, Sat. Rev. 11 (Dec. 31, 1966).
18. 1 Pound, Jurisprudence 371.
19. Samuel Johnson, quoted in Wain, Samuel Johnson 275 (1974).
20. Compare ibid.
21. Op. cit. supra note 1, at 326.
22. 62 A.B.A.J. 446 (1976).
23. Nisbet, op. cit. supra note 8, at 229.
24. Compare id. at 227.
25. Pound, The Spirit of the Common Law 184 (1921).
26. Holmes, The Common Law 1 (1923 ed.).

II.

The Law from a Broader Perspective

PERSPECTIVE OF HISTORY

Richard B. Morris*

When some forty years ago I started teaching legal history, I felt confident that I could differentiate the methodology and objectives of history and law. Then the differences seemed obvious, at least to me. History was essentially what von Ranke and Fustel de Coulanges had told us—a rigorous scientific discipline. Its purpose: to reconstruct the past *wie es eigentlich gewesen.* To perform the rites of the historian one had to see the past through the eyes of the past, scrupulously avoiding equally the fallacies of present-mindedness and that of endowing the past with a semblance of clarity and simplicity which it in fact lacked.[1]

If the purpose of history was to ascertain the truth about the past, the central aim of the law was to secure justice by a coercive set of rules providing the framework for social cooperation.[2] Unlike the historian who pursued an empirical discipline and the inductive method, the lawyer, trained in the Anglo-American school of adversary justice, was accustomed to deduce broad principles from discrete precedents. Ever the advocate, the lawyer saw the past through the felt necessities of his own time and selected facts and precedents which, hopefully, would win his client's case. At his worst he would cleave to a scintilla of evidence theory, accepting a proposition as proven on the basis of a minimum of citations without giving balanced consideration to precedents unsupportive of his argument or of the historical circumstances which shaped his "precedent." To me in those early years of teaching and writing it seemed inevitable that the office lawyer and the judge trained as an office lawyer would be more the advocate and less the objective scholar. In a mood of candor Horace Binney, the eminent nineteenth-century Philadelphia

Gouverneur Morris Professor Emeritus of History, Columbia University; President, American Historical Association, 1976.

barrister, once remarked that the practice of law added nothing to the lawyer's intellect. He was concerned to win, but win or lose, he forgets the case as soon as he has been paid. Unlike the physician whose new facts, sometimes gained at his patient's expense, increases the sum of his professional knowledge, "the lawyer's facts are unproductive of all benefits except to the fortunate client."[3] Perhaps Mr. Justice Holmes put it more elegantly when he declared: "I shall use the history of our law so far as it is necessary to explain a conception or interpret a rule *but no further.*"[4]

The more I analyzed my own research and writing and that of my contemporaries, both general and legal historians, the more convinced I became that present concerns in no small part motivated one's choices of the areas of the past to be investigated and that the historians' judgments were shaped by ethical and moral values perhaps as much as was the case with the bench and bar. Thus, the fact that I had devoted a substantial segment of my *Studies in the History of American Law*[5] to a section on "Women's Rights in Early American Law" may not have sprung inescapably from the advances so conspicuously gained by women in American law and politics during and after the First World War, but my preoccupation was clearly not unrelated thereto. Some years later I was to research the subject of *Government and Labor in Early America,*[6] an investigation which was indubitably a response to my curiosity to secure essential historical background to comprehend the revolutionary changes the New Deal was effecting in labor relations as well as to place in perspective the impact of World War II on labor-management relations, wage and price controls, and the newly emergent corpus of law on these subjects. The realization on my part that contemporary issues can stir historians to reopen the buried past brought with it an increasing awareness that history is an "unending dialogue between the present and the past"[7] and that soundly researched history will always have relevance.

If, then, the distinction between lawyer and historian on the basis of the former's present-mindedness breaks down in actuality, it is equally unreal to set up an artificial wall between objective history and subjective law. Most historians are not so naive as to view history as pure science. Perhaps Macaulay exaggerated when he said that history "begins in novel and ends in essay," but his conception of history as a branch of literature supports the notion that the function of history was to communicate as well as to entertain, and that if the historian was to succeed in communicating he was to eschew jargon so dear to the behavioral scientists or that dense prose style with which some judges are inclined to cloak their judicial thought.

Any analysis in depth of the historical process and of its various exemplars will disclose that the practice of history, much like the practice of law, is neither observant of strict logic nor of scrupulous objectivity. Since Henri Poincaré, it has become a commonplace that the scientist starts with a working hypothesis subject to verification, modification, or refutation on the basis of the evidence he turns up. This is equally true of the methodology of the historian.[8] Recently historians have been indicted by a humorless if exacting pedant for committing every logical fallacy in the book.[9] One historian after another over the past generation or two has taken the stand to attest to the subjectivity of his craft, to describe the historian's role as that of choosing and classifying facts according to the relentless direction of his "frame of reference," his choices unavoidably affected by his own values. Granted that he accurately reports events that have transpired, he so often ignores "non-events," what Macaulay called "noiseless revolutions," and by such emphases and omissions in fact distorts the past.[10]

Indeed, both the lawyer and the historian share guilt in this regard. Both, by their very selectivity, serve society or certain special interests in society. Both are called upon, as the late Richard Hofstadter perceptively reminded us, to provide society with a memory, but often a memory which knows how to forget as well as how to recall, one that will rearrange, distort, and delete as much as is needed to establish a workable legal principle or to make society's historical self-image livable if not agreeable.[11] Both deal with hypothetical absolutes like equality, liberty, and justice, concepts whose definitions vary from period to period, from nation to nation, and from Supreme Court to Supreme Court.[12]

To demonstrate that subjectivity is as evident in constitutional and legal as in general history, all one has to do is to note the biting polemical attack launched about a decade ago by H. G. Richardson and G. O. Sayles on poor old Bishop Stubbs or the well-known interchange between Professors Fairman and Crosskey. Or even better still, one has but to examine the productions of some of our greatest lawyers when they essayed historical writing. Consider for a moment the exalted Sir Edward Coke, who spared no pains to caution historians so audacious as to venture into the domain of the law.[13] Ever the advocate and politician, Coke approached the past, supremely confident but quite uncritical in the use of his authorities. "Out of the old fields must grow the new corn" was one of his favorite proverbs, one that led him at times to defend all the anomalies which disfigured English law, almost going so far as to justify trial by battle.[14] Or, to cross this side of the Atlantic, consider Thomas Jefferson, who borrowed so uncritically from the Whig historians for his idealized version of an Anglo-Saxon democracy undone by Norman treachery and feudalism.[15] Or his fellow Virginian John Marshall, preeminent among our jurists. Marshall's multivolume biography of George Washington leans so heavily on William Gordon's *History of the American Revolution* and the *Annual Register* that one must be very charitable in drawing the line between generous borrowing without attribution and flagrant plagiarism.[16]

To return to my original conception of the historian's duty, the point should be made that, even granting the unattainability of perfectly objective historical truth, one can hardly support the proposition that the historian should abandon the goal any more than that judges and lawyers should scrap the quest for justice, since perfectly impartial and equal justice is unobtainable in this world. The historian still has the obligation to treat history as a genuinely empirical discipline, conducted with as much objectivity and historicity as humanly possible.[17]

The same caution should be observed even when we concede that ethical and moral values are as much a concern of the historian as they are of the lawyer. Macaulay, were he alive today, would be sure to remind us that "we know of no spectacle so ridiculous as the British public in one of its periodical fits of morality,"[18] a quotation that a cynical world might re-address today to the American people whom it finds riddled by self-doubts and moral scruples. Macaulay and other scoffers notwithstanding, a concerned segment of the historical profession believes that the historian's quest for truth ought to be quite consciously suffused by a commitment to deeply held human values.[19] We expect the historian to inform us about what he adjudges good or evil about the past just as we consider such moral and ethical judgments to be central to the process of judicial decision-making. To excise moral evaluations from history is not only to confuse the aims and methods of the humane studies with those of the natural sciences, but, according to Sir Isaiah Berlin, constitutes "one of the greatest and most destructive fallacies of the last hundred years."[20]

When the late Alexander Bickel described the function of the Supreme Court as the maintenance of continuity in the midst of change, he was arguing for the relevance of the past, because, as he saw it, around the past "cluster settled ways of doing things and settled expectations which, for the sake of both stability and fairness to the individual, so often, as a matter of principle, control the rate of change in society."[21] To exalt reason and depreciate habit carries with it the risk of flying in the face of history, as Judge Charles Wyzanski reminds us.[22] Thus do these jurists of our own era join with Sir Matthew Hale in recognizing that history is an essential element in the legal process. Its comprehension serves to guarantee an age-old objective of the law—certainty or security, an element so essential to the growth and progress of our industrial civilization which rests upon decisions made by individuals, corporate entities, and even governments, decisions made with a reasonable expectation that they are enforceable.

In the Anglo-American legal system, rooted as it is in precedent, historical continuity, as Mr. Justice Holmes remarked, is not a duty, "it is a necessity."[23] On the very first page of his classic work, *The Common Law,* Holmes instructs us that "the life of the law has not been logic: it has been experience. The felt necessities of the time, the prevalent moral and political theories, institutions of public policy, avowed or unconscious, even the prejudices which judges share with their fellow men, have had a good deal more to do than the syllogism in determining the rules by which men should be governed."[24] Thus, the tenacity of a taught legal tradition and the implacable impact of changed socioeconomic conditions may have greater significance in decision-making than pure logic. It is not that history eschews logic, for as both Holmes and Cardozo pointed out, very often the effect of history is to make the path of logic clear. However, it is obvious that in some areas, such as real property, principles find their roots almost exclusively in custom and history and defy the logician's efforts to discover a rational pattern.[25] The reconciliation of the need of the law for continuity with the demands for progress are epitomized in Roscoe Pound's observation: "Law must be stable and yet it cannot stand still."[26]

If the lawyer brings to his craft a rigor of discipline and a power of logical analysis too often lacking in historical writing, the historian in turn is frequently aghast at what he sees as law-office history, of which the judicial reports are replete. History, so deeply imbedded in a legal system that gives daily lip service to *stare decisis,* poses continually embarrassing problems for the courts, and silently raises questions for which the courts have no consistent answers. Is the intent of the framers of the Constitution or the drafters of statutes governing? Does history involve a consideration of both the origins of a legal precept and the whole course of its development? Have we the right to expect judges and attorneys to observe in their briefs and opinions the canons of historical scholarship, in other words a professionalism as historians in addition to a professionalism as lawyers?

Twice a month the *Supreme Court Reporter* provides evidence that the United States Supreme Court, merely to take one example, has not made up its collective mind about the relevance of history. Let us consider, by way of illustration, a very recent case, *Michelin Tire Corporation* v. *W. L. Wages.*[27] In a unanimous decision the Court held that Georgia's assessment of a nondiscriminatory *ad valorem* property tax against imported tires which had been mingled with other tires imported in bulk, sorted and arranged for sale, was not within the constitutional prohibition against levying "any Imposts or Duties on Imports." In overruling a long-standing decision upholding the immunity of imported goods from local *ad valorem* property taxes, Mr. Justice Brennan has used history as a precedent-breaking device much as it has been employed by an activist Court that has in fact wrought a constitutional revolution over the past quarter century.

As the Court pointed out in the *Michelin Tire Case,* the principal motive, first, for the calling of the Annapolis Convention, and, then, for the summoning of the Federal Convention in Philadelphia the following year, was to resolve the problem created by the seaboard states' levying duties on imports bound for customers in inland states. This had created a situation, as James Madison was to later instruct us, that "never ceased to be a source of dissatisfaction and discord, until the New Constitution superseded the old."[28] Observing Chief Justice Marshall's classic distinction in *Brown* v. *Maryland* between goods remaining the property of the importer in his warehouse in their original container and those which lost their status as imports by being mingled with others imported in bulk,[29] the Court found the tax in the *Michelin Tire* case to be neither discriminatory nor selectively imposed.[30]

To discover the intent of the framers of the Constitution, Justice Brennan quoted the remarks of a delegate on this question when the last draft of the Tax Clause was submitted by the Committee of Detail at the Federal Convention, along with Hamilton's Twelfth *Federalist* letter. However, since the tires involved clearly came within Marshall's "original package" ruling, it is not apparent on the face just why the Court found it necessary to take this excursion into history to invalidate Taney's long-established holding in *Low* v. *Austin,*[31] giving imported goods immunity from local taxes, and, I might add, Mr. Justice White in a concurring opinion saw no necessity for overruling a case which was not challenged by the parties.

The explanation may well be that, history aside—and it is indeed hard to shove it under the rug where the issue involved is so central to the needs for and purposes of the Federal Constitution—courts everywhere are likely these days to uphold federal ,state, and local taxing powers in obeisance to the prevailing public fiscal stringency, if not fiscal crisis. Perhaps the Court let escape the real reason for its sweeping decision when it pointed out the unfairness of expecting local taxpayers to subsidize such services as police and fire protection accorded such imported goods. Considering the insistent pressures everywhere to find new sources for taxation, one can argue that the *Michelin Tire Case* could conceivably open a Pandora's Box, or at the very least prove counterproductive by impelling importers to utilize rapidly changing transportation technology to bypass large ports, railroad centers, and large airport terminals.

If the Import-Export clause of the Constitution has raised historical doubts in the Court's mind, just consider how the Court has manipulated history in interpreting the "obligation-of-contracts" clause. On its face no sentence in the Constitution seems clearer: "No state shall pass any . . .Law impairing the Obligation of Contracts."[33] One scholar has selected the Minnesota Mortgage Moratorium Case of 1933, wherein the Court upheld the moratorium partly on the historical ground that economic conditions in 1933 differed from conditions in 1787,[33] as an example of "intent" history, which he distinguishes from "ongoing" history. The former, he asserts, has been invoked in the name of change, while "ongoing" history has been exploited in the name of the existing order.[34] Needless to say, in freeing the Minnesota contract from the strictures of the impairment of contract clause the Court completely misread history. If there were foreclosure riots in the 1930s, what shall we say about the courthouse riots in Massachusetts in 1786 protesting foreclosures and the harsh sentences of imprisonment or sale into servitude imposed upon delinquent debtors, a series of riots which culminated in an open rebellion put down with state troops while federal troops stood on the ready?[35] Here was a classic example of the Court's rewriting the past erroneously in terms of present-felt necessity. Clearly the current fiscal crisis of the great municipality of New York offers the courts another significant moment to mangle history and rewrite the "obligation-of-contracts" clause, and although an historian should forgo prophecy, I cannot resist the prediction that they will once again rise to the occasion.

Since the early courts spoke on the basis of revelation[36] rather than historical research because the judges were present at the creation, one can find less fault with the historical judgments of the Jay and early Marshall courts than with those of their successors, notably with the historical dicta that the Constitution was ratified not by the several states but by the people of the United States in their sovereign capacity, the historical conclusion of Chief Justice Warren in *Reynolds* v. *Sims* to the contrary notwithstanding.[37] But how can one accept the outrageous mutilation of history by Chief Justice Taney in the *Dred Scott Case*? Therein he not only disavowed the stamp of constitutionalism that Congress had placed on basic legislation for the territories after the Northwest Ordinance but refused to recognize the fact that prior to the Constitution free Negroes in certain Northern states not only voted but were considered citizens of those states?[38] How can one accept as historical evidence the astonishing data adduced by Chief Justice Chase in the *First Legal Tender Case*[39] to support the strained view that there was an implied federal obligation-of-contracts doctrine?

The *Insular Cases,*[40] a deplorable pair of decisions, somehow managed through the use of "law-office" history to muster support for the Court's theory of the constitutional status of overseas colonies, a decision flying in the face of an older national morality, of the intent of the Founding Fathers, and of long-standing constitutional doctrines that there was no authority for keeping any territory in a position of permanent subordination.[41]

In the twentieth century we have been both edified and entertained by the High Court's use of history. Selectivity has marked the Court's use of history in the church-state and reapportionment cases.[42] History has been employed by the Court as a tool of judicial continuity and restraint while at the same time it has been wielded as a weapon of political interventionism, the latter occurring when the Court felt it was morally bound to act where the two other branches of the government had failed to confront long-standing grievances. Probably the best exemplar of the former is Mr. Justice Frankfurter, and a good illustration from many is his examination of the historic roots of the Fourth Amendment, including James Otis's notable dissent in *The Writs of Assistance Case,* on which he leaned heavily to buttress his dissent in *Harris* v. *United States.*[43] Such modern cases involving search or eavesdropping without warrant suggest the relevancy of historical principles in support of the constitutional right of privacy. The technology may differ but the issue remains the same.[44] Not only technology, but recent legislation like the much-disputed Bank Secrecy Act of 1970, which the Supreme Court has held not violative of the Fourth Amendment, along with revelations of the hitherto uncurbed invasions of privacy committed by certain federal bureaus operating under a veil of secrecy, disclose how narrowly circumscribed is our present area of privacy. This should concern us in the year of America's Bicentennial, which commemorates, among other things, the struggle of the American Revolutionary patriots to preserve privacy at all costs against government intrusion. Such revelations also should remind us that our republican institutions, as the Founding Fathers conceived them, must rest on morality and decency, for, as Mr. Justice Brandeis pointed out in a memorable dissent, our government is "the potent, the omnipresent teacher," teaching the whole people by example. "If the government becomes a law-breaker, it breeds contempt for law."[45]

One would expect that Justice Frankfurter would protest the anti-historicism of the judicial absolutists from whom he dissented so vigorously.[46] Possibly the most scorching piece of historical criticism ever delivered from the bench was Frankfurter's concurring opinion in *Adamson* v. *California*, where both sides of a hotly divided Court resorted to history to determine whether the Fourteenth Amendment had made applicable to the States all the provisions of the Bill of Rights. In a masterly encapsulation of the history of the Court on this question, Frankfurter noted that between the adoption of the Amendment and the beginning of the present membership of the Court, the scope of the Amendment was passed upon by forty-three judges, of whom only one ("an eccentric exception," Frankfurter labeled him) indicated that the Fourteenth Amendment was "a shorthand summary of the first eight Amendments," thereby restricting the powers of the States. In an emotional roll call of the great judges who had ruled on this question, he pointed out that some had been witnesses of the process whereby the Amendment had been incorporated in the Constitution while others were conspicuously "alert in safeguarding and promoting the interests of liberty and human dignity through law." Dismissing the remarks of one proponent of the Amendment who argued that it meant nationalizing the Bill of Rights as comments not to be deemed part of the Amendment, he pointedly added, "What was submitted for ratification was his proposal, not his speech."[47]

However, it was Frankfurter the judicial statesman not

Frankfurter the historian who tackled the problem of finding a common ground for the Court in the great school desegregation case of *Brown* v. *Board of Education*.[48] Considering his ingrained commitment to judicial restraint and his well-publicized views about the judicial history of the Fourteenth Amendment, Frankfurter was impaled on the horns of a great dilemma. An historian of the law who revered continuity and judicial restraint was confronted by social and moral imperatives that could no longer be ignored. It now develops that it was Frankfurter (as a delaying tactic to prevent a divided opinion at that time) who proposed that the Court seek advice on two main points. First, was there historical evidence as regards the intentions of those who framed and ratified the Fourteenth Amendment with respect to the impact of that amendment upon racial segregation in the public schools? And, second, if the Court were to find that racial segregation violates the Fourteenth Amendment, what kind of decree could and should be issued to bring about an end to segregation? An impressive historical team was recruited by the Legal Defense Fund of the NAACP in particular, and the fruits of the evidence set forth in enormous detail the background of the Amendment and the intentions of its framers and ratifiers. The historical evidence proved in fact inconclusive, and so the Court rendered its decision on other grounds, including socio-psychological ones. While Frankfurter might well have had qualms about founding the decision on history, he saw no conflict on the score of morality.[49]

The *Brown Case* suggests that in the final analysis and in most cases history is not the decisive factor in judicial decision-making, even in upholding a right such as trial by jury which has no meaning apart from its historical form.[50] There is in fact no reason that it should be so. The easy assumption that whatever happens to be the outcome of history is necessarily for the best or should be left undisturbed is a fallacious doctrine of a school of jurisprudence that has long outlived its usefulness.[51] Even so traditionally-minded a judge as Mr. Justice Sutherland, certainly one of the better historians on the High Court, pointed out over a generation ago that "regulations, the wisdom, necessity and validity of which, as applied to existing conditions are so apparent that they are now uniformly sustained, a century ago, or even half a century ago, probably would have been rejected as arbitrary and oppressive."[52]

Mr. Justice Holmes was prepared to subject traditions "which no longer meet their original end" to the critique of history so that the Court could dispassionately determine "whether the survival which we are enforcing answers any new purpose when it has ceased to answer the old."[53] On any matter of law through the perspective of history, Frederic William Maitland is still entitled to the last word. "Anyone," he reminded us, "who really possesses what has been called the historic sense must, so it seems to me, dislike to see a rule or an idea unfitly surviving in a changed environment. An anachronism should offend not only his reason, but his taste. Roman law was all very well at Rome; mediaeval law in the middle ages. But the modern man in a toga, or a coat of mail, or a chasuble, is not only uncomfortable but unlovely."

Maitland surely would not have meant to imply that judges have no obligation to take history into account. To shut history out would be to create a discontinuity in the law with disturbing effects on our entire society. Both in the realm of private law and signally in the area of constitutional law, where the courts, as Chief Justice Marshall instructed us, are expounding a Constitution, history cannot be ignored. If the past can be reclaimed to our understanding, not by choosing isolated, highly selective examples wrenched out of context, but through systematic research in which documents, constitutional provisions, and statutes are considered in relation to the circumstances which impelled their creation, history may serve as a useful, even an indispensable tool to give continuity and consistency to judicial decision-making. Continuity is not the only end of the law, however, and in adapting the law to a changed social climate history provides a good many answers, but not all of them, and it does not necessarily frame the questions. If employed with skill, perception, and good sense it need not bind the law in a straitjacket but, instead, can serve as an enlightening and liberating force in the quest for justice.

FOOTNOTES

1. See Schuyler, "The Historical Spirit Incarnate: Frederic William Maitland," 57 American Historical Review 315 (1952); Stern, The Varieties of History 58, 59 (1956); 5 Histoires des Institutions Politiques de l'ancienne France (6 vols., Paris, 1890), V. xiii.
2. Cf. Pound, The Formative Era of American Law 118 (1938); and Rawls, A Theory of Justice (1971).
3. Miller, The Life of the Mind in America: From the Revolution to the Civil War 182 (1966).
4. Holmes, The Common Law 2 (1881); italics added.
5. New York, 1930; 2d ed., New York, 1964.
6. New York, 1956.
7. Carr, What is History? 35 (1963).
8. Cohen and Nagel, Introduction to Logic and Scientific Method 496 (1934).
9. See Fischer, Historians' Fallacies (1970).
10. Macaulay, "History," 1 Miscellaneous Works 153-198 (Trevelyan ed. 1880).
11. Stern, op.cit. supra note 1, at 359.
12. Beard, "Written History as an Act of Faith," 39 American Historical Review 221 (1931); "The Significance of History," The Early Writings of Frederick Jackson Turner 43-67 (1938). Cf. also Higham, The Reconstruction of American History 22, 23 (1962); Ausubel, Historians and Their Craft (1950).
13. 3 Co. Rep. Pref. xiii.
14. See 5 Holdsworth, A History of English Law 472, 473.
15. Colbourn, "Thomas Jefferson's Use of the Past," 3d ser., 15 William and Mary Quarterly, 59-67 (1958). For an analysis of Whig history, see Butterfield, The Englishman and His History (1944).
16. Foran, "John Marshall as a Historian," 43 American Historical Review 51-64 (1937-38).
17. Veyne, Comment on Écrit de l'Histoire: Essai d'épistémologie 343 (1971).
18. Quoted by Clive, Macaulay: The Shaping of the Historian 493 (1973).
19. See Perkins, A Professor in a Quandary, 59 American Historical Review 277-278 (1953-54); Wright, History as a Moral Science, 81 ibid 1-11 (1976).
20. Berlin, Historical Inevitability 52-53 (1955), See also Commager, The Search for a Usable Past (1967).
21. Bickel, The Least Dangerous Branch; The Supreme Court at the Bar of Politics 108-109 (1962).
22. Wyzanski, History and Law, 26 University of Chicago Law Review 237 (1958-59).
23. Holmes, Collected Legal Papers 211 (1921).
24. Holmes, The Common Law 1. See also Pound, Formative Era of American Law 62, 63.
25. Holmes, The Path of the Law, 10 *Harvard Law Review* 465 (1897); Cardozo, The Nature of the Judicial Process (1922).
26. Interpretation of Legal History 1 (1930).
27. 96 S.Ct. 535 (1976).
28. Farrand, 3 The Records of the Federal Convention 542 (1911).
29. Brown v. Maryland, 12 Wheat. 419, 442 (U.S. 1827).
30. The Court made it clear, however, that a discriminatory tax would be invalidated. 96 S. Ct. 542 n. 7.
31. 96 S. Ct. at 548.
32. Art. I, sec. 10.
33. Home Building and Loan Association v. Blaisdell, 290 U.S. 398 (1934).
34. Miller, The Supreme Court and the Uses of History 28 (1969).
35. See Morris, Insurrection in Massachusetts, in *America in Crisis* 21-50 (Aaron ed. 1952).

36. See Kelly, "Clio and the Court, An Illicit Love Affair," Supreme Court Review 119, 123 (1965).
37. See Chisholm v. Georgia, 2 Dall. 419, 471 (U.S. 1793); McCulloch v. Maryland 4 Wheat. 314, 403 (U.S. 1819); Martin v. Hunter's Lessee, 1 Wheat. 304, 324-325 (U.S. 1816). For the relevance of this conception of the origin of the Union, see Richard B. Morris, "The Forging of the Union Reconsidered: A Historical Refutation of State Sovereignty over Seabeds," 74 Columbia Law Review 1056-1093 (1974). See also Klenkamer, The Use of History in the Supreme Court, 1789-1835, 36 Univ. of Detroit Law Journal 553-578 (1958-59). For Warren, C. J., in Reynolds v. Sims, see 377 U.S. 533 (1964).
38. Dred Scott v. Sandford, 19 How. 393, 536, 572 (U.S. 1857).
39. Hepburn v. Griswold, 8 Wall. 603 (U.S. 1870).
40. De Lima v. Bidwell, 182 U.S. 1 (1901); Downes v. Bidwell, 182 U.S. 244 (1901).
41. For an examination of the anticolonial impulse, see Morris, The American Dream Among Nations—What Promise? What Fulfillment?, in Foreign Policy Association, Headline Series, No. 227 (1975).
42. For a criticism of the historical reasoning of the majority in Everson v. Board of Education, 330 U.S. 1 (1947), see Griswold, Absolute is in the Dark, 8 Utah Law Review 167 (1963); and Mark DeWolfe Howe, The Garden and the Wilderness 180 passim (1965).
43. 331 U.S. 145 (1947). Frankfurter therein was pursuing the historic line laid down in the Brandeis dissent in Olmstead v. U.S., 277 U.S. 438 (1928). See also Frankfurter's dissent in U.S. v. Rabinowitz, 339 U.S. 56 (1950).
44. Morris, "Then and There the Child Independence Was Born, 13 *American Heritage,* 36 (1962). Frankfurter's excursion into the past had a less liberative result in his concurring opinion in Korematsu v. United States, 323 U.S. 214, 224 (1944). See also Kalodner, Mr. Justice Frankfurter's Views and Use of Legal History, in Forkosch, ed., Essays in Legal History in Honor of Felix Frankfurter 29-30 (1966).
45. Brandeis, J., dissenting in Olmstead v. United States, 277 U.S. 438 (1928).
46. See Leonard Levy, Liberty and the First Amendment, 1790-1800, 68 American Historical Review 22 (1962).
47. Adamson v. California, 332 U.S. 46, 62-64 (1947).
48. 347 U.S. 483 (1954).
49. See Kluger, Simple Justice 614, 716, 626, et seq (1975).
50. See dissent of Harlan, J. in William v. Florida, 399 U.S. 78 (1970). While the twelve-man jury was by the time of the American Revolution a long settled practice at common law, the colonies, owing to manpower shortages, had experimented with five- and seven-man juries, but only in civil suits or petty criminal cases. See, e.g., Morris, ed., Select cases of the Mayor's Court of New York City 162 (1703), (1935); Charter to William Penn and Laws of Pennsylvania, 1682-1702 33 (1676), (1879); McIlwaine, ed., Minutes of the Council and General Court of Virginia 482 (1632), (1924); 1 Public Records of the Colony of Connecticut 18 (1664), (1850-1890).
51. See Cohen, Law and the Social Order 69 (1933).
52. Euclid v. Ambler Realty Co., 272 U.S. 365, 387 (1926).
53. Holmes, Collected Legal Papers, 225.

PERSPECTIVE OF POLITICS

Robert W. Packwood*

I want to take you back a few years to 1956 in Oregon. One issue on the Oregon ballot in the general election was Ballot Measure Number Seven. The title read, "Prohibiting Certain Fishing in Coastal Streams."

Then I want to take you back 741 years to Runnymede, to Article 33 of the Magna Carta which reads, "All fish weirs shall be removed from the Thames, the Medway, and throughout the whole of England, except on the sea coast."

I was struck by the fact of how many issues seem to be eternal. They do not change. If you look at our two hundred years of government and England's for five hundred years prior to that, it is a continual struggle of men and women to free themselves from the strictures of governments which want to restrain their liberties.

The battle for preserving liberties is not usually fought against evil people. It is usually fought against those who are intent upon doing good—as they see it. Mr. Rosenthal's paper quotes Justice Brandeis: "Experience should teach us to be most on guard to protect liberty when the government's purposes are beneficient. Men born into freedom are naturally alert to repel invasion of their liberty by evil-minded rulers. The greatest dangers to liberty lurk in insidious encroachments by men of zeal, well meaning, but without understanding." I heartily second that.

This country is full of well meaning men and women intent upon helping us. They are going to prevent us, if they can, from driving cars in national parks, or make us wear motorcycle helmets when we drive our motorcycles, or limit or prohibit our access to tobacco or alcohol—for our own

**United States Senator from Oregon*

good, of course. These are well intentioned people. I have been in politics now from the year that I left New York University Law School, which next year will be twenty years. I have seldom met a truly evil minded person in politics. I have never met anybody in politics whose intention was to do *for* us or *to* us something which in their mind they regarded as against the common good. They intend to do what they sincerely believe is right. They are so convinced they are right that if you disagree with them, you are wrong. Then it is just a short step to the philosophy of the end justifies the means.

I have on my wall a quote calligraphied for me by a constituent. It is an anonymous quote, which says, "Power is the most subtle intoxicant known." A few weeks ago one of the reporters from a nationally significant paper was in my office and saw the quote and said, "Senator, after seven years in the Senate, have you become intoxicated with the power?" And I said, "I don't know." He said, "That is what makes it so dangerous."

As I read and reread history, and as I have the occasion more and more to observe people in powerful positions, political and otherwise, I am convinced that any man can stand adversity. If you want to test his character, give him power.

If we are going to protect ourselves against those who are in power, we must do battle in the first trench. We cannot wait until we are pushed and shoved to a hilltop where we are surrounded and circumscribed by a government intent upon doing things that, in its estimation, are good for us.

Usually the first battle is procedural, not substantive. Those who control the procedures of democracy are going to control the substance of democracy. Unfortunately the first battle is not usually to protect somebody whom you or I like or would choose to associate with. It is not somebody who is trying to prevent us from driving in national parks or making us wear helmets on motorcycles or stop us from smoking. It is usually some bomb-throwing radical who is repugnant to everything and to all institutions that most of us support. It is, however, imperative that the procedures to defend that bomb-throwing radical be secure, because the very government that can skew and turn those procedures against that person can skew and turn them against all of us when we are not ready to fall into line with whatever the goal might be of that beneficent government at any particular time.

I want you to go back with me a bit not in American history, alone, but in English history, because I think we forget too often our common antecedents. English protection of liberties is substantially different from ours. We wrote ours down in the Constitution and the Bill of Rights in a period of four years, ratified it, and said, "Here it is, mankind is protected, hopefully forevermore." England spent five hundred years learning by experience that free men and free women must be protected against government abuse of liberty. Let's go back to those days when Parliament was a fledgling, shortly after the Magna Carta. Parliament was having a difficult time getting established. Kings didn't like Parliaments. Kings didn't want to call Parliaments into session if they could avoid it. So the Statute of Sheriffs, passed in 1365, said, ". . . It is accorded that a Parliament shall be holden every year once, or more often if need be." How did we say it in our Constitution in 1787? "The Congress shall assemble at least once in every year." That we hoped would lay to rest the idea that the President could dispense with the Congress.

The King was troubled by the Parliament. Even the Statute of Sheriffs, requiring that Parliament meet every year, was not enforced for centuries. Finally, however, a Parliament did meet frequently and the King had to deal with it. The King thought at least he still should have the right to put into prison those who would utter things on the floor of Parliament adverse to what he regarded as the good of the government. So in the English Bill of Rights, the Bill of Rights of 1689, Parliament said that "The freedom of speech in debates or proceedings in Parliament ought not to be impeached or questioned in any court or place out of Parliament."

How did we say it in the Constitution over one hundred years later? "Senators and Representatives for any speech or debate in either House . . . shall not be questioned in any other place."

All right, says the King, you can meet, you can speak, I shall keep the citizens apart from Parliament and for those citizens who appear and have grievances against me and present petitions against me, off to prison for them.

So again, in the English Bill of Rights it is said it is the "right of subjects to petition the King and all commitments and prosecutions for such petitioning are illegal."

In our Constitution we simply said that "Congress shall make no laws . . . abridging . . . the right of the people . . . to petition the government for a redress of grievances."

Bear in mind that all of the acts the Parliament designed to preserve liberty were simply passed by a majority of those in Parliament and subject to repeal by any subsequent majority at another time. They were the distillation in England of centuries of experience. We felt so strongly about them in the United States that we wrote most of those English protections into our Constitution and our Bill of Rights and made it very difficult to change.

The King was becoming continually frustrated by the Parliament. When he wanted to call them to levy taxes so that he could fight his wars, Parliament was reluctant to levy the tax unless the King would meet with the Parliament to treat with other grievances that the Parliament had. Often if the King would not meet the Parliament would not grant the money for the war. Well, the King found a device, short-lived, but a device, to get around that and help reduce military expenses at the same time. The King would quarter the troops in the homes of the citizens. Let them pay the room and board and pick up part of the cost of the military in that fashion. In the English Petition of Right it is said: ". . . and that your Majesty will be pleased to remove the said soldiers and mariners, and that your people may not be so burdened in time to come. . . ." Again in our Bill of Rights we said, "No soldier shall, in time of peace be quartered in any house, without the consent of the owner, nor in time of war, but in a manner to be prescribed by law."

As far as justice is concerned, the words of the Magna Carta are of similar import to those of our Bill of Rights. The Magna Carta says, "No free man shall be seized or imprisoned or stripped of his rights or possessions, or outlawed or exiled, or deprived of his standing in any other way, nor will we proceed with force against him or send others to do so, except by the lawful judgment of his equals or by the law of the land."

We said it more simply in our Bill of Rights. "No person shall . . . be deprived of life, liberty, or property, without due process of law, . . ."

The Magna Carta said, "To no one will we sell, to no one will we deny or delay right of justice." Our Bill of Rights says, "In all criminal prosecutions, the accused shall enjoy the right to a speedy and public trial, by an impartial jury."

When the King found that he could not prevent trials, at least he could insist upon excessive bail or the threat of cruel punishment. The English Bill of Rights said therefore "that excessive bail ought not to be required, nor excessive fines imposed, nor cruel and unusual punishments inflicted." Word for word, we repeated that protection in our Bill of Rights over one hundred years later.

The King would try a person over and over, until the Crown finally could obtain a conviction. Parliament did not even have to rise to that occasion, because the common law courts in the pleas of *autrefois acquit* and *autrefois convict,* said, "A man shall not be brought into danger . . . for one and the same offense more than once." We said it in our Bill of Rights as follows: "No person shall . . . be subject for the same offense to be twice put into jeopardy of life or limb, . . ."

Lastly, although I could quote others, I think the greatest protection is that against self-incrimination, and there again it was the common law courts, not the Parliament, that recognized the plea. It was first raised in the time of Elizabeth the First, but finally fully recognized and firmly accepted by the common law courts by the time of John Lilburne's case in the early 1640's.

We did not trust so precious a protection to the courts. We said in our Fifth Amendment, "No person shall . . . be compelled in any criminal case to be a witness against himself, . . ."

Now, what was England learning, what was England telling us? What they were learning was that governments, any government, will naturally try to abridge our liberties, and it will not be evil-minded rulers that try to do it. It will be well intentioned men and women who are convinced they are right, who know that for the common good, some of your liberties must be circumscribed. And throughout five hundred years of often cruel and difficult experience, through measure by measure passed in Parliament and decision by decision in the courts, England fashioned a protection that we grasped onto, clutched to our bosom and said, let us make sure in this country that we don't have to live through the five hundred years of experience to gain the same liberties.

You can say, well, England was a monarchy. But England for a time had no King. Under Cromwell and the Puritans, the King was beheaded. Under the ensuing Protectorate, English liberties and freedoms suffered as great an abuse as they ever suffered under any royal decree. The English documents of liberty from the time of the Restoration in 1660 onward, while they are still addressed to the Monarch, say that it is the government, be it a government of the King or of Parliament, that shall not take away from the citizens certain inalienable rights.

As we discuss Watergate, the F.B.I. and the C.I.A. and the abuse of our individual liberties, the big question is not are we safe from Presidential domination. The key question is are we safe from Governmental domination?

We, too, should have learned that both the Congress and the President on occasion will abuse our liberties.

Take a look at our history. It was the Congress that got swept off its feet and passed the Alien and Sedition laws. It was Andrew Jackson who approved the interception of mail to the South by abolitionist groups in the North. It was Woodrow Wilson and his Attorney General Palmer who instigated the infamous Palmer Red Raids in New York City, whereby we swept up dozens of aliens and many American citizens who at the time were guilty of the crime of joining unions or other similar alleged radical activities and tried to deport them. It was President Franklin Roosevelt, with Congress concurring almost immediately, who interned American citizens of Japanese ancestry, native-born American citizens, of Japanese ancestry, in concentration camps, two or three or four hundred miles removed from the West Coast because they might be a danger to this country, an order in my mind shamefully confirmed by the Supreme Court.

In the mid-50's, it was the Congress under the McCarthyites that abused our liberties. In 1970, it was the Congress that passed the Preventive Detention Act under which you can be kept in jail prior to trial without bail, and among the factors that the judge can consider in deciding whether or not you shall be released are the following: your family ties, employment and financial resources, character and mental conditions, past conduct, and length of residence in the community. That is a dangerous power in anybody's hands. I hope that it is one day contested and found unconstitutional before the Supreme Court.

It was a President who violated our liberties in Watergate. All I am saying is that neither Congress nor the President guarantee a safe haven for our liberties.

From the perspective of one who is an amateur historian and a practicing politician, I realize that we can all foolishly be swept off our feet by the well intentioned passions of the moment. Without a fair grasp of American and English history, we fail to realize that on every occasion in the past when governments have been swept off their feet by passions of the moment and subjugated the rights of the citizens, it has, with very few exceptions, always been allegedly done for the common good. In every instance, as history later reveals, the common good was not served.

The only thing that distinguishes me from the rest of those contributing to this volume is that I have been elected to a position of political leadership. On occasion the exercise of leadership means flying in the face of prevailing winds, and on occasion doing that means you run the risk of political defeat. That is but a small price to pay for liberty.

As we celebrate this Bicentennial, I hope that we would remember it is not just two hundred years of American history we celebrate. It is really seven hundred years of English and American history during which free men and free women have been tortured and executed, so that we might have the right to say what we want and do what we want. In short, they have died to give us political liberty, and it is the greatest blessing we will ever receive. It is our obligation to try to pass that on to our children a bit more secure than we received it.

PERSPECTIVE OF JOURNALISM

A. M. Rosenthal*

Some years before his death, Justice Hugo Black visited *The New York Times.* The talk around the table turned after awhile to the question of limitations on freedom of the press.

Justice Black reached into his pocket and pulled out a thin pamphlet he said he always carried with him, the Constitution of the United States. "All I know about the First Amendment," he said, "is contained herein. It says that Congress shall make no laws abridging freedom of the press. It doesn't say some laws or just a few laws, or laws on certain rights of the press. It says no laws and that's what I know about the First Amendment."

For most of the editors at the table it seemed a fine, staunch answer and we were happy with it. Yet even then we knew that life was not going to be all that simple and clear-cut for us, that some judges did indeed believe that no laws of abridgment could really mean some laws or rulings of abridgment and that the press was in for something of a struggle. But we did not realize then how deep the struggle would go or how quickly it would come.

The last thing any sensible person would want to read in a commemorative volume is talk of another crisis. And yet I am afraid the press and the public do face a crisis in this Bicentennial year, the crisis of the First Amendment's guarantee of a free press. It is a crisis that will be fought out in the courts, but has its roots not only in the law but in politics and emotions, the high emotions that have so sapped this country in the past ten or twelve years.

Among the antagonists in the struggle will be the press and the bench. Or at least that part of the bench that feels it

**Managing Editor, The New York Times*

has the right to delineate or limit the right of the press to print information.

There is a sad and quite historic irony in this contest between the press and parts of the bench. Because it was the bench of the United States that was responsible in large measure for giving flesh and meaning and protection to those few words of guarantee in the First Amendment.

About a year ago, a group of editors, lawyers and judges got together for a few days to hash out some of the problems between bench and bar. One of the participants was a famous judge, and after listening to the complaints by the journalists about the conduct of the bench, he could no longer contain himself and this is what he had to say:

"Where, ladies and gentlemen, do you think these great constitutional rights that you were so vehemently asserting and in which you were so conspicuously wallowing yesterday, where do you think they came from? The stork didn't bring them. These came from the judges of this country, from these villains here sitting at the table. . . . They came because the courts of this country at some time or place when some other agency of government was trying to push the press around, or, indeed, maybe trying to do you in, it's the courts that protected you. . . . The very fact that these protections are available is attributable to the creative work of the judiciary over the last 190 years."

The fact that the angry judge was largely right does not change another fact—that it is indeed from the bench that much of the impetus for the creation of the present crisis comes. The heart of the crisis is the belief of some judges that they have the right to tell the press what not to print. For the first time in our history there is an epidemic of judicial restraining orders against the press, a fancy way of saying gag orders.

There are two kinds of gag orders. One is a specific order prohibiting a newspaper from publishing something that took place in court or some information relating to a trial, such as a defendant's previous criminal record. The second kind is an order closing a trial to press or public, which has much the same effect as a direct restraining order; it prevents the press from informing the public on what is taking place in the courtroom.

In 1967, there was just one order closing court proceedings to the press. By 1974 there were twelve, and in 1975 there were twenty-five. In 1967, not one judge in the country issued an order restraining the press from printing information it had obtained. In 1975 fourteen judges did so.

The chilling effect of this is obvious. We simply have no way of knowing how many editors or reporters refrained from printing what they might otherwise have printed for fear of bringing on a gag order or finding themselves involved in an expensive law suit. In state after state, newspaper editors themselves have agreed to so-called guidelines against the printing of certain kinds of information before and during trials. However well motivated, this is a kind of collective self-censorship. The danger is that non-conforming editors are subject to peer pressure to conform and that judges will transform so-called voluntary guidelines into law.

There have been ripple effects. Local restrictive ordinances have been encouraged. Police and prosecution, always eager for reasons to withhold information not to their liking, have hidden behind the restrictive, don't-talk, don't-publish attitude of some judges and used it as a legal curtain hiding some of their activities.

Just to give you some flavor of what has been taking place, here are some recent judicial decisions or governmental actions. I have taken them from the publication of The Reporters Committee for Freedom of the Press, a Washington-based group that has to struggle just to keep up with the flood of orders, and decisions, and restrictive actions of one kind or another around the country.

Congress and Justice Department move to seal criminal justice files; Charleston, West Virginia reporters jailed for silence in trial; Texas Supreme Court affirms gag order vs. *Austin Statesman*; U.S. Appeals Court upholds contempt and jail term vs. William Farr; Tennessee editor jailed for printing name of murder suspect; Florida newspaper indicted for murder story coverage; New Jersey court orders editor to print antigun editorials, and so on.

I think you can see what is taking place. The climate around freedom of information has been subtly changing. Not long ago it was taken for granted that the more information the public had, the better position it was in to make decisions and thus the stronger was the Republic and democracy. The basic concept was that the publication of information by the press protected the public from government.

Now there seems to be a growing counter-concept in government and among some judges, the concept that the public needs to be protected *from* the information gathering of the press.

One example of this is the gag orders. There are others. There is a bill before Congress, Bill S-1, that in effect amounts to a kind of official secrets act. It would make disclosure of classified information by a government official a crime. There are about twenty million classified documents in the Defense Department alone. Passage of this kind of bill would enable any of the thousands of employees with classification stamps not only to judge what the public should know—they already have that right vested in their rubber stamps—but would put in jail anybody in government who disagreed with them.

S-1 would also make publication of national defense information a crime—for the first time in our history. National defense information is so widely defined that publication of much information about military or diplomatic affairs that we now daily take for granted could become a crime.

Another example. Seymour Hersh of *The New York Times* gets stories about massive illegal activities in the United States by the CIA. At first he is denounced. Then the President appoints a Commission which turns in a report not only verifying Hersh's basic information, but going far beyond it. Hersh wins journalistic prizes and the President promises reforms. Among the "reforms" is legislation that would put in jail dissidents within the government appalled at the illegal acts of the CIA, who make it possible for reporters like Seymour Hersh to get his stories in the first place.

A final example. A House Committee investigates the CIA and finally produces a report. Much of it is printed in the press as the result of the work of inquiring reporters. The committee votes to make the report public. The full House disagrees and votes not to publish the text. Dan Schorr of Columbia Broadcasting System has the text and makes it available for publication. The House goes into a frenzy and votes hundreds of thousands of dollars to track down the criminal who made available to Schorr the text of a document its Congressional authors wanted made public and which was the result of the expenditure of public funds.

I am not saying that the First Amendment has been wiped out. I am saying as an editor looking at the state of press law two hundred years after the American revolution that there are clear signs that it is being endangered.

How did we get to this point? Some of the answers lie not in the nature of law, but in the nature of journalism and politics—and the catalytic effect on both of modern technology.

Journalism has become far more pervasive in our lives than ever in our history. Tens of millions of people see the same broadcast, millions read the same dispatch. The whole country is involved, almost instantaneously, in what politicians say and do and what the press reports or comments.

For the politician and the administrator, this has vastly increased the stakes in the relations between press and government. It has been said repeatedly that the new technology—radio, television, wire services, high-speed presses—has increased the influence of the press, electronic and printed, and this is true. But what is not usually mentioned is that this same technology has also increased the power and influence of government and politicians, and that it is they who are the greatest beneficiaries and whose dominance has increased to the danger point.

A President or a Secretary of State can command the attention of the entire nation at almost any time he chooses. State politicians, city politicians, and county politicians can reach their entire constituencies over and over. Quite properly, but quite interestingly, they can utilize not only the technological realities like the airwaves and channels, but the business resources of the press itself—the networks, the world wire agencies, the news syndicates owned by individual papers.

Through the modern press, electronic and printed, the public becomes an instant witness to what is going on. It is sitting in almost daily judgment not only on public affairs, but the way they are handled and reported. However aloof or objective it may try to be, the fact is that the very pervasiveness of modern journalism has made it a part of society that affects virtually every other part of society—and for this it has been paying a price.

Part of the price, inevitably, has been that politicians and government constantly seek to control or manipulate the press and public attitudes toward it. They seek more than ever to control the flow of news by releasing only what they consider in their own best interests and try to bottle up adverse information either through the classification stamp or the threat of punishment of those within the government who make known information their superiors do not want made known.

Presidents have traditionally disliked the press and attacked it, but the Nixon-Agnew administration raised this antagonism to an entirely different level. It made a carefully calculated decision to break the press, or that part of the press that Nixon-Agnew felt threatened the control of the American mind that the administration believed was its prerogative.

This campaign had several parts. Some of them related to the law. There was an attempt to destroy the ability of reporters to use sources of information that could not be identified. Without the privilege, only people and institutions strong enough to risk public identification would have access to the press, which would turn it into a handout press.

Nixon-Agnew also decided to use the courts in another way, which no other national administration had attempted. In the case of the Pentagon Papers, it went into court to impose prior restraint, and though it lost in the Supreme Court on the right of the newspapers to publish, it did establish the dangerous precedent of a government trying to prevent publication before the fact, a precedent that haunts and endangers to this day.

Finally Nixon-Agnew opened a propagandistic attack aimed at convincing the country that the press was biased and represented interests antagonistic to the interests of the public—that the government and the people were *we* and the press was *they*.

And there is no doubt that they did succeed in convincing millions of Americans that somehow the press had gotten out of hand and was a danger in a vague, unspecified way. Vague, unspecified dangers can be quite as frightening as clearly seen dangers, more so sometimes.

There is another historical irony in the fact that the very magnitude of the sins of recent administrations helped turn some of the public against the press that reported those sins. It was reporting upon all sorts of things that were unpleasant to hear about and the American anger at hearing the news rubbed off on the press. You hate the dentist rather than the toothache. So when the press day after day reported on the failures in Vietnam, on racism, hunger, corruption, and revealed as corrupt or stupid the politicians the reader had elected, nobody liked it very much. The press had become the Great American Dentist.

It was in this atmosphere, and perhaps because of it, that a number of judges in this country, on low benches and high, began to change one of the fundamental assumptions on which the free press rests, the assumption that no matter how angry government, bench or public might be about what the press prints, the right of the press to print is the rock of freedom.

Even those who felt the press could be punished for what it printed, believed that the decision on what to print must belong to the press. As far back as 1765, William Blackstone in his *Commentaries on the Law of England* wrote that liberty of the press consists in laying no previous restraint upon publication, not in freedom from censure for criminal matter when published.

Newspapermen know what lawyers know—you can always find a quotation to support a point of view. The literature of the relationship of the law to the press is full of references to the incompatibility between prior restraint and a free press. That is important, but less important than the consensus among the bench, bar, the press and every administration except Nixon-Agnew that prior restraint was a weapon not to be employed, or attempted.

That consensus lasted until the Pentagon Papers. Though the government lost its case, the fact that it broke the social and legal consensus emboldened others to try to do the same thing.

The wave of gag orders, whose constitutionality has just been tested in the Supreme Court, have to do mostly with matters before a court or with pre-trial publicity. The issue is usually put by those who support gag orders as one of a conflict between the First and Sixth Amendments. It is my belief that this is a false and contrived issue.

For one thing, there are virtually no cases presented where it is proved that the First Amendment destroyed the rights of a fair trial. On the other hand, the history of journalism in the United States is full of examples of the press preventing injustice from being done or uncovering convictions of innocents. A hypothetical danger—the conflict between the First and Sixth Amendments—is cited as an excuse for creating an actual danger, the muzzling of the press.

Gag orders rest on the thesis that jurors must be protected from knowing too much about a defendant, his background or the crime of which he is accused. To my mind, this runs counter to the whole institution of trial by a jury of peers. It was precisely because it was felt that jurors should indeed know something about the crime, the victim and the accused that the tradition of trial within the community, by the neighbors of the accused took root and became part of our law. It is for that reason that the Sixth Amendment guarantees not only a speedy and public trial by an impartial jury, but a trial within the district where the crime was committed.

So the argument against trial or pre-trial publicity rests on the belief that jurors cannot be trusted to be impartial if they have some knowledge—a belief which history has shown to be false.

In any case, if the trial judge believes that the jury has to be protected he has full power to do so without trying to censor the press. As Judge Harold Medina said recently, any trial judge "who knows his business and who has a stiff backbone" can "afford a fair trial without any invasion of the freedom of the press." He can control his courtroom, he can grant continuances or a change of venue, he can sequester the jury or witnesses, interrogate prospective jurors, and if all else fails, he can set aside a verdict of guilty. Some of these are irksome, but surely not as irksome as destroying the free press.

Instead of acting as judges, too many members of the bench have begun to act as censors, reaching out of the courtroom to try to control the reporter's typewriter and the publisher's press.

The bench is a branch of government, a branch to be respected but not submitted to docilely, which is why our laws provide for the rights of appeal. But the fact is that judicial orders can destroy the freedom of the press even though they are later overturned on appeal. By the time the appeal comes around, the issue is often moot, the story dead, the press successfully gagged.

As Floyd Abrams of the firm of Cahill, Gordon said in a speech at Harvard, journalists and lawyers are different and neither should confuse his role with that of the other. Mr. Abrams quoted Justice Brandeis as saying: "Men born to freedom are naturally alert to repel invasion of their liberty by evil-minded rulers. The greatest dangers to liberty lurk in insidious encouragement by men of zeal, well-meaning but without understanding."

Not long ago, Judge Medina gave some advice to the press which I think can stand as our attitude, our perspective and our task in a Bicentennial year.

First, he said, stand squarely on the First Amendment. Guidelines are a snare and a delusion and the same is true of American Bar Association proposals designed to bring about a certain orderliness in issuance of gag rules.

Second, said Judge Medina to the press, make no compromises and no concessions of any kind.

And finally, said the judge to the press: Fight like tigers every inch of the way.

PERSPECTIVE OF SOCIOLOGY

Andrew M. Greeley*

"*Timeo sociologos et data ferentes*"—attributed to Virgil (slightly modified)**
"Dem experts—dey don't know nuttin' "—attributed to Richard J. Daley (perhaps apocryphal)***

There is, as I am sure many of you are aware, a vast literature on the relationship between the two disciplines which are represented on the opposite sides of the podium here. My Jesuit training has made me dutiful about such things, and I did glance through most of it, growing ever more depressed with the melancholy thought that I was not competent in any of it. There really was no earthly reason for me to accept the invitation to contribute to this volume other than a reluctance to admit ignorance in a subject about which I cannot write an adequate paper. But then it occurred to me that the wise men who planned this volume probably know what my competencies are, and since this is clearly not an occasion for writing about the sociology of religion and the sociology of ethnic groups, I had been invited because of my competence, such as it may be, in empirical social research—in data collecting, fact grubbing, nose counting. And so therefore it is about the relationship between empirical data collection and the law that I will endeavor to write.

My thesis will be an exercise in sociological restraint, which, it seems to me, is even more rare today than that vanishing phenomenon judicial restraint. I state my thesis as follows:

The law would be very unwise to place undue emphasis in its arguments and decisions on the findings of sociological

**Director, Center for the Study of American Pluralism.*
***Freely translated, "Keep those sociologists away with their damn data!"*
****Freely translated as above.*

research. Rare indeed will be the sociological input in a legal and judicial process that is sufficiently definitive to tilt the balance of the scales of justice one way or another.

I clearly hedge. I do not want to rule sociology (or related empirical disciplines) completely out of order in the courtroom, but neither do I want to turn the legal process over to sociologists. "*Virtus in medio statu*," one of my tiresome predecessors once insisted. The dictum is unexceptionable, the problem is where the hell is the center? I would suggest that the center, or the mean, in this case is a minor footnote or two in a brief or a decision.

Or to put my heretical views in slightly different form: a good rule of thumb would be that when judges and lawyers find themselves listening to sociologists arguing with each other, it is time, perhaps past time, to declare a mistrial.

Let me be even more specific. I note that in *Brown v. Board of Education* there is a citation of social science research. As I understand it, this research was done by Professor Kenneth Clark about the harm that segregated schooling does to the self images of black children. I trust that this research was not decisive in the decision, and as I read accounts of the decision, it was not—though a lot of social scientists would persuade themselves that it was. There are, I believe, good and sufficient reasons for having ended "separate but equal" public schools quite apart from Professor Clark's findings. "Separate but equal" was a moral abomination, and while I am not a lawyer, I would be very surprised if someone told me that the legal and constitutional arguments against it needed social science support to be effective. It would be most unfortunate if that were the case, for Clark's findings do not, I think, stand the test of time. Human personality is remarkably resilient, and it takes a lot more than segregation and oppression to harm the tough self images of children. My own ethnic group, with a history of a thousand years or so of oppression and discrimination, would take strong exception to the notion that such an experience has particularly harmed our self image—though of course, characteristically, we would be perfectly willing to use the argument that it had done so if it suited our purposes on the occasion.

If I understand the state of the literature currently, it has been reasonably well established that poverty and not race correlates positively with low self image. The point is important, I think, if not for lawyers and judges then certainly for social policy makers. (Though in the present situation it would appear that a number of judges have decided that they are social policy makers.) You may very well wish to eliminate discrimination because it is an immoral and unconstitutional abomination; I shall applaud such a goal. But if you want to eliminate the effects that past injustices have imposed on minority groups, you will do so not by eliminating residential and educational segregation but by eliminating poverty. If you want to improve people's self images, improve their income and forget about where they go to school. Such a notion smacks of heresy. "What kind of school one goes to," you say, "certainly affects income levels." Alas, by and large, it does not. The greatest failure of the civil rights movement, it seems to me, in recent years was that it did not understand that fact. There may be moral, esthetic, legal, and religious grounds for campaigning for ever more school integration; but do not expect that by doing so you will make much contribution to improving the income of minority groups—to say nothing of improving their education.

But why am I willing, indeed eager, to restrain social research to a minimal courtroom role? I suppose the only answer to that question is to say that social science, despite its name, is not science the way other sciences are. Its claim to be a science is relatively harmless until it begins to interfere in the real processes of human life as though it had the same scientific certainty as physics and chemistry and biology. Quite simply, the predictive and variance-explaining powers of social science models that are other than definitions is appallingly low.

Social science is probably not nearly as good as meteorology in predicting what will happen. Imagine, if you will, making legal arguments and judicial decisions on the basis of the kind of certainties which weather forecasters have.

The reason for the low predictive and explanatory power of the social sciences is not the natural inferiority of these disciplines nor the stupidity of those who practice them. Social science is a very uncertain exercise because it deals with such a complex object—the social behavior of the most unpredictable and complicated creature in the universe. (Or that portion of the universe that is available to us to tap respondents for survey interviews; to my knowledge, no one has ever attempted to select a random sample of angels or devils. Of course the National Opinion Research Center would be willing to try if the proper funds were available and somebody could come up with a sampling list.)

Sociology is much less confident in its findings than microbiology because the matters studied by the microbiologists are a lot more simple than those matters studied by sociologists. Awhile back, it used to be complained that there was something wrong and perverse with our society because we could put a man on the moon and we could not educate children. The implication, of course, was that putting a man on the moon was a vast, complicated task and educating children was rather simple. In fact, putting a man on the moon is little more than a feat of engineering and administration; compared to educating even a single child, it is a pushover to get a man to the moon.

It is a pious fiction, but it keeps some social scientists going, that someday they will "catch up" with the hard sciences. Just now, they will admit, our explanatory or predictive powers are not all that good, but if we plug ahead with our theory formation and hypotheses testing, someday we will push our variance explaining up so high that we can swagger along in academic processions with every bit as much arrogance as the physicists and the mathematicians.

Okay, fellas, if that's what you want to believe. We all need our myths and our superstitions. I would be the last one to take yours away from you, but don't hold your breath.

My own perverse feeling is that the hard science model is a bad idea, that sociology is a different kind of science than physics and ought not to try to imitate physics. But still, when sociology came into being, the hard sciences were thought to be science par excellence; and between them and mushy-headed things like "the humanities" there was only a middle ground of disciplines striving mightily to achieve the same precision and certainty as the hard sciences. Well, like I say, if that's the way you want to divvy up the things that go on in the university, it's fine with me; but then, for the love of heaven, don't parade into a law court and claim that your knowledge about human society is roughly comparable to the knowledge of an astrophysicist about the galaxy.

Why should one have sociology then? I can think of any number of reasons. It keeps intellectuals off the streets where they could be looking for work or fomenting revolutions. It is a pleasant and interesting way to spend time. It broadens and enriches our knowledge about human behavior. It has some useful techniques for data collection. It's fun, and it doesn't do anybody a great deal of harm except when sociologists begin to indulge their apparently incorrigible messianic tendencies. "This is," you will say, "a very restrained justification for any professional discipline." Perhaps. Though I would contend in response that while it is surely the case that sociologists, plowing their own fields, do not do nearly as much good for human beings as do lawyers, it is also true that they do not do nearly as much harm. Anyhow, it's a living.

There is one sort of activity at which my kind of empirical fact grubbing is very good, I think, and that is refuting myths. It is a useful and instructive, if not socially productive, activity. Let us take three myths that are widely held in American society: (1) Attendance at parochial schools is likely to produce young men and women who are less sympathetic to other groups in the society than those members of their denomination who did not attend parochial schools. (2) The so-called white ethnics are more likely to be racists and were more likely to support the Vietnam war and are more likely to take conservative positions than are other Americans. (3) In a society like ours, few if any people will experience the intense ecstatic interludes of the kind described by William James in his *Variety of Religious Experiences*.

Now all three of those myths are so much part of the conventional wisdom that I dare say few would question them. Yet in fact each of them is totally unsupported by empirical evidence, and indeed, in each case, the evidence supports, and if I may say so, strongly supports, exactly the opposite position. Note that I do not say "proves"; I say "supports." But once we have refuted the myths, we are then in the awkward position of having to respond to the question, "how come?" How come Catholic school Catholics are more racially enlightened rather than less and are more ecumenically disposed rather than less? How come the white ethnics are more liberal on most social and political issues? How come mystical experiences have persisted into the contemporary world? One might also further ask, how come such myths can come into being and persist even though they are demonstrably false? It is possible to adduce explanations in response to this litany of "how comes." In some cases it is even possible to attach numbers to one's explanations; but anyone who does so with any degree of confidence or certainty is either a charlatan or a fool and should not be taken seriously—and certainly should not be testifying as an expert witness in a court of law.

Sociology, in other words, is quite good at refuting myths but not nearly so good at offering positive explanations. It is much less good still at dictating "scientific" social policy. To put the matter in mathematical terms, the standardized correlations (the "betas" for any initiate) on which most social policy recommendations are based are appallingly low. The honest sociologist will tell you this; he will even go so far as to make the extraordinary concession, "You know, I might very well be wrong on this."

When was the last time you heard a sociologist say *that*?

Let us take a case in point, the so-called "Coleman report" of the 1960s. (Coleman, *et al. Equality of Educational Opportunity* Washington, D.C.: United States Office of Education, 1966). Part of the incredible campaign of vilification against James Coleman consists of the assertion that his original report "proved" that racial integration improved educational achievement, but that more recently, like a lot of other "phony liberals," he has turned away from supporting integration.

Let us leave aside for the moment such questions of fact as to whether the press releases issued at the time of the publication of the Coleman report accurately described its findings. Let us also leave aside questions of whether Coleman's personal position on integration has changed (though I will not leave it without noting that Coleman was and is an integrationist, that he has not changed his mind, that his original stand in support of integration had little to do with the findings of his survey, and that his doubts about busing are not the result of a change of mind but rather of doubts about how best to achieve the goal) and ask whether in fact the Coleman report did prove that racial integration improves education achievement.

Now if one reads the report and looks at the data instead of reading what others write and listening to what others say about it, one will see that two facts emerge: (a) The report does not prove that racial integration, as such, will improve educational attainment. What it does show is that social class integration (and a natural as opposed to artificially manipulated integration, at that) does have some effect on the achievement of lower-class students. That is, when a relatively small proportion of lower-class students are integrated into an educational institution with a relatively large proportion of middle-class students, educational achievement of the lower-class children improves. (b) But the effect is a modest one—substantially lower, for example, than the impact of Catholic schools on adult religious behavior of Catholics.

These findings, I would suggest, are hardly enough to justify on their own merits immense and elaborate desegregation plans, to say nothing of busing. Note carefully what I am saying: I believe in desegregation (though not necessarily in busing); but I do not believe in it because of the impact that it will have on education, much less on economic success. Integration is desirable, to the extent that it is desirable, on political, constitutional, ethical, and moral grounds. If you cannot justify it in those terms, do not do so in terms of its educational or economic impact, because as far as such impact can be measured by the myriad indicators of social science, it is low to non-existent.

If there were serious intent instead of ideological rigidity about improving the educational experience of minorities—and non-minorities too, for that matter—a much wiser approach (though one which I would hesitate to say was established in social science either) would be to break up the vast monopoly of the public school system and provide more freedom of choice for parents and children rather than less. I am baffled by the assumption of the courts in many recent decisions that you can improve the quality of anything by restricting instead of multiplying freedom of choice.

Closely related to the low success of sociology in predicting behavior and its even lower success in suggesting social policy is the propensity of social science to generate the complex and usually unintelligible arguments about the data. It is rather like the old argument *ex enampasi* that we learned about from a professor in the seminary. "The weaker the argument," he said, "the stronger I pound the table." Precisely because the correlations are so low and the methodology so inexact, the arguments about the validity, the meaning, and the applicability of the data are likely to be "talmudic" (to use Nathan Glazer's word); and if the data only generates modest amounts of certainty but certainty is required for controversy and, *a fortiori*, for the adversary proceedings in the courtroom, then where is one to find it save by turning to ideology? One can take a set of data which show little correlation between social policy A and effect B, one can charge the researcher with ideological bias, one can raise grave methodological problems (one can raise grave methodological problems about any social science research that has ever been done), one can then play a thousand different mathematical games with the data and finally tease out something which may be in accordance with one's own ideology. One can then proudly announce that not all the research has been done, after all, and that it will take five or ten years more to tell whether policy A has indeed led to effect B. One can then conclude by remarking piously that the liberal turncoat who did the research ought to be cited before the ethical practices board of his professional association, harassed in classrooms, vilified in the newspapers, and driven off the lecture circuit. All of this may or may not be great sport, may or may not be serious scholarship; but I take it that most would agree with me that such proceedings have no place in a court of law.

I think my own research shows with reasonable persuasiveness that Catholic schools contribute to the economic and occupational success of their students under certain sets of circumstances. I think my research also shows that there is no evidence at all that Catholic education is socially divisive. I am willing to expect in a brief or a decision on aid to parochial schools a short footnote citing this research; I would be appalled if a court would lean one way or another in its decision because of such findings, and I would be seriously concerned about the future of the American judicial enterprise if a judge permitted protracted debate and discussion about my research, wasting precious courtroom time. I think there ought to be federal support for Catholic schools, but I think so for reasons that have nothing to do with my data. As for those who are opposed to such aid, I suspect that they too would admit that empirical evidence, no matter how powerful, does not get at their real reasons for their opposition.*

It is beyond the scope of this paper to discuss whether a major strategic mistake was made by the civil rights movement in using the school as the principal focus of its concern for correcting injustice in American society. Putting such confidence in the schools is certainly a thoroughly American thing to do; still it must be said that from what we know from social theory, empirical evidence, as well as common sense, we Americans have been unconscionably bemused by the power of the educational institution. How, after all, can one reasonably expect that an institution that interacts with children a mere five hours a day, five days a week, eight or nine months of the year, will effectively compete with such more powerful and pervasive influences as home, family, peer group, neighborhood, social class, ethnic group, and mass media? Why in the world would we expect anything more than very small standardized correlations? Still, we have had great expectations for the schools. First of all, they were supposed to "Americanize" us unruly Catholic immigrants with dark skins, funny names, and incorrigible propensities to consume alcohol. Well, they didn't "Americanize" us, thank God. And now the schools are supposed to bring about equality in American society. They can't do that either. At long last people are beginning to suggest that we might begin to look at the extra-school environment; and some black leaders, most notably Eleanor Holmes Norton, are calling for federal aid to strengthen the black family—only ten

I once played, against my better judgment, the role of an "expert witness" in a federal case. It is at least partially my horror at the uses that were made of the social sciences in that case (by both sides) and the mangling of social science terminology and evidence in the adversary proceedings that has led to the stand I take in this paper. In the outcome of the case, the judge (Julius "The Just" Hoffman, as opposed to another one time Chicago judge who was known as "Just" Julius.) came to what I think was the wrong decision for the right reason; viz., sociologists didn't know what they were talking about.

years after Daniel Patrick Moynihan was vilified as a racist for saying exactly the same thing.

Christopher Jencks has recently discovered that using brother's income as a surrogate variable to measure family environment explains as much variance in educational achievement as the education, occupation, and income of parents. Studies done by the National Bureau of Economics Research show consistently higher economic achievement for Jews and Catholics than for Protestants. And more recent research by Stewart and Hill seems to link these findings with more time and greater attention paid to children in the immigrant families than in the Protestant host culture families. (I have noted facetiously on occasion that if you really want to produce more equality in American society, you would forbid certain groups—the Armenians, the Greeks, Lebanese, Jews, Irish Catholics, Chinese—from having children; or if you do permit them to produce offspring, you would not authorize them to raise them. For surely people come out of such family environments disproportionately equipped to do well in the economic struggle.)

Let it be clear what I am saying. Evidence, theory, and common sense support the notion that the family environment is far more important than the schools. Social policy makers ought to take such matters into account. Lawyers and judges should not be unaware of them as they prepare briefs and decisions, but I think it would be a terrible mistake for such social science insights to be of critical importance in a decision, or for the courts to get distracted by wrong debates over such matters. If you don't know that the family is important without social science experts to tell you so, then you ought not to be sitting on the bench or arguing a case.

Eleanor Wolfe's scary (in my judgment) account of the use of social science in the Detroit school cases notes, "The court is a poor classroom. It is the only place where we can decide if a man is guilty of murder, but it is not a good place to study the causes of homicide." Ms. Wolfe's description of the interaction between the judge and the so-called "expert" witnesses in the Detroit case ought to lead to a serious reexamination of the sociological conscience. How can the discipline be anything else but distorted and violated in the adversary processes of the courtroom? For example, Ms.

Wolfe lists the social science evidence which the adversary proceedings somehow or other left out of the Detroit school case: such highly pertinent materials as Morris Gross's *Learning Readiness in Two Jewish Groups*, Gerald Lesser's *Mental Abilities of Children from Different Social Classes and Cultural Groups*, Kevin Marjoribanks, *Ethnic and Environmental Influences on Mental Abilities*, A. J. Schwartz's *The Culturally Advantaged: A Study of Japanese-American Pupils*, Colin Greer's *The Great School Legend*, Frederick Mosteller and Daniel P. Moynihan's *On Equality of Educational Opportunity*, and Nancy St. John's *Desegregation and Minority Group Performance*, as well as Christopher Jencks' *On Inequality*.

Now one merely has to say that no responsible professor who conducts a course on race and ethnicity and education could possibly omit any of those publications from his reading list. Ultimately, all of those research enterprises might be misleading, erroneous, and wrong-headed; but at least they are major contributions to the field and must be consulted in any attempt to understand the issue. That they were omitted from the discussion in the Detroit school case means that Judge Roth, for all his efforts—and according to Ms. Wolfe, they were prolonged and involved—to get at the relevant sociological information, made his decision without information and perspectives that would have been available to anyone taking an undergraduate course in the field. Whether Judge Roth's decision was the correct one is not at issue here; rather the point is that the decision was appallingly uninformed by social science despite the judge's strong efforts to incorporate social science into the proceedings and the decision.

And, incidentally, about that part of his decision which was overruled, it does not take social science to realize that the flight to the suburbs is the most powerful segregationist tool in our society. The lines which purport to be city boundaries are far greater restrictions than "separate but equal." Judges may sit secure in their bailiwicks in Flossmoor and Newton and manipulate other people's children in other people's neighborhoods in the name of enlightened social science. But when they do so, they indeed violate both social science and its theory as well as the most obvious common sense experience of driving across the street beyond the city boundary. Again, however, I would assert that the contribution of social science to a metropolitan approach to policy—and to policy-related judicial decisions—ought to be auxiliary, supplementary, and a minor footnote rather than an occasion for a disgraceful oversimplification of a very modest intellectual discipline in the ideological crucible, which some of our adversary proceedings have become.

A word also ought to be said about the weakness of most social science indicators. We do our best with our instruments, and, if I may say so, some of our instruments are pretty good and getting better; but they are not microscopes or radio telescopes or any of the other fantastically elaborate and precise instruments of some other disciplines. No one should begin to think that they are. I am endlessly amazed by the conflict over I.Q. tests. How could anyone take such an unreliable and indeed substantively undefined indicator all that seriously? As a general and vague measure of certain kinds of undefined intellectual abilities that are not all that important save in very gross ways, maybe I.Q. has some utility. But when I heard that the Irish were a standard deviation beneath the English in I.Q. scores in the British Isles, I said to hell with I.Q. The point is, of course, that if judges and lawyers permit themselves to be further seduced into taking sociological evidence with terrible seriousness in the courtroom, they are going to have to open up the whole can of worms of social science instrumentation.

My plea, as I say, has been restrained. You folks should take us with moderate seriousness—no less, I beg of you and no more, I implore you.

Should sociology fold up then? Well, probably no great harm would be done if it did, save to the families and dependents of sociologists. But one could respond with the ad hominem but always effective argument of "you're another!" Should law fold up because it is often wrong and because its history is made up mostly of reversals? Indeed, if only the successful professions are allowed to stay in business, I fear the mathematicians will possess the earth—and then only because no one else can understand their failures.

As a rule of thumb, the more modest and restrained the sociologist, the more low-key his findings, the more gray his world, the more cautious and hesitant his policy suggestions (something like, "Well, metropolitan voluntary subsidized integration might help a little, I think") the more likely he is to be a good witness in a court of law. What you will get from him, and you should value it, is a well-educated opinion and a sophisticated perspective. Do not expect anything else of him, for his discipline was never really designed to produce miraculous cures of social ills; and the good Lord knows that it has not surprised us by coming up with any such cures.

PERSPECTIVE OF ECONOMICS

Wassily Leontief*

The juxtaposition of human law and the law of nature was the subject of philosophical disquisition long before jurisprudence and, later on, economics evolved into two distinct academic disciplines. In the great theological systems both human order and the order of nature are usually fitted into a framework of a unified teleological design.

It is not surprising that the Scottish professor of moral philosophy, who in this year's Bicentennial of both the United States and of the *Wealth of Nations* could be celebrated as the George Washington of economics, found it appropriate to invoke in the context of his brilliant explanation of the operation of the competitive market mechanism the image, "invisible hand;" Hegel spoke in the same sense of the *List der Vernunft*. In contrast to Adam Smith the German romantic emphasized cunning deception serving eternal superhuman purposes rather than benevolent assistance in the pursuit of human aim.

Malthus made use of the same paradigm in formulating, or should one say discovering, his laws of population growth. Darwin's theory of natural selection in which the principle of deterministic causal explanation is blended dialectically with the teleological concept of purposeful design marks the triumphal culmination of that train of thought.

The mutual interdependence of the personal and institutional aspects of human experience, on the one hand, and of the natural material conditions that shape them from the outside, on the other, might ultimately be understood and spelled out within the framework of a very general but at the same time concisely structured historical approach. Nineteenth century social scientists such as August Comte,

**Professor of Economics, New York University*

Karl Marx and their twentieth century successors, for instance, Max Weber, envisaged articulation of an all embracing system as their ultimate goal. No one can seriously claim, however, that unified social science is still anything more than a gleam in an ambitious scholar's eye.

What can be said about the relationship of legal institutions and the economic processes as seen from the point of view of a working economist today?

Even as Adam Smith was about to demonstrate how the twin blessings of economic efficiency and distributive justice are automatically secured through the unfettered reign of the natural laws of the competitive price mechanism, Rousseau revived Hobbes's Theory of Social Contract that revealed a highly visible collective human hand behind it: without the legal institution of private property no private profit motive could exist and without a private profit motive there could be no competition, no efficiency, no maximization of economic welfare, and no distributive justice. This deterministic chain of causes and effects is very long, but when traced back it is found to be anchored in a man-made legal order.

As an economist I cannot help but examine and appraise every legal statute in terms of its effect on the structure and functioning of that complex mechanism to which, in our everyday work, I and most of my professional colleagues refer to as the economic and social system.

To assess the true significance of a given set of laws or of legal procedures involved in their execution, one must be capable of tracing their repercussions through the network of intricate interrelationships whose strength depends not only on the basic structure of the system but sometimes also on its passing transitory state.

Legal institutions are said to be establishing the "rules of the game." To judge and to design them one must, however, know what game is being actually played. The task of finding that out is difficult enough: it is complicated by the fact that those who know often do not want to tell.

Consider, for instance, our anti-trust legislation. The Sherman Act was designed some eighty years ago on the assumption that pure—the economist often characterized it as atomistic—competition would necessarily secure productive efficiency and just income distribution (whatever "just", in this context, might mean). To break up the steel or the oil companies would, under the present technological and social conditions, prove to be an impossible task. But even if it were possible to atomize them, there is a good reason to believe that the results would turn out to be quite different from those intended. The anti-trust procedure is being used now not to establish and to maintain perfect competition but to discipline selectively large corporations in the same way that the federal income tax was used to get at Al Capone.

With the economic and social systems being in a state of constant flux, laws that may have served their purpose adequately at the time they were enacted turn out to be ineffective or even harmful a hundred, fifty or even only twenty-five years later. Reference to past precedents as practiced in the courts seems under such conditions to have little sense. Judicial re-interpretation of old laws might, on the contrary, play the same beneficial role that accelerated depreciation plays in furthering timely replacement of obsolete, worn-out equipment.

For an economist there can be hardly any doubt that, at least in his own domain, to assess the actual impact as contrasted with the purported intent of a major piece of legislation, he has to understand the structural and operating characteristic of a very large portion, if not of the entire economic system; too often convenient theoretical assumptions are used for this purpose instead of systematic factual analysis.

Moreover, all other legal statutes that happen to be in force at the time a new rule is being introduced should be viewed as integral structural component parts of that system: In anticipating the effects of a new tax law it might be necessary, for example, to take into account the existing labor legislation. In other words, what has to be assessed is not a single law but the entire system of legislation.

Could the line of argument developed above apply as well to other areas of legislative and judicial action? To ascertain the actual impact of a proposed change in criminal statutes, it is clearly necessary to take into account not only the present state of criminal courts and of the administration of various penal procedures, but also to understand the nature of the social environment associated with specific types of crime; an environment that can be expected to react in a predictable way to any change in such statutes or in their practical implementation.

Between the law as a specific action and the concrete results that it is intended to achieve, lies the vast area of economic, social, often even physical and biological structures. Without a thorough understanding of these intermediate connections one never can be certain that a particular law does actually serve its avowed purpose.

When all the facts are in there still remains the unavoidable problem of value judgment. After the initial acceptance of Bentham's utilitarian calculus, economic theory passed through a long period of sceptical attitude toward the possibility of finding an objective natural measure of human welfare. It culminated in Kenneth Arrow's formal demonstrations of the impossibility of molding a given set of diverse personal preference judgments into a single internally consistent social "preference function."

More recently under the unremitting pressure of practical exigencies most of my professional colleagues seem to have flung caution to the wind and many of them are vying with each other in devising what they consider to be plausible sets of general postulates from which one can deduct or derive a complete internally consistent system of practical value judgments. Although not professional economists but rather philosophers, John Rawls and Robert Nozik exemplify, each in his own peculiarly single minded fashion, the possibilities—or limitations, if you want, of such axiomatic approach. Rawls opts for a set of moral postulates that logically lead to acceptance of complete and absolute distributional equality. Nozik demonstrates—at least to his own satisfaction—that the only reasonable foundation for a just social order can be provided by consistent application of the principle of unrestricted hereditary private property. The remaining, admittedly rhetorical, question is: What set of axioms or "self-evident" principles should govern the choice between such alternatives?

PERSPECTIVE OF ECOLOGY

Barry Commoner*

By now you know that Professor Schwartz has been very perceptive in organizing this symposium. In my case, he has done two very perceptive things: First, he has given me the task of discussing economics, which is what I am going to do, following Professor Leontief. Second, his introduction very accurately sets the scene for what I am going to say, which is: *mea culpa.* My main aim, here, is to consider the significance of the enormous legal constraints which have been imposed on this country as a result of environmental concern.

Now, it is clear, I think, that in the last ten years, with rather startling suddenness, we have become aware of our environment. We have suddenly noticed that the air, the water, the soil, are so fouled and degraded as to threaten the collapse of the ecological processes that, after all, are the ultimate support of our lives and livelihood. The oxygen of the air is both what we breathe and what is used for making steel.

It is also clear that we have undertaken to control environmental degradation largely by enforcing powerful legal constraints. In only a few years there have been enacted a series of major new laws, among them the National Environmental Policy Act, the Clean Air Act, the Water Quality Improvement Act, the Occupational Safety and Health Act, the creation of the Federal Energy Administration. All this has generated an elaborate system of regulation and a growing bureaucratic machinery, designed to set limits on environment degradation and to curtail activities that worsen it. For example, the laws now mandate that levels of the noxi-

Director; Center for Biology of Natural Systems; Washington University; St. Louis.

ous ingredients of smog may not exceed certain limits. These have been set by the Environmental Protection Agency, which also has the right to enforce these limits by requiring certain performance of automobiles, and if need be, by restricting the flow of traffic. In the same way, substances that cause cancer can be forbidden to commerce, restricting the use, for example, of DDT and other insecticides. Nevertheless, despite the new laws, the smog has not improved, the abuses continue, new toxic chemicals appear in the workplace, and old ones continue to spread in the environment. Further constraints seem to be needed to curb the hazards.

It is a fact, then, that the national effort to improve the environment has created a very considerable bureaucratic superstructure: regulations, reports, inspection, monitoring, hearings, civil and criminal proceedings, suits and countersuits, court orders, injunctions and fines. Our environmental concern has created a great deal of law. No matter how much we value the improvement of the environment, realism and candor require that we recognize the main outcomes of this concern for what in truth they are: stringent and pervasive limitations on freedom. And, the new bureaucracy which we have created to enforce these constraints adds new costs to a government which already inflicts on the nation's all too numerous poor a heavy burden of taxation. To quote one of the recent reports of the Council on Environmental Quality, the new environmental laws ". . . are weaving their requirements and constraints through the fabric of the nation."

Clearly, in our enthusiasm for improving the environment we have added to the increasingly fine net of burdensome regulations that enmesh our lives. We have increased the power of the government—which is already so powerful as to have engaged, as we know from the shameful revelations in Washington recently, in dangerous violations of the very laws that the government is supposed to enforce. Why should this be true? Why do we appear to be caught in a dilemma—that we can only improve the environment at the expense of added bureaucracy and added constraints on our personal freedom?

This is a question that involves issues much broader than

the environment. It is the same question that we need to ask about the government's growing power to regulate agricultural production, industrial practices, systems of transportation, patterns of housing or schooling, and the provision of medical care. These are the issues which—so long as they remain unsolved—discourage belief in the value of democracy that we celebrate this Bicentennial.

I am aware that this is the same issue which reactionary politicians are trying to exploit. But I think that the time has come to recognize the legitimacy of the issue, to remove it from the arsenal of reactionary propaganda and to discover a democratic and humane approach to the increasing burden of bureaucracy and government costs. It is a happy fact, that the environmental issue, properly understood, can lead us in this direction.

In order to understand the environmental issue we need to understand its relation to the three dominant systems that govern human activity:

First, there is the ecosystem, the thin skin of the planet; the air, the water, the soil, in which the biological processes that govern the interaction between living things and their physical and chemical surroundings take place. Together with the minerals that lie beneath the earth's skin, this is the source of all of the resources that support us—both as living organisms, and as the agents of productive activities.

- The ecosystem's resources support the production system—the factories and the farms that convert natural resources into the goods and services that we want.

- The production system generates wealth, which, taken up by the economic system, is converted into wages, profits, taxes, credit, capital and all the other representations of wealth that determine how it is distributed and used.

Logic would suggest that the production system, which depends on the ecosystem, ought to be designed to be compatible with it. In fact, things are the other way around. The reason why there is smog in the environment of New York is that the production system—in Detroit—has produced cars that generate smog. Cars that were built in Detroit before World War II did not produce smog because they had low-compression engines which operated at relatively low temperatures. Then, after the engines were made bigger and hotter, the nitrogen and oxygen in the air in their cylinders reacted chemically and nitrogen oxides was emitted in the exhaust; acted on by sunlight nitrogen oxides trigger the smog process. Smog—one of the worst environmental problems—is a consequence of a change in the technology of automobile production.

Nearly every environmental problem originates in this same way—in the production system. Why is there now a danger of cancer from exposure to vinyl chloride—a substance not found in nature? The reason is that the chemical industry decided to produce huge amounts of the plastic, polyvinyl chloride, which people wear as boots and raincoats, which coats the inside of motel rooms. To manufacture polyvinyl chloride, huge amounts of vinyl chloride have been produced—exposing workers, and perhaps the rest of us, to its noxious effects. And, again, the reason why we suffer pollution from detergents is that the soap industry decided to give up making soap and produce detergents. In sum, as I have pointed out in *The Closing Circle,* on the basis of these and many other examples, the basic reason for environmental problems is that there have been changes in the production system which are incompatible with the imperatives of ecology.

The changes made in the production system were governed by the economic system. Purely economic considerations have led to the redesign of the U.S. production system in such a way as to render it drastically incompatible with the ecosystem. To deal with the environmental question we must, therefore, enter the realm of economics.

For a biologist such as myself this is, of course, a rather risky step; if I survive with Professor Leontief's good will when I am finished, I will know that I have done moderately well. But environmental science is, after all, interdisciplinary; each of us involved in it must move outside our own discipline and accept the risk of criticism as a social duty. So with your forebearance, I will now perform this social duty, in the same locus as Professor Leontief.

To begin with, let us note that the relevant changes in the production system involve new relations between inputs and outputs. Natural resources are production inputs and among them energy is particularly important because it has so much to do with pollution. Other important inputs are labor and capital. Capital must be accumulated in order to produce the machines, the means of production; labor operates the machines.

Let us now consider how the recent changes in the production system that have led to the environmental crisis have affected the *productivity* of energy, capital and labor. Productivity is the ratio of the output to an input; it can be regarded as the efficiency with which that input is converted to output. For example, the most frequently discussed productivity—so common that the adjective is always dropped—is *labor* productivity. This can be measured as output per unit of labor (usually given as man-hours).

In order to express output in a way that is common to various industries it is usually measured as "value-added"—the value of the goods produced, less the value of the raw materials and energy needed to produce them. Value-added measures the contribution of the production process to the final value of the output. Thus, labor productivity is value-added per man-hour; energy productuvity is value-added per unit of energy used; capital productivity is value-added per dollar of capital invested.

Now let us examine the changes in productivities that have accompanied a transformation of the production system which has pervasively affected the environment: the substitution of synthetic materials for natural ones. One example is the substitution of detergents (which are made of synthetic materials) for soap (which is made out of fat, a natural material). Another example is the substitution of DDT and other synthetic insecticides for ladybugs.

Synthetics are produced by the petrochemical industry, which now dominates the industrial sector which is classified in Department of Commerce statistics as "Chemicals and Allied Products" (SIC Classification 28). As an example of a product which has been extensively displaced by a competitive product of the petrochemical industry—plastics—let us look at the leather industry (SIC Classification 31). Using data available for 1971, let us compare the productivities of the chemical and leather industries with respect to energy productivity—the efficiency with which energy is converted into value-added. The relevant data are: the average for all manufacturing industries is $14 of value-added per million BTU's of energy; for the leather industry it is $62 of value-added per million BTU; for the chemical industry it is $4.65 of value-added per million BTU. In other words, leather production is a more efficient way than the production of plastics to transform energy into economic gain. When you go to the store and buy a plastic handbag instead of a leather one, that plastic handbag represents a more intensive investment of energy than the leather one.

The data for capital productivity are as follows: For all manufacturing industries the average was $1.12 of value-added per dollar of invested capital. For the leather industry it is $3.64 of value-added per dollar of capital. For the chemical industry the figure is $0.80 of value-added per dollar of capital. The leather handbag is a more efficient way of converting invested capital into wealth than is the plastic handbag. Among manufacturing industries the chemical industry has one of the lowest capital productivities; it is rather inefficient in converting invested capital into value-added.

And yet the petrochemical industry has grown rapidly, while production of natural products with which it competes has declined drastically. How can an industry which is so inefficient in using energy and capital succeed? The answer is that there is one area in which the petrochemical industry is vastly more efficient than older ones, and that is in the efficiency of using labor, labor productivity.

Here are the relevant data: for all manufacturing industries labor productivity in 1971 was $12 of value-added per man-hour. For leather it is only $6.25 of value-added per man-hour. But the chemical industry has nearly the highest labor productivity of any sector of manufacturing, $27.25 of value-added per man-hour. Apparently the enormous efficiency with which the petrochemical industry uses labor overwhelms its inefficiency in using capital and energy.

(Professor Leontief, do I pass so far? This is the first time I have had an exam on this subject.

Professor Leontief: A-plus.)

What are the consequences of these differences in productivities? First, let us remember that labor productivity means different things to the entrepreneur and the worker. To the entrepreneur, rising labor productivity means more output, and therefore more economic gain from the same amount of labor. To the worker, on the other hand, increasing labor productivity may well mean fewer jobs. We can therefore make the following generalization which, in my recent book *The Poverty of Power,* is supported by extensive data from a number of technological displacements: In the post-war transformation of the United States' production system that has generated the environmental crisis, there has been a movement in the direction of a less efficient use of energy, a less efficient use of capital, and a less efficient capability to generate employment.

What is the relationship between these changes and the post-war proliferation of new regulatory agencies? As complex high-powered machines replaced hand labor, and the petrochemical industry introduced into the production system thousands of new synthetic chemicals—their biological effects always poorly understood and usually underestimated—workers began to experience more frequent work-related injuries. One result was the creation of OSHA, the Occupational Safety and Health Administration, in an attempt, which has been rather ineffective thus far, to control these environmental assaults on the workers. And, as these environmental hazards spread from the factory to the outside environment—and with the proliferation of the new industries' products which have themselves so often been harmful to the environment—there arose the need for EPA. And if, because of the transformation of the productive system industry has been inefficiently using energy, the energy supply/demand problem is worsened—which is one of the reasons for the creation of another new bureaucracy, the Federal Energy Administration.

And finally, if we are inefficiently using capital, then we have to bring the government in, as well, to help gather up enough capital, particularly to meet the needs of those industries which are least efficient in using it. As it happens, the least efficient use of capital occurs in connection with certain ways of producing energy: nuclear power, and the production of oil from shale and, synthetically, from coal. This is the rationale behind the recent proposal to create yet another Federal agency—The Energy Independence Authority—

which according to a bill introduced by the Administration would be empowered to disburse $100 billion of public funds to precisely those industries which are least efficient in their use of capital to generate power. This proposal, which would take a very long step toward state capitalism in the United States, would, necessarily, introduce new agencies to guard against the abuses that can readily occur when massive amounts of public money are applied to private purposes.

The same transformation in the production system is in part responsible for what is perhaps the most massive bureaucracy—that concerned with unemployment and its indirect but pervasive effects on social welfare. It has been estimated that changes in production technology eliminate nearly 2,000,000 jobs annually, while the entry of new workers into the labor market (in excess of those leaving it) creates a demand for about 1,800,000 new jobs. Thus, the transformation in production technology that is responsible for the environmental crisis, the energy crisis, and for the shortage of capital, is also responsible for a considerable share of the unemployment problem. Accordingly, we can assign the huge and so often lamented bureaucracy that has been created to provide for those who are unemployed and consequently in need of social support, once again, to this pervasive transformation of our system of production.

It is important to recognize that in a fundamental sense the agencies that have been thrown up by these problems usually do not act in such a way as to solve them by removing the *cause.* As a result, each separate effort—to solve unemployment, environmental, energy, or capital problems—may often worsen some other one. For example, when OSHA regulations require that production machinery be modified to protect workers from hazards, the necessary changes usually increase capital costs without increasing output—so that capital productivity falls. In the same way, when an EPA regulation requires that a factory install protective devices to reduce emission of pollutants into the environment, capital costs rise without an accompanying gain in output. And the proposed Energy Independence Authority would have the same effect, by providing public subsidies, and thus encouraging, precisely those energy industries that are least productive in their use of capital.

The falling productivity of capital plays a crucial role in these changes. Superficially it intensifies the "capital shortage" which has been the subject of a series of recent reports from the business community. According to these reports—from the New York Stock Exchange, The Chase Manhattan Bank and the U.S. Chamber of Commerce—U.S. business faces a thirty percent shortfall in the approximately $4,500 billion of investment capital that it will need in the next ten years. While one can argue about the accuracy of such forecasts it is difficult to dismiss an historical fact that has the same origin—the falling rate of profit, relative to invested capital. Capital is the denominator in this ratio, and as increasing amounts of capital are needed per unit output, the denominator swells and the ratio falls. Although it of course varies from year to year, the rate of profit, before taxes, of U.S. non-financial corporations has decreased by about fifty percent since 1948-50.

This process is bound to have a powerful impact on the economic system, for the rate of profit is—after all—what business regards as the "bottom line", the incentive for making an investment. In the last thirty years, there have been many thousands of decisions made regarding what to produce and how to produce it in the United States. Each one of these decisions has been made on the basis of this single criterion—the maximization of profit. Naturally any given decision may have some other immediate aim, such as expansion or winning a position in the market, which may defer increased profitability for a time; but whatever step is taken, the ultimate aim is always enhancement of profit. This is, after all, the basic precept of the private enterprise system. And guided by this precept, the production system has been changed in ways that have generated a deep-seated tendency to waste energy, capital and employment opportunities, to degrade the quality of the environment.

Here, then, is the common origin of all these problems—that the production system, the means of production, is private property and therefore governed, in its design, by the natural goal of enhancing the value of that property by maximizing the profit that it yields.

That the environment cannot logically be regarded as private property leads to some illuminating interactions between environmental and private concerns. New environmental laws and new interpretations of them have begun to have a noticeable impact on this relationship, tending to extend the domain of social interest into new areas. The new laws hold, for example, that land is not merely a private possession, but in some respects must be regarded as a social resource; that pollution of water is not to be opposed solely because it interferes with property rights in pure water, but more fundamentally because protection of the chemical, biological and physical integrity of the nation's waters is a social need.

But pure water, clean air, and unpolluted soil are also major production inputs. Accordingly, this new legal insight may help us recognize that, despite its present private ownership, the process of production is itself a *social* process, which logically ought to be governed by social rather than private concerns.

That the design and therefore the governance of the modern system of production is, indeed, an essential matter of social rather than private concern is, I believe, evident from the relationships among the ecosystem, the production system and the economic system. If it is acknowledged that the integrity of the ecosystem is a social concern and that its degradation is the consequence of the faulty design of production processes, then logic urges that society protect the quality of the environment by governing the design of production.

Here we can begin to see why our present social efforts to protect the environment have generated such large and complex bureaucracies, and what can be done to reduce these heavy and costly restraints. I wish to suggest the basic thesis that a social agency which seeks to protect the social interest in the integrity of the environment can do so much more efficiently if it is designed to *prevent* production faults, instead of to clean up the later consequences of these faults. This is evident, I believe, from the experience of our current attempts to remedy the environmental consequences of the faults of the production system—that have been imposed on it by a governance which seeks to serve, not the social interest, but the private interest of maximizing profit.

One example is the knot of serious and troublesome problems associated with nuclear power plants. One might imagine that such plants are designed by power company engineers, but in fact the real situation is rather different. After the designs are finished, they are submitted to an elaborate legal process—hearings regarding their safety and environmental impact—during which important changes in design are often made. Such hearings have introduced a series of major design changes: features intended to prevent earthquake damage; the emergency cooling system, design changes to reduce emitted radiation. This is not, after all, an efficient way to design a power plant. Indeed, a major part of the unpredicted increases in the capital cost of nuclear power plants is due to such design changes, which are introduced—at considerable expense—because the initial design has been found to be inadequate in its concern for the social interest in safety and environmental quality. It is clear, I believe, that if power companies were governed in the first place, in their operations, by a social concern for environmental quality it would be possible to exercise this influence more effectively, with less bureaucratic complexity and cost, than we do under the present arrangements.

Another example is provided by the smog problem, which is the inevitable consequence of a production decision—the introduction of large high-compression engines. Much of the present involved and costly environmental controls—requirements for exhaust devices, monitoring of automobile performance, environmental monitoring, traffic regulation—would be unnecessary if social interest had been brought to bear when the initial decision was made.

Thus, by allowing the production system to be governed by private interest, so that designs that violate ecological imperatives are likely to occur, and then building up a massive bureaucracy in order to try to remedy the inevitable environmental degradation, we incur both higher production costs and add to the bureaucratic constraints, and costs.

On these grounds, I conclude that the reason for the bureaucratic constraints that have followed in the wake of our determination to improve the environment, is to be found in the design of our systems of production and economics. There is a basic fault in these systems that is the common cause of both the degradation of the environment and the erosion of our freedom. The fault, I believe, is that we are governed in what we produce and how we produce it by the aim, which is a basic precept of the capitalist system, of maximizing private profit rather than social value. We can resolve this fault by creating a production system that is consciously intended to serve these social needs; and judges the values of its products by their use and not by their profitability; and an economic system that is committed to these purposes. Such a system is socialism.

There is a notion that is often put forward by conventional wisdom that our burden of bureaucracy and government costs is to be blamed on social concerns. But, it seems to me that this idea turns reality on its head. The reason why we need a massive and costly bureaucracy is to repair the faults of the private enterprise system. It is a matter of enormous historic irony that the fight to reduce bureaucracy and improve the efficiency with which the government operates, should be led by people who are defenders of the private enterprise system. Logically, it ought to be led by people who believe in socialism.

This is the outcome of the connection between the law and the environment. It brings us face to face with the most profound question that the United States must confront in the Third Century of its life: How can its failing economic system, which seems increasingly to destroy the resource base which supports it and to deprive the people whom it is supposed to serve of meaningful employment, be transformed into one which more effectively meets social needs and thereby sustains the personal freedom which is the historic foundation of the law and of our democracy?

LAW AND MEDICINE

W. Allen Wallis*

The most serious health problem in America today is the one diagnosed 40 years ago by Walter Lippmann, in his great classic *The Good Society*, as "the sickeness of an over-governed society."

"For more than two generations," Lippmann wrote nearly two generations ago, "an increasingly coercive organization of society has coincided with an increasing disorder. It is time to inquire why, with so much more authority, there is so much less stability; . . .

"Why should it be that, in a time when men are making the prodigious claim that they can plan and direct society, they are so profoundly impressed with the unmanageability of human affairs? . . .

"They find that the more they organize, the more general is the disorganization; the more they direct affairs, the more refractory they become. They find the directed society harder and harder to direct. For they have reached the point where the organization is too elaborate to be managed. The attempt to regulate deliberately the transactions of a people multiplies the number of separate, self-conscious appetites and resistances. To establish order among these highly energized fragments, which are like atoms set in violent motion by being heated, a still more elaborate organization is required—but this more elaborate organization can be operated only if there is more intelligence, more insight, more discipline, more disinterestedness, than exists in any ordinary company of men. This is the sickness of an over-governed society, and at this point the people must seek relief through greater freedom if they are not to suffer greater disasters. . . .

*Chancellor; University of Rochester

"The essential difference between the faith that our generation has embraced and the faith that it has forsaken is to be found in what it thinks some men can do to manage the destiny of other men. The predominant teachings of this age are that there are no limits to man's capacity to govern others and that, therefore, no limitations ought to be imposed upon government. The older faith, born of long ages of suffering under man's dominion over man, was that the exercise of unlimited power by men with limited minds and self-regarding prejudices is soon oppressive, reactionary, and corrupt. The older faith taught that the very condition of progress was the limitation of power to the capacity and the virtue of rulers.

"For the time being this tested wisdom is submerged under a worldwide movement which has at every vital point the support of vested interests and the afflatus of popular hopes. . . .

"The fact that the whole generation is acting on these hopes does not mean that the liberal philosophy is dead, as the collectivists and authoritarians assert. On the contrary, it may be that they have taught a heresy and doomed this generation to reaction. So men may have to pass through a terrible ordeal before they find again the central truths they have forgotten. But they will find them again, as they have so often found them again in other ages of reaction, if only the ideas that have misled them are challenged and resisted."

Lippmann may have been right when he predicted that men will find again the central truths about the evils of unlimited government that they have forgotten in this reactionary age. I hope that he was right; but I fear that he was wrong. The reaction of the current age is in fact moving at an accelerating pace toward mercantilism, Big-Brotherism, collectivism, and authoritarianism. We are surely approaching—indeed, we may have passed—the point of no return.

It was with these ideas in mind two years ago that I extended brief farewell remarks to the graduating medical school class of the University of Rochester. The remarks seemed to strike a resonant chord, and were widely reprinted—even *The New York Times* printed excerpts, alien though the ideas are to its editorial policies. Since those brief remarks represent my one and only sally into either law or medicine, it must be on them that you should blame my discussion of the subject "Law and Medicine." Since those medical school commencement remarks were brief I will quote them in full as a text for this paper.

"You who are receiving degrees in medicine or in the sciences related to medicine," I told the graduates, "undoubtedly realize that throughout the country at this season thousands of others are receiving similar degrees in token of their preparation, like yours, for devoting the best parts of their lives to improving the health of their fellow men.

"Most of you are vaguely aware, also, that all over the country even larger numbers are emerging from professional schools of another sort, namely schools of law. Probably few of you realize, however, that before your careers have run their courses those lawyers may have more influence than you have over what you do, how you do it, and how you are rewarded.

"You may find lawyers defining the range of treatments that you are allowed to use in specified circumstances. Lawyers may prescribe the criteria by which you are to choose among the allowable treatments. Lawyers may specify the priorities you must assign to different patients. Lawyers may require you to keep detailed records to establish at all times that you are in full compliance. Lawyers may punish you unless you can refute beyond a reasonable doubt their presumption that your failures result from not following all of their rules, regulations, and requirements. And lawyers may decide what incomes you deserve.

"Should you have the temerity to differ with the lawyers, you will be backed by the authority of your knowledge, your science, your skill, your art, your experience, your judgment, your dedication, and your conscience. Which is to say that in the eyes of the law you will have precious little backing; for knowledge, science, skill, art, experience, judgment, dedication, and conscience—whatever else their merits—do not constitute due process of law.

"This control of health care by lawyers will come about through a process in which many of you—and most of your contemporaries—believe unquestioningly. That is the process of turning to the government to solve all problems, real or imagined, large or small, widespread or confined. If research funds or training funds are less than you would like, have the government get them from other people by force. If you think that smoking tobacco or marijuana is bad for health, have the government prevent it. If you think that cars are too big, get the government to limit their sizes. If you think that people should not see obscene movies, get the government to ban them by force. If you think that professional wrestlers are often frauds, have the government license them. If you think that doctors do not always perform perfectly have the government establish professional standards and enforce them.

"Scarcely anyone has confidence in any branch of government (except, ominously, the military), so we create new government agencies to monitor the old ones. Increasingly, confidence in private institutions and professions also is eroding, and the accepted solution is to regulate them through government, even though government is respected and trusted even less than the institutions it is charged with regulating.

"It is this process of putting the least trusted of all institutions, government, in charge of less distrusted institutions and professions which may result in lawyers acquiring a far larger measure of control over health care and research than they have today. For what we call 'government' is, after all, made up of people, and not necessarily superior people, much less perfect people. While not all people in government are lawyers, lawyers usually participate in writing rules, regulations, orders, guidelines, and directives, and the adjudicators and enforcers almost invariably are lawyers. So we can expect the work of those now receiving degrees in health to be closely regulated by those now receiving degrees in law."

Since that talk was given a new periodical has been started, the *American Journal of Law and Medicine.* In its second issue, dated Fall, 1975, George J. Annas, (who is a Doctor of Jurisprudence, a Master of Public Health, and a faculty member of both the law and medical schools at Boston University) has an article on "Law and Medicine. . . ." whose second section is headed "Why Legal Medicine is a Requisite Component of the Medical School Curriculum."

"Almost everything the doctor does in the practice of medicine is in some manner governed by the legal system," Professor Annas writes. "The law defines what the doctor can or cannot do in terms of medical practice and the geographic bounds of his authority. It defines his relationship with his patient in terms of contract and implied contract, and it defines his duty to his patients in terms of obtaining both consent and informed consent. The law governs what drugs a doctor may prescribe and in what quantities. It defines the rights of patients and prescribes remedies for patients who are injured by doctors. This list is easily broadened to include staff privileges and duties, human experimentation regulations, privacy, confidentiality, privileged communications, abortion, sterilization, euthanasia, consultation, abandonment, referral, admission to hospital, emergency room duties, discharge from hospital, Medicare, Medicaid, private health insurance plans, comprehensive health planning, certificate of need, PSRO, licensing, physician assistants, anatomical gifts, and autopsy. Wherever a doctor turns, he is confronted by law—statutory, case, and constitutional—which governs or limits his conduct in one way or another."

Professor Annas points out that "A similar. . . list could. . . be constructed for policemen, dairy farmers, bankers, oil drillers, or for that matter, any American citizen," though he believes naively that the other lists are "probably not so extensive." Here he approaches the root of the situation of which the problems of law and medicine are merely one symptom, namely "the sickness of an over-governed society."

Professor Annas is not quite accurate when he uses the phrase "the law defines." Few of the entanglements between lawyers and doctors grow out of defined law, at least in the sense of statutory, case, and constitutional law. Often, they grow out of administrative law and regulations and guidelines issued by government employees—out of the edicts of bureaucrats, in other words. Sometimes they grow out of the activities of self-anointed groups who purport to represent the "public interest" as they define it—which is equivalent to "patriotism" as Samuel Johnson defined it. Sometimes they grow out of the disposition of courts to intervene in any area of social life.

The day will come, I fully expect, when case law or administrative edict will establish a sort of statute of limitations for refutations of research findings. Such a rule might say, for example, that a doctor may wait—or would it say that he *must* wait?—seven years before applying a new treatment in order to see whether any ill-effects turn up. This may sound preposterous, but courts already have made rulings on the maximum length of time following publication of a new finding during which a doctor may be excused for not knowing about it. No doubt some day, after an unlucky doctor has applied a new finding that is later discovered to have undesirable side effects, a court will set a minimum length of time that doctors should wait before applying a new treatment in order to see whether detrimental effects will be discovered. This would guarantee that no detrimental effects would be discovered within the stated time, since if the waiting period were observed no patients would receive the treatment during that period.

It is obvious (I hope) that any such uniform period, whether a minimum or a maximum, is obnoxious. Each physician ought to decide as best he can in each instance whether the unknown risks that always inhere in a new treatment should be accepted. If, for example, it is certain that the patient will die unless the new treatment works, or probable that he will lose a limb, or possible that he will lose his mind, it may be in the patient's interest to try the new treatment. But government cannot control conduct efficiently if it allows that kind of latitude. Mass regulation requires fitting all behavior into relatively few standard categories, within each of which all cases can be processed uniformly. As George Stigler has pointed out, we should refer not to Uncle Sam but to Uncle Same.

The meaning of the phrase "rule of law" is coming to be in practice the opposite of what we have traditionally understood by the phrase. Traditionally, the ideal of the rule of law has been that all men were equal before the law, regardless of rank, position, race, religion, income, occupation, politics, or any other characteristic; the law was blind. The ideal of the rule of law has precluded retroactive legislation, and it has precluded laws intended to burden or benefit some people differently from others in the same circumstances.

Now the term "rule of law" is coming to mean, as it did in the middle ages, that all activites and relations between people should be ruled by law. It is argued that in an interdependent society any action of an individual and any transaction between individuals necessarily affects other members of society, so it is intolerable that there should be any activities or transactions that are not regulated by society. Since human beings cannot exist except in a society, and a society is by definition interdependent, it follows that "Whatever is not compulsory should be prohibited." This is coming to be the new meaning of "the rule of law;" instead of protecting freedom, the new rule of law is annihilating freedom.

Alexander Solzhenitsyn has been quoted as making a statement about the Russian government that is too nearly true of ours, that it dislikes any relations between individuals which it does not supervise. In this country, it is not, of course, "The Government" as an entity that wants to supervise. Rather, for almost any relations between individuals there is some group which has a special interest in supervising, and the influence of special interests in our system of government is so strong that generally they get their way and are able to manipulate the coercive powers of the government to advance their special interests. (By "special interests" I refer not only to commercial and economic interests but to such organizations as the Sierra Club, Common Cause, Ralph Nader and his multifarious franchises, organized religion, higher education, the health professions, lawyers, journalists, and so forth.) As Walter Lippmann said in the passage I quoted earlier, "the attempt to regulate deliberately the transactions of a people multiplies the number of separate, self-conscious appetites and resistances."

To put the same idea rather differently: When government undertakes to bring about certain social results, instead of simply to establish and enforce constitutional and legal principles within which society will live—in other words, when government abandons the rule of law and undertakes the rule of society—people reduce their efforts to do things for which other people will voluntarily exchange their own goods and services, and increase their efforts to gain control of the powers of government through which they can coerce others; and in their direct relations with others, for example, in the practice of medicine, they divert their attention from consideration of what will best serve the client's interests to what will protect their own interests in potential legal proceedings.

Beyond its adverse effects on the practice of medicine and the care of patients in general, the new perverse rule of law, by which everything is coming to be ruled by law, has had detrimental effects on the quality of medicine available to be applied by doctors. The Food and Drug Administration's regulations, for example, together with certain acts of Congress, have changed the United States from a leader to a substantial laggard in developing new medicines. The U.S. drug lag is most pronounced in the cardiovascular, diuretic, respiratory, antibacterial, and gastrointestinal areas. In appearing before a Senate Committee in September, 1974, Dr. William Wardell, of the pharmacology faculty of the University of Rochester Medical School, testified as follows:

"The U.S. was at least the 30th country in the world to approve the bronchodilator metaproterenol; the 32nd country to approve the anti-cancer drug adriamycin; the 41st country to approve the anti-mania drug lithium carbonate; the 51st country to approve the anti-tuberculous drug rifampin; the 64th country to approve the anti-allergic drug cromolyn; and the 106th country to approve the anti-bacterial drug co-trimoxazole.

"Even when a drug is finally admitted to the U.S., the indications for its use are often ridiculously restricted and out-of-date. For example, the U.S. has more restrictions on the use of co-trimoxazole than any of the 107 countries in which the drug is currently marketed. Here, it is still only approved for the short-term treatment of chronic urinary tract infections. More important medically are situations in which this drug may be life-saving, in some of which no other effective therapy is available. Such situations were recognized as early as 1962, but are still essentially unknown (and certainly unapproved) uses in the U.S., some 12 years later.

"Perhaps the most astonishing recent example of the unrealistic gap between regulatory philosophy and medical practice is that of propranolol. It is hard to believe that an advisory committee was still debating the approval of this drug for angina at a time when a physician's *failure* to use this drug (e.g., as a trial in most patients prior to coronary artery surgery) would be regarded as substantially suboptimal medical practice. The regulatory fate of this drug, for an indication (angina) in which it has long been a therapy of choice, bodes ill for its regulatory chances in an equally important indication, hypertension. In this latter respect, American regulatory philosophy is already a decade behind medical practice."

It is ironic that the regulations which have greatly reduced pharmacological research have not harmed, but possibly have helped, the large established pharmacological firms. The effect of the FDA regulations has been to eliminate the most expensive form of competition among these firms, which has been the search for new drugs of sufficient value to be prescribed widely by the medical profession. This restriction of competition would have been illegal had it resulted from voluntary cooperation within the industry rather than from government compulsion—and it *should* be illegal, for competition to find new drugs has brought, in the net, incalculable benefits to consumers. The restraints on research give firms that already are well-established a considerable measure of protection not only against other established firms, but especially against would-be new entrants who might compete effectively with them.

All of these developments confirm the wisdom of the founding fathers in limiting narrowly the powers of the Federal Government. They did this only partly from antipathy to governmental control of private affairs. To be sure, such antipathy was strong at the time, because of direct experience in the preceding hundred years. But an equally powerful reason for restricting the power of the Federal Government was the realization that the form of government they wanted—a domocratic government—cannot endure if it intervenes extensively in the affairs of the people. Democratic processes—representative processes, if you prefer—simply cannot handle complex, highly technical matters satisfactorily.

A democratic government cannot design efficient automobiles, it cannot design a sound energy policy, it cannot eliminate prejudice and discrimination, it cannot manage transportation, it cannot assure the soundness of investments or the accuracy of information about them, it cannot guarantee the effectiveness and safety of medicines, it cannot assure standards of professional practice, it cannot eliminate risk from health care—it cannot, in short, do most of the things that our government undertakes to do.

Congress, perhaps partly in recognition of its own incapacity to do all the things it undertakes to do, has come increasingly during the past forty years not to legislate itself but to delegate to thousands of employees the right to make what are effectively laws, and the right to enforce them.

Another important fact about representative government that the founding fathers recognized is that direct election by the people is likely not to produce the most competent representatives to carry on the people's business, and furthermore is likely to promote demagoguery and instability of policy.

Thus, in the *Federalist Papers* one of the features described with pride, as an argument for accepting the proposed Constitution, was that the people could not get directly at the government. Only the House of Representatives was to be elected directly by the voters. Senators were to be elected by state legislatures; the President and the Vice President were to be elected by a special Electoral College; and judges were to be appointed by the President and Senate.

Perhaps in an unconscious response to the weakness of government by representatives elected directly by the people, there is currently a strong movement toward government by the judiciary, which is now the only part of the Federal Government that still is not elected by the people. A great deal of administrative business is now done by the courts.

It has been recognized for fifty years or more that the courts revise the Constitution through their interpretations and reinterpretations, and it has been recognized for perhaps twenty-five years that, in effect, the courts legislate in innumerable matters, including apportionment of Congress, legislatures, and school districts, and criminal laws and the operation of prisons, but it has not been widely recognized that currently the courts are assuming many administrative functions that formerly were regarded as executive responsibilities. A recent newspaper article suggested that more of the administrative business of Alabama is being done by a federal judge than by the governor.

The court system, especially the federal court system, in which judges have life tenure and the Supreme Court has power that is limited only by its own self-restraint, is the only part of American government capable of adopting policies on the basis of principle. The courts are the only part of the government capable of making its policies consistent throughout a broad range of diverse subject matter. And the courts are the only part of the government capable of adhering to policies steadfastly for decades. Perhaps the gradual evolvement of government by judiciary is to be explained by the default of the legislative and executive branches, which cannot act on principle, which cannot be consistent, and which cannot adhere to stable policies because of the vagaries of elective processes.

For decades, the apportionment of legislative and Congressional seats was allowed to depart further and further from both constitutional intent and the public's sense of equity. For decades the rights of criminals and prisoners were allowed to fall below constitutional standards and the public's sense of justice. Racial discrimination in public facilities was allowed to persist long after the public's sense of fairness had moved far toward the ideals expressed in the Constitution. In all of these matters, and many others, the Congress and state legislatures clearly defaulted until, finally, the courts took over, at first by directing adherence to constitutional principles, then by issuing laws, and eventually by direct administration.

But the courts, like all agencies of government, never know when to stop. Indeed, what criterion is there, once started down this path, by which the courts can discriminate between issues which they should take over from a defaulting Congress and issues which they should avoid, even though they involve social imperfections or injustices? Where can they stop, short of judicial autocracy?

But courts are ill-suited to dealing with many classes of

problem. Science in general, and medicine in particular, are fields in which the courts are fundamentally incompetent. The deference to authority and precedent, the respect for continuity and tradition, the rules of evidence, the adversary procedures, and concepts such as res judicata, collateral estoppel, fiduciary duties, advocacy, and summary judgment, that quite properly characterize the law, are all antithetical to science. Often the facts that are essential to understanding a legal case that involves science are quite beyond any possibility of understanding and comprehension by judges, much less juries. The impossibility of understanding and comprehending the essential facts of a case is even more complete when not only science is involved but, as in medical cases, the art of applying scientific knowledge which is incomplete and uncertain, to deal with conditions that cannot be known fully or instantly, under circumstances calling for prompt decisions which cannot be reversed.

Although at present medical matters are handled badly by courts and by the extensive catchment system of laws, regulations, and guidelines that channels medical matters into the courts, it seems to me possible that as we move increasingly toward government of the total society by judicial autocracy, the courts may develop better means of exercising their vast and intricate authority. Specialization is one possible device. Already we have a variety of specialized courts: small claims, tax, customs, probate, juvenile, family, and traffic matters are examples. Special judicial arrangements for medical malpractice cases have been suggested. Arthur Kantrowitz has been urging for some time that a special scientific court be established.

In summary: The sickness of over-government by which we are afflicted is leading to a transfer of governmental authority from representatives who are elected directly by the people for limited terms to judges who are appointed for life. Because elected representatives are subject to popular control by diverse constituencies, they are not able to act in principled, uniform, or consistent ways. Because federal judges are subject not to popular control but to a single authority, the Supreme Court, they are able to act in principled, uniform, and consistent ways, so authority is flowing to them by default of the legislative and executive branches.

The courts have not yet developed the competence to handle the infinite variety of subjects that are now coming under their administration. Medicine is just one of the innumerable areas in which the courts are heavily involved but for which they do not yet have the requisite competence. But as overgovernment continues to be elaborated, and as ever more authority devolves on judges, the courts may develop, as the legislative and executive branches did earlier, an intricate division of labor—in other words, a great bureaucracy of their own. This will not improve the health-care of patients—quite the opposite—but it should result in a stable—even static—system in which doctors will know what motions they should go through and will no longer be torn by the contradictory requirements of their patients' welfare, on the one hand, and the law on the other.

Doctors will simply conform to law. The government will have killed the patients, but it will persuade the public that the doctors, hospitals, and drug companies did it and must therefore be governed more stringently, more extensively, and more minutely.

The remedy for all this is obvious and simple, but implausible: *Return the power to the people.* Give each doctor and each patient the right and responsibility for making his own decisions freely in the light of his own best knowledge (or ignorance) and judgment (or folly). Inevitably, some doctors and some patients will make some unwise decisions, perhaps even some that harm other people. But there is no possibility that the greatest harm these errors could do would even approximate the least harm that the government can do—indeed, is already doing.

PERSPECTIVE OF PSYCHOLOGY
THE THEOLOGY OF THERAPY:

The Breach of the First Amendment Through the Medicalization of Morals

Thomas Szasz*

I

Expressing the "essence" of a nation in a single image is more like drawing a person's caricature than like painting his portrait. And as a good caricature reveals more about a person than does his portrait, so the true symbol of a nation reveals more about it than do its formal self-definitions.

We have no difficulty in compressing the spirit of America into a single word, symbol, or image. That word is "liberty." To understand the concept of liberty, and especially its characteristically American formation and deformation, it is necessary to understand the interests and institutions that encourage and impede its development. I shall assume that, in our national experience, we recognize the Rule of Law in general and the First Amendment in particular as encouraging and indeed creating liberty. And I shall argue that we ought similarly to recognize medicine in general, and psychiatry in particular, as impeding and indeed destroying liberty. The gist of my thesis will be that as the founding fathers regarded coercive religion as not religion but repression, and hence incompatible with the American political system, so we should regard coercive medicine (and especially psychiatry) as not therapy but tyranny, and hence equally inconsistent with the spirit of American liberty.

**Professor of Psychiatry, State University of New York, Upstate Medical Center, Syracuse.*

II

Sometimes it is convenient to view nations as if, like individuals, they would pass through a life cycle of childhood and youth, adulthood and maturity, old age and senescense, and would finally die. Consider the imagery that this metaphor generates: The American continent, dormant and virginal; the development of Colonial America under the protection of the mother country; the severance by the young adult of his ties to his parents; the Declaration of Independence; the self-development of the new nation, in a bare century-and-a-half, to the freest, richest, strongest, and most envied people on the face of the earth.

What are the main obstacles facing a young person in his quest for independent adulthood? On the one hand, there are the external obstacles—in particular, parents and other adults, who—whether altruistically seeking to protect a weaker person, or egotistically seeking to prey upon him—endeavor to keep him tied to them. On the other hand, there are the internal obstacles—in particular, the individual's own sense of weakness, his fears of the uncertainties and dangers of life—in short, his longing for the sort of protection to which he had become accustomed as a child. A person may thus remain immature either because his parents actively discourage his independence, or because he himself succumbs to the seductions of his own longings for security. Similar obstacles loom before people seeking independence as a nation.

Two-hundred years ago the American people were faced with the task that typically confronts the young adult—namely, securing a material existence separate from one's parents, and a spiritual existence separate from one's priests. The founders of this Republic were amazingly aware of both of these obstacles, and were boundlessly courageous, intelligent, and resourceful in overcoming them. Thus, on the one hand, they secured the military, territorial, and political independence of the United States from Great Britain and all other nations; and, on the other hand, they secured the separation of church and state.

Our situation today differs from that of Americans in 1776 much as the situation of an established middle-aged person differs from that of a young man or woman struggling to create his or her identity. To be sure, like the American colonists, we too face the unremitting danger of external obstacles to independence—that is, the ideologies and powers of other nations that would, if they could, subjugate and recolonize us. But I do not here want to address myself to that danger. Instead, I want to focus attention on our internal danger to independence—the perpetual temptation to reject freedom as a burden too heavy to bear.

We know how the American people and their leaders reacted to this internal—spiritual—danger two hundred years ago: by creating a societal arrangement with respect to religion such as the world had never seen before. Theirs was not just a struggle for religious freedom, although it assuredly was that too; it was also a struggle for freedom from religion, and, more particularly, from an alliance between religion and the state.

But that was in 1776. As the external danger to our independence is no longer Great Britain, so the internal danger to our independence is no longer "religion" in the sense in which people then used this term or in the sense in which we now usually interpret it. What, then, is the internal danger that faces us? It is simply the deeply human ambivalence about freedom and responsibility and the unremitting propensity to seek security by submission to individuals or institutions—whether clerical or clinical—that promise peace and protection.

III

It is no historical accident that the American struggle for religious liberty antedated the struggle for national independence. That struggle and the tradition it engendered culminated in the great writings on the separation of church and state by Jefferson and Madison, and in the First Amendment to the Constitution of the United States. For Jefferson and Madison, religious freedom—that is, freedom from religious coercion or constraint of any kind—was the crux of the struggle for freedom in general. Although this fact is familiar enough to historians, I am not sure that they, or others, have made enough of its psychological importance: namely, that men like Jefferson and Madison, who were themselves genuinely independent human beings, recognized that so long as a people want to submit themselves to a higher authority, whether it be king or pope, crown or church, their struggle for freedom will be compromised, and probably defeated, by their refusal to accept the indivisibility of freedom and responsibility across all areas of human concerns.

I realize that, today, my views on the alliance between medicine and the state may sound strange or even absurd. I dare say that in Europe in 1791, the First Amendment also sounded strange or even absurd. The point is that we, Americans, now live in a society in which we take the alliance between medicine and the state for granted, just as, for centuries, Europeans took the alliance between church and state for granted. Such habits beget closed minds filled with hatreds and follies which their owners mistake for love and wisdom.

I know that the mere suggestion of a separation of medicine and state is enough to make people raise horrified and incredulous questions such as: "You mean the government should not supervise medical education and license doctors? Should not support cancer research? Should not control dangerous drugs?" These questions leap out at one like flames at a heretic: they are not genuine inquiries seeking a dialogue, but rather accusations seeking to discredit the person to whom they are addressed.

Although we lack a tradition exalting a separation of medicine and state—indeed, we possess a contrary tradition exalting their union—we have an amazingly prescient warning, about precisely the sorts of dangers to which I am pointing, by one of the chief architects of the First Amendment. "Was the government to prescribe to us our medicine and diet," wrote Jefferson in 1782, "our bodies would be in such keeping as our souls are now. Thus in France the emetic was once forbidden as a medicine, the potato as an article of food."[1] These phrases highlight our medical-political predicament: with every forward step that we take holding the hand of the medical scientist, we take two backward steps holding the hand of the medical politician.

Jefferson was contemptuous of the French state for forbidding emetics and the potato. What would he think of the state he himself created that not only forbids the use of harmless sweeteners but also encourages the use of harmful contraceptives? That not only prohibits marijuana but also promotes tobacco? Surely, it is not mere self-serving if I suggest that were Jefferson with us today, he would conclude that the liberties he sought to guarantee for Americans have been subverted; specifically, that they have been undermined by the American Medical Association, the National Institutes of Health, the Food and Drug Administration, the Department of Health, Education and Welfare—that is, by the "unholy" alliance between medicine and the state which these agencies and organizations both symbolize and serve.

IV

The parallels between church and state relations two-hundred years ago, and between medicine and state relations today are close indeed. In each case, we are faced with a social institution to which men and women turn for protection when they feel most endangered. Hence, they want their "protector" to be as powerful as possible: for, so they reason, the more powerful is their protector, the more secure is their protection. It is usually useless to point out the fallacy in this belief; to demonstrate that protection from some things—for example, injuries and diseases—requires knowledge and skills, not power; that protection from some other things—for example, shame and guilt—requires honesty and courage, not power; that, in short, power is necessary to oppose the external, but not the internal, enemies of freedom. Why is it useless to demonstrate this? Because as soon as people set their sights on protection from responsibility, they lose sight of freedom. Two hundred years ago, many Americans understood that Jefferson and Madison were fighting not against religion, but for freedom. Today, few Americans understand that a person opposing government involvement in, or state support for, medicine—that is, medical care, medical education, drug controls, and psychiatric interventions—is fighting not against health but for freedom. It might be worthwhile to recall how Madison had put the case, in 1784, for freedom from an alliance between church and state:

> Because experience witnesseth that ecclesiastical establishments, instead of maintaining the purity and efficacy of Religion, have had a contrary operation. During almost fifteen

> centuries, has the legal establishment of Christianity been on trial. What have been its fruits? More or less in all places, pride and indolence in the clergy; ignorance and servility in the laity; in both, superstition, bigotry, and persecution.[2]

Such words betoken that both he who speaks them and those who listen to them dearly cherish self-reliance as a virtue. Although the spirit of independence has not been extinguished in our collective soul, it is clear that contemporary Americans have neither the same zest for life nor the same faith in themselves as did their colonial forebears. In what, then, do they repose their faith? To what ideas and institutions do they look, as people looked formerly to religion and the church, as sources of protection from the vicissitudes of life, as guarantees of future happiness, as substitutes for their own good sense and personal judgment? The answer is that they look to science, to medicine, and to psychiatry.

V

Medicine's hostility to liberty has a long and distinguished history, dating back at least to Plato, whose model for the benevolent despot was the doctor.[3] For our present purposes it will suffice to show how, even while seemingly fighting for political independence, one of America's leading physicians who signed the Declaration of Independence was already laying the groundwork for medical despotism.

Benjamin Rush—the author of the first American text on "diseases of the mind,"[4] and the "father" of American psychiatry (his portrait adorns the seal of the American Psychiatric Association)—never tired of insisting that therapy was more important than liberty. "Mankind considered as creatures made for immortality," he wrote in 1783, "are worthy of all our cares. Let us view them as patients in a hospital. The more they resist our efforts to serve them, the more they have need of our services."[5]

For Rush, just as for his disciples today, loss of liberty was, moreover, merely a prerequisite for the triumphs of therapeutic totalitarianism. Brutal coercion was the truly ideal therapeutic agent. "Terror," declared Rush, in one of his many Orwellian phrases, "acts powerfully upon the body, through the medium of the mind, and should be employed in the cure of madness."[6]

Finally, anticipating contemporary madness-mongers by two centuries, Rush asserted that virtually everyone is mad and advocated that political reform be replaced by "medical treatment": "The majority of mankind are madmen at large. . . . Were we to live our lives over again and engage in the same benevolent enterprise [i.e., political reform], our means should not be reasoning but bleeding, purging, low diet, and the tranquilizing chair."[7]

Because Rush had no intention to be as vigilant against the powers of physicians as he was against those of priests; because he was eager to redefine disagreements as diseases, and tortures as treatments; and because, in his passion to medicalize morals, he was at once an influential follower of our medical leaders and an influential medical leader in his own right—for all these reasons Rush's concepts and conduct exemplify the sort of danger that medicine posed to Americans even before 1776.

Clearly, the danger that medicine poses to our liberties today is infinitely greater than it was two hundred years ago. Although the encroachments of organized medicine on personal freedom have been numerous and widespread—affecting, for example, medical education and practice, abortion and contraception, the use of drugs, blood, and other organs,[8] the most obvious deprivations of individual liberties have occurred in relation to so-called psychiatric disorders and treatments. Actually, the birth and growth of psychiatry is itself a manifestation of this phenomenon.[9] That is why we now regard persons disturbed by their own behavior as suffering from a "neurosis," and those disturbing others as suffering from a "psychosis"; why we call the buildings in which such people seek retreat, or in which they are incarcerated, "mental hospitals"; and why we accept the things done with and to them—ranging from conversation and drugging to the artificial induction of epilepsy and the amputation of the frontal lobes of the brain—as "treatments."

Having thus medicalized morals, we are, nevertheless, surprised at, and revolted by, the so-called "abuses" of the healing professions. But I submit that the contemporary medical persecutions are the inexorable consequences of the alliance between therapy and the state, just as the earlier religious persecutions were the inexorable consequences of the alliance between theology and the state.

The facts are indisputable and are wholly analogous to those to which Madison pointed in the passage I have cited. We have witnessed the murderous alliance between physicians and the Nazi state in Germany; the similar alliance between physicians and the Communist state in Russia; and the only slightly less odious alliance between physicians and the Therapeutic State in America. These have been the "fruits" of the "legal establishment of medicine," and they are none the less poisonous even if, under propitious circumstances and in proper doses, they have had some beneficial consequences as well. Jefferson and Madison did not rest their case for a separation of church and state on the proposition that an alliance between them never had any beneficial consequences.[10] Thus, if we propose to accept, and indeed to embrace, the alliance between medicine and the state so long as it has any beneficial consequences at all, we might as well know it, as that is what we are now doing.

VI

The Virginia Bill of Rights declares "That all men are by nature equally free and independent, and have certain inherent rights. . .";[11] and the Declaration of Independence "that all men are created equal, that they are endowed by their Creator with certain unalienable rights. . ."[12]

It is no put-down to call these phrases noble rhetoric. I do it to emphasize that there remains the practical problem of demarcation or classification. Who are the "men" that are "by nature equally free," that possess "certain unalianable rights"? Are Negroes such? Are women? Are mental patients? For Negroes, the question was answered by Chief Justice Roger B. Taney in 1857, as follows:

> The words "people of the United States" and "citizens" . . . mean the same thing. . . . The question before us is, whether the class of persons described in the plea of abatement compose a portion of this people. . . We think they are not intended to be included, under the word "citizens" in the Constitution, and can, therefore, claim none of the rights and privileges which that instrument provides. . . [T]he negro might justly and lawfully be reduced to slavery for his benefit.[13]

I mention this opinion not to dwell on the injury done to

blacks, but to underscore that the identical problem has confronted, and continues to confront, Americans with respect to the religious clause of the First Amendment. What constitutes religion, within the meaning of this clause, and what does not? Analogies between the *Dred Scott* decision and contemporary interpretations of the First Amendment abound.

For example, a person is free to believe that the Jews are the Chosen People, but not that he is chosen to save the world; or that the pope is infallible, but not that he is infallible. The disjunction between the rights accorded by the courts to people who choose to be pious as against those who choose to be "psychotic" could not be more dramatic.

Illustrative of the Supreme Court's profound respect for religious piety is its decision to protect the rights of Jehovah's Witnesses who choose to believe that their God objects to saluting the flag. "[I]f there is any fixed star in our constitutional constellation," declared the Court in 1943, "it is that no official, high or petty, can prescribe what shall be orthodox in politics, nationalism, religion, or other matters of opinion. . . If there are any circumstances which permit an exception, they do not now occur to us."[14]

The amnesia here displayed by the Justices of the Supreme Court is reminiscent of their amnesia displayed toward slavery. For what was involuntary servitude if not an exception to the unalienable rights of persons to their life, liberty, and property? What are involuntary psychiatric interventions if not exceptions to the "fixed star in our constitutional constellation" restraining officials from prescribing what shall be "orthodox. . . in matters of opinion"? Surely, the fact that American psychiatrists now vote on whether a traditionally acknowledged mental illness—such as homosexuality—should continue or cease to be a mental illness establishes, beyond a shadow of a doubt, that definitions of mental illness and treatment are indeed "matters of opinion."

My point is that as formerly a human being was a person only if he was white, so now he is a person only if he is mentally healthy. The Negro was chattel, and the mental patient is a child. Such "objects" of benevolence need protection, not liberty. "If a man brings his daughter to me from California," declared a former president of the American Psychiatric Association at a 1961 Senate hearing on the Constitutional Rights of the Mentally Ill, "because she is in manifest danger of falling into vice or in some other way disgracing herself, he doesn't expect me to let her loose in my hometown for that same thing to happen."[15] Throughout American history, the courts have considered such loss of liberty not a penal but a medical matter, not punishment but treatment. Now they view reading the Talmud or the Bible as a matter of religion, but reading Freud or Spock as a matter of mental health. Thus have we transformed the cure of souls into the cure of minds, and our prohibitions against clerical coercion into our prescriptions for clinical coercion.

In short, I contend that we now classify many medical acts as scientific when, in fact, they are moral; and that we classify many psychiatric acts as medical when, in fact, they are religious. These opinions, which may seem strange or even outlandish today, are actually the opinions of the "founding fathers" of modern psychiatry.

VII

Toward the end of his life, Sigmund Freud asserted that "I have assumed. . . that psycho-analysis is not a specialized branch or medicine. I cannot see how it is possible to dispute this."[16] His reason for so classifying psychoanalysis was that "The course of analysis is most inconspicuous, it employs neither medicines nor instruments and consists only in talking and in exchange of information."[17]

If psychoanalysis is not a branch of medicine, what is it a branch of? According to Freud, it is a branch of religion:

> . . . the words, "secular pastoral worker," might well serve as a general formula for describing the function [of] the analyst . . . We do not seek to bring him [the patient] relief by receiving him into the catholic, protestant, or socialist community. We seek rather to enrich him from his own internal sources. . . Such activity as this is pastoral work in the best sense of the word.[18]

Carl Jung, the co-architect of modern psychiatry, was even more emphatic in rejecting the medical pretensions of psychotherapy (and psychiatry), and in reiterating the essentially religious character of soul-curing:

> [I]n most cases the sufferer consults a doctor in the first place, because he supposes himself to be physically ill. . . . That is why patients force the psychotherapist into the role of a priest, and expect and demand of him that he shall free them from their distress. That is why we psychotherapists must occupy ourselves with problems which, strictly speaking, belong to the theologians.[19]

These declarations of Freud and Jung are like the declarations, two hundred years ago, of the abolitionists and Quakers that Negroes are human beings. As the view that blacks are persons had the most far-reaching implications for the American way of life then, so the view that psychiatric (and certain other medical) activities constitute religious functions has the most far-reaching implication for our way of life now.

Slavery and psychiatry—these, in short, are the two great deformations of American liberty. The Declaration of Independence and the Constitution proclaimed lofty liberties for people and citizens. But who were "people" and "citizens"? Not Negroes; they were chattel. We now face the same problem in a different guise. Who are "people" and "citizens" today? Not mental patients; they are irresponsible children.

Moreover, we now face a serious problem concerning classification not in just one crucial area, but in two. Our forebears went astray in categorizing some people—that is, blacks—as non-persons. But at least they recognized religion when they saw it, and demarcated ecclesiastical from secular institutions and interventions correctly and wisely.

We go astray in categorizing some people—that is, mental patients—as non-persons. And we no longer recognize religion when we see it, demarcating medical from moral institutions and interventions incorrectly and stupidly.

As a result, medicine is now a threat to freedom—not because it is, in principle, an evil enterprise, but because it is, in practice, imposed by fraud and force on a deliberately confused and misinformed people.

FOOTNOTES

1. Jefferson, T., Notes on Virginia (1782), in Koch, A. and Peden, W., eds., *The Life and Selected Writings of Thomas Jefferson* (New York: Modern Library, 1944), p. 275.
2. Madison, J., Memorial and Remonstrance Against Religious Assessments (1784), cited in *Everson v. Board of Education;* 330 U.S. 1, 67, (1946).
3. See Szasz, T. S., The moral physician, *The Center Magazine;* 8:2-9 (March-April), 1975.
4. For a detailed discussion of Rush's views, see Szasz, T. S., *The Manufacture of Madness: A Comparative Study of the Inquisition and the Mental Health Movement* (New York: Harper & Row, 1970), especially Chapter 9.
5. Rush, B., Letter to Granville Sharp, November 28, 1783, *Journal of American Studies;* 1:1-32 (April 1), 1967; p. 20.
6. Rush, B., *Medical Inquiries and Observations upon the Diseases of the Mind* (1812) (New York: Hafner, 1962), p. 13.
7. Butterfield, L. H., ed., *Letters of Benjamin Rush* (Princeton University Press, 1951), Vol. II, p. 1090.
8. See Szasz, T. S., *Ceremonial Chemistry: The Ritual Persecution of Drugs, Addicts, and Pushers* (Garden City, N.Y.: Doubleday Anchor, 1974).
9. See, generally, Szasz, T. S., *The Myth of Mental Illness: Foundations of a Theory of Personal Conduct* (New York: Hoeber-Harper, 1961), Rev. ed., (New York: Harper & Row, 1974).
10. In this connection, see Moehlman, C. H., *The Wall of Separation between Church and State: An Historical Study of Recent Criticism of the Religious Clause of the First Amendment* (Boston: Beacon Press, 1951).
11. Syrett, H. C., ed., American Historical Documents (New York: Barnes and Noble, 1960), pp. 81-82.
12. *Ibid.;* p. 79.
13. *Dred Scott v. Sandford* (1857), in Syrett, H. C., ed., op. cit., p. 250.
14. *West Virginia State Board of Education v. Barnette,* 319 U.S. 624 (1943), at 642.
15. Braceland, F. J., Statement, in Subcommittee on Constitutional Rights of the Committee of the Judiciary, U.S. Senate, Constitutional Rights of the Mentally Ill (Washington, D.C.: U.S. Government Printing Office, 1961), Part I, p. 71.
16. Freud, S., The Question of Lay Analysis (1926, 1927), in Strachey, J., ed., *The Standard Edition of the Complete Psychological Works of Sigmund Freud* (London: Hogarth, 1959), Vol. XX, p. 252.
17. *Ibid.*
18. *Ibid.;* p. 256.
19. Jung, C. G., Psychotherapists or the Clergy (1932), in Jung, C. G., *Modern Man in Search of A Soul* (New York: Harcourt Brace, 1933), pp. 221-244; pp. 227, 241.

PERSPECTIVE OF SPACE

Isaac Asimov*

When asked to write this paper, I stated, quite frankly, that I knew nothing about the law and that I asked nothing better of life than to be forced into as little contact with it as possible. This objection was brushed aside and I seem to have gained the impression from what was said that I would not suffer, in this respect, by comparison with many of the other learned gentlemen participating in this volume.

Despite this possible community of ignorance (if, indeed, one exists) I am not so naive as to let myself be lured into a discussion of the fine points of the law, as I imagine them, or into a comparison of sea-law and space-law, for instance. I must leave this to wiser heads; or, at any rate, more specialized ones. I will confine myself instead to my own specialty—which is the construction of visions of the future.

Such visions may prove to be meaningless, but those who organized this commemoration were warned of this by me, and yet insisted, nevertheless, that I continue. My conscience is, therefore, as clear as a mountain spring.

Space—the vast realm beyond Earth's atmosphere—can not have a significant effect upon human society and upon the local rules of conduct on which it is based, as long as human beings have not invaded it in a significant manner.

What has happened so far, has been the temporary orbiting of the Earth, by ships carrying one to three human beings, at varying distances above the surface; plus six separate, but brief, visits to the Moon. These are *tours de force* and, as yet, nothing more. They have not yet given rise to the overwhelming sensation that new laws are needed or that old laws, based on the pre-space dispensation, are outmoded.

**Writer*

Things will change when human beings move out into space more or less permanently; when the Moon becomes a source of material over which human beings can quarrel; when the Moon or artificial structures in open space become suitable as the site of industries, laboratories or homes (or all three) under conditions so alien from those prevailing on Earth as to make Earthly law perhaps no more than a dim and, if anything, misleading precedent.

It is very unlikely that this can happen very soon, however. Unfortunately, there is a rising crisis on Earth generally that makes it less probable from year to year that resources, capital and effort will be put into building habitats in the sky, as long as the habitat on Earth continues to deteriorate. Our space effort will, in the short run, dwindle, and the question of the interconnection of space and the law will fade in consequence.

The long run is another matter, assuming that as far as civilization is concerned there *is* a long run. The rising tide of population and the dwindling ebb of resources will face humanity, alas, with the spectre of starvation—ourselves for food, our technology for energy and basic materials, our environment for viability.

Civilization may survive the crisis (and how awful the word "may" is in this connection) but, if so, what will emerge in the twenty first century will have to be quite different from anything we have seen before in history. The twenty first century will have to be a low-birthrate society if civilization is to make it, for population must be stabilized and, very likely, must be lowered in, we hope, a slow, steady, and humane fashion.

The effort to correct the cancerous growth of population and the open-ended ravishment of Earth's resources, together with all the ills this has brought about, will clearly have to be global in its nature. The problems created by the very success of human technology, human medicine and, therefore, human proliferation, are impossible to confine to one section or another of the globe. All the life-and-death problems of the world—population, pollution, scarcity and war—are, indeed, of the *world;* and there are no havens of refuge or avenues of escape.

Nor can any section of the world solve its own problems at

the expense of its neighbors. No section can flourish by looting another. However much against our will it may be, it will turn out that human beings, embedded in a globally-interconnected economy, can flourish individually only if all human beings flourish generally. The kick you aim at your neighbor will hit your own rear as well.

In short, then, if civilization does survive intact into the next century, it will be because there will be a kind of global organization, a kind of international cooperation, that will consider global problems, weigh possible solutions, decide on the most useful, enact it and enforce it. I don't know what to call this except "world government."

The concept of world government is not popular anywhere on Earth except in the case of occasional ivory-tower idealists like myself. Unfortunately, most people are quite convinced that they are superior to their neighbors (especially if their neighbors commit the unconscionable crime of looking, speaking, or behaving differently from themselves) and naturally resent placing those neighbors in a position to help determine the rules of society.

Even when vile necessity forces cooperation (as when wartime allies, with sidelong glances and under-their-breath mutterings, are reluctantly forced to march in unison against a formidable enemy) the slightest easing of the situation will produce instant enmity among the erst-while friends.

If the survival of civilization is to be more than a perpetual drunken stagger at the brink of the bottomless pit, the global community will have to be firmer and more steadfast than that. The great legal problem of the twenty first century will, then, have to be the establishment of a strong world government, capable of withstanding the centrifugal shocks of separatism, and yet one that will not drown out regional self-rule in matters that are not of global interest.

But how can that be accomplished?

One way, surely, could be to give the people of the globe some project that is large enough and glamorous enough to engage their hearts and minds: something to which all can contribute in one way or another and in which they can feel themselves to be global citizens, members of *Homo sapiens;* rather than members of this or that region inhabited by this or that sub-species.

In the past, we could sometimes rely on a war-crisis, for then it might happen that all questions of party were submerged in an orgy of self-immolation for the motherland or the fatherland or the grand old flag—or whatever combination of syllables could most easily tap reflex emotions.

War and civilization have become incompatible, however, and we must have something non-military and constructive for mankind to rally round.

It seems to me that the obvious project, large and glamorous, clearly global in scope, is that of colonizing space—of building cities on the Moon, or of building habitable doughnuts of glass and metal in open space.

For humanity to expand into space would entail enormous profits of all sorts.

It would enlarge knowledge, with incalculable and largely unforeseeable consequences, which we can hope that human wisdom (not always a markedly visible commodity) will guide into good and useful paths.

It would make possible industry and research of a kind that would profit in an environment that would include (depending on time and place) high vacuum, deep cold, or intense radiation; thus multiplying human ability to cooperate with the laws of nature.

It would lead to the construction of power stations in synchronous orbit that would collect Solar energy for human use with far greater efficiency than would be possible on Earth's surface, and thus solving our present problems of energy shortage and of pollution—or, at any rate, ameliorating them.

All these material benefits, and others, would become so obvious so soon that people will stare in disbelief or laugh in derision at the twentieth century accusations that space exploration is but a vast boondoggle, and those public men who will have commited quotes to that effect will achieve an unenviable immortality as cosmic examples of shortsightedness.

Yet it is not with material benefits I wish to concern myself here; but rather with something more. After all, nothing material space can bring us will be as great in value as the immaterial benefit of increasing humanity's appreciation of itself as a global set and as a single species; and of strengthening world government and making it workable—and therefore making civilization workable.

But can colonization possibly strengthen the concept and practice of world government and can it make possible the existence and development of global law?

If we eliminate simple assertion in one direction or another as a fruitful way of arriving at a clear view of the future, we are compelled to argue from analogy and to look back in history for incidents that might illuminate the future by way of the past.

When we think of colonization today, we are apt to think of a technologically superior society establishing itself on land occupied by "natives". A thin outpost-layer of the colonizing society then oppresses and, exploits the "natives", growing fat at their expense. This type of colonization has run its course and is viewed now with opprobrium.

This sort of colonization cannot, however, be viewed as analogous to the colonization of space where (at least in the immediate neighborhood of Earth, and perhaps in the entire Solar system) there is no intelligent life, or life of any kind, to displace, mistreat and exploit.

Must we then look to the past for occasions when some society occupied an empty land (at least as far as intelligent life is concerned) and established extensions of itself?

Such a search is not likely to be fruitful. The last occasions when this happened on a continental scale were when the forebears of the Indians passed from Siberia into Alaska and spread over the American continents, and when the forebears of the Aborigines travelled through the Indonesian islands from Asia into Australia. Much later, the same happened on an oceanic scale when, in the first millennium A.D., the Polynesians scoured the Pacific Ocean and settled the scraps of land they encountered.

These colonizers, however, possessed "prehistoric" societies, and had not yet developed cities and writing, those hallmarks of what we call "civilization." We don't know enough detail about such prehistoric colonizing ventures to shed the necessary light on what might happen in the case of space-colonization by societies that have reached such a pitch of civilization as to be virtually on the edge of suicide.

But there have been no *civilized* colonizing ventures of consequence that have ventured into empty lands. By the time civilization had arisen in the Middle East, there were no empty lands within reasonable reach of that civilization.

The next best thing is to find colonizing ventures which created their own empty land by pushing "natives" back, or exterminating them, or both. However morally reprehensible this is, the consequence is that the colonizing society produces a colony like itself without a significant residue of "natives" to exploit, and in this respect can be considered a possibly useful analogy to space colonization and its consequences.

Let us consider the Greeks of the first millennium B.C. It is from the Greeks that the modern western world traces its philosophy, art, literature, science, and even important strands of its religion. Generally, we of the west feel sympathetic to the Greeks and identify with them in their struggles against the non-Greek "barbarians," notably in their war against the Persian Empire.

Yet the ancient Greeks were not, at any time in their history, a single realm under a central government. They were a congerie of city-states, whose normal situation was that of mutual suspicion and hostility, and who would turn on any one of their number who showed signs of growing too powerful.

They could never, under any circumstances, truly unite even against an external enemy. Their closest approach to unity was in the war against Persia between 500 and 450 B.C. and even then substantial portions of the Greek world remained neutral—and in some cases even sided with the enemy.

This was true despite the fact that the Greeks recognized themselves to share a common heritage, a common language, a common literature, a common religion. It was true despite the fact that the Greeks recognized themselves to be a unity at least to the extent that they lumped all non-Greeks together as "barbarians."

After the successful fight against Persia, the Greeks could not maintain even the limited union that marked that war, and, through division, fell easy prey first to Macedon and finally to Rome.

Was there no great accomplishment behind which a pan-Greek spirit might have flourished?

Yes, there was, and it was even a great burst of colonizing energy that in some ways could offer an analogy to the projected twenty first century colonization of space.

The Greeks, between 750 B.C. and 550 B.C., expanded greatly, planting colonies all along the Mediterranean coast from the furthest eastern reach of the Black Sea to the coastline of Spain in the far west, pushing back the non-Greeks already on the spot and constructing extensions of their own culture.

Yet the period of colonization did not create the necessary spirit of union. For one thing, each colony was an independent city-state which promptly took up the task of fighting its city-state neighbors to the point where all could barely hold their own against the competing imperialisms of the Phoenicians, Carthaginians, Etruscans and, eventually, could not hold their own at all against the Romans.

Then, too, each colony was the product of the colonizing venture of a single city-state, so that Miletus was the colony of Athens; Syracuse of Corinth; Byzantium of Megara; Taras of Sparta, and so on. Many of the colonies then, in turn, founded colonies of their own.

Any political or emotional ties that the colonies might form were therefore never with the Greek world as a whole, but at best with the mother-city. The result was that when cities warred, each sometimes looked to a mother- or daughter-city for help, and disunion was exacerbated.

A curious parallel to the Greek experience was that of the great colonizing ventures of Western Europe between 1400 and 1800 A.D. As was the case with the Greeks, western Europe had never been unified at any time after the fall of the West Roman Empire in the fifth century, except for a partial and abortive union under Charlemagne about 800 A.D. This disunity, as in the earlier case, persisted despite a common heritage, a common language of learning, a common literature, and a common religion.

Nor did union develop through the great adventure of colonization.

Some of the colonization, it is true, took place in Africa and Asia and was of the sort that established the domination of a European minority over a non-European majority. If we ignore this as an aberrant form, there remains the colonization of the Americas and of Australia where the native inhabitants were pushed back or destroyed and in which extensions of the colonizing culture were established as had been the case, earlier, in the Greek colonizing period.

In the European case, unlike that of the Greeks, the colonies were not independent from the start. Instead, each European nation kept its colonies tightly bound to itself and exploited them economically. (Eventually, these colonies rebelled and broke away, of course.)

As in the Greek case, however, the colonies were established by single political units of the overall culture. No colony felt any allegiance to the European world in general, but only to individual nations. As a result, the colonies did not encourage union but rather exacerbated disunion, and colonial rivalries among the great colonizing powers became a new occasion for the endless wars that racked Europe as once they had racked Greece.

But now let us take a third case. In the period from 1600 to 1750, England (later Great Britain) had planted a series of colonies along the east-central coast of North America (pushing back the Indians and eventually destroying them in casual genocide)

These colonies had varying degrees of self-government, but whatever their ties to the mother-country, they were certainly independent of each other. There was no way in which the people of Massachusetts could help make the laws that governed Virginia, or vice versa.

In the Revolutionary War of 1775-1783, under the stress of the struggle for independence, the colonies joined in a weak and shaky alliance no stronger than the union of Greek city-states against Persia. Nor was it a unanimous alliance, anymore than the Greek one had been, for the colonists in Nova Scotia, Newfoundland, Upper and Lower Canada, and the West Indian islands did not join the rebellion. In fact, they wholeheartedly supported Great Britain. What is more, even within the thirteen colonies which were nominally in rebellion, at least as many colonists fought for Great Britain as for independence.

The war ended at last with American independence established, but that did not make the alliance of thirteen self-governing and essentially independent "states" any stronger. Few political observers in Europe thought that the "United States" would remain united for long.

There are a number of reasons why the Union persisted, but one of them rests with a crucial self-abnegating decision on the part of the infant states—a decision whose wisdom and critical effect has been underestimated by posterity.

The new states were primarily settled east of the Allegheny Mountains, but the territory of the new nation stretched westward to the Mississippi River. The royal charters that had originally established the colonies-turned-states were vague as to boundaries and generous in granting everything westward to the setting sun. The result was that nine of the states had claims, conflicting and overlapping, to the western lands. The land north of the Ohio River, for instance, (the Northwest Territory) was claimed entirely by Virginia and, in part, by Pennsylvania, Connecticut, Massachusetts and New York.

Had such conflicting claims persisted, there would have been an endless cause of wrangling among the states and the earlier Greek and European experiences would have been relived. Had the claims been straightened out and the western lands distributed among the states according to some compromise, conflicting imperialisms would nevertheless have been set up and each further extension of national territory would have been the occasion for endless rivalries. The nation in the end would have become a congerie of battling sub-nations.

What really happened was that one of the states *without* western claims, Maryland, refused to join the Union even under the weak terms of alliance that had existed during the

Revolutionary War until all western claims were abandoned and the western lands turned over to the weak and almost powerless Congress.

One by one, to appease Maryland, the various states abandoned their western claims.

Not only was a cause of rivalry removed, but the central legislative body, the Congress, now had something. Congress was so weak in the years following the Revolutionary War that it was almost a negligible quantity, as the United Nations is today. Like the United Nations, the early Congress could not levy taxes but had to wait, hat in hand, for contributions from the states that made up the Union—contributions that came reluctantly, sparingly, or not at all.

But Congress had the western lands! What was it to do with them?

On July 13, 1787, with only 18 members of Congress present (so moribund was the body), the "Northwest Ordinance" was passed. By that Ordinance, it was decided that when population reached a certain level, new states would be formed out of the Northwest Territory and these new states would be equal to the old ones in all political and social respects. No state would be the superior of another because it was older or because it had been one of the original thirteen. Had this point not been made clear, the Union might have become a mixture of dominating senior states and dominated junior ones and the stage would have been set for new rebellions.

The new states, like the Greek colonies, had equal status with the mother states, but unlike the Greek colonies maintained strong political ties with the colonizing power. These strong, political ties were not, as in the case of the European colonies, to a single segment of the colonizing culture, but to the culture as a whole. The new states became part of a central government which, in 1787, was made infinitely stronger by the working out of a Federal Constitution which was quickly adopted by the various states. (This adoption meant that the states voluntarily surrendered key portions of their sovereignty—again an enormously wise example of self-abnegation.)

There was another reason why American colonization, in

the form of new states, strengthened the Union—unlike the case of the earlier Greek and European examples.

The new American states were not officially founded by particular old American states. Most of the immigrants would naturally come from nearby states, but anyone could enter from any state—and did. The result was that, on the whole, blocs of states were not formed. There was not, from the start, a Virginia-bloc and a New York-bloc and so on.

The discords and dangers to which that would have given rise are clearly shown through the one case where blocs did form, but in a manner that did not arise out of the way in which the new states were formed.

Unfortunately, the states while they had still been colonies, had imported Black slaves from Africa and created a master-slave society where none need have existed. The unwisdom of this decision went far to neutralizing all the wisdom that had gone into the establishment of a working Union.

As time went on, some of the states outlawed slavery and a growing hostility arose between them and the other states that permitted it. The two groups were not scattered, but formed two compact blocs.

The consequences showed what might have happened if the United States had been broken up into half a dozen spheres of influence. In 1859, when Kansas was approaching entry as a state, possibly free and possibly slave, both sides attempted to influence the vote by subsidizing immigrants, arming them, and encouraging force. The result was a civil war in Kansas.

Within two years, there was a Civil War in the nation as a whole.

The United States survived, at great cost, partly because there were only two blocs. One could be defeated, the other be victorious. Had there been half a dozen blocs, the shifting alliances that would have resulted as each bloc perceived danger to itself every time a competing bloc seemed to grow too strong, would have made a clearcut conclusion impossible and the United States would have disintegrated.

What was more amazing than the victory of the Union in 1865, however, was the fact that it was followed by reconciliation. The defeated slave states, prostrated and humiliated, did not easily forget or forgive, and haven't entirely forgotten and forgiven to this day, but the spirit of revenge was contained. The embittered memory of defeat did not result in further revolts or in a guerrilla movement or a long-lived independence drive or appeals to foreign powers. Instead, reconciliation, while slow, was real and the United States has remained strong and united.

How did this come about? Partly the responsibility must surely rest with the historic accident that, in the decades immediately after the Civil War, what remained of the west was developed and a dozen new states were formed, states which were settled by men from the victorious north and from the defeated south on an equal basis; states which, therefore, owed allegiance to neither of the two sides but only to the nation as a whole. In the great task of the colonization of the west, the sectional wounds were healed.

If we agree, then, that the Greek civilization and the west European civilization each harmed itself enormously through an inability to unite, while the American civilization developed unprecedented power-plus-liberty over a vaster area than had ever before been the subject of such an experiment—and if we further agree that the Greek and European systems of colonization *did not* further union at home, while the American system of colonization *did* and was perhaps the key to American strength—then what can we say about the forthcoming colonization of space in the twenty first century?

1) The colonizing culture should be united to begin with, as Greece and Europe were not and as the United States was, even though the union might be excessively weak. This we may fairly hope for, since twentieth century civilization is not likely to survive without some form of Global cooperation and since a model for it already exists in the form of the United Nations (though one could scarcely imagine a more feeble and ineffective Global government.)

2) The space colonies must not be utterly independent as soon as they are capable of such independence, as in the Greek case; nor must they be subjected to such humiliating dependence as to be forced into rebellion and consequent utter independence, as in the European case. Either way, the

results will not be conducive to Global government. Instead, the space colonies must be tied to Earth but under terms which give them the full rights and privileges of the Earthly units themselves, as in the American example. This we may hope for, too, since the space colonies will not be sufficiently self-supporting for a period of time and can scarcely hope for complete independence very soon, and since colonial oppression has gone out of style and, we may hope, will remain out of style.

3) The space colonies must not feel bound, either politically (as in the European case) or emotionally (as in the Greek case) to one single colonizing unit of the greater whole, since that would encourage rivalry and disunion; but must feel bound to the central government only (as in the American case.)

This third requirement is the most crucial since it seems the least likely. To make it possible the Global government must be in charge of the colonizing ventures and the colonization must take place under Global auspices. Each colony must be open for colonization, without restriction, to people from any part of the Earth, and, indeed, a well-mixed population should be positively encouraged on every colony.

We should avoid, like the plague, the formation of colonies populated entirely by Americans, or by Russians, or by Uruguayans—or by any group that would then feel some emotional or traditional attachment to one section of the Earth more than another.

A well-mixed colony would, instead, be a microcosm of Earth and would be divorced from the local rivalries of the civilizing power. Naturally, we cannot expect perfection. On any of the colonies there will be occasionally-fashionable nostalgia that will make itself felt in the boosting of various ethnic heritages. We are experiencing this today in the United States, in fact, and it is a far cry from this to the deadly rivalries that result when opposing groups are armed and are ready to convert hatred into force.

And then, as the number of colonies increases, each with problems having nothing to do with Terrestrial localisms, those localisms will seem to grow progressively more picayune and meaningless, and the Global government will grow ever stronger and more meaningful.

My conclusion, then, is that if the colonization of space is carried through as wisely and as far-sightedly as the colonization of the American west, it will be a vast project that will unite humanity both in the performance and in the consequence, and may be the route by which we can establish a functional global law for the first time in history and, in consequence, make human civilization permanent.

So to those who cry out that space exploration is too expensive, I can only ask: How much is survival worth?

PERSPECTIVE OF LITERATURE

Ralph W. Ellison*

It is rather frightening to enter into what someone has called a legal thicket, if you don't know it as your own briar patch, but I will do my best.

I will begin with a bit of personal background because a writer's first impressions are apt to have a bearing on his later attitudes and opinions.

When I was a young boy I often went out to the Oklahoma State Capitol where I assisted Mr. J.D. Randolph with his duties as custodian of the State Law Library. I was about 11 years old at the time, quite impressionable, and very, very curious about the mysterious legal goings-on of the legislators. All the more so because while I was never able to observe the legislature in session, it was not at all unusual for me to look up from pushing a broom or dusting a desk to see one of the legislators dash into the library to ask Jeff—Mr. Randolph was always addressed by his first name—his opinion regarding some point of law. In fact, I soon came to look forward to such moments because I was amazed by the frequency with which Mr. Randolph managed to come up with satisfactory answers, even without consulting the heavy volumes which ranged the walls.

I wasn't surprised that Mr. Randolph was a janitor instead of a lawyer or legislator; Oklahoma was segregated at the time and Afro-Americans were strictly limited in their freedom to participate in the process of government. We could obey or break laws, but not make or interpret them. In view of this, I was amazed that Mr. Randolph had come to know so much about the subject. This was a tantalizing mystery, but the fact that white men of power would show no shame

*Albert Schweitzer Professor, New York University.

in exploiting the knowledge of one far beneath them in status aroused my sense of irony. That "after all" was simply another example of white folks taking advantage of black folks.

I was more impressed with the fact that Mr. Randolph could carry so many of the mysterious details of law and the laws which governed the State of Oklahoma within his own head. Now, I knew he had been one of the first school teachers in the city and the State, and that he read and owned a large collection of books. But just how he had come to learn the law was part of an experience about which I was never to hear him talk. I did know, however, that he had never attended college, and I was quite aware that many of our greatest lawyers had acquired their legal knowledge through the process of "reading" law with licensed members of the profession.

I only knew that Mr. Randolph appeared to possess a surer grasp of law than certain of the legislators, and my youthful sense of justice led me to see his exclusion from the profession as an act of injustice. I never heard him complain about the situation, but I felt that there was something shameful, even degrading, about such a state of affairs, and that there was something rotten in the lawyers if not indeed in the law itself.

Nor was it possible for me to ignore the obvious fact that race was a source of that rot, and that even within the mystery of the legal process, the law was colored and rigged against my people.

Later I became aware of the existence of a Negro lawyer, a Mr. Harrison, who was so skilled and eloquent that he got himself chased out of the State. Fortunately, he landed in Chicago where, in time, he became an Assistant Attorney General. Following this incident, however, there was much barbershop conversation centered around the Harrison affair, his legal skill, his way with words and the inability of white lawyers and judges to stomach a Negro more knowledgeable in the law than themselves. Interestingly enough, the men who engaged in these conversations while I shined shoes or swept the floors directed their disapproval not so much against law in general, but against those persons and forces which imposed the law undemocratically.

This was a period during which the struggle to attain an anti-lynching bill was at its height and Mr. Roscoe Dungee, the editor and publisher of our local black newspaper, was writing very eloquent editorials suggesting that the real clue, the real ground for solving the racial predicament, rested in the Constitution. I read his editorials, but I must confess that, with my youthful cynicism, I didn't quite believe them. But anyway, the men in the barbershop believed in the spirit of the law, if not in its application.

As for me, I saw no hope in the law. It was to be obeyed in everyday affairs, and in instances of extreme pressure, it was to be defied, even at the cost of one's life.

In our common usage, law was associated more with men than with statutes. Law enforcement officers in our usage were "Laws," and many were men with reputations for being especially brutal toward Negroes.

If such men were the cutting edge of the racially biased law, those above them were seldom better. "Alfalfa Bill" Murray, who took great pride in his knowledge of Roman constitutions, was Governor of the State and a very loud-mouthed white supremacist. And one occupant of the local bench, a certain Judge Estes, was famous for a quip made from the bench, to the effect that a Model T Ford full of Negroes ranging at large on the streets of the city was a more devastating piece of bad luck than having one's path crossed by a squad of thirteen howling, jet-black tomcats. Well, we laughed at it but held it against him. With such opinions issuing from the bench, I felt little inspired to trust the fairness of judges.

During the Depression, which occurred during this period, I noted something else about the relationship between the law and the attitudes of people, in this instance mostly white, who were suffering from the breakdown of economic order. This came in the form of their reaction to "Pretty Boy" Floyd, who at the time was in constant flight and on a rampage of lawbreaking; but he was frequently given sanctuary in Oklahoma City by law-abiding citizens. This was true not only of the city itself, but of towns all around Oklahoma.

Well, it puzzled me.

During June of 1933, I found myself traveling by freight

train in an effort to reach Tuskegee Institute in time to take advantage of a scholarship granted me. Having little money and no time left in which to earn the fare for a ticket, I grabbed an armful of freight car, a form of illegal travel quite common during the Great Depression. In fact, so many young men, young women, prostitutes, gamblers, and even some quite respectable but impoverished elderly and middleaged couples were hoboing that it was quite difficult for the railroad to control such passengers. I justify this out of sheer desperation, college being my one hope of improving my condition.

But I was young and adventurous and regarded hoboing as the next best thing to floating down the Mississippi on a raft. My head was full of readings of the *Rover Boys* and *Huckleberry Finn.* I converted hoboing into a lark, until I found myself in the freight yards of Decatur, Alabama, where two white railroad detectives laying about them with the barrels of long nickel-plated .45 revolvers forced some forty or fifty of us, black and white alike, off the train and ordered us to line up along the tracks. For me, this was a most frightening moment. Not only was I guilty of stealing passage on a freight train, but I realized that I had been caught in the act in the town where, at that very moment, the *Scottsboro* case was being tried. The case and the incident which led to it were widely reported in the black press, and what I had read of the atmosphere of the trial, led me to believe that the young men in the case had absolutely no possibility of receiving a just decision. As I saw it, the trial was a macabre circus, a kangaroo proceeding that would be soon followed by an enactment of the gory rite of lynching, that ultimate form of racial victimage.

I had no idea of what the detectives intended to do with me, but given the atmosphere of the town I feared that it would be most unpleasant and brutal. I too might well be a sacrificial scapegoat, simply because I was of the same race as the accused young men then being prepared for death. Therefore, when a group of white boys broke and ran, I plunged into their midst and running far closer to the ground than I had ever managed to do as a high school football running back, I kept running and moving until I came to a shed with a railroad loading dock, under which I scooted and there I remained until dawn, when I grabbed the first thing that was smoking and headed south.

A few days later I reached Tuskegee, but that scrape with the law, the fear, the horror and sense of helplessness, before legal injustice, was most vivid in my mind, and it has so remained.

Recently, a television dramatization of the *Scottsboro* case presented one of the judges that sat on the case as its hero. I was made aware of the snarl of personal and public motives, political and private interests, which had become the focus of the case. I was aware of the many factors locked in contention in the name of the purity of white womanhood, and as a writer I came to ask myself just why was it that American fiction had given so little attention to the law. Why, I asked myself, has the lawyer or the judge seldom appeared in our literature, serious or popular, in heroic roles?

One answer is that the presentation of the law in an unfavorable light allows for the formal expression and sharing of attitudes which are impious and irreverent, and that given such attitudes, they must be socially controlled, made visible, and socialized; otherwise they might be a force for the destruction of social order.

When one recalls Mark Twain's drawing of the judge in the *Adventures of Huckleberry Finn*, the judge comes across as something of a self-serving hypocrite.

Or compare the following incident from *Pudd'nhead Wilson:* Mr. Wilson appears before a reception committee expecting to make a name for himself in the town, but the proceedings are interrupted by the barking of a dog, whereupon Wilson says, "I wish that I owned one half of that dog."

And someone said, "One half of the dog? What would you do with one *half* of the dog?"

He said, "I would kill my half."

Whereupon these legal-minded gentlemen looked at one another and said, "Could he be serious? Doesn't he realize that if he kills his half of the dog, the other owner, the owner of the other half will be upset, will bring litigation against him, and that he will end up in all kinds of trouble?"

Well, for being irreverent on the matter of ownership, poor

Wilson was named "Pudd'nhead" and spent most of his life as an alien in the town.

When we recall Melville's *Benito Cerino,* and place it back in its historical perspective, we realize that it was influenced by the *Armistad* case, a case in which a group of Africans were brought to trial at the insistence of Spain because they had revolted against the Spaniards who had sought to enslave them, killed several of the officers, and in attempting to sail the ship back to their homeland, found themselves off the coast of New England. Melville takes the incident and makes of it one of his finest works of fiction.

But what puzzles me a bit, and I know better than to be puzzled about such things, was why he made nothing of the fact that these Africans were freed by having been represented in court by John Quincy Adams? Remember, this was a time of slavery in our own country. Remember that it cost Mr. Adams something just to take that case. But at any rate, Melville did not bother with the lawyer on that occasion.

But in *Bartleby the Scrivener,* we are introduced to the title character by his boss, a Wall Street lawyer who, for all of his goodwill, is as imperceptive in grasping the basic connotation as Captain Delano of *Benito Cerino* is unable to grasp the human complexity of the Africans who believed, like himself, so much in freedom that they were willing to kill for it.

I am not going to burden you with recounting the legal climate of 1894, when Mark Twain published *Pudd'nhead Wilson.* I will just remind you that it was a period of great theft, of much legal skulduggery, and no doubt this had something to do with the presentation. But if we think a little bit about Mark Twain as a humorist, and think about literary form as having a social function, then perhaps Twain was being far more than irreverent when he presented men of the legal profession in a comic light, because by so presenting them he allowed people who were very upset by some of the legal goings-on in the society to reveal their feelings, to laugh at themselves, and most impious of all, to laugh at the courts and perhaps at the Constitution itself.

At some point people, and especially American people, are pushed to recognize that behind the Constitution which we say rests in principles which lie beyond the limits of death and dying, are really manmade, legal fictions. That doesn't stop them from being precious; that doesn't stop them from being sacred. But we can only stand so much of the sacred. We can only stand so much of piety. We must be able to express our dissent, especially when the members of the bench fail to do so for us.

In the reading of *Bartleby the Scrivener,* Melville's story, we encounter a contest of wills between the lawyer, a genteel, learned lawyer who is admired by Mr. John Jacob Astor, a representative of the law and thus of order, a man with what de Tocqueville termed certain aristocratic propensities, and poor Bartleby, who owns hardly anything but the clothing on his back.

Bartleby has been hired to perform the job of copying, transcribing legal documents. The lawyer, as boss, is in the habit of sending his other employees to do various errands. Bartleby replies to each request with a simple phrase "I prefer not to." It is so unusual, this obstinate negativism, that the lawyer doesn't throw him out, but becomes locked in a psychological struggle through which he tries to bring Bartleby to his will. But in the process he reveals how little he understands of certain basic human attitudes which make the law and the order which it imposes quite necessary. Bartleby is never forced or persuaded or cajoled to agree.

In the reading of the story one has a sensation of watching a man walking backwards past every boundary of human order and desire saying, "I prefer not to, I prefer not to," until at last he fades from sight and we are left with but the faint sound of his voice hanging thinly upon the air, still saying No. Bartleby's last remaining force, the force which at the very last he is asked to give up, is the power of the negative, that capability of language which Kenneth Burke has identified as a symbolic agency through which man has separated himself from nature and gone on to establish this complex of human positives which we identify as civilization.

In this view, language is a primary agency of order. Why? Because it is the identifying characteristic of a symbol-using, symbol- misusing animal. It is through language that man has not only separated himself from his natural biologic condition as an animal, but it is through the symbolic action, the symbolic capabilities of action, that we seek simultaneously to maintain and evade our commitments as social beings. Human society in this regard is fictitious, and it might well be that at this point the legal fictions through which we seek to impose order upon society meet with, coincide with, the fictions of literature. Perhaps law and literature operate or cooperate, if the term is suitable for an interaction which is far less than implicit; in their respective ways these two systems, these two symbolic systems, work in the interests of social order. The one for stability—that is, the law is the law—the other striving to socialize those emotions and interests held in check by manners, conventions, and again by law.

"Does not law, like art," writes Professor Paul Freund, "seek change within the framework of continuity, to bring heresy and heritage into fruitful tension? They are not dissimilar, and in their resolution, the resolution of passion and pattern, of frenzy and form, of contention and revolt, of order and spontaneity lies the clue to the creativity that will endure."

Given the bits of personal experience which I outlined at the start of this paper, I must both agree and disagree with the professor. He states the ideal as a writer; with my background, I must state something of the exception. By the way, I always found Justice Holmes and Justice Frankfurter a bit less attractive as human beings than I did as men of scholarly excellence. But then I was always a bit impatient and something of the cat who was fated to stare at the kings.

I would also remind you, as one who somehow fits into the profession of Mark Twain, Emerson and Thoreau, that it is the writer's function precisely to yell "fire" in crowded theaters, and we do so, of course, through the form in which we work, and the forms of literature are social forms. We don't always take them seriously, but they are the start of seriousness, and an irreplaceable part of social order.

But if there is one Freund statement with which I could agree wholeheartedly, it is this:

"I have likened the Constitution to a work of art in its capacity to respond through interpretation to changing needs, concerns and aspirations," for I look upon the Constitution as the still vital convenant by which Americans of diverse backgrounds, religions, races and interests are bound. They are bound by the principles with which it inspirits us no less than by the legal apparatus which identifies us as a single American people. The Constitution is a script by which we seek to act out the drama of democracy and the stage upon which we enact our roles.

Viewed "dramatistically," which is Kenneth Burke's term, we can even suggest that the Declaration of Independence marked the verbalization of our colonial forefathers' intentions of disposing of the King's authority. The Revolutionary War marked the agonistic contest of wills through which the opposing forces were overthrown. The Constitution marked the gloriously optimistic assertion and legitimization of a new form of authority and proclaiming of a new set of purposes and promises. Upon these principles, which would be made manifest through the enactment of a new set of democratic hierarchal roles (or identities), the young nation would act. And through the dramatic conflict of democratic society it would seek to fulfill its revolutionary assertions.

But then came a swift change of direction in which the young nation was forced to recognize that the mere assertion of revolutionary will was not enough to lead immediately to domestic tranquility. It brought upon the stage a new alignment of political forces in which the collectivity that had made the Revolution became fragmented. Under the new dispensation the rights of individuals and minorities required protection from the will of the majority. As a new hierarchy began to function, those at its top were in better position to take advantage of the new-found benefits while those at the bottom were hardly better off than they had been under the Crown.

Ironically, the nation's recognition of the new problems of its hierarchy were coeval with its increasing concern with its language, with its linguistic style, which reminds us of the paradox that the revolutionary documents which formed the constitutional grounds of our new system of justice and which set the stage for the enactment of a new democratic drama of human rights—these documents were written in the language of the very hierarchy which they had overthrown. And indeed the new conflict of interest was foreshadowed in the very process of drawing up the new ground for action out of the English language. Even as the democratic documents of state announced a new corporate purpose, proclaimed a new identity, assigned new roles and aroused new expectations for a redistribution of material resources and authority, a conflict arose between the terms in which revolutionary action had been taken and those in which it would be fulfilled.

In drafting the Declaration of Independence, Thomas Jefferson had changed the old emotion-charged revolutionary slogan of equality, liberty and property, to equality, liberty and the pursuit of happiness. And his demands for eternal separation from England and its people were deleted. Also rejected was Jefferson's indictment of slavery in which he overloaded the scapegoat, King George III, with a malignancy that was all too obviously shared by Americans. There was mystification here, if not blatant hypocrisy, because as Katherine Drinker Bowen observed of Jefferson's discarded first draft, "in Jefferson's indictment of the King he nowhere states that slavery is a disgrace to America, and should be abolished root and branch by Americans. Instead, he turns his anger on the wrong culprit, twists a shameful fact of American life into an instrument of propaganda against George III, condemns the slave trade, then draws the sting by putting the blame and responsibility on the King of England."

Ironically, by his extreme eloquence, Jefferson provided his pro-slavery colleagues an escape from having to undergo the rigors of economic and perhaps spiritual mortification that would have given full credibility to their proclaimed principles of freedom and equality.

Thus the new edenic political scene incorporated a flaw similar to the crack that appeared in the Liberty Bell and embodied a serpent-like malignancy that would tempt government and individual alike to a constantly recurring fall from democratic innocence. With one of its cardinal principles violated, the drama of democratic equality began with its main actors revealing in their noblest gestures "mots vagues" that were at odds with their spoken lines. Indeed, more often than not they ignored the acting script and being good Americans, they improvised. Portentiously, the founding fathers' refusal to cleanse themselves was motivated by hierarchical status and economic interests. It was rationalized by the code of social manners that went with their inherited form and manner of speech, their linguistic style. Revolutionary fervor notwithstanding, they were gentlemen, and Jefferson's indictment provided these men the convenient excuse for not violating their private interests and their standards of good taste. Thus the glaring transparencies of Jefferson's rhetoric afforded them a purely formal escape from the immediate dilemma posed by the conflict between freedom and slavery, and allowed them to use social tact as a tactic of moral evasion.

One result of this evasion was to prove of far-reaching consequence, in that the principles of equality and freedom were splintered into warring entities, thus making for the unheralded emergence of a new principle or motive in the drama of American democracy. That motive or principle—and principles are motives, I will remind you—was race, a motive that would become a source of vast political power and authority and a major theme in American literature. And though not committed to sacred print, it was to radiate a qualifying influence upon all of the nation's principles and become the source of a war of words that has continued unto this day.

Men like John Adams fought against it as did Jefferson, who himself owned slaves. But because this principle operated in the ethical sphere no less than in the material world, the principle of equality being a command that all men be treated as equals, while some were very obviously being designated unequal on the basis of color and race, this made for a split in America's moral identity which would infuse all of its acts and institutions with a quality of hypocrisy. Worse, it would fog the American's perception of himself, distort his national image, and blind him to the true nature of his cultural complexity.

Later, behind the guise of States rights, it would explode the issue which led to the Civil War. So even as the English supports of the old hierarchical psychosis collapsed, it quickly reasserted itself in the immature and unfinished psyche of the new political order. That absentee authority and privilege once vested in kingship, now reappeared as the all-too-present authoritarian privilege of those possessing property and high social position. Social order is arduous and power filters down to the lower levels of society only under constant pressure. Thus new tensions arose and while the Bill of Rights was enacted to relieve the new imbalance, the manifestations of those rights in the lives of those low in the order of social hierarchy would require time, contention and endless improvisation and many lawyers. As this process ensued, not even the most optimistic citizens found an adequate fulfillment of revolutionary expectations. Indeed, these expectations seemed for some to recede before the anguishing complexity of the new social reality.

Instead of domestic tranquility, the Americans discovered that what their bloodshed and sacrifice had actually purchased them was not social perfection, but at best a firm new ground of hope. This was a great deal, but democratic equality remained the promise that would have to be achieved in the vividly imagined but illusory future.

At Philadelphia, the founding fathers were presented the fleeting opportunity of mounting to the very peak of social possibility afforded by democracy. But after ascending to within a few yards of the summit they paused, finding the view to be one combining splendor with terror. From this height of human aspiration the ethical implications of democratic equality were revealed as tragic, for if there was radiance and glory in the future that stretched so grandly before them, there was also mystery and turbulence and darkness astir in its depths. Therefore, the final climb would require not only courage, but an acceptance of the tragic nature of their enterprise, and the adoption of a tragic attitude that was rendered unacceptable by the optimism developed in revolutionary struggle, no less than by the tempting and virginal richness of the land which was now rendered accessible.

So having climbed so heroically, they descended and laid a foundation for democracy at a less breathtaking altitude, and in justification of their failure of nerve before the challenge of the summit, the founding fathers committed the sin of American racial pride. They designated one section of the American people to be the sacrificial victims for the benefit of the rest. And in failing their testing by what was later to be termed the American dilemma, they prepared the way for the evils that Jefferson had hoped to pile upon the royal head of England's King, and loaded them upon the black backs of anonymous American slaves. Worse, these Americans were designated as perfect victims for sacrifice and were placed beyond any possibility of democratic redemption, not because of any overt act of social guilt, but simply by virtue of their position in the social hierarchy. Indeed, they were thrust beneath the threshhold of social hierarchy and expected to stay there.

To further justify this act of pride and failure of nerve, myths of racial superiority and inferiority were evoked, and endless sacrificial rights of moral evasion were set in motion. These appeared in folktales, jokes, and then popular stories, indeed in some unpopular, but quite serious works. Ironically, however, this initial act of pride was to give the Afro-American an inadvertent and unrecognized but crucial role in the nation's drama of conscience. Racism took on the symbolic force of an American form of original sin, and as a man chosen to suffer to advance the nation's spiritual and material well-being, the black American was endowed linguistically with an ambivalent power like that vested in Elizabethan clowns, Christian martyrs, and tragic heroes. This is important if we are to understand the prevalence of black figures in our literature.

As a symbol of guilt and redemption, the Negro entered the deepest recesses of the American psyche and became crucially involved in its consciousness, subconsciousness, and conscience. He became keeper of the nation's sense of democratic achievement, and the human scale by which would be measured its painfully slow advance towards true equality. Regardless of the white American's feelings about the economic, psychological, and social conditions summed up in the term and symbol "Negro," that term and symbol was now firmly embedded in the operation of the American language. Despite their social powerlessness, Negro Americans were all unwittingly endowed with the vast powers of the linguistic negative, and would now be intricately involved in the use and misuse of a specific American form of symbolic action, the terminology of democracy. Not only in language, but through language into law and social arrangements, social ethics and manners, into sexuality and city planning (or no planning), or non-planning, and into art, religion and literature.

In brief, race became a major cause, form, and symbol of

the American hierarchical psychosis. As the unwilling and unjust personification of that psychosis and its major victim, the Afro-American took on the complex symbolism of social health and social sickness. He became the raw labor force, the victim of social degradation, and symbolic of America's hope for future perfection. He was to be viewed at least by many whites as both cause and cure of our social malaise.

This development, of course, contained a lot of mystification, for if there was hope for a cure to our condition, it lay in the direction of both white and black men undergoing that agonistic effort necessary to the fulfillment of the nation's commitment to those ethical principles compromised by the founding fathers. Until the time that this should come about, race would assert a malignant effect in areas of national life that were far removed from that of civil rights for black Americans.

It would function as a motive in Melville's *Moby Dick;* and, far beneath the fine prose of Henry James, it would goad the consciousness of his characters. It would form the moral core of Mark Twain's *Huckleberry Finn,* dominate the world of William Faulkner's fiction, and it would influence the attitudes of individual "secessionism" displayed by the heroes of Ernest Hemingway. Further, the contentions it inspired would hinder the establishment of a National Drama, a theater, and account for the dismal stereotypes of popular literature, plays, motion pictures and television dramas, and for their triviality and lack of moral seriousness. What is more, it would lead to the moral negations of the current crop of black films and to much of what we dislike in rock music.

But here we should pause. Here we will not recapitulate the Civil War. We know to what extent it was a war of words as well as of arms. We know to what extent the black American was involved. Very often, however, the issues of the Civil War and even the blacks appear in novels and other works of literature by other names. For instance, Crane's *The Red Badge of Courage* is about the Civil War, but only one black person appears, and then very briefly. It is concerned with the invasion of the private life by warfare, by the army, and by large impersonal social processes, a fact of American democratic life which was becoming a matter of consciousness some thirty years after the Civil War.

We are in a period today when many of the men of my profession complain that American life has gotten out of hand, that it is too much for the methods and modes of fiction. They say that it is too dramatic, that it overwhelms the fictional imagination. I am not so sure about that. I think that the resources are there, we have only to seek to use them. But I think something else should be said since much of the atmosphere of our time is created by major transformations in our way of looking at the law and looking at the racial aspects of the law, going back to 1954 and coming through the measures passed during the sixties.

We went about that with a feeling of good intentions, we sacrificed. We did much to rectify past injustices. But then with our usual American innocence, we failed to grasp that it was going to cost us something. It would cost us something in terms of personal sacrifices, it would cost us something in the rearrangement of the cities and the suburbs. It would cost us something in terms of the sheer acceleration of turmoil and conflict. And so, we became and have become a bit tired of this old business.

I, as a writer, would remind you, however, that when the Afro-American became symbolic of so many other issues in American life, that his increase in freedom acted on the youth at least as a sort of sudden release for which they were unprepared. It was as though the word had gone out, that the outsider, the unacceptable, was now acceptable, and they translated it to mean that all of the repressed psychological drives, all of the discipline of the instinct were now fair game. "Let it all hang out," they said. "We have all become black men and women."

This projection, this identification of the socially unacceptable with the blacks, must be raised to consciousness. We must be aware of what is going on because only through this will we be able to reassume that optimism so necessary for living and dealing with the many problems of this diverse pluralistic society. Democracy is a collectivity of individuals.

The great writers of the nineteenth century and the best of the twentieth have always reminded us that not only is the business of being an American an arduous task, as Henry James said, it requires constant attention to our consciousness and to our conscientiousness. The law insures the conditions, the stage upon which we act; the rest of it is up to the individual.

PERSPECTIVE OF ETHICS*

Malcolm Boyd**

One of my friend Langston Hughes's memorable literary characters is Jesse B. Semple, who was nicknamed Simple in the three books written about him. Simple invariably speaks his mind with wry understatement about a variety of issues. I was not disappointed when I looked to see if Langston Hughes had had Simple say anything about the law in the perspective of ethics.

'"If I was setting in the High Court in Washington,' said Simple, 'where they do not give out no sentences for crimes, but where they gives out promulgations, I would promulgate. Up them long white steps behind them tall white pillars in that great big marble hall with the eagle of the U.S.A., where at I would bang my gavel and promulgate.'

'Promulgate what?' I asked.

'Laws,' said Simple. 'After that I would promulgate the promulgations that would take place if people did not obey my laws. I see no sense in passing laws if nobody pays them any mind.'

"What would happen if people did not obey your promulgations?' I asked.

'Woe be unto them,' said Simple. 'I would not be setting in that High Court paid a big salary just to read something off a paper. I would be there with a robe on to see that what I read was carried out. I would gird on my sword, like in the Bible, and prepare to do battle. For instant, "Love thy

*Peter C. Schanck, B.A., J.D., M.L.S., Chief Reference Librarian of the Michigan Law School, generously and ably assisted me in the preparation of this paper. I offer him my gratitude.

***Episcopal priest; author; social critic.*

neighbor as thyself." The first man I caught who did not love his neighbor as hisself, I would make him change places with his neighbor—the rich with the poor, the white with the black, and Governor Faubus with me.'"[1]

Simple is fully aware of the ambiguities to be found where the law and ethics meet, or do not meet. A question that might intrigue Simple is: Can you legislate morality?

The initial trouble with the question is that, in our highly pluralistic society possessing massive competitors in self-interest, it is excruciatingly difficult for people to reach a mutually acceptable definition of what constitutes morality. For example, is it found in the arguments for, or against, legalized abortion—busing—the so-called right to die? Is it found in the arguments for, or against, free sexual expression of consenting adults—prison reform—government surveillance of people's lives—civil disobedience? One encounters bitter conflict among proponents of sharply divergent ethical propositions concerning these issues.

The first part of our discussion concerns the law as sacred. Since moral relativism has considerably replaced old clear-cut lines of authority, the burden placed upon the law by this society at the present time is a virtually insuperable one. For the law is, by default, presently supposed to be this society's moral spokesperson, its agency of ethics, its definer of what is right and wrong. There is a deep irony in this situation because the law is inescapably the definer of our surrogate morality instead of our morality itself. Indeed, morality forms the very foundation of law. As Peter Singer points out: "Our ultimate obligation to obey the law is a moral obligation and not a legal obligation."[2]

Nonetheless, there is anticipation and expectation on the part of the society that the law will speak from on high as well as the people's midst, and that it will make straight what would otherwise remain twisted, crooked lines; it will establish order in the stead of anarchy and chaos; it will retain a semblance of purity in the midst of vile motives and human deceits; it will be our god, or at least speak with a godlike authority and power in a godless age.

The law is the first to say, of course, that this situation is absurd, untenable, and beyond the pale of rationality. Yet it is the situation. This does not mean that the law is loved by the society or even universally respected. But the law exists; it is a given factor of stability, credible historical development, and yearned-for order amid the rise of violence, terror, and an unspeakable sense of insecurity that haunts the burnt-out souls of an anxious people.

At the same time that the society places the law inside a transitory and secular holy of holies, the law itself is torn by introspection concerning its identity and role. *Is* there a point of intersection between law and morals? Are what *is* and what *ought* to be indissolubly fused or inseparable? Legal Positivism has insisted on the separation of law as it is and law as it ought to be. It has viewed law as not being an ideal, but something which exists and must be considered in its actuality.

On the other hand, for Lon L. Fuller "It is in the light of [the] 'ought' that we must decide what the rule 'is.'"[3] He raises the question: "Is it really ever possible to interpret a word in a statute without knowing the aim of the statute?"[4] He claims that law possesses an "internal morality,"[5] and says: "The fundamental postulate of positivism—that law must be strictly severed from morality—seems to deny the possibility of any bridge between the obligation to obey the law and other moral obligations. No mediating principle can measure their respective demands on conscience, for they exist in wholly separate worlds."[6]

If we believe that the law, in its proper role, must reflect the ideal of a higher justice, how then are we to react when it violates that ideal? If the law seemingly institutionalizes injustice, is there a need to disobey it? Throughout my life, from childhood through school days and college, I understood implicitly that there was, in practice, one law for haves and another law for have-nots. (Anatole France perceived the law somewhat differently. To him, it was inherently inequitable rather than merely unequal in application. "The Law, in its majestic equality," he wrote, "forbids the rich as well as the poor to sleep under bridges, to beg in the streets, and to steal bread.")

Whether my own awareness came from early reading as a youngster—Edwin Markham's *The Man With the Hoe;* Charles Dickens' *Oliver Twist;* Victor Hugo's *Les Miserables;* "The

Scottsboro Boys," Richard Wright's *Native Son;* or from simply opening my eyes to life around me in the Great Depression, the metropolis in which I grew up, the racial maze in which blacks and whites were choreographed—I do not precisely know. But the awareness entered into my consciousness. So, in my teens I found that a Marian Anderson concert was not simply a concert. I knew that Marian Anderson was black. The manifold meanings of this escaped me, but beneath the surface of that knowledge there lurked a depth of tragic symbols that caused me to weep quietly in my seat in the concert hall when she sang "Sometimes I Feel Like a Motherless Child." I also knew in my bones that the racial tragedy had the sanction of law.

I was a student in high school when I listened to H. V. Kaltenborn—he was Walter Cronkite, John Chancellor and Howard K. Smith rolled into one—report over the radio about the rise of Hitler and a new anti-Semitism. Nazism was a distant but quite close-to-home monstrous force that repelled and frightened me, forcing me to look with apprehension and a new kind of wonder at my Jewish classmates. "Juden" became a chilling word in my limited, growing vocabulary that also included "nigger." The Nazis' destructive urges against Jews were bolstered by (I realized) the sanction of law.

What, then, was I to make of the law? It seemed to possess the power to do terrible things as well as good ones. I determined never to run afoul of the law, seemingly capricious with its potential Star Chamber aspects. I did not wish to find myself under any circumstances in its Witch-of-the-West clutches. Some people would say it was simply a good thing that I feared the law. But, alas, I did not respect it. Although I held it in awe as being sacrosanct, possessing even an element of the *mysterium tremendum,* I knew that it could be manipulated by the leverage of power. A demythologizing of the law took place in my early consciousness.

I had no way of knowing that later in my life I would actually test the law in the light of ethics as I understood them. Years afterward when I was a Freedom Rider, an earnest figure of the early '60s, I endeavored to test—and change—the law that enforced apartheid, the practice of separate lives and opportunities for blacks and whites, and even forebade racial mixing at a lunch counter. Often in the course of the Civil

Rights struggle, one found oneself stopped short by the stone wall of a dehumanizing system that was rooted in unyielding laws.

One felt a sense of wrestling with shadows or ghosts. Where was one's ground? As a middle-class white volunteer at work on black voter registration in the Deep South, I rode in a car on a highway one day with three young black men. We drove under the speed limit in order to avoid a confrontation with the police. But our car was stopped by the police, and we were placed under arrest on the actual—and utterly false—charge of speeding. The experience was a profoundly shocking one for me. I had always embraced the concept of law and order. But now I had to ask myself: Law and order for whom? What could one make of "order" that brought disorder into people's lives, tyrannizing them? More significant was the shady underworld of killings and lynchings. Emmett Till comes to mind as a latter-day example that at least became widely known and received new attention. For an agonizingly long time, such victims of torture and gross injustice had no access to justice. On entirely too many occasions, local laws apparently stood in the way of access itself even though this was guaranteed by the United States Constitution.

When the Vietnam War raged madly out of control, consuming human lives, a gutted portion of the earth, and an American generation's idealism, I found myself once again as a dissenter. This time I did not test or try to change laws; I merely wished to exercise responsibly the civil liberty that I believed was my right. Yet I recall how Vice-President Spiro W. Agnew attacked "the glib, activist element who would tell us our values are lies." He seemed not to understand that criticism of the state can be a high form of honoring it, and that without the honest and creative practice of dissent, democracy suffers irremediably. Concerning those who dissented, Vice-President Agnew proposed "to separate them from our society with no more regret than we should feel over discarding rotten apples from a barrel."

On two occasions I participated—once as the celebrant, once as the preacher—in Peace Masses inside the Pentagon, nonviolent and orderly demonstrations for the cause of peace. Laws of access at the Pentagon were not the issue; instead, it was the seeming irrelevancy of the law itself to the conduct of an undeclared war that profoundly tried the moral fiber of the nation. When we were arrested on the two occasions, the legal charge of disturbing the peace had to be juxtaposed against the reality of how many bombs the United States dropped that day on Vietnam. One thought inescapably of how many Americans and Vietnamese were killed on the same day when a few dissenters tried against clearly hopeless odds to disturb the peace of the Pentagon.

At the particular times when I have felt impelled to engage in acts of public dissent, I was neither so naive nor self-righteous as to feel that God was on "our side." Yet undeniably I believed that I was following the dictates of my own conscience as well as the fundamental precepts of what I had learned was the Judeo-Christian ethic. But this can be heady stuff. *Is* there such a thing as "law above the law" or "the moral code?" *Is* there "a lamp unto the feet and a light unto the path" and "a still small voice," or are these mere delusions in the place of serious reality? *Do* so-called moral values possess any ultimate sanction over legal sanctions?

1984 is but eight years away from us now. However, I do not ask you to look into the future or to inspect its implications, whether these be Orwellian or Disneyish. I ask you to look backward thirty years with me to the Holocaust. It is the single event in my own lifetime that has most deeply affected me. Millions of people participated in it. To observe a single aspect of it places us sharply in an existential frame of reference. One asks: How could the Holocaust have occurred in a highly civilized society rich in historical mores of morality, the practice of religion, and a vigorous intellectual life? We need to hold the Holocaust in a precise perspective of near-contemporary occurrence instead of letting it become an abstract symbol of universal numbness. In the interest of specificity, this is part of a German engineer's sworn testimony at the Nuremberg Trial:

"I went round the mound of earth and stood before the gigantic grave. People lay in it so closely packed one upon the other that only their heads could be seen. The trench was already three-quarters full. By my reckoning there were already about a thousand people lying in it. I looked round to see who was shooting. An SS man sat at the edge of the trench letting his legs dangle in it; he had a submachine gun resting on his knee and was smoking a cigarette.

"The completely naked people went down a few steps which had been dug in the wall of the trench, scrambled over the heads of those who were lying there to the position that the SS man indicated. They lay down among the dead or wounded people; some stroked those who were still alive, and spoke quietly to them. Then I heard a succession of shots. I looked in the trench and saw how the bodies twitched; blood spurted from the necks. I was surprised that no one told me to go away, but I also saw two or three postmen in uniform standing nearby."[7]

Could anything demonstrate more vividly the crying need of a higher judge of law? What judges justice? This event judges justice! It took place at a particular time and place, and certainly with the compliance of the law.

So we have learned that the law, sometimes mistakenly equated with justice, cannot be considered sacrosanct. But does this mean that we must accept, for example, Philip Berrigan's dictum that "Given America's crimes, keeping the law is rejecting Christianity?"[8] Surely one cannot insist upon a utopian ideal of an absolute moral purity as a prerequisite of keeping the law in human society, where there can be only approximate justice, and moral ambiguities are as much parts of life as idealism and spirit.

"Let justice roll down like waters, and righteousness like an everflowing stream," wrote Amos. But, Giorgio Del Vecchio tells us, justice can be hard to grasp or neatly define. "Justice is sometimes taken to be synonymous with or equivalent to law, sometimes to be distinct from law and superior to it. Justice in one of its aspects is held to consist in *conformity with law;* but it is also asserted that *law must conform to justice.* What at one moment is taken as the standard whereby to judge what is just and unjust can in turn, in its manifestation as mere empirical fact, be itself judged in the same way; this happens when we appeal, in the name of justice, to a higher ideal criterion which transcends all rules of positive law and must therefore rest on some other foundation."[9]

When is it possible for a society to agree upon this "higher ideal criterion?" Is it not by means of perversely appealing to such an undefined "criterion," which is said to transcend "all rules of positive law and must therefore rest on some other foundation," that the door is opened to the "transcendent" or "divine" or absolutist rights of those who do evil even as they claim to stand above the law? If, as citizens, we are told that it is our duty to hold conscience above the law, what collective conscience can save us from the sheer anarchy of a legion of individual consciences?

Most people's individual consciences will be informed by the individual consciences of peers and colleagues, and the collective represented by these. But collective consciences can create the most barbarous evil, as witnessed by Nazi Germany or South Africa. There is a profound need for these individual consciences to be nurtured by morality in the sense of a universally accepted ethical context. Few would argue with Lord Devlin when he says: "The idea that you must not seek without restraint your own profit and well-being but must be careful that in so doing you do not injure others is a moral idea that is part of the foundation of every good society."[10] And this is surely not the only universally accepted moral principle. When the law is true to its nature, it provides a parameter for the implementation of this principle and others like it.

However, to accept this role for law and to put it into practice are quite different things. There's the rub. I could ask you to accompany me in this Bicentennial Year to a thousand different American communities, and in each of them I could show you human tragedy directly based upon failures of justice and the breakdown of moral ideas, this in the face of operative legal systems.

What hope is there that the law can make any difference in these fragments of an impending social tragedy that are as much parts of the American Bicentennial observance as TV specials and patriotic oratory? What is the law in perspective of ethics supposed to mean when it comes to the needed growth of genuine social morality and the injection of hope itself into human lives?

Apparently we must hold in some kind of a workable balance (1) the demands of individual conscience, (2) the extenuating demands made upon individual consciences by the often competing realities of society and the world, (3) the dangers inherent in postulating an undefined higher ideal criterion which is said to transcend all rules of positive law, and (4) the moral vision inherent in a higher ideal criterion that takes positive shape in the service of human needs and justice.

A sick, badly wounded or endangered society is addressed by occasional surrogate prophets. A healthier society is informed by a prophetic instinct—even a body of knowledge—that is generated, nurtured, and shared by a larger number of different people. This prophetic instinct needs to provide the foundation of a responsible, self-challenging, socially-challenging, humanly responsive community of law.

Let the law be the servant of justice. Justice needs to be informed by love and mercy. Surely these words do not comprise mysterious cunundrums or puzzles within puzzles that are incapable of being understood in this moment of the age-old struggle between the individual and constituted authority. Let the law not reduce itself to letter-perfect casuistry that denies its own servanthood to humanity. Humanity is never a cut-and-dried entity. Brand Blanshard usefully reminds us: "However capricious or selfish or brutal a man may be in actual behavior, if we are right in calling him a moral being at all, what he is trying to be and do is never exhausted in what he is."[11]

Yes. On this point our best poets and playwrights agree with our best explicitly moral prophets. This is an essentially optimistic, generous, openended, and hopeful view of the human endeavor. The law must maintain order, yet recognize that order is changing, adjusting, relating to the human beings whom it encompasses. Order is fluid, not constant; it is not a strait jacket, but a garment that adheres naturally to the body following long use.

One thing is clear. Internal morality is not essentially different from external morality. So, the law is judged by the law. The law above the law, and the law within the law, are the same and cannot be seen as standing separate from the essence of the law itself.

As a people, we do not wish to see the law as holy. At its best the law is a guide to motives and actions that point toward what is holy. As a people, we do not wish to suffer under the law as institutionalized injustice that stands in the way of justice and decency. We seek a balanced vision of the law as necessary, and based on justice and suffused with love and mercy. We yearn, and are sometimes heard to cry out, for this.

As we need the law, so does the law need us. It needs us to irritate, prod, disturb, and criticize the law. Why? Because the law needs people as human reminders of what the law ought to be, and is capable of becoming, so that it will not arrogantly and comfortably settle for what it is. Let the law be honored in its own practice.

FOOTNOTES

1. Langston Hughes, *Simple's Uncle Sam.* Hill and Wang, 1965, p. 160.
2. Peter Singer, *Democracy and Disobedience.* Oxford University Press, 1973, p. 3.
3. Lon L. Fuller, "Positivism and Fidelity to Law—A Reply to Professor Hart," *Harvard Law Review;* Vol. 71, No. 4, February, 1958, p. 666.
4. *Ibid.;* p. 664.
5. *Ibid.;* p. 645.
6. *Ibid.;* p. 656.
7. Joe J. Heydecker and Johannes Leeb, *The Nuremberg Trial.* Trans. and ed. by R. A. Downie. World Publishing Co., 1962, p. 334.
8. Philip Berrigan, *Widen the Prison Gates: Writing from Jails.* Simon and Schuster, 1973, p. 51
9. Giorgio Del Vecchio, *Justice: An Historical and Philosophical Essay.* Ed. by A. H. Campbell. Edinburgh University Press, 1952, p. 1.
10. Sir Patrick Devlin, *Law and Morals.* The Holdsworth Club of the University of Birmingham, 1961, p. 3.
11. Brand Blanshard, *Reason and Goodness.* George Allen and Unwin Ltd., 1961, p. 397.

PERSPECTIVE OF PHILOSOPHY

H.L.A. Hart*

I

As an Englishman I am delighted to add my contribution to this celebration of the great events of 1776. You did well, if I may say so, for yourselves, for us, and for the world to make that break, of which not the least important product has been the development here of fresh and, as we see them, characteristically American interpretations of the nature and significance of law.

The perspective in which I shall invite you to see the law is to relate certain ideas now astir, particularly in this country, in political philosophy and jurisprudence to those which sprang into vigorous life just two hundred years ago. No English lawyer, certainly no English philosopher of law, could forget that the year of wonders 1776, which saw the publication of the Declaration of Independence, the first volume of Gibbon's *Decline and Fall of the Roman Empire,* and Adam Smith's *Wealth of Nations,* was also the year of the anonymous publication of Jeremy Bentham's first book, *The Fragment on Government,* which contained his first formulation of the Principle of Utility and the germ of nearly all his later thinking about law and the sciences of law. It is, I think, less well known that in the same year, 1776, Bentham contributed, again anonymously, to *An Answer to the Declaration of the American Congress*[1] a brief, brusque and satirical attack on the philosophical preamble of the Declaration and on the doctrines of the natural equality of men and of their unalienable rights.

In *The Fragment on Government,* published four months be-

**Principal, Brasenose College, Oxford; former Professor of Jurisprudence, Oxford University.*

fore the Declaration of Independence, Bentham described the Principle of Utility as "the fundamental axiom according to which the greatest happiness of the greatest number is the measure of right and wrong." In Bentham's hands this maxim was to provide among other things the justification for the exercise of government of men by coercive laws and the justification both for obedience to laws and, when occasion required it, for withholding obedience. So Utilitarianism became a justificatory theory of Government and of the limits of Government. In his contribution to the *Answer to the Declaration of the American Congress,* Bentham attacked the alternative justification for these things which was offered by the doctrine of unalienable rights of man. In so doing he fired the first, light shots of destructive analysis, which developed into a lengthy and heavy bombardment when seventeen years later the doctrine reappeared in the French Declaration of the Rights of Man.[2]

Jeremy Bentham thus opened in 1776 with these two works a whole epoch in that area of philosophy which is of peculiar relevance and concern to the lawyer. Moreover even if, in the narrow English style, we conceive of jurisprudence as lying outside the scope of political philosophy or theory, it is true that in jurisprudence also Bentham's thoughts, published just two hundred years ago, have been enormously influential and persistent. During the years since his death in 1832 much argument and counter-argument about the nature of law, about the relation between law and morality and about the forms of legal reasoning appropriate to legal adjudication have circled round ideas to be found in Bentham's works. The most fundamental of these ideas is that law, good or bad, is a man-made artifact which men create and add to the world by the exercise of their will: not something which they discover through the exercise of their reason to be already in the world. There are indeed good reasons for having laws, but a reason for a law, even a good reason, is not a law any more, so Bentham thought, than "hunger is bread".[3] On this foundation rested the famous definition of laws as the commands, prohibitions or permissions of a sovereign legislature, either issued explicitly and directly by the Sovereign, or indirectly through subordinates whose mandates the Sovereign explicitly authorises or tacitly adopts.[4]

With these fundamental ideas went the sharp severance which Bentham made in *The Fragment on Government* between law as it is and law as it ought to be (and between an analytical or, as he termed it, expository jurisprudence and a critical or censorial jurisprudence), and his insistence in the same work that the foundations of a legal system are not to be found in any moral or justificatory theory, but are properly described in the morally and evaluatively neutral terms of a general habit of obedience to a sovereign legislature. This cluster of ideas opened the long positivist tradition in English jurisprudence. Transmitted through the medium of John Austin's work, in a style more easily assimilable than Bentham's by lawyers who were not also philosophers, this tradition has of course profoundly and, as some think, disastrously, influenced English legal education and the English conception of the judicial function, and left its profound imprint on English legal thought in general.

Even in the United States the leading themes of Benthamite jurisprudence have reverberated though, to continue the musical metaphor, they have been transposed into another key, the American law-making court replacing the British sovereign legislature as the chief focus of attention. John Chipman Gray in *The Nature and Sources of Law* explicitly endorsed and indeed applauded the Benthamite and Austinian distinction between law as it is and law as an ideal of what ought to be,[5] and Holmes, who had read with care and responded to much of Austin's work, finding its apparent toughness congenial to his temperament, was advocating what was in essence the same distinction when he argued that the clear-minded jurist should wash the notion of legal obligation and duty in "cynical acid"[6] so as to free law from a perennial and obscuring confusion with morality.

Such then were the leading ideas with which an epoch opened in both political and legal theory in 1776. But there are signs that this epoch may now be closing. Utilitarianism, which for long was regarded as the sober, workmanlike English manifestation of the European Enlightenment, and was certainly the fountain of great reforms of the archaic English legal system and the inspiration of progressive thought in England and elsewhere, is now seen by many thinkers to have a darker, more sinister side licensing anything to be done to individuals, any sacrifice, in the pursuit of the ultimate goal of maximising the aggregate or average welfare of a community. Moreover, much of the most interesting current work among American political philosophers—and I am thinking here of John Rawls's *Theory of Justice* and Robert Nozick's *Anarchy, State, and Utopia*—is not only frankly hostile to Utilitarianism but identifies as Utilitarianism's cardinal sin its failure to recognize that the division of humanity into separate individuals is a fact of great moral importance which confers on certain interests of individuals a title to inviolability, to be maintained even where to maintain it may reduce the level of aggregate or average welfare below that which could otherwise be achieved. Plainly a social philosophy in this temper has much affinity with the eighteenth century doctrines of the unalienable rights of man which were for long thought to have succumbed to their great Utilitarian critic. In jurisprudence, in suggesting that we may be at the end of an epoch and the beginning of a new one, I am thinking of the work of my American successor in the Chair of Jurisprudence at Oxford, Professor Ronald Dworkin. This is marked by the same antipathy to Utilitarianism[7] and the same insistence on the independent importance of individual rights, but is also marked by a new form[8] of the ancient theory that there are vital conceptual connections between law and principles of justice which justify the law, to which, it is said, positivism has been blind and blinded its victims.

Of course criticism of Bentham's form of Utilitarianism is no new thing. For a century at least in England and America there has been a stream of intermittent, unsystematic and piece-meal criticism of Bentham's legacy to political philosophy and jurisprudence. Till recently the criticisms had been absorbed as matters calling for refinement, qualification or re-interpretation of the doctrines and not outright rejection, even if in the case of some of the re-interpretations, notably John Stuart Mill's distinctively libertarian and individualistic version of the notion of Utility, it might seem that the spirit of Bentham's doctrine was quite transformed and only the terminology in which it is formulated remains the same. But the three contemporary writers whom I have mentioned are different and it is a phenomenon of importance that in spite of many differences of doctrine and political implications, the liveliest and most interesting modern writings in political and legal theory contain frank and fundamental challenges to Bentham's thought about law and politics. So in the remainder of this short paper I shall take two examples of the new ideas and I shall raise the question—no more—whether we should do well to regard them as disposing finally of Bentham's thought in these fields.

II

First then the doctrine of natural unalienable rights. In his attack in 1776 on the Declaration of Independence Bentham allows that the concept of a non-positive right, that is one not created by the law or social custom, is coherent and not self-contradictory, though his own view was that it was indeed self-contradictory and a species of nonsense. Within the framework of this provisional concession, Bentham focussed his criticism of the Declaration of Independence on the absurdity of combining the assertion that there are unalienable rights with the assertion that government is necessary to protect them and legitimate when it does so. This was absurd in Bentham's view because the exercise of the necessary powers of any government must constantly restrict the exercise by the individual of his alleged unalienable rights. "They see not or will not seem to see that nothing that was ever called government ever was or could be in any instance exercised save at the expense of one or other of those rights: that, in as many instances as government is ever exercised some one or other of these pretended unalienable rights is alienated . . . . If the right of pursuit of happiness is a right unalienable, why are thieves restrained from pursuing it by theft, murderers by murder and rebels by rebellion?"[9] Taken strictly as offering unqualified guarantees of certain liberties, the doctrine is essentially anarchical, and anarchists have not been slow to invoke it in support of their claim that the State is, morally speaking, illegitimate. Bentham insisted that no political principles with the rigidity of the doctrine of unalienable specific rights could have any application in the real world where men live their lives. Such principles belong to Utopia; that is Nowhere or an imaginary world, and accordingly he stigmatised the doctrine as the product not of reason but of mere imagination,[10] and complained that such principles were "deaf, unyielding and inflexible, principles which will hear of no modification, which will look at no calculation,"[11] which, if instead of imagination reason were consulted, would be seen to be unnecessary.

This form of criticism was amplified by Bentham when he came to deal with the French Declaration of the Rights of Man by the demonstration that unalienable rights construed as guarantees of specific liberties of action were not only incompatible with government but were doomed to constant conflict with each other. Simple and crude as this form of criticism may seem, it became and remained for decades the standard objection to the doctrine of fixed natural rights. Indeed its vitality is paradoxically confirmed by one of the works which I have already mentioned, Nozick's *Anarchy, State, and Utopia.* For at the outset Nozick raises precisely Bentham's question and asks "How much room do individual rights leave for government?"[12] What is astonishing is that Nozick in effect gives Bentham's answer: "No room except in an imaginary world." For that is the message of his ingenious and brilliant work. Thus Nozick argues that, granted a set of natural rights, such as not to be killed, assaulted, coerced, and not to have property taken or destroyed, and not to be limited in the use of property, only a minimal form of State, the so-called nightwatchman State, whose functions are limited to the punishment of violations of such rights, can be legitimate. Moreover given these natural rights even this minimal form of State could be justified only under conditions of which Bentham never thought and might be forgiven for failing to do so, for they are conditions produced out of Nozick's lively imagination which are highly unlikely to be satisfied in the real as contrasted with the imaginary world. The conditions in question are that the State should have arisen through individuals voluntarily joining a private protection association which might eventually achieve, without infringing any natural rights, dominance in a limited territory even if not everyone joined it. But all this seems indeed imaginary and to have little relevance to a world where States do not arise in this way.

So Nozick's theory seems just tailor-made for Bentham's accusation that talk of unalienable rights taken strictly belongs only to the world of the imagination. Bentham of course realized that defenders of the doctrine would disclaim such rigid unqualified interpretations of it and while speaking of rights as "unalienable" would admit limitations of scope, qualifications and exceptions and balancing, both of right against right, and right against general welfare or would even be content to view them merely as ideal directions to governments to do the best they can for certain individual interests. But he claimed that the doctrine would then be nugatory. To support this point he could have cited some famous—or infamous—examples from America, where express declarations of natural rights to liberty incorporated into State constitutions were held not to affect the slave owner's rights to property in his slaves.[13] So he depicted the French advocates of natural rights as on the horns of a dilemma between the impossible and the nugatory.[14] In this I think he was wrong: there is certainly more to be said about the relationship between basic human rights and other values than he allows. But in spite of recent work I do not think we yet have a satisfactory theory showing how respect for such rights is to be combined with the pursuit of other values. Some theories seem to me to throw out the baby (that is basic rights compatible with each other and with government) with the bathwater of excessive rigidity. Other theories—perhaps Professor Nozick's among them—do worse; they throw out the baby and keep the bath water.

III

I turn now to my second topic, the modern challenge to the legal positivism inherited from Bentham. Here I can only consider, although very briefly, one aspect of this modern challenge: namely the new form of the old indictment that the positivist has misrepresented the nature of the judicial process. Here there has been an astonishing volte face among the critics. Indeed, if I may use the language of 1776, it is "the world turned upside down". I say this because twenty years ago when I came to Harvard to lecture on my own brand of legal theory, the sin imputed to positivist conceptions of the judicial function was 'formalism', 'conceptualism', 'mechanical' or 'slot machine jurisprudence' or an excessive belief in the use of 'logic' in reaching decisions. The positivist was said to believe (though in fact neither Bentham nor Austin ever did believe this) that correct judicial decisions were always the conclusions of syllogisms reached by pure deductive reasoning from clear pre-determined legal rules serving as major premises. It was said that the positivist jurists, and judges misled by them, ignored the indeterminacy at the borderline of many constitutional provisions, the open ended character of many statutes and the unsettled or conflicting scope of many precedents which left leeways open to the judge and made a choice on his part inescapable. So that ultimately, the critics urged, to reach a decision, the judge has to choose between competing alternatives and such a choice, if rational, would have to be made in the light of social policies and values that took him outside what the positivist called law. So on this view, intended to correct the then errors of positivism, the judge sometimes made law though unlike a legislator he was no doubt constrained in various ways, hemmed in by the existing law which ruled out many alternatives and imposed on him a duty to weigh, as best he could, before reaching a decision various, sometimes competing, presumptions representing the received values of the legal system.

But the new critique of positivism expounded with great power and subtlety and also complexity by Professor Dworkin reverses these accusations against positivism and holds the positivists' cardinal sin no longer to be 'formalism' or belief in a 'mechanical' theory of judicial decision but to consist in a mistaken assimilation of the judge's task in deciding hard cases to a legislative or law making choice.[15] Litigants, it is said, are always entitled to have from judges an application of existing law to them, not the making of new law for them. For a judge to make such law would not only be unjust where decisions have retroactive force, but, where judges are not elected, they would be undemocratic.

But the old and new errors of positivism do not, according to this new critique, exhaust the alternatives. There is a third alternative which is also a *via media* between classical Natural Law theory and positivism. For over every legal system—or rather over the mass of constitutional law, statutes and precedents which a community at a given time accepts as clear and settled law, there is exactly what Oliver Wendell Holmes denied, "a brooding omnipresence" of general principles of fairness and justice. These are not to be identified with positive constitutional provisions, enactments or authoritative decisions but are pre-supposed by these taken together as their implicit justification and are to be inferred from them. From

this body of principles, which, in our system, includes conceptions of individual dignity and freedom, rules can be deduced to solve correctly those hard cases when separate positive constitutional provisions, enactments and precedents give incomplete, ambiguous or conflicting guidance. It is to these implicit principles manifested in the body of existing clear positive law that judges must turn to find the law which will serve to decide hard cases, and they exist as law before he turns to them. So the belief that judges can in deciding such cases properly make law even "interstitially" can be discarded as a misleading positivist error. On this view Holmes was wrong in stating that when the law is in doubt "even if it is disguised and unconscious the judges are called upon to exercise the sovereign prerogative of choice."[16] On the contrary, according to the new theory with its expanded version of what law is, there always awaits the judge's discovery some pre-existing law adequate to dispose of the case with superior claims over competing alternatives, which might also be regarded as implicit in the body of existing positive law, to be best fitted to it.

Of course only a superhuman being (Dworkin calls him "Hercules") commanding a god's-eye view of the whole legal system could be certain that he had identified correctly the one consistent set of principles which will both explain and justify the whole mass of clear and settled positive law, and also yield *the* correct rule of decision for the instant controversial case. Ordinary mortals, including judges, can only infer from the body of already decided or settled law these general abstract principles. They can only attempt to determine them by framing explanatory and justificatory hypotheses. The hypotheses of different judges may conflict but when a judge adopts one rather than another he is not on this theory choosing what is to be the law and so "making" it, but acting on what he thinks is the best evidence as to what the law already is; for the law itself on this view is not, as the positivist claims it sometimes is, ever incomplete or indeterminate. The fault is not in *it;* but in *our* limited powers of discernment. Even when the positive law has proved to be unsettled something always already was the law for every case however "hard".

Professor Dworkin has recently provided a most striking example of the working of this theory in his recent reflections on Professor Cover's admirable study of anti-slavery and the judicial process.[17] Before the Civil War famous judges like Joseph Story and Lemuel Shaw in Massachusetts, who were passionately opposed to slavery, nonetheless after much agony enforced the Fugitive Slave Acts passed by Congress and ordered slaves who had escaped to free States to be taken back by their masters. The judges did this, distasteful as it was to them, because according to Professor Dworkin they thought it was their judicial duty to follow the clear intentions of the legislators in Congress who had enacted the Fugitive Slave Acts and the clearly manifested intention of the Constitutional Convention embodied as part of the grand compromise between the slave States and free States in Article 4 of the Constitution. This provided that the escaped slave "shall not in consequence of any law or regulation of a State to which he had escaped be discharged from that service but shall be delivered up on claim of the party to whom his service or labour may be due." The judges who with such agony suppressed their own moral qualms in this way in order to do what they saw as their duty to enforce the law were guilty according to the new theory of a "failure in jurisprudence". If only they had been willing to think along the lines proposed by the new theory, they could have found implicit principles better fitting the existing law than any rivals and strong enough to yield a clear decision in favour of the slaves. For according to this theory "The general structure of the American Constitution presupposed a conception of individual freedom antagonistic to slavery, a conception of procedural justice that condemned the procedures established by the Fugitive Slave Acts, and a conception of federalism inconsistent with the idea that the State of Massachusetts had no power to supervise the capture of men and women within its territory. These principles were not simply the personal morality of a few judges, which they set aside in the interests of objectivity. They were rather, on this theory of what law is, more central to the law than were the particular and transitory policies of the slavery compromise." So judges like Story and Shaw could and should have given effect to them in discharge of their duty to apply the law.

Much that Professor Dworkin says in the course of developing this conception of the unity of law with its justificatory theory seems to me exceedingly well taken against some incautious descriptions of what judges do, and against some hasty claims as to what they should do in those cases where particular parts of the law offer no clear guidance. As he rightly says, judges on reaching that juncture do not and should not put their law books aside and choose without fuller reference to the existing law, according to their own social policy or moral intuition. They do seek and often find fuller guidance in the body of existing positive law which imposes constraints upon their decision and exercises what, in a striking phrase, Professor Dworkin well calls "a gravitational pull" (even if it is only one of analogy) over it. So that the decision, when it comes, may seem to the judge to have been latent or immanent in the law. Nonetheless anyone considering this theory and especially its application to the Fugitive Slave cases must I think be visited by doubts on two main scores. The first is the latitude which Professor Dworkin permits himself and so would allow to the courts in drawing the line of distinction between what is to be taken as settled law from which the guilding justificatory principles are to be derived, and what as unsettled law providing the hard cases to be decided by reference to the principles so derived. Thus for the theory to have any application to the Fugitive Slave Act cases the relevant law must at the time of the decision be taken not to have been settled. But the judges themselves as Professor Dworkin says, said that it was settled. "The law was not already settled though the judges said it was." He implies that the judges could not have believed what they said for according to him in spite of what they said they believed they were making new law. "The decisions were surprising not because the judges refused to bend the law to their own convictions but because though they believed they were making new law they made law they themselves thought immoral."[18]

More important is the doubt whether Professor Dworkin has established something which is central to his case, viz: that a judge will not frequently be faced with alternative equally correct ways of applying this theory, when in seeking to avoid "the failure in jurisprudence" of which Story and Shaw were guilty, he tries to extract from the existing law the principle that will yield the correct decision in a hard case. It is right and illuminating to speak of the existing law as exerting a gravitational pull over the judge, but that there will not quite often be equal gravitational pulls in different directions seems to me something still to be shown. It is plain from Professor Dworkin's exposition that the underlying justificatory theory of the existing law from which the judges are to extract rules of decision include principles that are hugely general and abstract and I find it difficult to believe that among these just one principle or set of principles can be shown to fit the existing settled law better than any other. Principles *supporting* the decisions against the slaves seem to fit the then existing law at least as well as those proffered by Professor Dworkin.[19]

How would Bentham have viewed this intriguing and suggestive new theory and the claim that in failing to take this wider view of the law judges like Joseph Story were guilty of a failure in jurisprudence, exposing themselves to needless agonies? He would undoubtedly have thought it was an extension to the law as a whole of Blackstone's theory of the common law according to which the judge's decisions do not make the law but are merely evidence of what the law is. The crucial question is whether the new theory can escape the criticism which Bentham made of Blackstone's theory, namely that it was a fiction which would enable the judge, in the misleading guise of finding what the law behind the positive law really is, to invest his own personal, moral or political views with a spurious objectivity as already law. All depends on the claim which Professor Dworkin makes with great power and subtlety, to which I have been unable to do justice here, that when hard cases arise equally plausible and well based explanatory hypotheses as to what the latent law is will not be available. This is a claim I think still to be evaluated.

So to sum up: In my perspective for the future of law and philosophy, there is much unfinished business. At a time when, both in my country and in yours, substantive issues of social policy are much discussed in terms of individuals' rights, we still need a satisfactory theory of basic human rights and their relationship to other values pursued through law. So too, if positivism in jurisprudence is to be finally laid to rest, we still need a demonstration that an expanded concept of law which includes for every legal system a unique set of justificatory principles as a reserve for the solution of hard cases, will illumine and not obscure the description and the performance of the judge's task. But judging from the work in progress the prospects that we shall have at least some of these things are good. Certainly American philosophers are more likely than any others to provide them; but let us hope it will not take them another two hundred years.

FOOTNOTES

1. An Answer to the Declaration of the American Congress (London, 1776). The author of the main part of this work was John Lind (1737-1781), Bentham's close friend and collaborator who began with him the project of a critical examination of Blackstone's Commentaries from which grew Bentham's Comment on the Commentaries and of which A Fragment on Government was an offshoot. Bentham's contribution is included in the "Short Review of the Declaration" at pp. 120-122 of Lind's book and is identified as Bentham's work by his letter to Lind written in September 1776 now published in The Correspondence of Jeremy Bentham, Vol. 1, pp. 341-344 in The Collected Works of Jeremy Bentham (London, 1968).
2. *Anarchical Fallacies* being an examination of the Declaration of Rights issued during the French Revolution in Bentham's Works (ed. Bowring), Vol. 2, pp. 491-534.
3. *Op. cit.* n. 2, p. 501 and *Pannomial Fragments* in Bentham's Works, Vol. 3, p. 221.
4. See *Of Laws in General;* chapters 1 and 2, pp. 1-33, in Collected Works of Jeremy Bentham, London, 1970.
5. *The Nature and Sources of Law* (first published New York 1909), Chapter 4, sections 213-214.
6. Oliver Wendell Holmes, *The Path of the Law* (an address of 1897) in Collected Legal Papers, London 1920, p. 174.
7. *On Taking Rights Seriously;* in Oxford Essays in Jurisprudence, 2nd series, ed. Simpson.
8. *Hard Cases* (1975), 88 Harvard Law Review, 1057.
9. The passages quoted here are from Bentham's draft of his letter to Lind of September 1776 (see n. 1 supra). The text published by Lind in his Answer to the Declaration of the American Congress differs in certain points of detail but reproduces the substance of these passages. The published text adds however (p. 122) the words "Here they have put the axe to the root of all Government."
10. "Imagination with its favourite instrument the word 'right'". *Plan of Parliamentary Reform* in Bentham's Works, Vol. 3, p. 515, cf. Anarchical Fallacies, loc. cit. p. 523.
11. Plan of Parliamentary Reform, Bentham's Works, Vol. 3, p. 467, n.
12. Nozick, *Anarchy, State, and Utopia* 1 (1974).
13. E.g. the interpretation of the "free and equal" clause of the Virginia Bill of Rights (1776) in Hudgins v. Wright 11 Va. (1 Hen & M.) 133 at 141 discussed by Professor R.M. Cover in *Justice Accused: Anti-slavery and the Judicial Process* (Yale 1976) pp. 52-54. See Bentham's observations on such declarations of rights in An Introduction to the Principles of Morals and Legislation, pp. 309-10, in Collected Works of Jeremy Bentham (London, 1970).
14. *Anarchical Fallacies;* loc. cit. pp. 493, 502 ("nonsensical or nugatory and in both cases mischievous: such is the alternative"), 502, 507, 510 and 534.
15. See his *Hard Cases;* op. cit. n. 8 supra.
16. *Law in Science; Science in Law* (address of 1899) in Collected Legal Papers, p. 239.
17. Review of Cover, *Justice Accused: Anti-slavery and the Judicial Process;* in Times Literary Supplement, December 5th, 1975, p. 1437.
18. Compare Times Literary Supplement, December 5th, 1975, p. 1437, with Professor Dworkin's letter in Times Literary Supplement, 9th January, 1976, p. 35.
19. Thus Joseph Story and Lemuel Shaw had they followed Professor Dworkin's

theory might have extracted from the then existing law the following principles instead of those formulated by Professor Dworkin (pp. 16-17 supra):

(1) The general structure of the American Constitution presupposes that a compromise between different states with different institutions is to be maintained even at the cost of individual liberty involved in the effective enforcement of a slave owner's rights, where slavery is recognized by an individual state.

(2) The conception of federalism and procedural justice presupposed by the existing law consequently requires that a slave owner's claims to the return of an alleged escaped slave be adjudicated in the owner's state which recognizes the institution of slavery and where the best evidence of the status of the alleged slave is likely to be found.

(I am indebed to an unpublished paper by Mr. J.L. Mackie for the suggestion that principles of this kind might be extracted by Professor Dworkin's method from the then existing "settled" law.)

III.

CONCLUSION

THE RULE OF LAW

Lord Widgery*

The subject which I am invited to present covers the widest possible field because the Rule of Law connotes the general supremacy of law over anarchy. Nevertheless, to ask a Judge to comment on the rule of law is like asking a Bishop to give his views on sin. The Bishop's answer, you will remember, was that he was against it. My view on the Rule of Law must be that I am all for it.

This Rule starts for present purposes with King John and the Barons at Runnymede, and has since marked the defeat and disgrace of Kings, Dictators and Presidents who sought to seize power or to exert authority in excess of their constitutional limits.

It has thus demonstrated its powers against the highest in the land, but this is not necessarily the point where people today are looking for a victory of order over anarchy. It is a good thing for the giant democracy to flex its muscles occasionally, but a disregard of the law in high places is happily so unusual that it does not strike us as the real threat to life, liberty and the pursuit of happiness. Instead, the field in which the public ask for a sign that the forces of good will triumph over the forces of evil lies much nearer home in the streets in which we live, and it is that aspect of the rule of law that I would like to discuss here.

Two hundred years ago—the date which we commemorate in this Bicentennial year—there lived in England an artist who was a notable illustrator of birds and whose name was Thomas Bewick. Such was his renown that the swan which we now call the Bewick swan was named after him, and every winter we look forward to the arrival of these gorgeous

**Lord Chief Justice, England*

creatures as they leave their summer territories in Russia and come to spend the winter in Southern England.

To the expert each of these birds is recognizeable and distinguishable from the remainder. Tiny differences in facial detail are as positive as the human fingerprints for purposes of identification and when in October they begin to arrive, watch is kept for them as individuals by this means. One such place where the Bewick swans winter is at Slimbridge in Gloucestershire and great is the rejoicing as the favourites return each year. Romeo and Juliet, Castor and Pollux, Romulus and Remus, are signalled in, and one day I heard the message for which the whole world waits. It said simply "Law and Order are back".

It is a terrible condemnation of our management of our affairs, that after two hundred years in America, and far far longer in England, we have not succeeded in giving the ordinary citizen the most elementary freedom of all, namely, the right to walk freely and safely in the street and public places, and to be secure from attack or disturbance in his own home. Saddest of all is the fact that this freedom, or "law and order" if you will accept the shorthand version, has been achieved on both sides of the Atlantic, but is now slipping away again through fingers which seem powerless to resist the slide. In view of these developments we might, I suggest, be concentrating much of our effort on discovering *why* we are now in retreat, and what it is which has made our city parks and open spaces dangerous at night when only a few short years ago you could walk in them with impunity. To do this involves going back over well trodden ground, but no apology for that is expected. Somehow, somewhere, and by some means, we have lost our way. We must go back and find the right road again. If we do not, our civilization cannot survive.

This is a two-fold problem because we are concerned with both law and order. The laws which are enacted by Congress or Parliament, or made by the Judges, lay down the rules by which the game is controlled. If these laws are not wise and appropriate, "order" will not follow. Order comes from the efficient enforcement of good laws. If laws properly made are not enforced and obeyed, the whole business of law enforcement falls into disrepute. When we retrace our steps, one of the things we must be alert for is to decide whether we have been making bad laws, or whether we are just failing to enforce the good ones. As we retrace our steps we shall not lack advice from well-wishers. Some will contend that all our ills stem from poverty and a lack of social justice. Others will say that we are reaping the whirlwind of permissiveness which has swept the western world since the Second World War. Much, of course, is due to the mis-use of drugs, but this is itself a symptom of the malaise and not the root cause. Some friends will find it possible to blame all on the Republicans or the Democrats or the Conservatives or the Socialists, and others will seek inspiration from the stars. I suggest that we go back to read the signposts along the road again.

In 1968 the American Bar Association did me the honour of inviting me to attend their annual meeting which that year took place in Philadelphia, and in the course of the programme there was a valuable discussion on the proposition that crime was the product of poverty and social injustice. In my metaphor of today we were examining a signpost which said "To law and order through social justice," and we were debating whether it was true that law and order lay at the end of that particular road. At the time I expressed the view that we should not be side-tracked into thinking that the problem of restoring law and order was as easy as that, and nothing which has happened in the intervening eight years has altered my opinion. *Of course,* the strongest motive to steal is a family with empty bellies. Unhappily such families are found in abundance in Africa and Asia, but are they really to be found in any significant quantity in the United States of America or the United Kingdom? I think not—certainly it is not my experience that persons guilty of crimes of violence generally come from below the poverty line. We are, I think, in danger here of confusing want with envy. Those not in actual need may still be jealous of their better-off brethren and be tempted to commit crime to counter this imbalance, but since we are all guilty of the sin of envy from time to time, we can hardly regard its elimination as a practical step with which to conquer crime. In any case the logic of associating crime with social injustice is destroyed when one looks at recent history. The last twenty years have seen enormous strides in the creation of social equality, but have we seen any reduction in crime? The sad and clear answer is no; instead it has increased to the point when we are beginning to despair of the future. If we have spent the last twenty years following the sign which says "To law and order via social justice", I fear that we have got lost and must start again.

What is it which we had twenty years ago and no longer have, and which might have had some influence on the level of crimes in the street? It is not something in the world of science because, there again, the trend has been all the other way. Law enforcement agencies now have sophisticated devices for the detection and prevention of crime which were unheard of twenty years ago. Even the development of radio whereby the individual police officer can call for instant reinforcement has made the task of the vandal and the mugger infinitely more difficult, but their crimes flourish and increase.

But what we did have twenty years ago was discipline. A deep rooted conviction that modern urban society was intolerable unless everybody conformed to the rules, and a sense of shame and disgrace to be, or to be associated with those who broke them.

It was in the home that these lessons were first learned, and mother was the principal teacher. The current sense of values rated this as a more important task for the mother of the family than going out to work in order to buy a second automobile or a television set or an expensive summer holiday to keep up with the Jones's. Parents did not lie fast asleep in bed whilst their teenage children roamed the streets, nor did parents endeavour to avoid the obligation to train their childrens' character by putting it on the shoulders of teachers at schools. There were, of course, delinquent families, where the parents did not help, but the great bulk of parents then, as now, were and are, decent law-abiding people, and they used to make a definite and highly effective effort to see that their children conformed to social standards and did not bring upon the family the shame of public delinquency.

This *public* concern for law and order gave much additional strength to the organized police forces. A police officer who caught a young vandal red-handed, and who administered some mild corporal punishment on the spot, would be thanked by the culprit's father instead of being sued for damages. By contrast is the modern case of a police officer who found two youths ransacking his aged mother's apartment, and who made them clear up the mess in double quick time, with the encouragement of a certain amount of force. The officer incurred a substantial fine for assault.

Now I can fully understand the apprehension of those who are afraid that the police may become above the law, and there is much to be said for treating unlawful use of force as being more serious when committed by police officers than by ordinary citizens. Nevertheless, let us not be self-satisfied or smug about it, or pat ourselves on the back at such a demonstration of the impartiality of our courts. Our object is to discipline the vandal and the mugger. If all that we have to be proud of is that we have disciplined a policeman, we are not doing very well.

One of the things which we shall notice as we retrace our steps is the very different attitude towards offenders which the courts have adopted in the last twenty years. The trend has been away from sentences which are retributive or punitive in character, and towards sentences which are designed to reform. Capital punishment and corporal punishment have disappeared over large areas of the Earth's surface, and the concern of the courts has been as much to rehabilitate and reform the individual offender as to deter others from following his example. This is a development of the utmost importance and it cannot pass unnoticed because the area in which it has been most widely used is amongst juvenile offenders who themselves constitute the class in which the growth of crime has been most marked. I have no desire to return to the dark ages and throw away all we have learned about criminology during this century, but we must be honest with ourselves and recognize that the increase in juvenile crime must be more than simple coincidence. The lowest intelligence soon realizes that if fire burns it should be avoided, and it has always been a feature of criminal law to discourage crime by pointing out its unfortunate consequences to the offender. The psychiatrist's couch may in a given case be the supreme instrument for reforming and straightening out the individual offender, but it contains no terrors which will deter or discourage his friends.

To suggest that there is a connection between on the one hand the softer and more progressive attitude of the courts, and on the other the vast increase in juvenile crime, will be unacceptable to many who will contend that there is no evidence to prove that punishment deters. That may be so, but where must one expect to find evidence to prove this essentially negative proposition? I find it frankly inconceivable that the rise in juvenile crime is not associated with the relaxation of the punitive character of the sentences imposed. This does not mean that we must immediately put the clock back to the dark ages, but we shall never solve these problems unless we first identify the causes, and do not pretend that things are really better than they are. There is no painless way to restore law and order, as we shall surely find.

Another manifestation of calculated disorder in recent years has been the outdoor demonstration. Persons have gathered in large numbers with banners proclaiming the faction which they support, and the resultant crowds have filled the streets, and all too often provided cover for those whose only concern is to cause a riot and to make as much damage as possible. Many of these demonstrations in the past have been arranged by students with unimpeachable motives, and no interest beyond putting the world to rights (which, after all, is every young man's privilege). But they have constituted a serious threat to public order, if only for the opportunity which they give to evil minded men to hide behind them.

Happily this particular threat to public order has abated somewhat in the last two years. It is not easy to say what the cause is, but in Britain, at all events, the demonstrations are smaller, less frequent and much better behaved. It is annoying that the explanation for this change is so elusive since it may represent a valuable lesson to be learned. But I suggest, as the most likely explanation, that the sincere and well-intentioned organizers have become tired of being associated with the rabble and have withdrawn their support.

We have also suffered greatly from the so-called football rowdies, who consist of hundreds of teenagers who gang up together ostensibly to support the local football team, but often, in fact, to fight the supporters of the opposing club. These gangs disrupt the game, run wild in the locality of the ground where the game is played, and break up the special trains which have been laid on to bring them to the scene. We have not found an answer to this problem, and it is contained only by the deployment of an excessive number of police who are needed elsewhere, or should be enjoying time off themselves, but I have no doubt that a serious cause of this disorder is the inadequacy of the penalties which the courts can now impose upon teenagers. We are experimenting with the idea of making these youths miss their football matches, and wash floors in hospitals instead, but this very attractive idea presents serious practical difficulties in regard to supervision and enforcement.

Now, let us assume that we have retraced our steps and examined these follies and triumphs of the last two decades. What are the lessons learned, and how are we going to apply them?

First, it must be obvious to all that the Rule of Law will not govern us unless we have a fierce and burning determination that it shall do so. It is not enough that those of us here today should realize the importance of its restoration, or that this should be pursued by any limited class of people. We must somehow make it fashionable to be law-abiding, instead of being fashionable to be smart. In Britain we have recently relearned a lesson which had been forgotten in the long period of domestic peace which followed Hitler's war. It is that the most efficient law enforcement agencies are powerless unless they have the active assistance of the public. We, as you know, have suffered from a plague of small bombs, mere toys compared with those which fell on London in the war. But nasty, vicious things nevertheless, which can kill at short range, and be very damaging to property. We should have suffered far more if the public generally had not become alert to spot suspicious parcels and give the alarm. Some have done far more than this, and have shown bravery far beyond the line of duty. For example, a young West Indian immigrant who had become the driver of a suburban train, which was chosen for a bomb attack, was so incensed that *his* train should have been thus treated, that he chased the bomber only to be shot dead for his pains. I do not suppose that he had ever heard of the Rule of Law, but if everyone prized it as this hero did, we should worry about it no more. But it is not given to everyone to have courage of that order. It is, however, open to us all to be observant, and to make a conscious effort to play some part, however small. We cannot afford to pass by on the other side; it may be us next time. We must, above all, get rid of the canker inherent in an over-permissive society which refuses to recognize responsibility towards anyone but self, and takes pleasure in flouting the minor laws merely to show that it is above them. We must keep a deterrent element in our criminal law, and for this purpose, we must make sure that existing punishments, or methods of treatment, are not thrown away until other and more suitable alternatives have been worked out. In Britain we have abolished the death penalty, but no clear alternative has emerged. Nominally a murderer is sentenced to imprisonment for life, but the view is frequently heard that imprisonment for more than ten years is inhumane, and if that view should prevail it will mean that the bank robber who shoots a policeman in order to escape will incur no more penalty than the robber who does not carry a gun. This surely cannot be right, but in the desire to get rid of the death penalty these issues have been shelved. It goes without saying that we must have an efficient Police Force, that suspects must be brought promptly to trial, and sentences must be sufficiently unattractive to discourage emulation. We must show the younger generation the well defined paths, and warn them of the quicksands which lie on either side. In many respects that younger generation seemed to be superior to their predecessors, and not least in the self reliance which their freedom has enabled them to develop. But there are some who cannot manage on their own, and all will profit from sensible guidance, however unwilling they may be to admit it. It is with the parents that the ultimate hopes of restoring law and order depend. Discipline starts in the home, but many parents are afraid to teach it lest they and their children should appear to be out of line with prevailing opinion. The slightest restriction on the freedom of a teenage daughter will be met with the objection that "every other girl in our school is allowed to do it". It takes courage and dedication for the parent to meet and deal with that situation, and it is astonishing to me to find that the mother who stays at home to help the children through these crises is, in some quarters, regarded as undertaking menial work unworthy of her sex.

Our present state is due to a cause which is common

enough, namely that we have tried to get on too far and too fast. By taking the stigma out of juvenile crime we have undermined the family discipline which heretofore kept it in check. The loss of that same discipline has allowed the young to reject the standards and code of conduct of their parents when they have no alternative to fill the vacuum thereby created. We see the results in hippy communes and other exaggerated indications of independence. Obviously the young people who demonstrate their independence in these ways are not necessarily guilty of offences against law and order, but how much greater the risk of moral corruption when compared with the sort of background in which most of us were brought up.

I have spent perhaps over long on that aspect of the supremacy of law which is needed to enable our people to enjoy themselves in peace at home and in the neighborhood streets. I have done this because if you cannot count on law and order in the streets you can count on little else. The greater the threat outside, the greater the tendency to create siege conditions in which each family retires behind barred doors and locked windows, there to await the relative safety of the new day.

If the Rule of Law is to prevail the very opposite must happen. People must come out into the open to talk and reason together, to help and support each other. Then alone can public opinion have a chance to form; then alone can the public restore its confidence in the power of the authorities to enforce the law; then alone can we restore respect for the law, and allow it to rule, guide and govern us.

And may I make a special plea to the lawyers, because although the Rule of Law demands the support of every citizen it is the lawyers who must ensure that it works. They cannot do this unless they are accessible to those who need the protection of the law, be it as civil litigants or defendants in a criminal charge. They will not be accessible for this purpose if their offices are too grand, or their charges are too high, and we fail in our duty unless and until we have removed all the obstacles which separate the courts from the litigants who require their services. It used to be said that the doors of the Royal Courts of Justice are open to all, like the doors of the Ritz Hotel, and there is still too much truth in this saying for my liking. In Britain today financial considerations may still deny a litigant access to the civil courts unless he is very rich (when it does not matter), or fairly poor (when he gets free State legal aid), or a member of a labour union (when he will probably be looked after by his union). There remains a large number of people of modest means to whom the Rule of Law is an empty concept, and who are beginning to say again—"The law is for the rich." At the beginning of America's Third Century may we dedicate ourselves afresh to producing universal respect for the law and universal protection for those who desire and deserve it.

RETROSPECT AND PROSPECT

Warren E. Burger*

One important benefit of this Bicentennial celebration is that it prompts organized programs, such as the one to which this volume is devoted, in which we pause, look back and try to look ahead. Our profession likes to think that the discipline of the law has made important contributions to the stability, continuity, and cohesion of what we have come to recognize as a very fragile society in which we live. The speeches of lawyers, judges, and statesmen in the Centennial celebrations of 1876 and of the Supreme Court in 1890 speak eloquently of the "indestructible Constitution," the "indestructible union of indestructible states," but we delude ourselves with such terms if we take them literally. Our society and its institutions are destructible and fragile, as the human body is, and, like the body, need nourishment and renewal, and they must adapt in order to survive.

As lawyers, we naturally tend to draw on the past because our discipline is one of evolution rather than discovery. It is important, therefore, that on an occasion of this kind, New York University included other disciplines less bound to the past and hopefully more resilient in contemplating the future. We are here neither to glorify the past nor condemn it, but to do our best to evaluate it fairly and try to peer into our Third Century in an effort to discern what problems it will bring and how we, and those who will follow us, can cope with those problems.

We are told that the lowly ant has had a highly developed society for 65 million years but that it has remained essentially static. I am not sure just how scientists make such evaluations but it is quite clear that the human race, unlike the ant, has slowly but steadily changed its institutions and

**Chief Justice of the United States.*

improved the quality of life in many respects over thousands of years.

This volume is a manifestation of the spirit of inquiry concerning needed change. By its very nature, although there are some who disagree, the law responds to change for the most part rather than initiating it. But it should initiate when change is overdue. The special quality of the common law has been what Professor Plucknett terms its capacity for "slow adaptation to new social conditions" and some historians have suggested that, although each has had revolutions, this explains why England and the United States have suffered less than other societies from internal violence. This is attributed—correctly, as I see it—to the essential nature of the common law as a generative mechanism, sharing with nature the capacity for growth and adaptation, steadily renewing itself with a minimum of disruption, thus responding to changed conditions.

If we accept the idea that the primary function of every society is to create the kind of environment in which people can develop their God-given talents free from interference by other individuals or the state, certain rules of behavior must be established and enforced. I mean to include here not simply the criminal code but all law. The effectiveness of a system depends not merely on the soundness and fairness of the substantive rules but upon the capacity of the system to enforce them. In contemporary terms this is sometimes referred to as the "delivery of justice." The late Professor Edmond Cahn spoke of the "consumers" of justice, and in the sense he used the word, that includes all of us.

In the very Bicentennial we celebrate, we can observe the gap between the promises of the Declaration of Independence and the performance or "delivery" with respect to some promises. The lag between promise and delivery is alone enough to suggest the crucial importance of the means, the methods, and the mechanisms of giving meaningful effect to substantive rules and constitutional guarantees.

This volume, both in the diversity of its composition and the breadth of its purposes, seeks to address broad fundamental issues relating to our legal system. It is consistent for me, therefore, to focus on large objectives even though it may be necessary to deal to some extent with specific and concrete problems in order to relate the objectives to reality. Accordingly, I invite you to consider with me some fundamental aspects of our system of justice.

I.

The literature of the 1876 Centennial naturally reflects the belief of people in that time that enormous changes had taken place in our first hundred years, as indeed was true. Yet the changes which have occurred in our second hundred years tend to make the first century look like a period of relative stability. Perhaps this is because distant times, like distant fields, look greener than what is under foot.

As I see it, three conditions stand out as we look back at the society of 1876:

(1) A century ago our society was still largely rural, relatively simple, and compared with the present day, it was non-mobile and non-technological.

(2) Business relations and disputes were generally between people who had some acquaintance with each other. And again, generally speaking, those disputes were resolved within the community and influenced by attitudes of community, of family, and of church, and only finally by courts.

(3) The judicial system was primarily the state court system and state judges were engaged almost exclusively in the resolution of individual disputes. The federal judiciary had barely 100 district and circuit judges in the entire United States. Litigation in the federal courts was truly within the special and limited jurisdiction contemplated by the authors of the Constitution, and, as we know, that jurisdiction has been enormously expanded.

There have been significant changes in each of these three conditions.

(1) Contemporary society is urban, highly complex, highly mobile, technological, and volatile in transition.

(2) A large volume of the litigation occurring today involves adversaries who are not acquainted with each other. And the dispute-resolving mechanisms of 1876 have now, to a large extent, been altered by the addition of layer upon

layer of administrative and regulatory agencies at both federal and state levels and expanded pre-trial procedures. These were instituted in the name of more efficient and speedy dispositions and I leave it to experts in administrative law and other litigators to assess whether that has been achieved.

(3) Courts are increasingly organized in an institutional or administrative sense; they are perhaps less common-law oriented and probably more remote and impersonal than a hundred years ago. The influence of the judiciary, taken as a whole, with more than 20,000 state and local judges and more than 500 federal judges, is more pervasive today than a century ago, partly because our society and our economy are more complex. Courts today have an impact no one dreamed of in 1876.

If I have stated the conditions with moderate accuracy, the next question is: what are some of the major problems we should address in looking into the next century in relation to the needs and demands?

(1) Despite the increase in the number and variety of dispute-resolving mechanisms by the addition of the administrative process, and modern pleading for example, there are still injustices and inequities that are not resolved. This is due in part to the fact that the institutions and mechanisms we have established are not geared to resolve certain disputes that are minor in an economic sense although very real to the victims, and in part because new demands have outstripped capacity.

(2) The institutions and mechanisms, such as traditional courts and the administrative or regulatory agencies we have created, today impose inordinate expense and delay on the parties. Old and established institutions and procedures to deal with such mundane matters as the probate of estates of decedents, the acquisition and financing of homes, and more troublesome matters such as divorce and child custody are not adapted to the twentieth century and surely will not be adequate in the twenty first century.

(3) The gradual entry of traditional courts into what can be called *problem* solving as distinguished from specific *dispute* resolving has given rise to new questions as to the proper role of courts and the limits of the judicial function. Courts

are increasingly confronted with resolution of problems that the traditional political processes will not or cannot—or in any event do not—remedy. There was a time when a serious problem—as distinguished from a specific dispute—exerted sufficient pressure upon the political branches of government so that the problem would finally become resolved or partially resolved. This was because the problem remained a political problem, with pressure on the political branches until some response, however inadequate, was made. This is not an entirely new phenomenon. For example the problem, and I emphasize *problem* rather than *dispute,* that existed in the *Dred Scott* case could and should have been resolved, as it eventually was, by the political branches of government. Similarly, the problems of *Brown v. Board of Education* and *Baker v. Carr* theoretically could have been resolved by the political branches long ago.

Recently Simon Rifkind, a distinguished lawyer and formerly a federal judge, pointed out that in a sense the judiciary is a victim of its own success in that in the decision of *cases* and *controversies* it has also resolved great political questions, giving fresh proof to what de Tocqueville said long ago that "scarcely any political question arises in the United States that is not resolved, sooner or later, into a judicial question." Perhaps the political scientists and historians will say that this is inherent under a system of divided and coequal branches of government operating under a written Constitution. This, I submit, gives rise to some very profound questions as to the nature of a representative government and the scope of power of the one branch of government which is not elected, which is protected by long tenure, and is virtually beyond recall. But that is another tale for another occasion.

What we are confronted with now is a reality, not a theory, that unresolved social, political, and economic problems do in fact tend to wind up in the federal courts and the impatience for solutions in this age of "instant gratification" places an increasing and hydraulic pressure on the courts to solve difficult and important questions within the framework of a particular case when, by its very nature, the question is one historically and logically a subject for the slow, painstaking, cumbersome political process. That process, of course, calls for patience, compromise, and acceptance by the constituency, as the late Alexander Bickel reminded us.

II.

What I have said up to this point about the need to review the functioning of the judicial system represents a distillation of conversations I had beginning last summer between Chief Justice Charles House of Connecticut and other leaders of the Conference of Chief Justices, and President Walsh of the American Bar Association. These conversations culminated in the calling of a conference convened jointly by the Judicial Conference of the United States, the Conference of Chief Justices, and the American Bar Association. Apart from a relationship to Bicentennial thinking, this year is the seventieth anniversary of the speech familiar to all of us made by Roscoe Pound to the American Bar Association entitled "Causes of Popular Dissatisfaction with the Administration of Justice." In 1906 Pound was a young, relatively unknown dean of the Law School at the University of Nebraska and his remarks were not received with great enthusiasm by what may be called the "establishment" of the American legal profession. They were largely quite content to continue with things as they were. The impact of Pound's speech has been felt ever since, however, and borrowing his title to describe the conference held in St. Paul in April, 1976, suggests something of its continuing influence. For the first time in our history the Chief Justices of the highest state courts, their counterparts of the federal judiciary, and leaders of the legal profession, together with legal scholars and leaders in other disciplines, assembled to engage in what has been called "systematic anticipation" about the future. Because the one major topic dealt with an examination of which disputes belong in the courts and which disputes can better be resolved by other means, we anticipated that the conference might be viewed as a means of denying or limiting access to the judicial process, and we were not disappointed. I may add that intimations to that effect were relatively insignificant. Thoughtful people recognized both from what was said and the speakers who were treating the subject that the true object of the Conference was to make more certain that people's conflicts and disputes would have available a forum of some kind that would bring fair dispute resolutions to the greatest number of people at the lowest possible cost in the shortest possible time. We remember that the Magna Carta denounced delay and denial of justice as twin evils.

Two challenges were inherent in holding the St. Paul conference and in microcosm they represent tensions which our whole society must face up to sooner or later. One is how to enlarge the availability of dispute resolving tribunals and mechanisms while reducing the unnecessary expense, complexity, and delay that are now common experiences. The other is how we will resolve the growing tension between the concepts and traditions of democracy, on the one hand, and the growing, inexorable tendency to use the courts as a "shortcut" for the solution of problems—as distinguished from disputes—problems that in a true democracy should be solved by elected representatives of the people.

In opening the St. Paul conference, as well as on other occasions, I have suggested some of the areas which called for careful in-depth study, all leading, I repeat, to widening the availability and enlarging the access of all people to some adequate dispute resolving mechanisms. I tried to avoid specific and concrete proposals, except by way of illustration, and, in a capsulized form, I would like to review some of these points here.

If we turn to look honestly at our own system of criminal justice in which the enforcement is dispersed among fifty states, and within each state much of it is dispersed into local subdivisions, we will find with few exceptions that law enforcement agencies in the broadest sense of that term have been the stepchildren of government.

Our police, as compared with the police in many other civilized societies, can be fairly described as poorly trained, poorly paid, and poorly regarded. Yet this is the first point of contact that our system of justice has with people whose lasting impressions and attitudes may be formed by the contact.

The second phase of justice begins when the courts take over, and here again our federalism divides responsiblity among fifty states and myriad local subdivisions, with limited judicial authority in the hands of the national government. The courts, both state and federal, like the police, have also been society's stepchildren, and they suffer from the same kind of deferred maintenance as law enforcement agencies.

A third phase of criminal justice begins with the sentencing process and concludes technically when a prisoner is discharged. This is perhaps the most difficult, the most neglected, and the least understood of the three phases of criminal justice. No one really understands what we ought to do with the delinquents and misfits of society who refuse to abide by its rules. Even a greater tragedy is that we are not applying what little we do know by way of intensive and selective education, vocational training, counseling, and continuing support after release. As a consequence we see a rising curve of criminal activity and recidivism.

The inadequate performance at all three levels of criminal justice has contributed to giving our country a crime rate unparalleled in history and probably without parallel among the developed societies of the world.

Each of these stages must be reexamined and submitted to a critical analysis in terms of the objectives of a civilized society. This is not the occasion to probe at the causes of crime or try to evaluate the oft-repeated suggestion that the way to cure all crime is to eliminate all poverty.

It would be unfair not to take note that there have been substantial improvements in the performance of the police function due to intensive training sponsored by the Federal Government and that there have been significant improvements in the judicial processes and promising developments such as the creation of the Federal Judicial Center, the National Center for State Courts, the Institute for Judicial Administration, and the Institute for Court Management. Similarly, for the first time in its history, the American Bar Association in 1969 embarked on an important project in the form of its Commission on Correctional Facilities and Services, first chaired by the present Chief Justice of New Jersey, Richard J. Hughes, and now chaired by the former dean of New York University Law School, Robert B. McKay. In most of these areas, however, what we have been doing is tinkering when, as Pound said seventy years ago, we should be addressing ourselves to comprehensive change. Comprehensive change is desperately needed in correctional processes.

Assuredly, tinkering is important with our legal institutions as it is important to keeping an airplane or an automobile in safe functioning order, but along with the tinkering we have reached a point in history when we must have profound in-depth examination with respect to all of the legal institutions we employ. It is not enough to continue to employ given methods simply "because that's the way we have always done it", which is often the only reason given for an obsolete practice.

III.

Turning to problems of justice other than the criminal area, I suggest that the area of civil problems also deserves the kind of inquiry I have just suggested:

FIRST: Ways must be found to resolve minor disputes fairly and more swiftly than any present method makes possible. The late Edmond Cahn, to whom I referred earlier, reminded us that few things rankle in the human breast like a sense of injustice. The powerful and the affluent may experience that same reaction, but it is likely to be accompanied by successes and other satisfactions that balance out. This is far less frequently so with the wage earner who has a meritorious claim for shoddy merchandise or shoddy services—concretely on a washing machine, a refrigerator, a poor roofing job, or a usury in any one of these purchases. With few exceptions it is no longer economically feasible to employ lawyers and rely on conventional judicial processes for such claims. Yet the legal profession cannot justify refusing to deal with these relatively minor cases on economic grounds and still insist that only lawyers can deal with litigation. The advent of the "paralegal" in law offices may afford some relief, but I suggest it is time to consider a new concept that has been approached from time to time in some places. To illustrate rather than to propose, we should consider the feasibility of a tribunal of three representative citizens or two nonlawyer citizens and one lawyer or paralegal to decide certain kinds of minor claims. Flexibility and informality are essential in such a process, and this kind of tribunal should be available at a neighborhood or community level, not only during traditional business hours but evenings as well. New York and Philadelphia have much experience with this kind of tribunal. I hope they will export it.

SECOND: As the work of the courts increases far more

rapidly than court personnel is provided, delays and costs will rise, and we should make a substantial effort to encourage a wider use of the arbitration process. Lawyers, judges and social scientists of other countries are baffled by our failure to make greater use of the arbitration mechanism to settle disputes.

THIRD: Basic to our way of life is the concept of transmitting property to family or other loved ones at the death of the owner. The traditional probate procedures are largely obsolte and unnecessarily cumbersome. The way has already been found in the Model Probate Code to eliminate much of the complexity, to speed the process, and to reduce the costs without any jeopardy to the certainty of ownership. It has been adopted in a few states and, even if it is not the perfect solution, it is a starting point.

FOURTH: We must find ways to simplify and reduce the cost of land title searches and the other expenses involved in acquiring and financing purchase of a home. The rise in land and construction costs have already created significant barriers to home ownership, and the legal profession must see to it that archaic, obsolete, and unnecessary legal barriers will not add to the cost. Few things would seem to be more likely adaptable to the proper maintenance of land records and the examination of land titles than modern computer technology, with a consequent reduction in cost to the consumers.

FIFTH: Belatedly we have discoverd that certain of our natural resources are not inexhaustible, and also belatedly we have become aware of the destruction and pollution of our environment, sometimes thoughtlessly, sometimes callously. This has given rise to a large amount of litigation, and here again we see the courts being called upon to engage very often in what is essentially problem-solving rather than decision-making. There should be no retreat from the protection of our environment, but ways must be found to give adequate weight to ecological and environmental factors without inordinate delay and expense that forecloses or delays needed public works and industrial expansion. We have appropriately committed ourselves to protecting the environment, but we must also build needed schools, homes, and highways, and in the process provide jobs.

SIXTH: We must look for new ways to compensate people

for injuries from claimed negligence of others without having the process take years to complete and consume up to half of the damages awarded. Beginning early in this century a comparable problem was resolved by the development of workmen's compensation laws, which may be a useful guide.

SEVENTH: We must explore new ways to provide reasonable compensation for injuries arising out of medical treatment without the distortion in the cost of medical and hospital care witnessed in recent years.

EIGHTH: For centuries the problems of family relationships—marriage and divorce, child custody and adoptions—have been assigned to the courts. We must probe to see whether there are not better ways to deal with relationships of such sensitivity and intimacy outside of the potentially traumatic atmosphere presently inherent in the American judicial process.

NINTH: Seventy years ago Pound vigorously criticized the "sporting theory" of justice, and since then there have been some improvements aimed at simplifying litigation procedures at both trial and appellate levels. The modern rules of civil procedure in both federal and state courts were an improvement, but increasingly, after more than a third of a century of experience, we hear widespread complaints that some of the modern procedures, including pretrial discovery, are being overused and abused. The common complaint is that the "case must be tried twice." This is strictly and exclusively the responsibility of practicing lawyers and judges. The Judicial Conference of the United States maintains a Standing Committee on Rules of Practice and Procedure and an Advisory Committee on Civil Rights. If any procedure is obsolete or if it causes delay or increases expense, then practicing lawyers should promptly present the problem to the Judicial Conference of the United States.

Still other valid complaints are made at the spectacle of lawyers using the jury selection process to condition a jury to a particular result or to secure, not a fair, impartial jury, but a favorable jury. Another chronic complaint of long-standing was renewed in the April, 1976, *American Bar Association Journal* in an article written by a business executive recounting the dismal experience he encountered as a juror in the United States District Court in New York City. That this could happen after our major program to train court personnel in efficient juror utilization proves that even our relatively simple problems are never fully solved.

I will close with an observation I made in opening the St. Paul Conference: as we try to peer into the future and engage in a process of inquiry, we should do it boldly, not timidly—candidly, not apologetically.

